T0290697

Your Call Is Very Important to Us

Your Call Is Very Important to Us

Advertising and the Corporate Theft of Personhood

Richard Hardack

ROWMAN & LITTLEFIELD
Lanham • Boulder • New York • London

Published by Rowman & Littlefield
An imprint of The Rowman & Littlefield Publishing Group, Inc.
4501 Forbes Boulevard, Suite 200, Lanham, Maryland 20706
www.rowman.com

86-90 Paul Street, London EC2A 4NE

British Library Cataloguing in Publication Information Available

Library of Congress Cataloging-in-Publication Data

Names: Hardack, Richard, author.
Title: Your call is very important to us : advertising and the corporate
    theft of personhood / Richard Hardack.
Description: Lanham, Maryland : Rowman & Littlefield, 2023. | Includes
    index. | Summary: "In a unique exploration of how corporations take on
    rights and identities of people, Hardack reveals corporate America's
    quest to dominate every aspect of our culture. Making a seemingly
    complex topic accessible, the book recontextualizes the inordinate
    influence of corporations as a legal, political, psychological, and
    sociological phenomenon"-- Provided by publisher.
Identifiers: LCCN 2022051072 (print) | LCCN 2022051073 (ebook) | ISBN
    9781538177730 (cloth) | ISBN 9781538177747 (epub)
Subjects: LCSH: Corporations--Public relations--United States.
Classification: LCC HD59 .H273 2023 (print) | LCC HD59 (ebook) | DDC
    659.2--dc23/eng/20230227
LC record available at https://lccn.loc.gov/2022051072
LC ebook record available at https://lccn.loc.gov/2022051073

Contents

Chapter One

A Conceptual Overview

> Here is how to get free sticks and strings and clothes and gear from Dunlop, Inc. as long as you let them spraypaint the distinctive Dunlop logo on your sticks' strings and sew logos on your shoulder and the left pocket of your shorts and use a Dunlop gear-bag, and you become a walking lunging sweating advertisement for Dunlop, Inc; [as long as you keep your rank, the] New New England Regional Athletic Rep will address you as "Our gray swan."
>
> —David Foster Wallace, *Infinite Jest* (175–76)

Several years ago, without my consent, a dentist who works for a corporate chain forced me to watch, or at least view, an infomercial for a teeth-whitening procedure while I waited in the exam chair. She had blocked in an extra fifteen minutes for each patient to make them watch this video, which she either was being paid to show or whose product she had a financial incentive to promote. That experience represents the way most of us are treated in our daily lives: we incessantly encounter corporations that try to sell us things we don't need and sell our information against our interests; violate professional ethical norms we don't even recognize have been lost; and subject us to an unavoidable barrage of advertising. Most of all, we become captives of systems that treat us as objects. The video reminded me that advertisers would have us believe we're all ugly ducklings who cannot be transformed without corporate fantasies and interventions. It also served as an example of how corporate personhood—the idea that corporations are people—functions, and the ways corporations communicate with and depersonalize people. Experiences of this kind are increasingly emblematic of our contact not just with corporations, but also with people who have internalized corporate modes of behavior. Each such individual

1

transaction might seem trivial, but they cumulatively dominate and shape our lives. Smile—you're continuously interacting with the premises of corporate personhood. As David Mitchell suggests in *Black Swan Green*, almost every aspect of culture, and the identities we derive from it, reflects a masochistic incorporation of the tenets of corporate personhood:

> "What is that advertisement you are wearing on your chest?"
> "What advertisement?"
> "*That* advertisement on your sweater!"
> "This is my Liverpool F.C. top. I've supported them since I was five."
> "What signifies Hitachi?"
> "The F.A.'ve changed the rules so football teams can wear sponsor's logos. Hitachi's an electronics firm. From Hong Kong I think."
> "So you *pay* an organization to be their advertisement. *Allons donc*. In clothes, in cuisine, the English have an irresistible urge to self-mutilation." (152)

As Colson Whitehead puts it in *Apex Hides the Hurt*, "It was progress, and progress was Windex, Vaseline, Band-Aids: pure brand superiority. Beyond advertising. Why advertise when the name of your product was tattooed on hearts and brains, had always been there, a part of us, under the skin" (172). And as Richard Powers proposes in his novel *Gain*, we internalize the literal and figurative productions of corporations into our bodies and psyches: "Traders on the Frankfurt Burse mouth 'Clare' [Corporation] at the mention of Lacewood [its 'home' town]. . . . Teens in Bangkok covet anything bearing the company's logo" (6). The corporation, or its form of personhood, has become the dominant celebrity of US culture.

In this book, I focus on the ways advertising language has helped bolster the idea that corporation are people, and how corporate personality has come to supplant human personality in many aspects of US culture. Corporations use advertising to create an impersonal persona—some form of stand-in—to convince people they have a relationship with the things (products) they buy. (Apple here serves as a useful example of an entire cult of impersonality.) Drawing on Sharon Cameron's work regarding impersonality in somewhat different contexts, I argue that the mechanisms of advertising, which simulate and manipulate human emotions and relations, are intertwined with the creation of corporate personhood, the cultural and legal contrivance through which corporations attain more rights than people, and exceptional religious, political, economic, and speech rights.[1] In addition to the "nonhuman" attributes Cameron identifies with the impersonal, I would add, in the context of corporate personhood, the mechanical, artificial, generic, and parasitic: producing an array of detrimental effects, corporate systems simulate human behavior and siphon personal qualities from people (x). Advertising, the corporate speech I depict as impersonal and depersonalizing, provides a primary register for creating corporate "autobiographies"—the networks of representation that make corporations appear to be coherent and personalized entities, rather than inhuman legal fabrications. Because they are inherently impersonal, or without persons, corporations incessantly impersonate people and parasitically acquire their traits and rights. I explore the history of such impersonations as they relate to the corporate form, for example in the guises of con men; corporate mascots and spokespersons; CEOs; AI; and discrete fantasy constructs that resemble, possess, or dispossess people. These issues pertaining to advertising, language, and corporations are intimately connected—one can't apprehend the corporate person separately from the language of corporate advertising, its most "autobiographical" medium. Though it is precisely mediated, advertising is the most (quasi-) autobiographical utterance a corporation can make; most biographical representations of a "corporation" serve to ratify the pretense that it can be a singular and personified entity.

Briefly defined, corporate personhood is the concept that corporations have the legal rights, but also human attributes, of persons, including the right to sue, obtain damages for being defamed, and even hold religious beliefs. But it's also a justification for corporations being granted exceptional, virtually unlimited rights—for example effective immortality through succession—tethered to exceptionally limited liability. In other words, corporate personhood stands for having great power in inverse proportion to accountability. Corporate personhood has a specific history and legal meaning; but it also encapsulates a diffuse range of concepts, mechanisms, and forces that directly and indirectly shape and define human individuality, agency, and identity. As it operates in US culture, corporate personhood is predicated on an impersonal, collective, transactional, and instrumental notion of identity, and I try to trace the cultural and legal development of such conceptions. Some of that history emerges through the connections between advertising—its premises, sources, and effects—and corporate personhood, because advertising is the primary communication of corporations. I don't endeavor to write a history of advertising practices or the economic rationales for the corporate form, which others have provided. Instead, I try to bring to light the assumptions behind advertising, what they say about society, and the effect ads and the premises of corporate personhood have on daily life. One of my grounding assumptions is that advertising, commerce, and corporate enterprise are not predominantly economic activities; while people are of course motivated by economic incentives, all human activity can best be understood in terms of its ulterior psychological and sociological causes, effects, and motivations. Put simply, one can interpret economic behavior through psychology and sociology, but one cannot interpret psychology and sociology through economics, much as economic considerations affect us and impinge on how psychology and sociology function. Concluding that a civil war broke out because of disruptions in supply chains or that corporations burn rainforests for profit is inadequate. One must assess why people turn to violence when they feel destabilized and what profit means to people and why. That is, one must understand how, in psychological and sociological contexts, the prioritization of short-term private gain displaced, or was normalized instead of, the prioritization of long-term sustainability. Economic systems, most of all, though or because they appear to many people as the primary drivers of behavior, are not just shaped by ideologies but are also understandable in terms of the way those systems satisfy (often irrational or at least hidden) psychological needs. Under the guise of the rational pursuit of profit—often treated as if it were an independent law of nature—advertising and the rituals and endeavors of corporate personhood ultimately seek not just profit but trust; psychological and sociological payoffs; forms of power; an ordering of hierarchical social relations; the preservation of social order; the inculcation of behavioral imperatives; and the marshalling of identity and behavior through manipulation, fantasy, fear, anxiety, envy, lust, and the incessant simulation of (putatively) noneconomic human interactions, especially those involving love and family.

What is an advertisement in contemporary terms? In contrast with a label, which identifies the contents of a product in neutral and verifiable terms, an ad is an inhuman entity's attempt to manipulate human emotions and create a relationship between persons and things. The point of an advertisement is to tether something that has nothing to do with a product—a feeling, fantasy, or value—to that product. This process is deleterious to individuals and society, and it is reflected in the way we're saturated by, yet largely unaware of or indifferent to, its corrosive influence. Ads are incommensurate with objective, empirically verifiable information, and usually rely on deception, fantasy, and misleading claims about how products, images, and branding affect the consumer's identity. A sinister premise is behind many of these maneuvers; advertisements must pretend a corporation's interests are aligned with yours when in fact they're almost categorically antithetical. Ads by their nature misinform, distort, insult, degrade, demean, and distract. As Louis Menand observes, "Advertising has become for most people the primary symbol of the thoroughgoing commercialism of American life" (*American* 142). We live in a society dominated politically and ontologically by corporations, and in less recognized ways dominated culturally by the advertisement. (By ontologically, I mean the nature of being—in this case, the status and identity of humans as situated against corporations.) People who resist or oppose corporate culture and branding aren't just anti-bourgeoisie (Danesi 133) or Luddites; they're rejecting our dominant, and in some contexts, pathological form of culture and values.

Advertising and corporate personhood obviously aren't directly generating all our social ills, but the cultural forces and trends they represent are causes and effects of a range of related phenomena, particularly in the context of how we define human identity and behavior. Corporations helped rewrite the definition of their "personhood," but they also helped re-create humanity in their image, which is the language of impersonal and depersonalizing commercial speech. Most of the problems I address of course existed in a wide range of contexts before corporations and corporate personhood. But their frequency and ferocity increased in connection with the corporate enterprise in specific ways I try to illuminate. The corporate form is different from that of other organizations: it achieves more, but we tend to suppress the harm and the costs, and rush to defend capitalism, conflating the corporate structure with free enterprise when the two are in many ways incompatible. The corporate form affects not just predictable aspects of our economy, such as production, but an array of unexpected social relations, such as the scope of our legal system, family relations, and our sense of human identity. While writers have addressed elements of corporatization in discrete frameworks, none have systematically explained how the corporate system has transformed our notion of public and private identity and the public and private good.

I argue throughout this book that only an individual person can possess subjectivity and agency in terms of legal and moral responsibility; no collective entity can attain personhood or have intentions. People influence each other in groups and through group dynamics and can reach group decisions or consensus. But these are individual actors reaching an agreement; no group per se decides or acts. Organizations that sustain themselves usually rely on elaborate fictions of cross-generational coherence and consistency. The Catholic Church, for example, can act in part though the pope and can survive generations, whereas a partnership might not, because it is impersonal, slightly belied by the necessary facade of having a charismatic leader. The corporation is as numinous as a church, in that it's imbued with contradictory and insupportable, artificial, inhuman, and superhuman characteristics. The notion that organizations or institutions can think or act as agents is a heuristic fantasy, or instrumental falsification. But in the context of corporations, this fantasy creates a kind of negative space that hollows out and affects everything around it; it allows and possibly compels individuals to act in ways they otherwise never would. This fantasy acts as a screen for both large-scale enterprise and individual antisocial behavior, both as part of corporate praxis and in ways that spill over into our personal lives. Many individuals wouldn't, for example, risk endangering an ecosystem unless they were doing so within corporate structures that encourage and shield such actions. Many organizations prompt individuals to engage in behavior they likely never would on their own, but corporations have wide-ranging purchase in getting people to act against their interests.

Corpography is a term I devised to identify a series of memes and effects involving advertising, the legal status of the corporation, and corporate modes of "self"-representation—the forms of life writing or autobiography that corporations use to disseminate semblances of human personality and personhood. But "life writing" is an oxymoron in the corporate context—the corporation has no life, self, being, or agency, and its personhood exists only as a fiction and contrivance. (Fictions are often more germane to corporations in the context of life writing than other forms of biography.) The corporation can be represented only by partial surrogates, most obviously executives such as officers, advertisers, accountants, lawyers, celebrities, and mascots. As another index of the ways we need to personify and humanize the corporate edifice, most people would see executives, yet not employees, as representing a corporation, but that perception mistakes forms of ownership for forms of identity. None of these figures are the corporation, nor can they author its autobiography. However, their external "biographical" representations retroactively generate the corporation, in much the way one might say priests create a god. In this sense, advertising and corporate autobiographies and biographies don't describe or correspond to existing "persons," but create them. No organizations or groups—agencies, institutions, corporations, universities, and so on—can coherently represent themselves, since they not only have changing constituents, but are by definition mutating fictions. While some might imagine a corporation can have a "biography" through a CEO, imagine how odd it would sound if we said that the United States had a biography. Such entities can have histories written about them, or issue reports, or be represented through agents, but they cannot have inner (or any other kind of) lives or express themselves; the corporation can speak in the ways that matter most only through advertisements, and, despite the pretenses on which it relies, it posits not a self, but an identity. In these contexts, however, all advertising is speech without a speaker. Lisa Siraganian proposes that corporations use forms of autobiography to convey their intentions, but I would argue such "autobiographies" are deployed to hide the fact that corporations have no intentions at all ("Theorizing" 101). Most of all, as I elaborate in numerous contexts, the corporation is an artificial, virtual entity, and the perfect catalyst and emblem of internet culture, because, like our lives online, it is by definition disembodied. The inability to locate a self or moral agent in the corporation bleeds into our difficulty in locating a self and moral compass in our personal lives. I try to assess the ramifications of the appropriation and disappearance of our personhood.

Speculating about the future has become closely associated with the corporate form, which transcends individual life by creating a fictional, artificial being that never dies, never transmits an inheritance, has no "soul," and so forth—it's a monstrosity that is everywhere, yet locatable nowhere. True to its designation, the corporation is an animated corpse, an undead body imbued with artificial life that haunts our civilization. (I argue in "Pure Formalities" that contemporary representations of inhuman life—including zombies, aliens, and forms of altered or collective, but unintelligible, sentience—often bear a corporate residue because they reflect our anxiety not just that corporations are creating alien forms of life, but that they reflect and have instigated the ways our own lives have become alien and inhuman.) As I try to document throughout this book, the ultimate goal of the corporate form is not just to monopolize core sectors of the economy, but to monopolize, control, and displace nature, reproduction, personhood, and life itself. This is a trajectory it has followed for hundreds of years, with technology and socioeconomic transformations enabling each next step. And as the response to the pandemic in the Unites States—from bailouts to gouging to the move to virtual life, all of which we might call aspects of corona–capitalism—further highlights, corporations are dead things that have inordinate influence over all living things.

Because corporations are fictional contrivances and kinds of chimeras, they cannot be described literally, but through or even as a series of seemingly fluid metaphors. The range of metaphors I invoke reflects the inconsistency of the entity being described.[2] The apparent inconsistencies in these metaphors constitute and define the corporate form. Because corporations aren't coherent entities, but artificial nonentities, they rely on ontologically and culturally mixed metaphors, but relatively stable legal tropes regarding their exceptional or enhanced rights. Corporations are less coherent forms with wholly defined features than Mephistophelean structures whose legal status allows them to take on superhuman and often contradictory attributes. At any given time, the law delimits how corporations operate and must be funded and organized, in relatively stable terms; but in cultural contexts, corporations often mutate and become amorphous, sinister in overreach, and diabolical in "temperament." The corporate form is designed so no person *can* represent it. The similes that best evoke the corporate "person" remain consistent in their connotations; the monsters, phantoms, shadows, and scarecrows, for example, that often "embody" or evoke the corporate form are unnatural, ventriloquized, and lacking in independent interiority. Because it's a metaphorical contrivance, personhood is often represented through images of artificial, mechanical, and vampiric modes of existence. In other words, impersonal corporate systems poorly or eerily imitate and siphon the personal qualities of people or mimic human interactions—they steal identities. As I try to demonstrate throughout this book, the idea that corporations are persons has a perverse cultural logic that shields them from scrutiny and distorts and inverts reality. Corporations are not just impersonal: they ultimately cannot be identified with and are the antitheses of people, and their "goal," or trajectory, is to control or eliminate them.

Chapter Two

The Zero-Sum Game
of Corporate Personhood

Because corporations operate in different cultural registers and function as fictional entities and personae, I address them in multiple contexts, invoking not only economists and political theorists but also writers and social theorists who explicate their day-to-day and symbolic operations. I chose writers who offer accessible insights into these phantasmic entities and capture the distorting language and premises of corporate personhood, as well as the laws and court holdings that codify them, and who trace the effect of advertising and the twisted relationship between human and corporate personhood. I try to weave together this historical, legal, and cultural background in ways that are partly analytic and partly contemplative. This book develops an etiology of the ailments and symptoms that conjoin corporate personhood and advertising—in other words, it is a deep dive into the connections among numerous fields that show how the corporate view of the world pervades society. We know that large corporations do appalling things to the environment, workers, and competitors, as well as undermine democratic institutions. What we don't apprehend sufficiently is their ulterior function: how they communicate, why they have the power they do in society, beyond the obvious factor of money; and how and why we allow entities without agency, responsibility, or accountability to control so much of our lives.

Corporations are not monolithic; CEOs can make a significant difference in influencing corporate culture, and corporations approach issues of social responsibility with varying levels of commitment. Countries have distinct and sometimes disparate inflections of corporate regulation. I am not writing about those differences but about the disturbing commonalities that define most corporations and afflict most contemporary societies; the corporate form limits the range and possibility of commercial and personal behavior and generates an almost ineluctable set of outcomes. I don't contend the development of the corporation has been uninterrupted, without setbacks, or uniform. Corporations under the New Deal or in partly state-controlled or socialist economies might have little in common. But the trajectory of the corporate form tends to move not only toward deregulation, but to the generation of an increasingly consolidated corporate form, with the corporation accruing an escalating array of personal rights and privileges as well as impersonal immunities. Corporate personhood is coterminous with having four chains control most of the supermarkets in the country, four major airlines, and a handful of banks; though smaller competitors exist, they're largely irrelevant to the larger functioning of the system. Though these things are pernicious, the worst effects of corporate personhood aren't the externalities society pays for, such as widespread pollution and toxicity, a poisoned food supply, or even economic polarization and the erosion of democratic norms. Rather, the worst effects are the legitimation, absorption, and dissemination of the idea of corporate personhood and all it has represented in its evolution. Corporate personhood delimits perception and normalizes a view of the world that is pathological, reduces our expectations, and seems irrevocable and irremediable. Corporations are attack dogs that the law has bred over generations to be feral in their relation to society as a whole.

I develop a genealogy of the premises and consequences of corporate personhood, especially as manifested in the context of advertising, the primary communication of the corporate "person." Corporate personhood reflects a number of economic, legal, and cultural developments; foremost is the idea that corporations have the legal and even personal rights and attributes of human beings. But personhood turns out to be a zero-sum game: as corporations attain more "personhood" and human rights, people retain less. (In a zero-sum game, one has a fixed amount of some property—in this case rights and personhood—and the more one entity gains of that property, the more another must lose.) Each right and attribute corporations gain is siphoned from people. In many ways, the ever-increasing wealth gap in the United States is a personhood gap, and corporations have perpetrated the greatest identity theft in history. The effect of corporate personhood, which operates conterminously with privatization, is to dehumanize people, turning them into things that have no rights—not to health care, education, retirement, speech, or even enfranchisement. Those rights have been transferred to corporations that can lobby and set agendas for issues ranging from taxation to military spending, election rules, gerrymandering, and campaign spending. As Paul Hawken succinctly comments, if you consider history since the industrial revolution, it's "impossible not to find a period when business," for which I would substitute the emerging corporate form, "didn't have a disproportionate share of rights in the world" (62). Where do corporate rights, wealth, and finally souls come from in a closed system? Corporations suck them out of you.

My overarching argument is that corporate personhood is part of a zero-sum game, one in which human traits and privileges—including privacy, legal rights and exemptions, and traditional forms of continuity—are being transferred to corporations (and not shareholders per se). As corporations attain personhood, persons become, largely without their realization, more impersonal, generic, and increasingly defined by their relations to things. As corporations are granted human rights, people lose them. Equally ominous is that corporations operate within a framework that presupposes that limitless growth is possible, while they function as part of a zero-sum game economically, environmentally, ontologically, and culturally.

One of my goals is to define the effects of this zero-sum game of corporate personhood, and the disturbing strangeness of the corporate form in our lives. In summarizing how Freud's theory of the uncanny applies to "mechanical entities that appear human," Mark Fisher emphasizes that "*repetition and doubling*—themselves an uncanny pair which double and repeat each other— seem to be at the heart of every 'uncanny' phenomen[on]" (*Weird* 9, emphasis in original).[1] Fisher adds that the eerie "is fundamentally tied up with questions of agency. What kind of agent is acting here? . . . [These questions] apply to the forces governing capitalist society. Capital is at every level an eerie entity. . . . The metaphysical scandal of capital brings us to the broader question of the agency of the immaterial and inanimate" (11). In other words, as Marx proposed, the market (and capital) appears to be a living entity with its own will and agency. Fisher's comments apply even more forcefully to corporations—immaterial, inanimate entities that nevertheless seem to possess agency and human attributes. As such, corporations channel repetitions and doublings, patterns of eerie communication and uncanny disjunctions in their "self-representations" (especially advertising), but as part of a zero-sum game in which they accrete their "life force" from society. The "repetition without origin" (93) that Fisher notes is common of eerie science fiction also demarcates corporations, not just in franchises, but also in their parthenogenetic self-replications; we repeatedly see corporations bootstrapping identity and relying on inconsistency, contradiction, and sleight of (missing) hand to advance their status. In addition, as Fisher notes, eerie texts often conjure ontological confusion or an inappropriate intrusion from one level of reality to another, for example, when characters talk to authors or figures from a simulated computer world suddenly emerge into this one (53). But that's exactly what corporations do continually; they speak to us without agency, source, or intention from another ontological register or an artificial world, irruptions of the unnatural into our world.

The many "fictions" or artificial attributes of the corporate identity also warp the definitions of human personhood on which they're ineluctably based. In part because corporations are theoretically immortal collectives, locatable nowhere as an agent, yet operating everywhere, they've been able to claim the legal right to elide most individual human limitations regarding continuity, embodiment, inheritance, criminal liability, and mens rea. These considerations help explicate principles of corporate exceptionalism, which then precipitate a number of other inversions, polarities, and ontological exchanges; corporations are exceptional, for example, because they can be multinational or transnational in ways people and most other institutions cannot.

The dehumanization corporate personhood precipitates is structural—manifested in the way we're treated in a corporate economy—and personal, reflected in the way we internalize a corporate view of life and treat others as commodities. As codified by the ironically titled *Citizens United v. Federal Election Commission*, 558 U.S. 310, 351 (2010)—the Supreme Court (hereafter "Court") case that held that corporate money is speech and affirmed that corporations are people—corporations have come to control speech and representation in almost all media.

Citizens United is simply the most recent extension of a long line of legal holdings and cultural paradigms, a distinct teleology, that enable corporations to impersonate people. It therefore becomes critical to track the cultural, aesthetic, legal, and ontological inversions that have allowed corporations to regulate the state. The causes and effects of these inversions affect society at all levels. As one irritating example, it's now commonplace for many corporations, even those not immediately involved in information technology or social media, to refer to persons as the products rather than the consumers. Most media, which now includes everything from entertainment to politics, serves primarily as a pretext or lure for corporate advertising and manipulation and a distraction from corporate maneuvering. All these inversions and effects are predicated on the notion that the corporation is now the person.

The legal contrivance that protects corporate agents from bearing personal responsibility for the acts they perform on behalf of corporations also obscures the fact that many assumptions in our daily lives are predicated on an "Oz effect." It's telling that courts use the term *corporate veil* to describe how corporations function; the veil separates corporations from the people who own and direct them, but the veil also hides the fact that no one is behind the curtain legally, ontologically, and ethically. Corporate personhood veils the fact that no human persons can stand in for the corporation. Corporations cannot possess human agency and intention or "speak," and the attribution of fantasized human qualities to such organizations reflects an antidemocratic, anti-individualistic and what I will address as an impersonal network of "post-social" relations. Like advertising, corporate personhood requires the performance of a confidence game, in this case one that manipulates not only consumer desire and behavior, but also the relationship between individual and group, and state and organizational identities. Everyone representing the corporation is a kind of actor, because the corporation is a kind of machine for producing actions without agents and consequences without liability. And advertising ventriloquizes this corporate personhood—it's the quintessential speech without an identifiable author, the soundtrack of Oz. In the United States, corporations reflect and enact a destructive social, structural, and in-dividual urge to transcend the self—to exist as some collective, conformist, and merged entity without individual agency or liability. One of my primary arguments is that corporate personhood represents a series of reifications, or the mystification of economic and political processes, typically to make them seem natural or inevitable. When corporations speak or advertise, you cannot locate any intent or person behind the communication; the speech and acts are divorced from the corporation, in the way shareholders are divorced from employees, and the corporate entity from management. (These dislocations mirror the way signifiers or signs are divorced from signifieds, the things they're meant to represent—a decentered postmodern world in which what you say need not or cannot coincide with what you mean.) Speech without a speaker is a terrifying instance of reification—a concealment of agency and responsibility that naturalizes a process and suggests it is ineluctable and immutable. Corporate personhood attributes omnipotence and autonomy to impersonal structures that produce action and speech without actors. Put more simply, the corporation is a materialization of the premise that shit just happens, without an asshole to hold accountable.

It's a great irony that corporate advertising represents and presupposes the antithesis of individuality but relies on and manipulates the discourses of in-dividualism to sell products. Corporate influence on consciousness and most aspects of social and economic interaction at such a mass level raises the ques-tion of where we can locate agency and morality in US culture. As Shoshana Zuboff documents, corporations gather unprecedented amounts of data about our behavior, which they use not just to predict but also to influence and control what we do (7–10). When consciousness isn't locatable in individuals but dif-fused throughout a corporate entity or network, morality becomes a virtually inapplicable concept. Even if mass consciousness and collectives could be at-tributed with will or intent, they couldn't be held responsible or liable (75). One might argue that corporations represent a distillation of the population or its unconscious; they especially reflect attitudes about the worth of the individual and individual willingness to relinquish agency and will to collective forces. Corporations are always enemies to the individual—they're incompatible with

small businesses, nonconformity, and any form of non-systemization. Ironically, Jefferson hoped "to crush in its birth the aristocracy of our moneyed
corporations," which he knew would always attempt to circumvent not just
governmental authority, but democracy (Ignatieff 72). Zuboff assesses how
corporations, particularly those that mine data, "circumscribe democracy"
by interfering in the political process and, through their agents, by contending they must remain above the law to advance technology and safeguard
the economy (107). In other words, they blackmail society. The post-national
expansion of corporate power and reach realizes Jefferson's worst fears; as
Joel Bakan notes of one of the most egregious and transparent examples, the
World Trade Organization is an exceptionally undemocratic body that incessantly manipulates world governments (23–25).

I try to provide a novel overview of how and why the corporation developed; how it has come to be regarded under the law, but also by the media
and culture at large, as a person; and the disturbing and sometimes humorous
implications of the attribution of personhood to corporations. In a series of
connected political, legal, and historical contexts, advertising was integral to
the exploration, development, economy and culture of the New World, and
dispersed to the rest of the world from there. Fledgling configurations of the
corporation used early discourses of advertising to express themselves, but
also changed how we define agency, actorhood, individual and collective
identity, novelty, speech, and social responsibility. The state first chartered
corporations for the limited function of colonizing the New World, but these
entities gradually became Frankenstein monsters that supplanted their
creators and took possession of that New World.[2] In that new arena, the
body of the king, and all it represented, was eventually replaced by the
virtual body of the corporation and all it represents. Concepts related to
power, speech, and agency were transferred from God to the state to the
private corporation that has taken over many state functions. Supersed-
ing nature and the state, the corporation now represents the increasingly
artificial body, or corpus, of power in society, and in multivalent ways
became a form of artificial intelligence. I trace the unexplored connections
between the colonization of the New World, as facilitated by the corporation, and the corporation's primary form of expression, advertising, which
encapsulates an entire way of structuring society—including its economic,
aesthetic, political, and, most of all, psychological components. The development of social and legal notions of an exceptional corporate soul (and
other corporate rights) was an integral part of the colonization, branding,
marketing, and social construction of the New World.

The history of the corporation is intertwined with the history of the New
World, which was a putative state of nature settled by what were ultimately

designated as soulless corporations. From the charter companies to the East India Company to the military corporation in the film *Avatar*, colonization long has been associated with corporations. The corporation was created as monarchy began to wane. The state created sponsored entities with limited liability that could do what no individual or small group could do: expend, transfer, and generate extraordinary sums of money, as well as shield individuals from liability, all of which was necessary to colonize the New World. But the incentives defining these entities from their inception gave them not just license and leave but a compulsive obligation to harm the public good for private gain. As I later argue, the New World should have been called the new and improved world. "The New World" is itself an early advertising slogan, a fantasy fabrication to lure new customers, echoed from New Coke to every "new and improved" product. That embryonic advertising phrase encapsulates the ideology of a new system of representing the world, whose successors have implemented the corporate colonization of language, territory, and culture throughout the developed world over the past century.

The fiction of corporate personhood is tethered to a trope that situates the United States as the apotheosis of this New World, developed in and as a series of propositions that were generated as part of a corporate origin fantasy whose task, as Edward Said might put it, was to elide actual historical beginnings (10, 13, 19–24). Part of my goal is therefore to trace the cultural trajectory from the charter companies (proto-corporations) that settled the New World to the new and improved world of New Amsterdam, New York, and New England, and finally to corporate personhood. When the United States achieved independence, corporations were effectively banned, except for those formed on a temporary basis for specific, enumerated purposes that benefited the public; in contrast to some of those of the Old World, these corporations were precluded from influencing public policy, public officials, laws, or elections (see, e.g., Safina, 41). The anomalous grant of limited liability was supposed to remain tethered to a limited purpose; the corporation would receive state protection in order to accomplish some grand undertaking for the benefit of the nation as a whole. To incentivize large-scale projects to advance the public good that no individuals could undertake, the government granted these corporations immunity from negligence or error, but only in the context of their public task and for a specified period; in other words, their limited liability was itself highly limited. Instead, except in the narrow context of product liability, that relationship largely has been inverted, so the corporation has become unaccountable for its effects on the social and natural world and its immunity has become permanent.

As Malick Ghachem notes, historians tend to assume the priority of the nation-state over such entities as the corporation as a subject of inquiry; but colonialism involved wars between national trading companies as much as it did colonial powers. (Ghachem argues that these "forever companies" of the seventeenth and eighteenth centuries—quasi-state enterprises such as the Dutch, French, and British East India Companies that merged colonialism and commerce—were already too big to fail.) According to Ghachem, the only check on corporate malfeasance now comes in the language of fraud; unless an endeavor amounts to conspicuous fraud, a corporation's power is largely treated as a matter of right. Ralph Clare contends that in Richard Powers's 1998 novel *Gain*, which traces corporate history in the United States, "the only resistance to the corporation remains" through "legal recourse," but the law largely has become an ancillary tool for corporate expansion (175). The tendency of the corporation is to concentrate wealth and power, eliminate competitors and make conceptual alternatives impossible, and reduce/consolidate the range of speech. This is another facet of the corporate zero-sum game, which most disadvantages, and often displaces, small business and dissenting voices, all in the name of putatively individualist free enterprise.

The corporation signaled a displacement of what we would consider the commons (public space or the public good itself), nature (even if our modern notion of nature was also being created to fulfill some similar cultural functions), and finally a diminution of the state. I assess the way language and concepts used to describe nature in the nineteenth century became used to describe the pointedly artificial corporation; in many instances, one can, rather unexpectedly, substitute the word corporation for nature in the passages I cite. The issues I address raise numerous correlative questions regarding the agency and intentions of an inhuman entity—are nature (represented, for example, by Moby Dick) and the corporation benign, indifferent, or malevolent? Melville gradually decided that the giant mass of nature was not just indifferent to humanity, but a kind of confidence trick, an assessment he transferred to the corporate form as its ulterior manifestation. The indifferent, impersonal nature of naturalism returns in even more dangerous form in the "behavior" of the inhuman and agentless corporation, which is indifferent to life in such a reckless way—in the way of a motorist driving 200 miles an hour on a cul-de-sac—that it must be held to have an intent to kill.

As corporations' liability became ever more limited, their rights and attributes became almost unlimited, or exceptional. As part of the zero-sum game of corporate inversions, the public good was redefined as the good of the corporation/corporate person. The government proceeded from shielding corporate representatives from financial liability (bankruptcy when a company loses money) to shielding them from criminal liability (when a company's actions harm people or the environment). The trajectory that led to corporate personhood required not just large scale enterprises but also quasi-governmental institutions that would exist above the law. The corporate form that developed, which shielded individuals from most liability for actions undertaken in corporate contexts, provided not just an incentive but a directive to engage in antisocial and reckless behavior. The corporation itself ultimately stands for deregulation—the transfer of power from the sovereign (including the people) to an unlocatable fiction, and the grant of impunity for private behavior that harms the public good. And many large corporations wield more influence over the public sphere than governments, but with little transparency or accountability.

I also provide an alternate cultural history of the New World by looking at the laws and beliefs that facilitate the institutionalization of supra-individual agency and speech, which ultimately produced an ethos of corporate exceptionalism—that is, that enabled the corporation to attain rights, privileges, and immunities beyond those of any individual or state. (This ethos also comports with what Zuboff terms surveillance exceptionalism, reflecting the ways corporations advocate not just complete deregulation, but the right, particularly in the post-9/11 shift from protecting privacy to sacralizing security, to unfettered access to data [112–15].) I chart the sequential attribution of personality, agency, and voice to impersonal, fantasized, and unstable aggregations—to God, nature, the state, collectivities, and organizations, and finally the contemporary corporation. Societies have imbued these entities with superhuman and quasi-mystical properties. Recently alleged to have religious rights and beliefs, the corporation has taken on characteristics of a divinity in our society: it exists everywhere and forever, and seems to transcend space, time, and individuality. The corporate person is a kind of golem, zombie, or alien—it impersonates or displaces human beings.

I first provide an overview of the principles of my argument, which operate a bit like a mathematical proof: I can't address every point at length, but I try to document overlooked connections between corporate status, corporate advertising, and social personhood. Advertising might seem secondary to the issue of corporate influence and control, but the two are closely linked. The corporation and the advertisement wind caduceus-like around our culture and economy. Corporations specialize in producing junk culture even more than junk food, and the effects of that continuous contamination on our minds are even more harmful but less easily diagnosed, harder to elucidate and trace, than their effects on our bodies. The advertiser's goal is to control subjects; to get you to watch a TV show, billboard, movie, game, video, screen, surface, anything, at all times, so you will see and respond to the ads. Stay tuned, stay with us, don't touch that dial, we control the airwaves. But for corporations, content is tertiary if not irrelevant; the ad matters. And to those who object that the ad is just a means to an end, a sale, I attempt to show that the ad has in many ways superseded the sale in its significance, effects, and function.

I argue throughout this book that all corporate speech is commercial speech—it's the only kind of speech corporations are legally capable of making, or ultimately authorized to proffer. On legal and philosophical grounds, advertising is the primary way corporations can "speak" or express something. I treat all corporate speech as commercial because, by charter and law, corporations still can act only in ways that promote their business interests. Corporations cannot speak "privately" or in terms of other human emotions, ambiguities, or beliefs, but, as emblematized by the notion of corporate personhood, must imitate those forms of communication incessantly.

Here it is useful briefly to address the quintessential commercial speech, the corporate commercial, or language that is, in effect, always already "as seen/heard on TV": consumers often buy products simply because they've seen them advertised. An advertisement typically refers to itself, not a product, because the campaign is arbitrary—time travel, e.g., tends to have little to do with snack food. Consumers are lured into an endless closed loop of references that has no original source or exit. (The ideal ad would simply announce, "as seen in other ads.") At their most fundamental level, many ads assert a mere name as an identity. People in local elections often vote for candidates whose names appear on signs, which are meaningless assertions, conveying no information whatsoever (except, for some people, perhaps ethnic, gender, or party affiliations). Any politician is emphatically "as seen on TV": the ability to post signs and slogans has no correlation to an ability to be a good leader, so why do we rely on this method of communication as a primary component of our electoral system? A similar process works with Bounty—many people buy this brand, which is nearly identical to any other, because it's had an arbitrary association attached to it, much as they want to visit places that they've seen on TV when they travel. This isn't confirmation bias, but a tautological closed loop. The problem is that we confuse the familiar with the informative; but ads, and corporations, are engineered not to provide information or communicate any empirically verifiable data. Designed to manipulate and obfuscate, ads exist in far more than literal or obvious form. Nothing is wrong with legitimate endeavors to inform consumers, market products, or influence opinion. But the agenda of everything you read that's part of a corporate advertisement or sponsorship isn't to debate or inform, but exclusively to manipulate behavior. The psychology behind and practices of advertising foster what economists term alienation, which leads the public to think and act against its own interests. And almost all communication in the United States, from political discourse to health data, has come to resemble corporate advertising, or corporate "self"-representation. Though they sometimes are infected by the ethos of advertising, we expect reviews of books or products to be disinterested evaluations, but increasingly every form of message is tainted by the ethos and mechanisms of advertisements and corporate personhood—by virulent, colonizing strains of (anti-)culture. Advertisers (and especially political advertisers) who carry out the marching orders of corporate personhood aren't trying to convince you of the soundness of an argument or point of view, which would be laudable: they're using the pretext of arguments to get you to do something—to vote or buy.

Advertising represents one of our last forms of common culture: tastes in music, film, literature and news have become fragmented, yet most people will be familiar with the same ads. As the (sometimes problematic) centers of our culture have disintegrated—shared news sources, values, and aesthetic canons and epistemological assumptions—advertising and consumer culture fill the void. Filmmakers, novelists, newscasters, and professors no longer can assume their audiences will have any mutual frame of reference for their allusions to history, authors, films, or other cultural touchstones, but they can still refer to a repository of ad clichés and images. Aside from representing a dreary cultural heritage, this state of things suggests the disturbing power of advertising to shape our collective values. The techniques of corporate advertising, the history of the rise of the power of corporations and film, fiction, and culture are inextricable because almost all culture has become sponsored—culture no longer exists independently from the impersonal corporate form. I ask readers to consider how we fund entertainment, politics, news, and research almost entirely through corporate systems of advertising, and the unexamined effects pervasive corporatization has on civic society.

In explicating the attribution of human traits to corporations in neoliberal cultures, and its manifestations in advertising, I try to unearth phenomena throughout our culture involving false personalization. For example, the discourse that supports corporate personhood generates a need to have CEOs and celebrities represent corporations; such spokesperson figureheads are metaphorically scarecrows and masks, whose purpose is to make you believe they speak for something ulterior in the corporation, when the disembodied corporation is by legal definition an empty shell—no person(s) can fully represent it. I also examine the way people interact continuously with corporate personhood in their daily lives. When you see actors feign ecstasy at the prospect of using corporate products, or corporations attach their brands to events such as weddings, you witness the imitation of human emotion, and the parasitic attachment of corporate persons to real persons. (It's appropriate that advertising is called copy because it's all a simulation of human relations.) As an important qualification, while I emphasize globalization and the universality of corporate culture, I don't wish to overlook or diminish the importance of local resistance, problems of translation, anomalies and exceptions, and social practices and movements outside the corporate domain. But my focus is on how the arc of corporate personhood led to the creation of universalizing networks of communication and assumptions about identity and behavior, and on the often unseen effects that teleology has across contemporary society. Corporate personhood has numerous features consonant with digital media because the corporate person is by necessity a kind of digital effect, a copy without an original. Advertisers are inserting ads in old music videos and other visual content; in much the way characters and events can now be digitally placed into or even replace analog content, corporate persons are fabricated and placed into ads or the representations of companies to fool us into thinking something dead, or that could never attain life, is alive.

This book does not present a history of corporations or advertising, nor does it reflect on the business practices of advertising per se. Instead, it develops a sustained exploration of the effects of ads on culture, but also their causes; and their effect on individuals, relationships, ethics, aesthetics, and politics. I don't develop a linear analysis of how corporations function but rather an assessment of how they reflect and affect our culture across a range of registers, and how they "speak" through advertising. Ads have become a kind of unregulated, toxic cultural pollution, but most people don't seem to realize they're being poisoned. Worst of all, ads have been normalized and glamorized, so most of us no longer notice, let alone object to, each new encroachment on what had been a private or public sphere. Whenever I walk around Berkeley, I pass rows of sponsored bikes with giant corporate logos on them—ironically, always sponsored by a car company or bank that has an appalling record on environmental and other corporate social responsibility (CSR) issues, and in one case fought ferociously to block the development of forms of public transportation and electric vehicles. (In this case, the bikes are sponsored by Citigroup, which has an especially reprehensible environmental record and recently rejected a shareholder resolution to meet climate change mitigation targets or stop funding fossil fuel industries.) These wildly overpriced bikes are a fitting emblem of corporate sponsorship and CSR— they serve little purpose beyond providing the corporation with outlets for low-cost advertising, and it is dispiriting but emblematic that even cities such as Berkeley would engage in such deals. These corporate bikes represent the way the public good, through the medium of advertising, is sold out to corporations, which then represent themselves as stewards of the public good.

In these contexts, I address the ontology or phenomenology of advertising—that is, what effect does it have on our sense of identity? How and why does advertising in unacknowledged and overlooked ways affect most aspects of our lives? Economic factors obviously are important, and they propel the escalation and acceleration of advertising practices at least at the level of conscious decision-making. But at the level of our culture as a whole, advertising and the predicates of corporate personhood are inflected far more by unconscious factors than by individual decisions. Even when corporate and advertising practices seem driven by profit motives, their specific manifestations are shaped by deeper, noneconomic cultural assumptions about society. Corporate personhood is a critical part of a corporate ethos that helps regulate and control organizational behavior, and our notions of individual desire, hierarchy, self-worth, and identity, all of which involve cultural behaviors that enact different and usually hidden logics, and often make little sense from an economic perspective.

By focusing on the connection between corporate personhood and advertising, this book brings together a number of flashpoints and controversies in contemporary culture: the unprecedented influx of corporate money into US politics; the power and influence of corporations from big pharma to big agriculture and big media; the corporate domination of debates concerning technology and privacy; and the effect of *Citizens United*. Why focus on those connections? Because corporate advertising is a kind of universal graffiti that confronts us not just on television but at hospitals, on elevators, on the backs of menus, in textbooks, on highways—figuratively at every turn. The fact that few limits apply regarding where advertisers can encroach and what tactics they can use characterizes the shamelessness and rapaciousness of our cultural and political moment. Little public space is left anywhere, which reflects how little sense of community we retain.

Advertisers are incessantly making money off us, and it's no wonder we start unconsciously feeling as if parasites are sucking our blood: they are. Yet we don't often locate advertising as a source for our widespread sense of anxiety, discomfort, and disaffection. Advertising works by manipulating envy, insecurity, masochistic fantasies, and addictive behaviors (ads that fabricate and foment social anxiety rely on what's termed *whisper copy*). Drawing on Vance Packard's 1957 work *The Hidden Persuaders*, Tamara Piety treats advertising as a form of conditioning and experimentation on human subjects; she justly concludes that "[l]ittle thought seems to have been given as a policy matter to what all of this may be doing to us as a society." Advertising is an often-overlooked barometer of the state of our individual and national psyches. Often puerile, trivial, antagonistic to history, unctuous, crass, manipulative, pandering, and accelerating in ferocity, ads characterize contemporary culture. If, as I try to demonstrate, all advertising is by definition false advertising, truth in advertising is a contradiction in terms. Not only are ads forms of fiction but effective ads work only through their falsehood. Claims that corporations engage in more sound environmental or labor practices generally are distractions; certainly, some boards of directors are more conscientious than others, and one should welcome corporate attempts to be socially responsible. And corporations have disparate economic interests, structures, and impacts on environment and infrastructure. But they share a legal and ontological form and imperative that cannot be elided. While people directly can represent organizations and partnerships, anyone representing a corporation does so indirectly, at a remove, and can neither coincide with nor alter the nature of that entity. Because I focus on the overlooked implications of corporate person-hood, I don't here attempt to differentiate corporations in terms of their local variations and anomalous actions. As Ralph Clare concludes, the fact that corporations must remain antidemocratic, exist only to pursue private profit, and never have a human face—that is, be reconciled with individual needs or the public good—"should serve as a warning for those who today distinguish "good" corporations from "bad" ones" (199–201). I explore what it means to have a culture that fetishizes individuality, but, as advertising helps reveal, pro-duces depersonalized corporate commodities.

Advertising also is a wellspring of fake news—both the generation of false claims and stories and the ability to challenge facts and science as relative. Advertising stands for the proposition that there's no truth, only competing economic and political assertion, and viewers are free to decide whatever they want. The right to be willfully ignorant or wrong becomes the emblem of consumer choice, which supplants any meaningful notion of individual liberty. Many ads are designed to look like news stories, and erode the distinction between fact and opinion, and expertise and manipulation. Trumpism in part is the outcome of the language and premises of decades of advertising and corporate culture; corporations stoke desire, anxiety, and envy; make unfounded claims to the point where people don't care or become unable to discern whether they're true; and rely on slogans, sound bites, and memes. In multiple contexts, advertisers not only have revised but reviled facts. As one of thousands of similar contentions, Al Ries and Jack Trout assert that marketing involves a battle of concepts, not products: brands "appeal to aspirations and not reality" (90, 142). In such a warped economy of signs, no product or truth exists, just a will to concept; alternative facts are by-products of such an approach to communication. One might counter that deflection tracks the nature of desire, or that desire is predicated on fantasy that's incompatible with facts, but such suppositions let advertising off too easily. Advertisements are responses to desire, but also cause and heighten destructive impulses and help erode social relations.

Part of my goal is to alienate the reader from what has come to seem normal, to help us see anew that much of what we've come to take for granted is damaging, unnecessary, and more far-reaching in its effects than most people realize. It might sound polemical to claim advertising offers nothing of value—but that's because we're so used to it that we fail to perceive its consequences. The premises and effects of advertising have permeated and warped politics, media, music, dating, the food industry, news, academia, research and scientific studies, social relations, and, perhaps most ironically, the world of entertainment itself.

Finally, I hope to illustrate the skein between advertising, romanticism, and corporate personhood, one that offers the seductive promise of an allegiance with the forces that oppress us. Perversely, the corporate person represents both a betrayal and fulfillment of a kind of romantic notion of literature, one that links naive readers with what René Girard describes as the victims of advertising, who give themselves over to powers larger than themselves (31). In other words, readers of corporate advertisements and certain forms of romantic literature want to be seduced by lies, but those lies can be socially and psychologically carcinogenic. The corporation is both the cause and effect of a semiotic, ontological, and psychological erosion of language and culture, a series of related and intercalated phenomena. The terminus of corporate personhood in turn is a source and consequence of many of the premises of advertising, through which human personality is overlaid onto corporations, brands and sponsored entities.

In later sections of this book, I address the legal framework that creates and protects corporations in the context of the cultural background I discuss. Throughout this book, I situate the corporation in terms of economies of scale: the effects I address are generally neither visible nor at issue in small corporations—which I would define as oxymorons—but only in those that have achieved sufficient market domination to operate across time zones and begin to appear always and everywhere—beyond culture as a force of simulated nature. Thom Hartmann contends that few small or medium-sized businesses ever avail themselves of legal features or attributes related to corporate personhood (308). Genuinely closely held corporations, which are owned by a small group of "insiders," sometimes retain the governing mechanisms and characteristics of partnerships, which still acknowledge the critical role of individuals and hold partners accountable for the actions of their partnerships. (Close corporations, as codified for example under Delaware law, typically are restricted to thirty shareholders.) But even small companies generally must emulate large corporations to compete, and "are forced to engage in and emulate the corporate model" (Moore 217).

Chapter Three

You're Soaking in It

I won't try to convince you that modern advertising began, as a new-historicist Monty Python might propose, at 2:18 p.m. on October 14, 1784, or that ads always have been part of culture or, conversely, that ads are part of nature, in which peacocks always have been selling themselves. I'm interested instead in the effect ads have on our daily lives, psyches, and relationships. Advertising is what most people in America read most: it's their primary form of communication. We see ads everywhere: buses and public transportation; billboards and store windows; the clothing of people we pass on the street; print media and the margins of web pages; and in product placements in movies, TV shows, and music videos. We live in a sea of them, so thick they've become the medium we inhabit. What most people are most exposed to are endless variations of the art of lying. If we allow ourselves to be bombarded with misinformation, trivial distraction, and a pernicious set of beliefs about what it means to be a person, our lives will be dominated by misinformation, trivia, and depersonalization. But advertising is neither trivial nor secondary; by examining its causes and effects, one can reverse engineer how our culture works at a systemic level. Advertising has become the way we relate to the world, yet we rarely examine its deep-structure causes and effects. We don't like to look too closely at the ways advertising influences us because our sense of identity, and our desires and hopes, can be threatened. Ads stand for the proposition that everything is for sale: our integrity, identity, allegiances, data, objectivity, and opinions.

Ads increasingly distract not only in their content, but their presentation. They simultaneously seek to monopolize your attention and to erode the meaning of language. Many email servers feature ads that block the side of the page and your emails, so you can't access them: the intent isn't just to distract, as the jiggling ads that pop up on your browser do, but to interfere. Many of these scrawls assail you with moving images, flashes, and overlays,

---

making it difficult to read the main pane. Advertisers incessantly attempt to make you think ads are email messages or news, anything but advertisement, as part of their relentless campaign of misdirection to draw your gaze. A recent trend is to feature distorted faces to attract your attention to ads. Almost every credit card mailer that says "important account information inside" is only advertising high-interest loans—any sensible definition of "important information" has been subverted. Everything from bad breath to a life-saving drug is reduced to the same level of triviality by being elevated to the same level of urgency. Networks and websites need to generate revenue—but all this is something of a different order. Ads distort reality and distort and trespass on every person who views them; many distort and trespass on public space.

The rationale for advertising and sponsorship has undergone a radical transformation in the past fifty years that paces the premises of corporate personhood. With broadcast television you at least have the semblance of some kind of exchange: you pay for programming by watching ads. But with ads confronting you at gas stations, on the sides of buses, in every literal walk of life, you're being subjected to advertisement without even the pretense of recompense. You're being taken advantage of, incessantly, because public space has been sold at your expense, without your consent. Cities in financial crisis have started to sell ad spaces on public buildings and even fire hydrants—erasing the distinction between public and private, and essentially selling you out. Public entities from universities to government itself no longer generate the mere appearance of partisanship; they have come to endorse and be endorsed by products, a process that reached bathetic depths in the Trump administration's continuous association with Trump's own products and those of his cronies. (Many of Trump's allies, from Herman Cain to the CEOs of Goya and MyPillow, embraced corporate personhood as a con game.) New York subway cars often repeat a single ad throughout the compartment: you're meant to be unable to look at anything else. Advertisers seek to trap you in confined spaces with their ads, creating what they call a "captive audience." Venturing forth in this society effectively places you in a hostage situation. I often feel like Alex in *A Clockwork Orange*, eyes pinned open and forced to view horrible acts of idiocy, violence, and intrusion. Credit cards directly sponsor government programs such as TSA-Pre. At the California DMV, you're subjected to screens that show commercial ads interspersed with public service messages, conflating the two and undermining the government's claim to be a public service. Interacting with government becomes almost indistinguishable from interacting with corporate stores, restaurants, airlines, and so on, which all subject us to screens everywhere we look, meaning we spend much of our lives in modified panopticons, always forced to watch. Aside from selling our trust and eroding the vital distinction between the public and private sectors, advertisers here shift the balance of the social contract and encroach on the public good—public space, public trust, and public services.

In his 1975 science fiction novel *The Shockwave Rider*, John Brunner predicted the way an initial resistance to advertising would give way to co-option and addiction:

> Traditionally one had defaced or scrawled on posters and billboards, or sometimes—mainly in rural areas—shot at them because the eyes or nipples of a model formed convenient targets. Later, when a common gadget around the house was a set of transparent screens . . . to place over the TV set for mock tennis and similar games, strangely enough the viewers' ratings for commercials went up. Instead of changing channels when advertising began, people took to switching in search of more. . . . To the content of which they were paying no attention. . . . With horror the advertisers and network officials discovered that in nine cases out of ten the most dedicated watchers could not recall what product was being promoted. . . . Saturation point, and the inception of diminishing returns, was generally dated to the early eighties, when the urban citizen of North America was for the first time hit with an average of over a thousand advertisements *per diem*. (189–90)

An American Association of Advertising Agencies study, more than twenty-five years old and not reflecting current internet and smartphone usage, found that average consumers viewed 1,600 advertisements per day, which now likely has doubled (Fox, 328; Sivulka, xiii). Andrea Bennett in an article in *Adbusters* contends that advertisers cumulatively spent $498 annually on every American by 2011 (16, 18). In other words, what many of us see, hear, and read most aren't the utterances of people—writers, artists, entertainers, politicians, or even loved ones—but of corporations.

Chapter Four

He Can't Be a Man 'Cause He Doesn't Smoke the Same Detergent Pack as Me

Although I watched only a moderate amount of TV growing up, I can remember the entirety of the idiotic jingle for Beautiful Mount Airy Lodge but not the Yeats or Dickenson poems I once knew by heart. A Poconos resort, Mount Airy Lodge was hardly a national or even an impersonal business—but it participated in the same aesthetic, moral, and persuasive economy as larger corporations. Most ads are designed to function like viruses, to infect and colonize your mind so you associate a phrase or tune with a product in a purely meaningless way that is instrumental—in other words, programmatic. Corporations write code into you through ads. Most people will hear the jingle for a car insurance company far more than they'll ever hear anything by Bach, the Beatles, or Beyoncé. A performance I saw in a retirement center in Florida consisted of skits and songs from radio plays from the 1940s; but what most people recognized most, and reacted most enthusiastically to, were the ad jingles for detergents. Those commercials triggered memories of what were likely the happiest years of their lives, so their nostalgia was not necessarily directed at and only triggered by the commercials, but what does it say about our culture if our deepest bonds and fondest memories are cathected to advertisements?

What's the cost of being lied to hundreds of times a day? What would it mean if a thousand individuals lied to you to your face each day? Advertisers marshal a complex apparatus whose output rivals most countries' GNP, all to manipulate your behavior. This process has nothing to do with rational persuasion or the political speech of free debate in a democracy, and advertisers have little accountability to the public (only to their clients). Advertisers have become so aggressive that they will suggest, usually without irony, that you'll be shunned or even harmed if you don't buy a brand of product. Most peddlers of addictive substances go to prison, or at least are regulated, but advertisers—whose aim is to induce anxiety, discomfort, fear, envy and unhappiness, entirely to get you addicted to buying something—are glamorized. Many of us respond by coming down with Stockholm Syndrome: we identify with the process that indoctrinates us. Much of the time—when we fly, arrive early at movies, watch most Hollywood films, or simply venture out in public or interact with virtually any aspect of our culture—we're paying to be subjected to advertising, a scenario that reflects a culture of wide-ranging masochism and exploitation. Advertising is at the center of a serious public health issue. It perhaps affects women most, whose body image and sense of self-worth are targeted by the beauty industry, but no one is immune, because advertising relies on insecurity, self-doubt, envy, and disaffection to convince everyone that they're inadequate. We're incessantly told we can become whole by not only buying products that are deleterious to us and our environment, but by internalizing an allegiance to the corporations that produce them and accepting the premises of corporate identity.

What enabled contemporary corporations and advertising to turn people into consumers in political and cultural contexts and corporations into super-persons? How did corporations come to exploit so effectively the gap between product and ad, fantasy and reality, and human and corporate personhood? Some of these contemporary contradictions and schisms can be traced to the nineteenth-century split between domestic/private and business/public ethics. What was acceptable behavior at home was cast against what was acceptable in business—many other splits arose from these bifurcations and helped generate a business persona that could be rigid, rapacious, corporate, and in some cases effectively sociopathic. By the mid-nineteenth century, pacing the country's industrialization, acceptable domestic behavior began to be cast and defined against what was acceptable in business. That division complemented the split between the human and corporate person. Where the former was supposed not to lie and to assume responsibility and liability for actions, the latter was growing freer of constraints in speech and action (a conceit literalized in the TV series *Severance*, whose corporate historian is an analogue to the corporate ethnographer writing the Great Report in Tom McCarthy's 2015 novel *Satin Island*).[1] A businessman increasingly was expected to be ruthless and disingenuous in his work, but still meticulously honest at home. It's as if the deceptions of business became necessary to underwrite the fantasized candor of homelife. But that border between public and private now barely exists even in fantasy: the public self has displaced the private, even as private enterprise increasingly displaces the public sphere. The granting of ever greater personhood to corporations and the invasiveness of contemporary marketing is commensurate with Judge Richard Posner's notion that everything is commodifiable—especially the most intimate aspects of human relations—and can be priced, advertised, bought, and sold. (The culturally bankrupt law and economics movement, which evaluates human behavior, laws, and incentives in purely monetary terms, reflects the final eradication of any lingering nineteenth-century distinctions between public and private space, and work and domestic spheres.) Companies never have been in the business of telling the truth but of selling—using whatever rational or irrational methods work best. But corporate advertising presumes the only way to communicate is to manipulate. The ways we might market ourselves or lie as individuals—for example, on résumés or dates—and even the "hard-sell" are distinguishable from the structural misrepresentations endemic to advertising. Advertising tracks and precipitates an encroachment on public spaces, values, and objectivity that, as Brunner suggests, we once resisted. More specifically, sponsorship has become a wide-ranging means of co-option and control. In conjunction with other forms of advertisement, the consolidation of media, the denigration and defunding of public education, and the erosion of attention spans and literacy, it's managed to generate a culture of intrusion and distraction whose primary and highest form of expression is akin to visual yelling.

Corporations have accreted and magnified the positive traits of persons—for example, agency, legal and human rights, speech—while minimizing or eliminating their limitations and negative attributes—responsibility and liability, susceptibility to social constraints, and mortality. In this sense, corporations adapt the self-definition of the United States in claiming to be exceptional. To help explain how we got here, I trace a teleology of corporate exceptionalism and examine how certain legal conceptions of personhood in the United States—from those attributed to fetuses and corporations to those denied to non-US citizens and enemy combatants—have come to be predicated on artificial and dangerously mutable conceptions of who and what can possess human identity and rights. For example, corporations counter-sue human rights lawyers for libel, as if corporate entities had personal qualities or human characters one could defame (Meier, B2). Inhuman things are systemically using personal discourses against people. Because we lack coherent accepted definitions of personhood, corporations have been able to hijack and co-opt the very notion of human identity and rights, and they have precipitated and benefitted from an inchoate patchwork of laws and cultural beliefs regarding personhood, speech, and agency. The next chapters address the dense historical backdrop of the corporate form, which might not be of interest to readers who would prefer to focus on more familiar and accessible examples of contemporary corporate malfeasance. In which case, they might want to skip to chapter 8.

Chapter Five

The Nature of Corporations

The history of corporations must be considered as part of another history: of the attribution of personality, agency, and voice to impersonal and non-individual entities—God, nature, the state, and other collectivities and organizations. Even legal codes often implicitly imbue corporations with the superhuman and quasi-mystical properties of divinities (these entities usually are imagined to be immortal, for example). We have personalized such forces to provide causal explanations for systems we don't understand, and we do something similar with corporations, assigning personhood and personality to what we pretend is an impersonal market force that somehow allegedly operates independently of people and culture. As I elaborate, corporations are designed to elide personality and responsibility. Fisher contends that "centerless impersonality" defines corporate behavior and malfeasance; trying to impose ethical responsibility in such a corporate system is hopeless and pointless, in part because no individual can be held responsible for structural and systemic mechanisms, imperatives, and behaviors (*Capitalist* 68–9). Who's to blame in an impersonal system of transactions that disconnects individuals from actions and human valuations? Can one hold the agent who answers the phone for a corporation accountable for anything the person says or the corporation does? We're inclined to think we can blame the corporate board or CEO, who might be guilty of illegal or questionable behavior, but who are ultimately as fungible as cans of soda. As one example that might seem counterintuitive, replacing a corporate board usually would change little; it's the permanent impersonal structure that makes genuine human agency nearly impossible in such a system. Fisher attributes the persistence and power of the corporate system to capital, the ulterior impersonal mechanism and god that drives the economy, but it's the corporate form that's most responsible for the evacuation of human agency and personality in many contemporary societies (80–81).

Some of us retain the illusion that we can speak to a corporation, when we never can. It doesn't matter whether we reach a disempowered agent in a cubicle or a megalomaniacal CEO. We could speak to an infinite and arbitrary series of agents and we never get through to the corporation, because it doesn't exist in that sense. Reacting to what a corporation does is hopeless and pointless—you might find sympathetic employees, but you cannot encounter the corporation. People might say institutions are just made up of, and are as good as, its employees—but people who work for corporations don't set the rules, especially with regard to the corporate form and its demands and constraints. When an oil spill destroys an ecosystem, some engineer or ship's captain was negligent at a local level, but it's the corporation—the corporate ethos, imperative, structure—that exists above and beyond and persists long after such individuals that remains the culprit. The idea that individuals can buck or reform corporations is usually a romantic fantasy and a Hollywood reification that allows people to imagine safety valves that don't exist. No Warren Beatty character from *Heaven Can Wait* can reform a corporation's directives; corporations can never be the good guys because they never can *be*.

One should also situate the corporation as a quasi-transcendental or metaphysical construct, whose lineage can be traced to impersonal divinities. Sociologists John Meyer and Ronald Jepperson, who study organizations, propose that in

> modern Western ontology, there is an ongoing diminishment of the domain under direct transcendental-spiritual control. . . . [As God recedes], agency and authority are relocated immanently in society's structures and rationales. Some agency is built into modern pictures of the agentic authority and responsibility of the state and other organizations; much devolves to the modern individual, who is empowered with more and more godlike authority and vision. (105)

But the modern individual is much less empowered in the context of corporate personhood than such analyses assert. In focusing on the distinction between "man" generally and previously divine forces of agency, Meyer and Jepperson fail to differentiate adequately between individual and corporate agency: they assert that "'Man' as actor—individuals, organizations, states—carries almost the entire responsibility for the now-sacralized human project, with gods, other spiritual forces, ancestors, or an animated nature drained of agency" (105). In many ways, the corporation has filled the role of those gods and forces. And the organization of the corporation is exceptional—it has attained super-agency but jettisoned responsibility. Sociologists tend to treat agency, or actorhood, as a given and then address how it functions in different regimes (rather than question the premises of agency ontologically): according to Gili Drori, John Meyer, and Hokyu Hwang,

The organization is an "actor" rather than a passive instrument of an external actor. Extending beyond the legal dimension, this actorhood is expressed, for example, in the organizations speaking in a singular voice: corporation A denies this. . . . Actorhood of this sort is also a feature of workers and participants in such organizations: they are responsible for and initiators of the organization's tasks rather than servants of an executive head. (40)

But as I attempt to demonstrate, such formulations fundamentally misunderstand the nature of corporations, which are devices that suppress human agency and actorhood, and the range of behaviors possible within corporate systems is exceptionally circumscribed for structural reasons. Corporate workers and consumers are often passive and disempowered. As a tangential but telling example, an ad for the drug Xeljanz, in a tactic many drug ads use, scrolls a litany of horrific side effects. But the ad then concludes by subtly eliding the agency of either the corporation or the consumer; we're told serious illnesses, negative test results and deaths from infection "have happened," because the advertiser is trying to hide the fact that these things resulted directly from taking the drug. In other words, there's no agent acting here at all, no active ingredient causing anything to happen; no speaker ever exists behind corporate speech. More broadly, corporate actorhood is always that of the actor in an ad representing the corporation; a falsification that encapsulates the disconnection between person and corporation, act and missing actor. The conceptual and grammatical passivity of this ad reflect the foundational fact that corporations are constructed to deny liability and agency. They have super-agency to commit acts no individual can, but they remain unlocatable when serious side effects just happen.

Surprisingly, the corporation represents an ongoing mutation of what the nineteenth-century transcendentalist Ralph Waldo Emerson formulated as the impersonal transcendental collective (which he designated Nature, natural law, the Over-Soul, and the All). The contemporary corporation functions as a collective fiction that replaces its apparent opposite of nature: the Over-Soul, the figurative soul of nature, or "the All" is subsumed by the corporation that's continually identified as having a mechanical, but lacking a human, soul. The corporation is also in a zero-sum game with nature, and finally even the state. Transcendentalism and pantheism—the extreme form of transcendentalism that treated natural law as a precisely impersonal deity—emerged in a narrow but influential strain of US culture. Primarily reflecting elite Northeastern views of nature, transcendentalism didn't represent a "national" culture, but it did voice persistent fantasies about universality, nationality, and impersonal forces and laws. Emerson believed that God was not an anthropomorphic figure, but an impersonal system of natural laws, designated under the umbrella term of nature; that deity was universal and omnipresent, and could have a personality attributed to it—that is, it could be personified. But it was not human in any way; Emerson could never have a personal Jesus. The impersonal God, or All, was a mediating structure, a regulatory system that governed all forces of nature, mechanisms of communication and exchange, and principles of rationality.

Emerson claims, for example, that in all conversation, "tacit reference is made, as to a third party, to *a common nature* . . . [that] is not social; it is impersonal; is God" (*Works*, "Over-Soul" II, 277, emphasis in original). Nature or God here mediates as a language might; we cannot converse directly to another without invoking or relying on this common intermediary force or language. But as Emerson emphasizes, this god and common nature are impersonal: they're not modeled on individual human personality or identity but on an impersonal (and potentially mechanical) collective or interpersonal entity. All communication passes through that ubiquitous common impersonal entity, some form of a Lacanian Big Other—a fantasized omnipotent entity that sees and mediates all we do. (Emerson also became the transparent eyeball on the commons—that is, on the common space of that impersonal nature.) The often invoked "common nature" has become the province of the corporation; ironically, most of our personal lives are now mediated by impersonal corporations, from Tinder to Instagram, and many would argue that social media has made our lives far more impersonal. Our common nature, our common culture, is wired through the corporation. But the corporation always impersonates the personal and infiltrates the private and social spheres. Facebook emblematizes how the impersonal inhuman corporation imitates and regulates personal human interaction, while incessantly advertising to you.

Nineteenth-century transcendentalism remains germane to this discussion because many of the assets and qualities of universal and once divine impersonal nature, from ubiquity to immortality, have been transferred to the universal impersonal corporation. Leo Marx exposed the machine always present in the garden or nature of nineteenth-century US culture, for example, in the way the railroad effectively intrudes into even Walden Pond. (This machine eventually takes the form of artificial intelligence that mimics and supplants nature.) But it was also the corporation that owned the railroad, and not just a machine, that intruded into the transcendental garden. The transcendental or collective commons has become the province of corporations, and some of the numinous attributes and discourses of religion have been subsumed by the language of advertising. The corporation turns out to be an unexpectedly transcendental entity. As one emblematic example of the fusion between pseudo-religious, new age transcendental "spiritualism" and corporate personhood and advertising, Gopi Kallayli is described, on the back of his book *The Internet to the Innernet*, as "Chief Evangelist for Brand Marketing at Google . . . An avid Yoga practitioner . . . [Burning Man devotee and speaker at] the World Peace Festival, Wisdom 2.0 . . . and Yoga Journal Live!"

As I briefly argue in *Not Altogether Human: Pantheism and the Dark Nature of the American Renaissance*, some of our contemporary debate about the corporate form can be traced to nineteenth-century religious arguments about the nature of divine personality and impersonality. Many Christians have a personal relationship with a personified son of God: God is never impersonal, but often all too human. By contrast, transcendentalists were impugned for depersonifying God—for believing that nature controlled and was All. Emerson in particular developed a theory of pantheism in which every aspect of the impersonal world was alive and interconnected, and governed only by a universal nature. Partly with Emerson in mind, the New York–based Reverend Morgan Dix titled a critical 1864 work *Lectures on the Pantheistic Idea of an Impersonal Deity*, and it was common to consider nature the emblem of an impersonal God. Contemporary critics frequently charged that Emerson's deification of an impersonal nature would eviscerate human personality and personal relations. Another critic of Emerson, Andrews Norton, describes pantheism in terms of how it defines human and divine personality and impersonality, and in ways that will resonate with how we come to describe corporations. Norton denounces pantheists' attempts to merge with a deified nature as destructive to human personality: for the modern German pantheists who influenced transcendentalists,

> religion is the sense of the union of the individual with the universe, with Nature, or, in the language of the sect, with the One and All. It is a feeling; . . . independent of the idea of a personal God. And the belief and desire of personal immortality are "wholly irreligious," as being opposed to that which is the aim of religion, "the annihilation of one's own personality" . . . "becoming, as far as possible, one with the universe." (*Discourse* 11, 44)

Debates over whether god had a human personality were partly coterminous with debates about whether corporations were persons. In his biography of the Swedish mystic Emanuel Swedenborg, Edwin Hood asserted that for pantheists, "God is not a personality": The writings of this day are greatly imbued with the spirit of this great fallacy. . . . The essays of Emerson . . . [generate] a state beyond the pantheistic" (49–50, 60). Pantheism depersonalizes an anthropomorphic god and identifies divinity with impersonal systems. Reverend Jacob Manning, a Boston pastor, rebukes Spinoza for postulating a "being to whom understanding, will, and even personality is denied; a being who does not create, but simply is; who does not act, but simply unfolds. . . . Such a being cannot be a father, a friend, a benefactor; in a word, cannot be a God to man" (76). This evacuation of personality is as critical to transcendentalism as it is to the corporate form. Charles Feidelson declaims that "in order to become god-possessed, [transcendentalists] deny a personal god. By the same token, in order to unite themselves with nature, they also deny personal identity" (33). Relative to the universality of divine nature, for Emerson human "personality is a parasitic deciduous atom" (*Journals* V, 272). Americans could transcend that personality, or the individual, by merging into divine nature or the supra-natural corporation.

To Emerson, the self is the parasite, and a deficient fragment that can find a unified identity only by joining with collective nature, not society. Contrary to the popular perception that he championed the self, Emerson attributed true *personhood* only to the impersonal—to archetypal nature, universal truth, and traits that transcend the self. Emerson's nature—also universal, immortal and omnipresent—consequently begins to bear many of the attributes of corporations. Pantheists "worship" an impersonal God that is omnipresent, but locatable nowhere specifically.

As Mary Cayton documents, the early nineteenth-century use of the word *personality*, still common during Emerson's life, connoted being a person and not a thing; the transcendental and pantheist god is primarily a thing, and an impersonal abstraction (76–77, 223). In 1840, Tocqueville predicted that what we might now deem to be corporate religions would be popular in the United States because they allowed its isolated and exceptionally individualistic (enfranchised white male) citizens to submerge their solitary identities in a unified whole:

> [Any] philosophical system which teaches that all things material and immaterial . . . are to be considered only as the several parts of an immense Being, who alone remains eternal amidst the continual change and ceaseless transformation of all that constitutes him . . . such a system, though it destroy the individuality of man, or rather because it destroys that individuality, will have secret charms for men living in democracies. . . . It naturally attracts and fixes their imagination. (II, 31–32)[1]

In other words, Tocqueville situated nature as the American leviathan, but it turned out to have most of the qualities of the corporate octopus. As Tocqueville anticipates, Americans' extreme individualism poses the risk of a dangerous form of isolation and antisocialism, and it comes to generate a countervailing need to be immersed into some collective mass that effectively annihilates the individual.

I digress briefly here to lay the groundwork for several arguments, which will apply in multiple contexts, about the corporate mass. The transcendental system Tocqueville evoked initially took the shape of nature, to a lesser degree the nation-state, and finally the immense Being of the corporation. As Tim Wu remarks of corporate culture generally, "The urge to surrender to something larger and to transcend the self can be just as urgent, if not more so," than the predilection for individuality (*Attention*

120). That desire to "transcend" the individual in the immense mass defines transcendentalism as well as the ethos of the corporation, which in many ways fulfills this ontological imperative. Tocqueville concluded that Americans, because of their atomization in a society of inordinate or radical presumed autonomy, would be attracted to systems or religions that merge their individuality into the mass of nature or the state—that is, that subsume their autonomy to some transcendent and collective force. In the United States, corporations began to supplant nation-states as they started in systemic ways to take on the transcendental functions of nature. They also imposed a false form of cosmopolitanism based not on the universal franchise of democracy, but the universal franchise of corporate outlets. As I later argue, Nature was always a "transcendent" fiction of collective identity in US culture, one that not only bore strong affinities with the corporation, but also was ultimately revealed as its predecessor.

Many of the tenets of pantheism serve as precursors to corporate capitalism because the corporation becomes the "immense being" that supplants nature as well as the state. Reverend Dix proposed we conjure "this immense condition, or mass, or state (or by whatever name you wish to call it) and you have before you the only eternal being. Let us apply to it, for the sake of convenience, the term God" (22). What is consistently referred to as this immense, immortal, mass body symbolically has been sacralized in the corporation as well, for which we're expected to sacrifice ourselves. (As anyone who deals with corporate customer service can attest, the corporation is often as capricious in its communication as a deity.) The immense "body" we belong to isn't that of community but corporation, which participates only in transactions that are part of a zero-sum game. While writers such as Hobbes, Tocqueville, and Emerson invoke a language that seeks "common" nature that will create a common wealth, the mass, immortal corporate version of that common body winds up absorbing and dissolving its members. As noted, one of Emerson's terms for the immense being of divine nature was "the Over-Soul." It's particularly ironic that the corporation, which is immaterial, attains a body with the most mass in the world. That immense corporate body was intermittently imagined to possess a(n over) soul, but as it became increasingly impersonal, it also became clear it functioned without a mind.

The corporation translated and reduced most human endeavors, motives, capacities, and interests to purely economic contexts. Emerson already worried that modern US and British society had become "a great industrial corporation" that rewarded and valued only commerce (Sealts 222). But nineteenth-century US formulations of nature contained incipient premises of industrial globalization, the process that connected the world not through nature, but corporate transactions and power. Though he was averse to travel, Emerson, perhaps unwittingly, attempted to tether natural science and certain kinds of technology and evoke universal (worldwide) laws of nature, forces, and flows of communication that augured and helped foreground a form of globalization. In some perversely surprising ways, contemporary forms of nomadic globalization, in which labor migrates with the flow of capital, have roots in romantic transcendentalism, a discourse that sought to universalize culture through both nature and technology (for example, the emblematic railroad and telegraph that would link all time and space, and were built by nomadic workers whose presence displaced nomadic Native Americans). Transcendentalism combined a resistance to travel with a contradictory fetishization of technology and a "nomadic" state of nature.

I here share a brief anecdote that encapsulates how these transcendental US notions of nature are, at a more literal level, easily commodified in a corporate ethos. In the 1990s, I participated in a joint Japanese-American conference on environmental issues and encountered a Japanese version of Thoreau's *Walden* (which is in the public domain, and so can be translated and revised at will). A Japanese sporting goods corporation sponsored the edition; the message of the radically revised text, the only version of *Walden* many of the Japanese readers had ever encountered, was that nature could be experienced properly only with the right gear. While Thoreau himself embellished his tale of solitude and self-reliance considerably—his cabin was not especially remote, and he didn't spend as much time there as he claimed—he never would have brooked sponsorship. But it turns out that transcendental nature had been sponsoring or guaranteeing our sense of identity in ways that made it easy for the corporation to take over that function. In an unwittingly perceptive comment on American culture, the Japanese corporation turned *Walden* into a version of *Tom Sawyer*—a paint job, a cover up, an endless practical joke, that we've been taught to pay for and enjoy. REI's corporate personality is based on similar premises—only corporations can mediate your experience of the world, natural or otherwise. Emblematic of corporate culture, *Walden* became just a surface for advertisements for other products. Around the world, culture, which had once been the loss leader for the ad, has become subservient to it through the corporation.

As I elucidate, before the Civil War, some of the transcendental rhetoric regarding merger with universal nature reflected Northern attempts to counter Southern sectionalism. The "demonology" of or exception to that rhetoric involved forms of disunion and dismemberment, initially figurative, but ultimately literalized in the carnage of the Civil War itself. Transcendentalists encouraged individuals to transcend individuality in nature; the state then urged them to relinquish their individuality to the nation in war, in the cause of union. As Elizabeth White Nelson documents, it was critical for the North to incorporate or merge with the West as an extension of itself, as part of its overarching directive to achieve "cultural unity in the face of Southern political dominance" (15). Northern exhortations to pursue a more perfect union, and the perfectibility of man, often invoked a more perfect merger into a federated whole. After the Civil War, almost all transcendental rhetoric regarding *union* with nature (or merger with a larger whole or All) was deflected to rhetorics of *incorporation*. In other words, once political union had been secured, the rhetoric of consolidation and progress began to focus more directly on the corporation rather than the state. The sometimes seemingly abstract contest between the individual and the immense corporate mass is evident in more concrete terms, for example, in the jury instructions of an 1886 Mississippi Supreme Court case:

> This poor negro has the same right to have his matters adjudicated as the defendant, but things have come to such a pass in this country that a railroad company is very much injured if an humble man dares to bring them into the courts. If he dares to appeal to the juries of the country, it is high treason. I say you must consider who the parties are, and who is more likely to overawe witnesses,—a corporation of this sort, or a private individual. I put it to your own knowledge of human nature, whether it is not true that immense corporations, controlling immense armies of operatives, are not more likely to overawe witnesses.

Newman v. Vicksburg & M. R. Co., 64 Miss. 115, 122 (Miss 1886). (As I address in more detail, it is illustrative that the personhood of African Americans is pitted against the immense personhood of the corporation in terms of legal speech.)

Subsequent cases often have referred to the unprecedented power of "immense corporations," *St. Louis Gaslight Co. v. City of St. Louis,* 84 Mo. 202, 204 (1884), and corporations as immense aggregates: *Nw. Union Packet Co. v. Shaw,* 37 Wis. 655, 660 (1875) (acknowledging that "that the transportation of the products of the country is mainly controlled by powerful corporations, representing immense aggregations of capital"); *McCarter v. Firemen's Ins. Co.,* 74 N.J. Eq. 372, 381 (1909) (addressing "the enormous extension of this business, by its concentration in the hands of immense corporations, by state regulations that amount to privileges"); *Com. v. Copperman,* 26 Pa. D. 763, 769 (Pa. Com. Pl. 1917) (stating that we live in the "days of giant corporations, great railroad companies, immense industrial and financial organizations"); *Race Safe Sys., Inc. v. Indy Racing League,* 251 F. Supp. 2d 1106, 1108 (N.D.N.Y. 2003) (referring to "an immense multi-national corporation"). Brook Thomas contends that in the early nineteenth century, when the country's new market economy required great expenditures, common law that bound private corporations to serve a public good was abandoned to favor private first developers, ever-increasingly turning chartered limitations into special privileges and rights (259). The once aptly named common law was supplanted by corporate law effectively written by and for the corporate person. As the Court recently noted, apparently without irony or alarm, most recently and disturbingly in *Citizens United*, 558 U.S. at 351, "media corporations accumulate wealth with the help of the corporate form, [and] the largest media corporations have 'immense aggregations of wealth.'"

This immensity is captured throughout contemporary culture, from images of megalithic corporations to the notion that banks are too big to fail; their very size often seems to produce an anxiety that we're irremediably dependent on these corporations. And as Don DeLillo conjectures in his 1976 novel *Ratner's Star*, we come to fear "Absorption by the shapeless Mass. Total assimilation. They would be incorporated, transformed and metabolized" (132). This incorporation is a form of mass assimilation, a nightmarish version of the earlier dream of absorption into nature, and of a collective corporate identity that transcends and digests isolated individuality. The primary economic force of US society is structurally antithetical to democratic institutions, processes, and values. Aside from retail, much of media in this country is controlled by a handful of corporations. As Naomi Klein notes, in film or television you "have to be huge to stay in the game. Here once again is the strange combination of a sea of product coupled with losses in real choice" (159). Only the largest firms can survive in many industries, let alone enter them or speak. The *Citizens United* holding ratified the insidious notions that corporations are people and money is speech, which means that corporations can simply outspend/outspeak everyone at will.

I return to this fantasy of merging with the mass—and ideas of mass identity, production and consumption, and the corporate mass itself— throughout this book because it evolves across multiple contexts in multiple periods. Wu contends that the purpose of German fascism was to "smelt an entire people into a single mass consciousness" (*Attention* 109). But much the same could be said of American transcendentalism and the corporation. Addressing the crowd psychology of Gustave Le Bon to explain Nazism, Wu adds that "it is loss of individual responsibility that makes the individual in the crowd more malleable," and the same proviso should be applied to the corporate form, which is designed to eradicate individuality and liability (113). (As I elaborate, we should in such contexts contrast the partnership with the corporate form.) Though he doesn't reductively equate the techniques of fascist propaganda with those of advertising, Wu proposes that the goal of broadcasters is "to mold that relative sameness [of national sensibilities] into a single, national consumer mass," and that mass will have secret charms because it helps us escape our dismal individuality (175). As Wu intimates in somewhat different contexts, the Western state after World War Two abdicated the use of overt propaganda and mass propaganda campaigns (though certainly not the manipulation of media), as the corporation took on their use (*Attention* 121). Ironically, many Americans retain a wariness of government as manipulative and untrustworthy but have much less wariness or perception of the workings of its successor. In whatever ways one might claim media or audiences have become fragmented, corporations have attained state-like influence that rivals that of any achieved by state propaganda. If you think billions of people drink an acrid, enamel-destroying liquid because they choose to of their own will, you've drunk the cola. Corporations influence and impact daily life more than governments, and it's almost impossible to go for a few days, let alone a more protracted period, without seeing corporate ads, using corporate products, or visiting corporate franchises.

As noted, critics of pantheism often targeted its proponents' tendency to personify and deify abstractions, especially the impersonal mass and impersonal laws of nature. In "Transcendentalism," Cyrus Bartol asks whether events are "determined by persons, or by laws? . . . Personality is nothing, or it is all. . . . If we are personal, we have a destiny; if impersonal, only a doom" (120–22). Pantheists tried to redeem the impersonal principle of divinity on the grounds that it afforded permanence. Responding to such maneuvers, Reverend Manning assails Emersonian beliefs by invoking an "intuition of the immortal, a consciousness that the essential element of man, that *principle* of individuality, never dies." But pantheists make the corporate attributes of nature benign, much as we've made them seem natural; Manning complains that what Emerson's Christian devotees "took for the immortality of the person as now living and conscious, [Emerson] seems to have meant *only for the eternity of the impersonal 'soul'* which fills all things" (345). For Reverend Morgan Dix, pantheists reject the personality of God: "the personality of almighty God is either in terms or by implication necessarily denied, even by those who admit of His existence" (18–19). In other words, Emersonian pantheists sacralize an impersonal soul, which becomes the hallmark of the corporation. Sounding as if he has Emerson in mind, Dix proposes that for pantheists, "God developed into trees and animals . . . took this higher form and passed to consciousness, then . . . God arrived at the knowledge of God in becoming man. . . . God has no personality and no consciousness but in man. . . . [Man] was God coming to the consciousness of Himself" (25). Even sympathetic critics such as Émile Edmond Saisset, a French philosopher whose works recall those of early Emerson, argue that "liberty without responsibility, morality without duty, immortality without consciousness, mad idolatry of self—these are the practical conclusions of Pantheism. This is what it makes of human personality." Saisset believes we must safeguard "two poles of all human science—the personal I, with whom all begins, and the personal God, in whom all ends" (II 122). A central question for pantheists is then whether *impersonal* resurrection in nature can guarantee the resurrection of actual persons. Late in life, even Emerson accedes that only laws and impersonal forces abide: "I confess that everything connected with our personality fails. Nature never spares the individual" (*Works*, "Immortality" VIII, 342). In other words, the price for impersonal immortality in nature (or the corporation) is the personal self. When human personality fails, the residue that survives is that of corporate personhood. According to Cameron, Emerson

> disdained "the personality of the deity" (the "soul knows no persons"), rather discovering manifestations of deity everywhere, which throughout his essays he variously called "the Over-soul," "the moral sentiment," "virtue," law," and "nature." His pantheism depended on the liquidity of foundational terms like "God," "Nature," and "self," terms which— offering no resistance to each other—were permeable. (*Impersonality* xv).

In the American Renaissance (the period of the 1840s–1850s), laying the groundwork for the great awakening of the corporation, the precepts of transcendental nature become incommensurate with those of a humanistic identity and nearly coterminous with those of corporatism.

An Edinburgh Divinity Professor and author of *Modern Atheism: Under Its Forms of Pantheism, Materialism, Secularism, Development, and Natural Laws*, published in the United States in 1857, James Buchanan treats the Dutch philosopher Spinoza as a source of many fallacies of American pantheism: "With him, God is not a person but personality which realizes itself in every human consciousness, as so many thoughts of one eternal mind, apart from, and out of, the world; therefore there is no god, and so apart from the universal consciousness of man there is no divine consciousness or personality" (134).[2] To the pantheist, human individuality and personality are insignificant and illusory: divine "personality," whether in a collective god or deified natural laws, is impersonal and therefore authentic in transcending limited and partial personality. Emerson believed only in an "aboriginal self," an archetypal self that exists before and after individuality, and one displaced by the Over-Soul ("Self-Reliance" II, 63). In the above contexts, Emerson's vaunted representative men are exemplary precisely to the extent that they've transcended individuality to become impersonal, or finally corporate, types. (Corporate products, franchises and experiences "transcend" particularity and are meant to be identical everywhere). As Emerson admonishes in his lecture "Love," "Thus even Love which is the deification of persons must become more impersonal every day" (*EL* III, 64). For Edmond Holmes, in *All Is One: A Plea for the*

Higher Pantheism, God "entirely transcends" the category of personality as anthropomorphically defined. Echoing Emerson, Holmes wonders, "can one give love to an impersonal deity? . . . The words personal and impersonal have gone into the melting pot; and there is no telling what they will mean when they re-emerge from it" (113). (Those shuffled words and precepts have reemerged in notions of corporate impersonality and personhood, forms of our new post- and transhuman deities. In corporate contexts, the American trope of the melting pot has quite different connotations, and we will see it recur with regard to the absorption of individual identity). Even Emerson's would-be acolyte, philosopher and general Ethan Allen Hitchcock, grandson of Revolutionary War hero Ethan Allen, proposed that "generals and great men are pygmies. Principles, laws of nature, truth—these alone seem grand" (*Fifty* 134). Persons are incessantly displaced by these "grand" archetypes and impersonal principles, by structures and attributes that outlive them.

In incipient ways, some critics of transcendentalism were criticizing its proto-corporate ethos of human personality. Manning, for example, reminds us that "personality is properly but another name for determinateness," and that pantheists such as Emerson "deny all personality. Man, to their view, is essentially impersonal; a person only a personification" (372). An impersonal nature, and later its successor corporation, becomes the putative guarantor of the personal attributes lost as the norms that attend an anthropomorphic god recede. From the composite figures of the white whale to the Confidence Man, Melville imagines the results of this "personification" of the impersonal in both nature and the corporation. Melville most famously dramatizes this prospect in *Moby-Dick*, "incarnating" the universal mind in one allencompassing mass body. Simply put, "all those malicious agencies" larger than the individual male self, and "all evil, to crazy Ahab were *visibly personified* and made practically assailable in Moby Dick" (184). In complex ways, *Moby-Dick* stages a contest between the personified forces of capital (in the way monomaniacal Ahab, against Starbuck, genuinely represents the emblematically corporate whaling venture) and the personified forces of nature (in the white whale).

According to the critic Leon Chai, for transcendentalists, "this "personified impersonal" is but another name for God" (324). (It turns out to be another name for the business of America. The corporation is quintessentially impersonal, but we interface with it by imposing human faces and features on it. If nature or God must be personified, so must the impersonal corporation, in the use of mascots, CEOs, and brand images). For Emerson, man becomes divine by becoming impersonal—by transcending individual personhood. For the Unitarian Reverend Orville Dewey, a contemporary of Emerson's, impersonality is a key attribute of Emersonian pantheism: "If we deny [Divine intelligence], rational religion is impossible. Such denial leads directly and inevitably to Pantheism. . . . [Pantheists] give up the personality of the Supreme Being" (202). Pantheists seek not to attain salvation from, but merge with, this inhuman impersonal god. Even a relatively positive anonymous assessment of contemporary US religion in an 1844 issue of *The United States Democratic Review* stresses that "the tendency to merge the universe and man in God—to make all things deity, and Deity all things— is the peculiar pantheism of the present day," a trend that, as Tocqueville declaimed, reflected the need for Americans to subsume themselves to larger, ultimately corporate forces (*Spirit* 30). Famously wanting to merge directly into nature, Emerson writes that within the "plantations of God . . . in the woods . . . [I am] bathed by the blithe air and uplifted into infinite space,— all mean egotism vanishes. I become a transparent eyeball. I am nothing; I see all; the currents of the Universal Being circulate through me" ("Nature" 10–11). Emerson would merge with deified nature only, and he awaited "that rapture of absorption into the divine life" ("Natural Religion," *Uncollected* 60–61, 65). In important ways, his valorization of merger with nature was as anti-social as merger with the corporation. Absorption into the All of nature or larger impersonal corporate systems allows one to transcend (or as Melville concludes, erase) individual personality. As the TV series *Made for Love* (which in critical ways replicates the virtual ontology of *Avatar*) emphasizes, corporations, and especially tech corporations, not only supplant nature with virtual nature, but symbolically prompt people to merge their minds into single, virtual entities.

Accumulation and aggregation are usually zero-sum games; the more money, power, sheer mass, and ontological privilege corporations attain, the less is left to individuals. Transcendentalists fantasized that nature was a bulwark against and alternative to the mechanistic corporation and the emerging corporate society, but the language used to evoke both sides of this equation revealed a discursive and ontological commonality. Emerson wanted men to merge into (a corporate, impersonal) nature and not society; he notably warned in "Self-Reliance" that "Society is a joint-stock company, in which the members agree, for the better securing of his bread to each shareholder, to surrender the liberty and culture of the eater. The virtue in most request [*sic*] is conformity. Self-reliance is its aversion" (II, 49–50). But by the term *self-reliance*, Emerson unequivocally meant God-reliance— reliance on an archetypal self that transcended individuality and became representative. Transcendentalism asks us to transcend the self/autonomy as false concepts. Here, Emerson sounds strikingly like an inverted Hobbes, inveighing that individuals shouldn't surrender their liberty and autonomy in exchange for security. While Emerson championed the individual, his definition of individuality was anomalous, and it was predicated on the transcendence of what most people would consider the particular self. Appropriately, Richard Garnett describes Emerson as an isolated crystal, "the last of mankind to be merged into a joint-stock association" (103). Wanting to avoid joining with the joint-stock entity of society, however, Emerson didn't fully or consistently glean that his nature was even more corporate, demonological, or collectively irrational. Ironically, in trying to avoid merging with the corporate society/state, Emerson proposed merging with, and surrendering one's autonomy to, a nature just as corporate, immense, impersonal, and dispossessing.

Emerson's conception of nature turns out to be compatible, and even a kind of screen for, the corporation (e.g., in offering a collective identity that's everywhere the same, and in transcending individual mortality). Emerson's relinquishment of personal autonomy to the laws of nature reifies the relinquishment of autonomy to corporate capitalism and culture: in such a system, we ultimately aren't responsible for our actions, because they're controlled by larger forces. Emerson's proviso reflects a kind of cultural automachia (or self civil war), in which individual autonomy turns out to be predicated on corporate conformity: one's identity is largely defined by mass production and culture, and one's agency—whether in political or economic terms—is reduced to what we might call manufactured autonomy. The precept of autonomy is here automated, yet it perpetuates the illusion that we make free choices.

One of my overarching claims is that several prominent proponents of individualism and presumed autonomy in US culture have been widely misappropriated or misinterpreted, and that such misprisions are structurally necessary (misappropriations that represent a different version of a Bloomian strong misreading). This logic of inversion attaches to much of corporate history, in the way corporate language inverts or warps meaning, predicates qualities on their opposite (e.g., defines individuality as conformity), and conceals similarities between alleged opposites (nature and corporation). For example, Ayn Rand—and this is not any defense of her work—would have vehemently opposed the right wing that incessantly invokes her ideas; she opposed the criminalization of drugs; thought governments have no right to make decisions about gay marriage, abortion, and so on; and thought religion was a form of psychosis. Emerson even more than Rand has been misappropriated and inverted by the right wing, but neither would be assimilable to the general culture if their work weren't misread and misapplied. One could say this phenomenon pertains in a generic sense to figures from Christ to Gloria Steinem, but a particular and exigent dissonance applies in the context of American self-reliance, which always was predicated on a history of genocide, slavery, denial, and corporatism. Though entirely disparate in most aspects of their beliefs and influences, Emerson and Rand, in consonant ways, don't laud individuality, but its dissolution into an archetypal and hierarchical higher self purged of human particularity and idiosyncrasy. In Rand's play *Night of January 16*, we're advised to "value a strength that is its *own motor*, an audacity that is *its own law*," an exhortation that defines a kind of radical sui-generis autonomy; we must develop a "self" that coincides with universal law (118). Auto/nomy means, as Cornelius Catoriadis would note, by itself law, a law for/from itself, as opposed to heteronomy. Emerson also had insisted, in disturbingly Randy language, that "*The height of culture, the highest behavior, consists in the identification of the Ego with the universe. . . .[But]* communication [between man and his work] follows *its own law*, and refuses our intrusion"—that is, we surrender to something autonomous from us, the common communication that exists between us, the nature or corporation that mediates everything (*Works*, "Natural History," XII: 62). Emerson's concept of self-reliance, which advocated harmonious merger with a generic self in nature, has been appropriated to represent an antagonism to government, which was once the primary, if during many periods theoretical, check on corporations. But the ethos of self-reliance also reified and hid the fact that an incipient corporate economy was, even in the North, dependent on the opposite of self-reliance— the exploitation of slave labor.

In Melville's *Moby-Dick*, Ishmael tries to imagine an alternative to the social-commercial enterprise of his nation, even as he embarks on a commercial whaling expedition, by "merg[ing his] own individuality" with Queequeg's "in a joint stock company of two" (320). (Ishmael's opinion of corporate enterprises is evident in his observation that, much as men in the ideal might be commendable, they "might seem detestable as joint stock-companies and nations" (117). Whaling, however—a venture whose camaraderie Ishmael admires, despite its bloody and predatory mechanics—was a precarious joint-stock enterprise that had to be funded by corporate shareholders, and the scale of the venture meant partnerships generally were not feasible). Ishmael is repeatedly tempted to merge into nature, but also is repeatedly chastened by the risks, as emblematized by the fate of various disillusioned and deranged pantheists and Pip, who loses his mind when he confronts and merges into the overwhelming vastness of the ocean, an incarnation of the mass of the All itself. In letters to Hawthorne, Melville expressed a similar longing to merge male bodies to create a composite body, even while acknowledging that such desires for transcendence were absurd or potentially self-destructive: "spread and expand yourself, and bring yourself to the tinglings of life that are felt in the flowers and the woods, that are felt in the planets. . . . What nonsense! . . . This 'all' feeling, though, there is some truth in it" (*Correspondence* 193–94). Many of Melville's young white male protagonists expressed this longing to transcend themselves, to become one with the world. What Romain Rolland later terms the oceanic feeling turns out to represent a longing to be immersed in a corporate form; we don't transcend painful, isolated individuality by merging with nature, but the corporation. The language of merger, often used to describe reverie with nature, is the language of both social connection and utter disindividuation.

These ideas about merging with an impersonal but deified nature are germane here because they come to apply in many ways to the corporation. The emblematically artificial corporation is the final materialization of a commercial, historical, and epistemological teleology begun in antebellum America. Beginning roughly in the two decades before the Civil War, the corporation starts to take over the function of transcendental nature—it becomes ubiquitous, universal, and impersonal, and, most oddly, seems to speak to and instead of us. The corporation becomes our new "common nature." Through the corporation, individuals achieve impersonal succession and a common or impersonal immortality. It's the corporation's very impersonality, which is related to a myriad of legal contrivances afforded to it, that ultimately allows it to manipulate personal desire. Despite its name, the corporation precisely can have no body. But in a number of senses, it is defined by its incorporation (a magical and pseudo-numinous term); in law and literature, the most critical enabling fiction or artifice is that the corporation can be physically located and personified.

As he grows more cynical than even Ishmael, Melville's young pantheist Pierre begins to realize his longing to transcend isolated individuality and merge with nature is a ruse of corporate pantheism: the merger of self into the impersonal corporation. At first, *Pierre* assures us, "You lose your sharp individuality, and become delightfully merged in that soft social Pantheism, as it were, that rosy melting of all into one . . . no one draws the sword of his own individuality" (250).[3] Like Emerson, Isabel in *Pierre* similarly longs to transcend isolated individual existence and experience. If she too can merge with rosy nature, Isabel will never be cut by the sword of male individuality: "I pray for peace—for motionlessness—for the feeling of myself, as of some plant, absorbing life without seeking it, and existing without individual sensation. I feel that there can be no perfect peace in individualness. Therefore, I hope one day to feel myself drank up into the pervading spirit animating all things" (119). Isabel iterates the premise of Melville's own literary proposal to Hawthorne—that they might live together in an animated/ ensouled pantheistic nature, because, as Tocqueville admonished, an individual "separate identity is but a wretched one" (*Correspondence* 193).[4] In his pantheistic novel *The Overstory*, Richard Powers recuperates Isabel's language of absorption into floral nature,

When the lateral roots of two Douglas-firs run into each other underground, they fuse. Through those self-grafted knots, the two trees join their vascular systems together and become one. Networked together underground. . . . There are no individuals. There aren't even separate species. Everything in the forest is the forest . . . branches running into each other, too mazy and fused to trace. . . . There are no individuals in a forest. (142, 264, 280)

But as Powers knows, as evident in his novel *Gain*, there also are no individuals in a corporation. As Kathy Acker paraphrases Flaubert in *My Death My Life by Pier Paolo Pasolini*, "[H]e seeks to merge with unnameable nature, fleeing the weight of nomination in the unnameable texture of things, I want people to treat me as an animal in the irregular indefinable movements of the foliage, of the waves. To be matter" (*Literal* 183). But the longing to merge with the transcendental force of nature itself merges into the longing to merge with the corporation.

The definition of individuality attributed to nature and the premises of corporate personhood implicate our sense of what makes us human, of what it means to have an identity and some version of a soul or personality. In passages Powers recuperates almost verbatim in *The Overstory*, Emerson initially described nature, in positive terms, as a kind of aggregate collective or corporation: "Nature can only be conceived as existing to a universal and not to a particular end. . . . When we behold the landscape . . . we do not reckon individuals. Nature knows neither palm nor oak, but only vegetable life, which . . . festoons the globe with a garland of grasses and vines" (*Works*, "The Method of Nature" I, 201). (As I elaborate, if you translate these organic metaphors into mechanical ones, you evoke the Borg world of *Star Trek*.) Like the corporation and Emerson's representative men, nature is disindividuated; for Emerson, transcending individuality makes us universal (or one might say, infinitely franchiseable). As noted, near the end of his life, Emerson acknowledges that everything connected with our personality fails, and that nature never spares individuals (*Works*, "Immortality" VIII, 342). Only *impersonality*, in failing nature or the ascendant corporation, survives. Perhaps tragically, Emerson did realize in his darkest moments that transcendental systems—nature and then corporations—are profoundly anti-individualistic; that's one reason he remains a useful heuristic for understanding the contradictory meta-mechanics of a profoundly anti-individualistic corporate ontology or worldview. The more reflective transcendentalists came to the same conclusion: that nature regards only the species, and knows not the individual.

In his novel *Mardi*, Melville's narrator, in explicitly Emersonian mode, concluded that, "Through all her provinces, nature seems to promise immortality to life but destruction to beings. . . . *Nature is not for us*" (210).

It turns out that the corporation most fully delivers on this false promise of immortality. In *The Gold Bug Variations*, Powers similarly situates the individual's irrelevance to the species: sounding like Melville's Pierre, Dr. Ressler claims that "Nature cares nothing about the calculus of individuals" (165). Such passages are intimately related to corporate biography—one can substitute the corporation for nature in all these utterances; it transcends and cares nothing about particulars, and it promises immortality to an impersonal fiction and destruction to the individual and individual personality. As Bakan documents, the legal theorist John George wrote in 1825 that "the law looks to individuals," but with corporations, "it sees only the creature of the charter, the body corporate, and *knows not the individual*" (16). The *corporation* never knows or spares the individual, isn't for us, and has been lurking behind nature all along.

Chapter Six

Pumpkins and Sugarplums

The history of the corporate person in the United States is also the history of the collective or exceptional person, which in some ways overlaps with that of the celebrity, the outlaw, or the maverick. But in a corporate culture, these figures are feints for individualism, and usually represent a fake rebellion or freedom that's essentially corporate. One of the surprising conclusions Melville reached through his evaluation of Emersonian transcendentalism was that nature and the corporation are equally anti-individualistic. The individual never survives the process of being a spokesperson for nature, or the corporation that Melville came to equate it with. In the end, even Emerson, the supposed champion of American individualism, is a corporatist interested only in the "moments in the history of heaven when the human race was not counted as individuals, but was only the Influenced, was God in distribution, God rushing into multiform benefit" (*Works*, "Method" I, 210). Emerson's god of nature or the corporation gathers these distributed individuals or fragments into a collective mass existence that transcends locality and particularity. Contrary to popular conceptions of his notion of self-reliance, Emerson rarely considers anyone or anything in individual terms: as he admonishes with unusual precision, "We fancy men are individuals; so are pumpkins" (*Works*, "Nominalist and Realist" III, 246). In other words, the system of nature, like the corporation, doesn't rely on individual biography (individual pumpkins), but transpersonal, transgenerational, transnational, and transcendental impersonality. Throughout his essays and journals, Emerson averred that God is "no respecter of persons," and that for our truest relations, "there is no personeity [personality] in it" (*Journals* 5, 170). For Emerson, the representative man must "disindividualize himself" and align with "the universal mind" (*Works*, "Art" VII, 48–49). This is what the corporation requires of those who represent its impersonal universality; it turns us into pumpkins.

Emerson is certain that the "individual is less than what is universal. . . . Than the individual, nothing is less; than the universal, nothing is greater; that error, vice, and disease have their seat in the superficial or individual nature; that the common nature is whole" ("The Philosophy of History," *Lectures* II, 11). This often-iterated notion of "common nature" is central to transcendental thought, but also to the corporate form that derives from it. In "Fate," Emerson both promises and warns that the Law of Nature "dissolves persons" (*Works*, VI, 49). The corporation now implements this law. Though his Laws of Nature promised a compensatory unity, Emerson periodically concedes the cost: these forces "seem to leave no room for the individual" (*Works*, "Perpetual" X, 72). As Emerson writes, Pan (or the All) "disdain[s] particulars" (*Works*, "Natural" 35–36). As Emerson's influential concept of the "representative man" suggests, one becomes great by leaving individual identity behind; the true taxonomist sees only the type, the ideal, the national, and the ahistorical. Emerson at least implicitly views white male individuality as universal: but an individual white male is irrelevant. For Emerson, "the individual is always wrong" (*Works*, "Experience" III, 69. Such sentiments recur throughout the works of Emerson, Melville, and transcendental writers, reflecting a process of disillusionment in which some form of corporate collective betrays the individual. Emerson finally fears that "nothing is of us or our works—that all is of god. Nature will not spare us the smallest leaf of laurel. . . . I can see nothing at last, in success or failure, than more or less of vital force supplied from the Eternal" (*Works*, "Experience" 69). The corporation again seems to displace the function of nature; it bears the transcendental, collective identity that speaks through us. More disturbingly, the apparent opposition between nature and corporation disappears, a process symbolically concluded as corporations begin to control most forms of speech, patent genes and seeds, and effectively modify and create life. As we see in many forms of popular culture, the ultimate incarnation of evil is the corporation that creates alien, monstrous, zombie, or deformed life—life forms that emblematize corporate personhood.

Individuality in the United States—especially male individuality, as Emerson attests—often is submerged in some form of collectivity, and finally in the corporate person. For pantheists, nature, and especially plant life, is collective: plants lack separate identities, and represent a pre- or post-human existence. This language of merger and incorporation that defines the pantheistic impulse—and the desire to attain an undifferentiated existence in nature—morphs into the business-speak of corporate mergers and incorporations. Ironically, though it's the symbol of capitalism, the corporation from Thomas Hobbes onward is fiercely anti-individualistic in its organization, operation, premises and effects.[1] Corporate mergers consolidate power and make it difficult for small independent businesses to survive; as Matt Stoller contends, it is especially distressing that policymakers see monopolistic corporations as "exemplars of the American spirit, instead of the dangerous re-creation" of the East India company that we sought to escape (250). If Hobbes conceived of the sovereign as a "God on earth" (Hardt and Negri 85), as the divinity's extension and successor, the corporation attains not only its own soul, but the power to create and steal souls, making it a kind corporate Over-Soul. Corporations have become forms of sovereigns themselves, primarily by acquiring human rights and "personalities" and tethering them to the corporation's inhuman attributes. Though credited with personhood, corporations cannot act with univocal intention or possess agency. But they aren't just simulacra that mimic human behaviors; corporations challenge and destabilize the status of personhood and what it means to be a person.

Today, super-personality is concentrated in the corporation and its products; the corporation's lack of identity is inversely proportionate to the degree to which people imagine that corporations, and their brands, have intrinsic identities and attributes. Marcel Danesi alleges, after Scott Bedbury, that brands have a "fundamental essence" (21). Such language is naively essentialist, attributing to corporate products the culture- and history-transcending qualities many once attributed to an essentialized nature. John Hunt, a nineteenth-century Emerson manqué, summarized the impersonal collective of transcendental nature as having a universal, shared *essence*: "*God is the impersonal—the common nature*—which appears in each of us, and which is yet higher than ourselves. We, as individuals, live in succession, in division, in parts, in particles; but within, in the universal-soul . . . to which every part or particle is equally related—the eternal One" (322, emphasis in original).

We repeatedly encounter this language of common shared nature and communication that transcend individual existence; but these formulations now apply to the corporate form. Once the domain of the personal family, succession becomes the domain of the impersonal corporation. Sounding in the first part of this passage like Emerson, the Lacanian critic Slavoj Žižek contends that "Nature has an ineradicable tendency to 'speak itself out,' it is caught in the search for a Speaker . . . whose word would posit it as such; this Speaker, however, [only] can be an entity which is itself not natural, not part of Nature, but Nature's Other. . . . It can 'find itself,' attain itself, only in a medium which is itself not natural" (*Indivisible* 47). Again, transcendental mergers become corporate mergers; it's the "unnatural" corporation that now needs "natural" human speakers to legitimate it and act on its behalf. Instead of merging with nature, we merge in a different sense with corporations. Emerson's universal nature is being replaced by universal monopoly, franchise, and corporation, or what Žižek calls "Capital's universalism" (*Universal* 27).

The impersonality codified and sanctified in antebellum transcendentalism is further developed as an aesthetic and political concept in modernism.[2] In ways consonant with Emerson's disdain for idiosyncrasy and personality, and with the valorization of archetypal impersonality, some modernists, most notably T. S. Eliot, averred that romantic glorifications of an author's personality were distractions, and treated inspiration, aesthetic canons, and genius as aspects of impersonal tradition. Along with a variety of modernists, Wyndham Lewis believed that personality was a festering illusion—artificial, imitable, and akin to a superficial, detachable adornment (Rives 26). Lewis fulminated against the fetishization of personality as a democratic fantasy that induces its opposite: the drive to attain individualized personality emerges from and leads to a society based on automation, disindividuation, homogenization, and externally imposed behaviors. Lewis warns that the capitalist imperative "to 'develop the personality' is an alluring invitation, but it invariably covers some process that is guaranteed to strip a person bare of all 'personality' in a fortnight" (Arvidson 798–800). Heather Arvidson concludes that for Lewis, "the ruckus about personality in self-help and newspaper rhetoric succeeds only in habituating the crowd to individualist mannerisms that become ludicrously synchronized across a population," and the same could be said about the rhetoric of corporate personhood and advertising (800).[3] Emblematic of modernism, however, Lewis still champions a corporate model of the self. A belief that, in William Carlos Williams's encapsulation of a modernist credo, there are "no ideas but in things" can precipitate a pursuit of impersonality as a medium and authenticator of truth.

Modernism placed a new premium on originality, but one defined in the use of juxtaposition, pastiche, and plagiarism as forms of impersonation.[4] An emphasis on copying and (re)combination, or on disingenuous self-representation, reflected a belief that no preexisting, stable, non-recombined original self was available to modern persons. The artist individually could be glorified, but primarily for undermining the shibboleths of individuality. (Positing a magpie of personhood, the corporation well suits such an ethos of amalgamation). Lewis famously mocked anyone attached to individual personality as bearing a form of false consciousness: "He has been supplied with this formula, 'expressing the personality,' as a libertarian sugar-plum. He has been taught that he is 'free'" (151). Such sentiments comport with Emerson's dismissive remarks that men think they're individuals, while "Most men and most women are merely one couple more," duplicates creating more duplicates (*Works*, "Fate" VI, 11). Lewis's distaste for the overvaluation of individual talent recalls Emerson's insistence that individuals are only conduits for the impersonal. As Emerson iterates in dozens of formulations, "The reference of all production at last to an aboriginal Power explains the traits common to all works of the highest art" (*Works*, "Art" II, 358). The impersonal of nature or the corporation provides that common language, and makes individuals superfluous, except insofar as they channel these universal forces.

Chapter Seven

The Animated Corporation

To explain the ways the corporation emerges as the successor to transcendental nature, I briefly address an array of primarily American pantheistic/animistic writers who also serve as harbingers of contemporary corporate culture. Their evocations of the attributed power, scope, and functions of an animated nature with a soul comport with the vectors of the corporation. Many transcendental depictions of merger with nature predict or are co-opted by the corporate age that soon follows. For example, in Holmes's description of man's fall from nature,

> The animism [that] peopled the outward world with nature spirits was the instinctive protest of man's heart against the materialism of his conscious thought. . . . [When] animism fell into disrepute . . . it made possible . . . scientific exploration. . . . [But] as belief in the supernatural waned . . . especially in Protestant countries . . . materialism reject[ed] the supernatural, and [gave] a mechanistic explanation of life. . . . [The loss of animism] empt[ied] nature of her own spiritual life. (16–17)

The corporation both disembodies and reembodies this lost animism in the guise of a mechanistic and deterministic artificial life, overlaid with a human face and soul. Perverse as it sounds, the animated spirit of nature is infused into the animated corporation that has a soul. In an 1885 address to the Concord School of Philosophy, John Fiske asserted that everything is animated or alive: the whole universe thrills

> in every fibre with Life,—not, indeed, life in the usual restricted sense, but life in a general sense. The distinction, once deemed absolute, between the living and the not-living is converted into a relative distinction; and Life as manifested in the organism is seen to be only a specialized form of the Universal Life . . .

Chapter Seven

reappearing from moment to moment under myriad Protean forms . . . [through] this animating principle of the universe. (149–51)

This process of animation is a kind of predicate for being imbued with a soul; for transcendental pantheists, all things have souls because nature, though impersonal, is a living, personified entity. But we will see this ascription of a soul to an impersonal abstraction transfer to the animated corporation. Animism, the notion that the world itself is inspirited, here is often conflated with the related but distinct idea that one can animate or give life to inanimate things. The corporation, which many would see in its present form as the most modern of institutions, is a repository of many of our most "primitive" beliefs, and functions as a numinous, transcendent entity. Some cannibals believed they could incorporate the traits of enemies by eating them (as some hunters believe of prey); people in some cultures presume that taking daguerreotypes or photos steals people's souls. Such beliefs are apropos of the corporation, which symbolically appropriates the souls of the real bodies that do its bidding. (What we now incorporate into ourselves literally and figuratively is largely dependent on the corporation. In *Brave New World*, Aldous Huxley channels a Rabelaisian eating of words to mock what we consume in consumer culture: "Back to culture. Yes, actually to culture. You can't consume much if you sit still and read books" [33].)

Transcendentalists thought that a mysterious, ubiquitous principle or force infused nature and "animated" all people. (They often [mis]translated such a cosmology from native sources, typically formulated in the notion that the earth or nature has a soul.)[1] This animation couldn't be restricted to people or even organic matter; as Melville suggests throughout *Mardi*, the entire world is alive or has a soul. Transcendental nature animates—vivifies and connects—all life: "With Oro [Pan], the sun is coeternal; and the same life that moves that moose animates alike the sun and Oro" (615). Babbalanja describes his world of Mardi as an enormous mass that's collectively alive and possesses a soul:

I live while consciousness is not mine, while to all appearances *I am a clod*. And may not this same state of being, though but alternate with me, be continually that of many dumb, passive objects we so carelessly regard? Trust me, there are more things alive than those that crawl, or fly, or swim. Think you, my lord, there is no sensation in being a tree? . . . Think you it is nothing to be a world? . . . what are our tokens of animation? That we move, make a noise, have organs, pulses, and are compounded of fluids and solids. And all these are in this Mardi as a unit. Daily the slow, majestic throbbings of its heart are perceptible on the surface in the tides of the lagoon. Its rivers are its veins; . . . and as the body of a bison is covered with hair, so Mardi is covered with grasses and vegetation. . . . Think you there is no sensation in being a rock? Mardi is alive to its axis. (458)

Here, the world itself has attained personhood. (As I later argue, this pantheistic notion of a living world is appropriated to develop a corporate fantasy of the living world in *Avatar*, whose planet of Pandora is a variation of Mardi). Consciousness here becomes fungible or transitive, and nature guarantees our continued existence and bridges gaps in our "consciousness" and identity (in ways that adumbrate the function of the corporation). As Babbalanja indicates, we're not identical to ourselves or self-contained—we live while our consciousness is subsumed by nature. Without any intervention of an anthropomorphic deity, nature's "animation" turns mere matter into an entity possessing some form of life. (As Nietzsche might say, the problem is that if you discard an anthropomorphic god, you create a non-human one). Adumbrating *Mardi*, James Russell Lowell rebuked Emerson's Divinity School Address because he refused to "hear the anointed Son of God / Made like themselves an *animated clod*" (McAleer 250). Under the extended terms of such debates, corporations also come to be animated persons and possess some form of consciousness. One consequence of the impersonal animation of all matter is that life itself becomes impersonal and transitive—as we see in works ranging from Melville's novels to contemporary horror films, limbs, bodies and even dead bodies can move on their own (via what Melville terms St. Vitus), because life and personhood are detachable and we're not identical with ourselves or whole. In a system in which corporations can steal and transfer human personhood, life resides everywhere and nowhere, and like agency is transferred impersonally among objects.

For transcendentalists and some political theorists, nature served as the universal force that authorized American democracy as well as the expansion of manifest destiny. But as the nation-state came to be unified not by nature—which was imagined to be everywhere the same—but corporate technologies such as the railroad and telegraph, the corporation became the new form of animated clod. Emerson believed that "The Soul which animates nature" is "published in the figure, movement and gesture of animated bodies" (*Works*, "Behavior" VI, 169). As Hawthorne uncannily writes in *The Marble Faun*, which chronicles the animation of a statue into a Pan figure, Americans easily are seduced by "the mystery, the miracle, of imbuing an inanimate substance with thought, feeling, and all the tangible attributes of the soul" (271). As the United States industrialized, however, that belief in a living, animated nature turned to nostalgia. As I elaborate in "New *and* Improved," the corporation voices this once silent speech of nature, serving as the repository of collective speech and numinous, impersonal or trans-personal life. The naturalist Annie Dillard asks, "Did the wind use to cry, and the hill shout forth praise? Now speech has perished from among the lifeless things of earth, and living things say very little to very few" (69). In the transcendental American grain, nature is a personified social construct and force that has an alleged intent and animates people. As the corporation takes on the function of nature, it is supported by an ever-increasing array of technologies that enable it to simulate the ubiquity of natural forces and speak to everyone. (As Ned Beauman intimates in his novel *Glow*, animism in contemporary terms has been channeled into a corporate materialism: "Marx's creed seemed to be that material things had more power over people than people had over material things, which struck [him] as not all that different from the animism of his grandparents" [141]). Around the 1840s, some Americans already began to manifest anxiety that some collective—nature or the corporation—could take over their bodies: the transpersonal corporation represents action without actors, speech without a source, and an immense mass that could absorb us.

Some twentieth-century legal cases specify that the state animates or gives life to corporations, in language that echoes but tempers the transcendental ascription of nature's animation: "A corporation is a creature of the State. It owes its very being to the State. "Into its nostrils the State must breathe the breath of a fictitious life for otherwise it would be no animated body but individualistic dust [citation omitted]." *Cloverfields Improv. Assoc. v. Seabreeze Props., Inc.*, 32 Md. App. 421, 425 (Md. Ct. Spec. App. 1976). Such cases appropriately treat the corporation as a kind of closely held Frankenstein monster, an animated thing of dust: "While the directors are chosen by the stockholders, they become, when elected and properly organized as a board, the agent of the corporation. It is by such means that animate force is given to an inanimate thing." *Lamb v. Lehmann*, 110 Ohio St. 59, 65 (1924).[2] Contrary to most representations of corporations in films and texts, these courts treat the corporation as a contrivance without independent life: "Corporations are animated by people; those who control such corporations hire others to perform on the corporation's behalf." *Chemtall Inc. v. Citi-Chem, Inc.*, 992 F. Supp. 1390, 1403 (S.D. Ga. 1998). This language recalls that of *Mardi* in addressing the ways people and things manifest agency (and the natural and artificial signs of life), but the reality is that corporations are no longer animated people, but the reverse. While they capture the way corporations operate, these cases overlook their symbolic and figurative functioning; the corporation that attains personhood might be a fiction, but it's one that has dramatic effects. The rhetoric of these judges also eerily is co-opted in the recent tenets of vitalism, the conjecture that all matter has some form of life and identity, which can be used to attribute the traits of nature to corporations.

Chapter Eight

Truth and Soul

[This advertising] agency is [now called] Truth and Soul [Inc.]! . . . "[For this campaign], you got to get a young girl with soul. . . . Putney says the Borman Six girl has got to have soul! Putney says the Borman Six girl has got to have soul! Putney says the Borman Six girl has got to have soul! Got to have Soul!

—*Putney Swope* (1969)

Transcendental animism—the rhetoric that attributed life, soul, and impersonal personhood to aspects of nature—was gradually transferred to the corporate form that gained a soul. According to Gregory Mark, the idea of a corporation imbued with life initially didn't hold great influence in the United States: "Equally ill-fated were the attempts to animate the corporation, which were not generally taken seriously in America. Nonetheless, commentators recognized the births and deaths of corporations, and accepted that they possessed lives and the powers to will, to act, and to create" (1987). But this idea of animation, even if not (consciously) familiar to the general population until recently, has had profound ramifications and effects and is an essential facet of a quasi-religious and ontological discourse that pervades US culture. The corporation has come to possess a life independent of the people who allegedly animate it.

Some post-humanist and neo-vitalist theory (also termed the new materialism), which tries to erase hierarchical distinctions between species and organic and inorganic matter, can play into the notion that the corporation is itself alive and has personhood, rights, and a soul. For example, under Roberto Esposito's resuscitation of vitalism—a theory that's meant to transcend the limitations of the human or humanism and contends that all existence is equal and should be approached impersonally—the precisely impersonal corporation is also alive. Here, the corporation, in structural/ impersonal terms, is effectively able to appropriate post-humanist person- hood as, we shall see, it did the personhood of African Americans. Similarly, Jane Bennett's notion of enchanted matter, impersonal affect, and heteroge- neous agency—another affirmation that everything is alive and that agency isn't confined to individual beings but involves swarms of interacting "vitalities"—can also apply to the animism that gives corporations the onto- logical status of persons (31–32). Thomas Pynchon long has attributed con- sciousness to all forms of matter, from Byron the Bulb to Iceland Spar, and dramatizes the prospects of what I term consciousness without borders; like Melville's, his characters frequently wonder, for example, whether "the earth [might be] alive, with a planet-shaped consciousness" (*Against the Day* 939). Almost anything in Pynchon's works, from the wind to gravity, egg yolks and railroads, can have intention and agency. But Pynchon also acknowledges the demonological or dark implications of such fantasies.[1] Bennett, for example, in advocating for an egalitarian and expansive (and finally nearly indiscrimi- nate) application of personhood to everything, which could give rights and protections to all species, also inadvertently lays the groundwork for corpo- rations to become exceptional persons. To deny the distinction between the living and the nonliving can play into the absent hands of the corporation; one consequence is that an entity such as the animated corporation becomes not just equal to any other form of existence but superior, attaining exceptional rights over them. When theorists try to expand the definition of personhood, they often generate a host of unintended consequences, marked by a confla- tion of categories and a failure to distinguish and evaluate. Anna Grear sagely proposes that "corporate rights, animal rights, the rights of eco-systems, 'post-human' rights and human rights need not be reduced to one monolithic category," and, as Grear intimates, the conflation of nonhuman rights with human rights is based on faulty premises (47). The question isn't just whether we should grant all disadvantaged subjects rights, but whether we should treat all inhuman things as persons.

Other strains of recent critical theory at least implicitly address how corporate personhood distorts the premises of human personhood. The contemporary corporation represents the apotheosis of a kind of existen- tial posthuman identity—the corporation isn't tethered to any "natural" or traditional notion of human subjectivity, and need have no biological body, personality, or limitations. A post-human theory of identity can embrace new concepts of personhood, including nomadism, animality, AI, and so on, but it also can validate the concept of purely artificial corporate person- hood. In Paul Giles's estimation, via N. Katherine Hayles, post-humanism doesn't signify the end of humanity, but questions "comfortable liberal assumptions about the sovereignty of the human subject":

> If the emergence of postmodernism can be attributed contextually to the aftermath of the Second World War, when the collapse of grand modernist narratives centered on a utopian state paved the way for the liberal agendas of multiculturalism and diversity, the provenance of posthumanism can be traced to more specific concerns around the mid-1980s about the extent to which a politics of human identity might ontologically be differentiated from other categories of scientific and biological existence. Such anxieties were impelled partly by rapid developments in information technology. (165)

But we can trace the social and political causes and effects of the corporate form to the beginnings of the modern Western era. Corporations were created to supplement but ultimately replace people and replace the construct of nature; they were early forms of artificial intelligence, meant not only to undertake risky and large-scale endeavors but also to sustain themselves as self-perpetuating and impersonal systems that controlled and finally obviated persons.

For Walter Benn Michaels, on ontological grounds, "corporations must be persons even if persons aren't"; the corporation must have a body and a soul and represent a new kind of person (205–6). That new entity is again post-human, a disembodied agent that cannot speak, have intent, or bear true liability yet is afforded unlimited speech, presence, and "mass," and unprecedented social, economic, and political influence. Perhaps most incongruously, impersonal corporations are responsible for much of contemporary culture, telling people what it means to act like men, love, be loved, be cool, desire, and so on. Speech should be considered a human right, and corporations, which possess a virtually unfettered ability to monopolize speech in almost every register—including most broadcast media and publishing—appropriate and agglomerate this right from individuals. That domination of speech is most obvious in the form of advertising, but it extends to most media. Wu observes that "On popular prime-time television, all but the highest commercial bidders—America's largest corporations—[a]re priced out of each time slot" (*Attention* 140). We might call this a speech network effect—only those who already have a seat at this small, absurdly expensive table ever will have a voice at it. But what's more sinister is that corporate monopolization prices people out economically, politically, and culturally, and, in less acknowledged ways, ontologically. The corporation is a kind of computer simulation that mimics people and nature; it might appear to act as a human being, but because of the corporate form, one can rarely, as a structural matter, even trace corporate acts to a specific person. Corporations are series of effects without causes, and their personhood is a series of accumulated thefts, and more recently gifts, that codify their legal exceptionalism, escalating in consequence as they hoard rights at the expense of persons.

Recent changes in the conception of corporate personhood are both cause and effect of such transformations in information technology, and the corporate form exploits technology to undermine human identity, privacy, and rights. Though its political lineage still can be traced to the Hobbesian Leviathan—the impersonated person of the state—the corporation culturally has become a post-human entity; it is in some ways analogous to a poststructuralist text produced without an author, and it acts without an actor, agency, or intention behind it. Republican ideology in such contexts often seems commensurate with aspects of posthuman and postmodern relativism and indeterminacy. While Republicans tend to be absolute about effectively naturalized rights—for example, those of individual gun owners and fetuses, illegitimately ascribed to the Constitution—they often try to relativize facts and scientific theories whose implications they dislike, and reverse engineer artificial rights for artificial persons such as the corporation. (These artificial rights are designed after the fact to meet the economic demands of corporations and not on the basis of any coherent or legitimate theory of personhood, save in so far as corporations become the default repository for the rights transferred from persons.)

The age of disruptive corporations is also the age of the disruption of persons. Cultural movements that attempt to normalize, promote, or help you cope with these disruptions, sometimes in the guise of pseudo-religious advice, self-help guides, or allegedly holistic and anti-corporate platforms, tend to draw on a consistent set of corporate premises and values. As Žižek has noted, such apparent alternatives provide mechanisms to justify and help you accept corporate culture rather than question or transform it; Žižek often evokes the image of the corporate banker who practices yoga and meditation without ever changing his predatory behavior. A line of TED Talks specializes in promulgating a fake new age liberalism, or a neoliberal ethos that relies on narratives of perfectibility/self-perfection achievable through corporate products. Many of the assertions about the internet and technology one hears in such talks present an odd mix of numinous nonsense and ulterior right-wing politics, or just gibberish. Speaking on Forum on KQED (May 19, 2015), Charles Murray claimed that disruptive technology companies such as Uber were making government regulation superfluous. (One is reminded of the way corporations obtain free labor by enlisting consumers to write reviews; while these can help consumers, they in no way represent any alternative to a corporate culture, a "share" economy, etc.) It's as if the corporate ethos that can produce self-driving cars also agitates for every aspect of its economy to be self-driven. Driverless cars are another apt emblem of corporate personhood—and for an enterprise without a self, or one replaced by AI. (In this sense, Steven Spielberg's film *Duel* was a prophetic documentary.) Uber is among the worst companies in terms of its treatment of women and employees (the latter of whom it wants to consider impersonal contractors), and people such as Murray, who bury their politics under the facade of manipulated data, pseudoscience, and misrepresentations of workers' views, might seem to "personalize" corporate malfeasance, but they're in the larger view enacting an impersonal corporate code that has little variability.

For corporations, technology presents new possibilities to cultivate an impersonal, collective, pre- or post-human existence. Benjamin Sovacool argues that the corporation itself has emerged as an unrecognized form of instrumentally successful, but socially failing, technology (2–5). Much as workers often become irrelevant to corporations—that is, most corporations symbolically and practically strive to reduce the number of people who work for them—human personhood becomes less and less relevant in the wake of corporate personhood. (Perversely, cases that litigate the right of "corporations" to impose religious or personal beliefs on corporate governance belie and distract from the exigently impersonal nature of the corporate enterprise.) It's not contingent that corporate technology and directives aim to automate work and people—the trajectory of the corporate form has been to replace human personhood with corporate personhood. In this light, the New World has developed along an asymptotic curve that arcs toward the wholly depopulated corporation, a kind of *Terminator Matrix*. The teleology of the corporation runs not just toward monopoly but toward the ontological elimination of people as workers.

One of the many ironies and dissonances of current right-wing rhetoric, which claims that immigrants are taking the jobs of US citizens, is that it is corporations that most threaten conservatives' putative "way of life." Melville already was perturbed by the manifold routes through which the corporation could replace persons with mechanisms and monstrosities; in his 1857 novel *The Confidence Man,* the Missourian declaims, "I am now started to get me made some kind of machine to do the sort of work which boys are supposed to be fitted for" (108). The early twentieth-century populist orator Cyclone Davis asserted that he "would not be surprised to hear that some man had invented a machine for making books that dispensed with [the] author . . . and ground out paragraphs by steam" (Michaels 209). The corporation relies on numerous machines that dispense with authors and agents, or people altogether, effectively validating the corporation itself as the ultimate author function. Corporations dispense with people not just in their modes of production, but in their essence; their teleology is to accrete the personhood of those who serve them. Henri Bergson argued that a comic effect is produced when a person is momentarily transformed into a thing, but he was referring to momentary entanglements, for example, of machine and person;

in our current corporate system, we've instead the horrific and systemic transformation of persons into impersonal things, and of things into persons (57). Corporations can attain the identity and personhood they don't have only at our expense. Lars Christensen and George Cheney propose broadly that all contemporary organizations, regardless of their sector, "are in the communications business," and that corporations generate their identities less through sales than messaging (247, 249). But corporations aren't primarily communicating about products or even themselves: they're communicating, performing, and appropriating epistemology and ontology, and in this sense, they serve not just as an author function but perhaps as our last Big Others: systems without centers, disquisitions without speakers, a constellation of effects and processes without causes or affect.

As Klein notes, citing reporter Aaron Bernstein, "Outsourcing started in manufacturing in the early 1980s," but soon expanded into nearly every sector of the corporate world (229); shifting employees into gig or part-time work is another way station in this process, and further turns people into expendable contractors who have little direct connection with the corporation. Just as owners are separated from the corporate form, so finally are workers/people. (Republicans often bandy about the euphemisms of independence and rights in such contexts, with the right to work meaning that corporations have the right to set all terms of employment and bust unions, and independence meaning your right to fend entirely for yourself in a world dominated by corporate power.) Much as corporations such as Facebook treat you not as a person/customer but as data/product, many corporations treat workers as fungible hindrances. In this zero-sum game, as many corporations grow, they outsource work abroad as much as possible (depopulate themselves of persons and treat foreign workers as less than human or nonpersons). As Klein illustrates, the trend is for corporations to divest themselves of direct production and exist as shells that simply design products, market the brands, and collect the profits. (See chapter 9, "The Discarded Factory," whose title echoes the narrative of Philip K. Dick's short story "Autofac," a megacorporation whose self-replicating factory and robots continue to produce junk goods after most humans have been wiped out; the *Electric Dreams* version of the story, in which the auto-corporation has displaced all actual people, emphasizes that corporations will consume all resources and accelerate consumerism in ways suicidal for their creators.) "Restructured companies" that outsource and rely largely on brand rather than employment and production become 'hollow corporations,' because their goal seemed to be to transcend the corporeal world of things," or to divest "of the world of things" and become pure, disembodied, floating brands (xvii, 4). The corporation again fulfills the basic goal of Emersonian transcendentalism, to transcend the material world and body and become an invisible all-seeing, demateralized orb. Klein consistently invokes this language of a vacated body politic. In a corporatized state, the government also is "hollowed out, handing over to the private sector many of the most essential functions of government," as we've seen in terms of security, education, health, and environmental protection; in this "auctioning off of the state," we're left with "only a shell—or a brand" (xix). (That hollowness is reflected in the way corporations incorporate and maintain invisibility; corporations that register but do no business in Delaware, for example, pay no state taxes. The fiction of the corporation adds another layer of fiction through such contrivances.) The hollow corporation also becomes a figurative thing itself—a symbolic, fictional, and ultimately monstrous, invisible mass body.

Klein traces the way companies such as Nike and Microsoft "pioneered the hollowed corporation," generating brand facades and providing the templates for corporations such as the military contractor Blackwater, which could deny responsibility for their crimes and negligence and simply rebrand themselves. These entities are like empty storefronts or the PO boxes that serve as addresses for offshore corporations: they exist as brand names, but the production, operations, and employees are outsourced and disassociated. As Klein proposes, this is all part of the "dream of a hollow state" (xx–xxi), of attempts not just to deconstruct the state, but disembowel it so it resembles the corporation. The Trump administration, which grafted the most horrific aspects of corporate personhood onto the state, was the logical and almost inevitable outcome of this process, the wholesale sell-off of government assets and hollowing out of the state, State Department, and any department that might resist the corporate ethos that prioritizes profit and modes of communication that rely on the tactics of advertising (i.e., the distortion and denigration of facts and science, reliance on bombastic assertion, and indifference to contradiction). It's no accident that so many positions in the Trump administration were handed to corporate cronies or left permanently vacant; like the corporation, the corporatized state tries to function as much as possible without persons (and in this case like a closely controlled corporation run by a crime family). This inexorable assault on civil government "hollows out" all centers of civic society (Klein 130), from downtowns to the social safety net, but also personhood itself. Its end is the hollow man/woman.

Chapter Nine

Your Call Is Very Important to Us

One can find an accessible colloquial example that illustrates how corporate impersonality generates a specious corporate intention in almost any interaction with a corporation: when an automated on-hold message tells you "Your call is very important to us," or a recorded announcement "thanks" you for choosing to fly with that airline, there's no person and no intent behind the message, even if a human, rather than a tape, conveys the message and happens to believe it. These generic corporate voices, feigning personal relationships, mock your personhood; making such statements is akin to telling every person you pass on the street, or as you enter Costco, indiscriminately and idiosyncratically that you're in love with them. All ads and corporate communications are variations of spam that begins with "Dear beloved friend" or tells you, "I'm horny to fuck you!" When the recording tells you "Your call is very important to us," you are speaking to corporate personhood—even if the person you eventually reach is interested in you. There's no "us," intention or person behind corporate communications; the corporate configuration creates an absolute separation between owners and operators, form and content, and finally advertisement and advertised. Our diurnal experience of the corporation inures us to this systemic depersonalization, and the degradation of genuine human interaction. (No wonder people are starting to adopt robots and AI programs as pets and friends; the associational logical is unassailable.) It's obvious that your call isn't remotely important to the corporation—which has outsourced its customer service and intentionally made it difficult to reach anyone who can take action—and that you'll be on hold indefinitely, and these ubiquitous lies insult anyone who hears them. But worse, these imitations of human interaction debase human communication and personhood.

When flight attendants or any corporate spokespersons say, in necessarily perfunctory fashion, we appreciate your loyalty, there's no "we," no
locatable intent, behind the utterance. (I here leave aside the larger issue of
how we ever locate univocal intention; with regard to corporate speech, the
primary obstacle isn't finding a consistent intention, but the impossibility of
locating an identifiable source.) Most communication from organizations
similarly invokes an authoritative we; communications without an identifiable source are imbued with an air of specious authority that's reified. But
corporate speech and advertising are the most widespread and pernicious
manifestations of this sorcery. In terms of communication and relationships,
no corporation exists to thank you or to be loyal to. In a variety of cultural
registers, advertising exemplifies speech without a speaker; much as they're
created to escape liability, corporations are engineered to have no center or
tangible core. In most contexts, the corporate form inverts the relationship
between speaker and utterance, and human emotion and whatever triggers it.

When I email my bank, I receive the following automated message:
"Thank you for sending your service request to [us]. As one of our most valued customers, your questions and concerns are our highest priority." These
sentences likely were at some point written by a person (though a functionally
illiterate one, since my questions aren't one of their most valued customers).
But the absurdity of sending rote, automated replies that claim to value you
personally communicate the essence of the artificial intelligence and impersonations of corporate personhood. When I email a tech company's customer
service, a chat-box bot says, "Let me introduce you to my favorite colleague,
Steve," which of course is not the person's real name, and not an associate of an
automated program. Ads for the internet cloud that feature the voice of Watson,
a form of AI, also express the voice of corporate personhood: speech without
a speaker; a fake personality without a person; and a pseudo-consciousness
without responsibility. Strictly speaking, there's never anyone at the other end
of the communication if you're interacting with corporations. All corporate
employees are Watsonized and Siriated.

A widely disseminated jingle from the mid-1970s for Chemical Bank
proclaimed, "Yes is a chemical reaction (yes, yes, yes!)." Like many ads, it
reveals more than its creators likely intended. Aside from the perhaps unintended Joycean sexual innuendo (from the end of *Ulysses*), the ad asserts that
decisions don't require individual will, or even something organic, but entail
an impersonal, autonomic chemical function. The person has been excised.
As such, the ad for the corporate bank performs the corporation's ontology—
human cerebration, evaluation or response are removed from the transaction,
and assent becomes a verification of corporate autonomy. This ad effectively
predicts the financial crisis that Chase, which in a kind of ironic raid took

over Chemical Bank, helped precipitate. Banks were automatically giving out loans and mortgages; Wall Street increasingly was relying on algorithms; and corporate capitalism was "directing" its flow of capital divorced from reality. Many sectors of society are funded by the future fantasies of advertising, in ways that parallel the overvaluation of the future worth of corporations on stock markets. David Graeber notes that "by allowing any corporation to become part of the financial services industry, government was granting them the right to create money" (77). Deregulation has allowed financial corporations to become the greatest usurers in history, and some can lend ten times as much as they hold in reserve, meaning they're creating money, or borrowing from the future.

Culture based on corporate personhood helps occlude human personhood and agency; no specific people finally are responsible for the consequences of financial crashes, decades of corporate environmental contamination, or unpersoned drone missions. Yes is a chemical reaction, but possibly also a nuclear one—corporate personhood is part of a process that rationalizes and foments ever more impersonal violence and exploitation. The impersonality of the corporation by design generates a template that occludes personal agency and responsibility.

Chapter Ten

There's No Their There

When Facebook incessantly tells you, "We care about your memories," no "we" exists to utter that claim. No difference exists between this form of AI and the corporation itself. (Even if you somehow could locate a rare anomalous group of persons who work at Facebook who do care about your memories, they would not be that we.) Much as shareholders by design cannot represent corporations, these speakers, when they even exist, can't represent a corporate person or intention. The nature of the corporation is that there's no "their" there. This scenario illustrates the way the immense mass of the corporation serves as what Žižek, via Lacan, calls the Big Other—it's a repository for an ideological fantasy of some external godlike and omniscient agency that speaks to and watches us (*Ticklish* 398). Even when we know the Big Other doesn't exist, we cannot stop imagining that some all-knowing mass knows what we don't. The issue is that we give rights to this Big Other as if it could be a person, when it can function only like an idol. The cultural logic embedded into our ethos seems to be generated by the nonexistent corporate person in a kind of automated program. Our remarkable failure to hold corporations accountable for legitimating a culture of fraud and malfeasance reflects an unconscious acceptance that no specific agency resides behind them—that they behave like some kind of collective id or daemon. Trying to hold corporations liable is like trying to have a conversation with their automated messages.

Anything corporations do to exhibit a noncommercial affect involves a form of impersonation, which is most problematic when corporations overtly manipulate politics and social policy. Corporations do have political interests, and commerce always overlaps with politics. But in the context of ontology and the legal frameworks that create and define them, corporations are imaginary constructs engaged in exclusively commercial endeavors. If natural persons under US law and its cultural ethos were imbued by God or nature with certain inalienable rights, corporations became imbued with those rights unnaturally, through legal fictions and forms of graft(s). Legislatures and courts developed the law related to corporations entirely in that commercial context—to allow them to make contracts, own property, and sue and be sued, and to differentiate them from people, especially shareholders, in virtually all scenarios. Many corporations now claim to be the most embattled, most personal of all persons—to have merged with and superseded them.

Corporations endemically invoke the right of "free speech" to escape scrutiny for advertising and spending under the First Amendment. But because their personhood is, or at least should be deemed, univocally commercial, all their speech should be regulable under the Commerce Clause, which provides the government leeway to regulate and constrain commercial statements, such as clams about product safety. (Under Article 1, Section 8, Clause 3 of the Constitution, Congress has the authority to regulate interstate commerce.) Throughout the critical recent holding of *Citizens United*, the majority alleged it was protecting political speech, but corporations by their nature cannot, unless they represent the fourth estate, engage in political speech.[1] (Much as religious organizations, to retain their tax-exempt status, are meant to function without engaging in politics, corporations shouldn't be allowed to exceed the scope of their charters and engage in politics if they retain limited liability.) Corporations were devised as commercial entities with strictly delimited rights and aims. Created by charters at the largesse of governments, corporations are a priori regulable. It seems absurd to have to make such a point—that the charter grants the corporation certain rights, but also many limitations—but in the present political climate, many commentators allege that corporations have innate rights. Because they've been turned into persons, corporations no longer have their rights defined by charter—the entire basis of their existence—but by unjustifiable analogy to persons.

US corporations also are established under the aegis of individual states. As publicly chartered entities, corporations were initially restricted to specific purposes, and often for limited periods and with caps on their accumulation of capital, in almost all states; they existed through the consent of the sovereign, and were chartered to reflect not only their uses, but their potential dangers, particularly with regard to their concentration of power. Corporations were created to take on tasks putatively too large, complex, risky, or specialized for government, but they've since conceptually, practically, and ideologically eclipsed that government. The corporate form did need to evolve over the past century; but the need to delimit and control its power and the scope of its endeavors also increased, even as the will and ability to do so diminished. As Gregory Mark notes, recent Court holdings selectively ignore history and precedent and treat corporations as independent entities whose effective superpowers, which the state helped create, need no longer concern the government: "In *First National Bank of Boston v. Bellotti*, the Court rejected and characterized as 'extreme' the view that "corporations, as creatures of the State, have only those rights granted them by the State. 435 U.S. 765, 778 n.14 (1978)" (The Personification, 1442). In other words, the completely artificial corporation suddenly had independent natural rights. The chartered corporation has been used as a kind of spearhead to privatize all aspects of the commons and social goods, from charter schools to hospitals to every aspect of government, from social to military security. As Tyler Coburn tracks in different contexts, one current trend is even to charter cities, and to turn states into privately held aggregations of corporate cities operating under laissez faire principles of voluntary "citizenship" and market competition, which leaves only the wealthy as free agents or citizens, an exacerbation of a "preexisting" condition. (One recent example of this principle was the Trump administration's directive to let states not only fend for themselves to obtain PPE, but to compete with each other for it.) But we also shouldn't imagine that the wealthy are immune from corporatization, much as we shouldn't imagine that CEOs represent or control corporations. In the most deleterious contexts, corporations aren't doing the bidding of the superrich; the superrich are unwittingly doing the bidding of the corporate form. Like Trumpism, corporate personhood is a pathology that cannot be tempered or tailored and will come to overtake and take over all those who think they can control it.

Courts have tended to be incoherent at best in addressing the vexed issue of whether corporations, as legal fictions, can be identified with the beliefs or rights of owners; their confusion destabilizes the identities of people as well as corporations. Courts now routinely grant impersonal and abstract corporations exceptional rights and exemptions based purely on "personal reasons." As Judge Rovner observes in her dissent in *Korte v. Sebelius*, 735 F.3d 654, 688 (7th Cir. 2013), addressing the religious claims of a corporate person, "The court extends a highly personal right to a secular corporation, a man-made legal fiction that has no conscience enabling belief or worship." Rovner logically asks, what if

> one of a corporation's two equal owners is Catholic and the other is Protestant, Muslim, Jewish, or an atheist—are the beliefs of one or both attributed to the corporation, and if the beliefs of only one count, which does? Are the beliefs a conglomeration or neither? Or suppose that both owners are Catholic, but only one of them claims that his beliefs are burdened by some legal requirement (like the mandate at issue here) imposed on the company, whereas the other professes either indifference or support for that requirement. (704)

In a rare judicial insight in this context, Judge Rovner admonishes that "To say, as the court does today, that the right to exercise one's religious faith may be asserted on the same terms by a legal construct—an incorporated currency exchange, accounting firm, or automobile repair shop, for example—as by a human being, is, to my mind at least, irreconcilable with the very essence of religious faith and, for that matter, humankind" (701–2). If corporations can have no feelings to hurt, how can they have faith to defend? Corporate personhood and personal rights are irreconcilable with their human counterparts.

Chapter Eleven

You Can't See the
Corporation for the CEOs

Courts generally maintain the distinctions between corporations and executives and shareholders when addressing liability, but increasingly erase them when it comes to rights:

> It is true that a corporation is a fictional entity, separate and apart from its association of individuals, and it enjoys certain privileges benefitting both the association as a whole and the individuals alike. But the individuals are the real parties that make up the association and these individuals bring with them certain rights that, unless incompatible with the corporate form, should not be relinquished. It cannot be said here that the exercise of religion by an individual in association with other individuals is incompatible with any of its corporate privileges, whether we speak of the privilege of a shareholder to enjoy limited liability or the privilege of a corporation to exist in perpetuity. Put simply, an individual's right to freely exercise religion includes the right to exercise religion in association with others under the corporate umbrella. See generally *Citizens United [v. Fed. Election Comm'n*, 558 U.S. 310,] 392 [2010] ("But the individual's right to speak includes the right to speak *in association with other individual persons*.") (*Beckwith Elec. Co. v. Sebelius*, 960 F. Supp. 2d 1328, 1342 [M.D. Fla. 2013]) (emphasis in original)

Of course, the court here doesn't consider what happens when those speech rights conflict, or that it is privileging the religious rights of some owners over others, and of impersonal corporate persons over human employees. Courts are willfully obtuse and incoherent in holding that personal rights are commensurate with those of fictional legal entities, and in failing to consider any of the implications of conflating the identities and rights of individuals with corporate "associations." Individuals can exercise their personal rights only as individuals, not as somehow merged into commercial corporate fictions; it's completely incoherent even to suggest that an individual can "cross over" into the corporate form, or that a group of individuals in a corporation could have uniform views about religion or anything else. The purpose and rationale of the corporation is commercial; the deleterious effect of such holdings it to degrade personal beliefs and rights into commercial considerations—to turn us into corporate persons—and elevate corporations into super-beings. *Citizens United,* and cases such as *Beckwith* in its wake, upend all (still often misguided) justifications for creating the corporate form, and the philosophical and legal gravamen of these holdings boils down to "all rights, and no liability." Claiming that an "association's" (corporation's) right and ability to speak are equivalent to those of an individual is as specious and fatuous as claiming an individual litigant's rights and abilities in a lawsuit are equivalent to those of a multinational corporation.

Courts unwittingly reveal the ulterior logic of the ways corporations can hide behind veiled inhuman impersonality in achieving immunities yet simultaneously claim the privileges of personal rights: for example, the Maryland District Court held that "Beckwith Electric *is inculcated with the beliefs of its owner* and CEO. Beckwith manages the day-to-day operations of Beckwith Electric and is responsible for establishing all its operational policies." *Beckwith,* 960 F. Supp. 2d at 1344 (emphasis added). If such is the case, that corporation has been infiltrated by or commingled with the personal assets of an owner outside the commercial arena; it is by definition no longer a corporation, and the corporate form, with its rights and immunities, should be dissolved or pierced. The rationale of the corporate form is to be impersonal and preclude any such "consanguinity" between owners and operators. Even contemporary charters specify that corporations are impersonal entities whose purpose is to seek profit; in exchange for their directors being granted limited liability, those directors are proscribed from treating the corporation as an extension of their personalities. Further, CEOs and managers matter as individuals, but they're largely irrelevant cogs in the structure of corporations. As Aaron Ritzenberg contends, writing about the early twentieth century,

> Even as the visible hand replaces the invisible hand, as managers replace market forces, the power of individual managers—indeed, of any individual—is rendered miniscule by vast managerial networks. . . . A widespread crisis of lost personhood occurs when economic networks become ossified—hardened into permanent skeletal structures whose existence no longer corresponds to human life. (*Sentimental* 91)

That ossification and crisis has become even more pronounced as the premises of corporate personhood infiltrates all aspects of society. We lose sight of the impersonal and fixed corporate structure or network when we focus on the arbitrary personalities of what are in effect corporate celebrities. Especially in the context of technology, people as agents have been replaced. Directors and employees, of course, work at Facebook and Google, and they design their algorithms, but those algorithms are designed to work autonomously, in ways divorced from any person. Those algorithms are another emblem of corporate personhood—autonomous inhuman systems, designed by persons, that manipulate and dehumanize people. Granting personal rights to corporations is as sensible as granting them to those algorithms.

Peter d'Errico proposes that the modern legal doctrine of corporate personhood coincided with the separation of finance capital from corporate management (105). In this regard, one might say that the "real" actors and persons of corporations are those few individuals, such as the Koch Brothers or the Waltons, who own or effectively control corporations larger than some countries yet are shielded from many forms of scrutiny, liability, and civic oversight. But even those anomalous families are subsidiaries of the corporate enterprise and not the reverse. CEOs such as Beckwith and the Green family that owns Hobby Lobby are largely irrelevant distractions—the problem isn't that the owners of a few atypical corporations have been given the ability to impose their (no doubt sometimes problematic) human beliefs on their corporate enterprises. It's that the overwhelming majority of corporations have been given the right to impose their personhood—which as we'll see, tends be sociopathic—on the vast majority of people.

The only interests corporations have under their charters are commercial—they're created for a strictly mercantile purpose. (Nonprofit corporations—for example, most universities—are distinct entities, but even they are increasingly infiltrated by the strictures, expectations, and behaviors of for-profit corporations. Even most B corporations, the relatively miniscule number of corporations dedicated to social causes such as renewable energy, are still defined and constrained by the corporate form. While some of these businesses behave much more responsibly than the average corporation, they still use their social agendas to promote their businesses, and to brand themselves as putatively anti-corporate, while still taking advantage of the corporate form.) No autonomous person exists in the formal corporate domain to generate views or voice speech, other than agents who make commercial representations on the corporation's behalf. But these agents are imitations or copies without an original—while executives issue directives, there's no "corporation" to locate as having a will and intention. Many other groups and associations can voice any kind of speech—they're not bound by corporate charters, and their privileges were not designed to be balanced by equivalent restrictions. No doubt, such entities face their own problems in voicing the views of a collective, but they are in critical ways disconnected from the imperatives and constraints of for-profit corporations. Unlike NGOs, partnerships, and most organizations, large corporations create a nearly absolute separation between not only owners and actors and agents, but also between the empty, unpeopled structure of the legal entity and the dehumanized people who serve it. No partnerships have ever claimed personhood or a soul, and far fewer of them than corporations ever have threatened the ecosystem, a national financial system, or the health and welfare of their customers.

Chapter Twelve

Unpersoned

The corporation that has limited liability perhaps also should be designated as having limited labiality—it's an unspeakable and unspeaking thing that's spoken for. (I here think of the title and narrator of Harlan Ellison's 1967 short story, "I Have No Mouth and I Must Scream"—whose consciousness is controlled by a self-aware computer that has eliminated most of humanity and who is turned into a monstrous immortal thing—as emblematizing the corporate person. One could rewrite that title as "I Have No Mouth and I Must Advertise, Constantly and to the Point of Psychosis." Or as Thomas Ligotti's "The Wages of Life: My Work Is Not Yet Done," in his *Three Tales of Corporate Horror*, "Her mouth, which had once talked so much Sherry-thing talk, tried to scream. But no sound came out of that mouth" [93]). Certain people must have authority or legal agency to act on behalf of corporations, but in Lacanian terms, corporations produce communications without origins and that no one can be fully identified with except through fictions. Corporations have stolen the mouths and speech of persons. As Tom McCarthy conjures the ubiquitous nonexistent corporate body in *Satin Island*, "In not having a face, or even body, the [corporate] Project garnered for itself enormous and far-reaching capabilities, while at the same time reducing its accountability and vulnerability—to almost zero. . . . [There was] no Project Headquarters. . . . The Project was supra-governmental, supra-national, supra-everything—and infra too; *that's* what made it so effective" (123–24, emphasis in original).

Beginning with their Hobbesian chartered inceptions, corporations have been artificial entities imbued with personhood, or souls. The deafening, largely unregulated speech they make in our society is perversely proportionate to the absence of an identifiable speaker (behind the spokesperson): ultimately, theirs is speech without an individual orator or source, but it generates a discourse that permeates everything. As Paul Maliszewski notes, in Richard Powers's *Gain* the protagonist's central mission is to discover the corporate source of her cancer, but no personal agency, no person, exists to be found (163). The spirit animal for that contemporary corporation should be the unpersoned drone, whose recent emergence seems not accidental but an outgrowth of assumptions related to corporate governance, responsibility, and rights. Robert Mankoft, a *New Yorker* cartoonist, depicts God affirming that "Switching to drones has made having to be everywhere at once much more manageable" (Sept. 23, 2013, 56). As Herbert Marcuse observed of advanced industrial culture, "There is only one dimension, and it is everywhere and in all forms" (11). The potential ubiquity of the all-seeing drone matches the omnipresence of the corporation. Representing a kind of technocratic "evolution" of Moby Dick, the whale that was spotted in multiple locations at once, the drone that is everywhere simultaneously is an appropriate mascot for the corporation: it elides agency and liability, is part of a tangled network of corporate profits and governmental/military collusion, and creates another nexus for a kind of corporate management of life and death. *Unpersoned* is a word that describes the effect of corporate culture on individuals, but also on social values; corporations and drones are designed to separate individuals from responsibility. Hobbes thought we needed to submit to state power and violence to guarantee safety and security, but we now submit to corporate power, control, and violence. Though in less obvious ways than the state on which it relies, and whose military it directly and indirectly uses, the post-Pinkerton US corporation often deploys various forms of violence abroad to achieve its ends, from effectively engineering coups throughout Central and South America to covertly instituting contemporary forms of servitude that treat workers as serfs. What only states and sovereigns could once do has become the domain of the corporation.

Through the corporate entity and the conceptual corporation, we've created a system that encourages and necessitates the concentration of wealth and the circumnavigation of liability. Though the power behind a corporation is normally diffuse in the sense of being unlocatable, Barry Lynn documents the rise of a powerful class that "communalized all its holdings" in corporations and "thus escaped the legal strictures that tie individual owners to real property. Even when that power is momentarily concentrated in the body of a real person . . . the interest remains only to maximize capital and hence power" (242). Corporations are structured to minimize accountable agency, to split act from actor, and act from consequence. In *Collective and Corporate Responsibility*, Peter French argues that just as the president of the United States is authorized to take acts that represent the country, corporate boards are authorized to take acts that represent the corporation (Garrett 263). We don't in this context encounter the problem of singular intention—that is, the distinct but separate inability to state credibly that someone acts with a single, purely conscious intent that can be known; the problem instead is that claiming to represent a fiction doesn't make the fiction real. (In this sense, any nation is also a collective fiction. No definition could cover what it means to be an American or establish what constitutes the United States: Does one have to be pro- or anti-abortion to be American? Pro- or anti-gun rights? No trait or combination of beliefs could definitively exclude or include the citizens of any country. But such limitations in defining a collective are different; the democratic nation isn't being treated as a person.) French's claim that corporate acts that are consistent with corporate policy enact corporate intentions is circular, and bizarrely ratifies agency in acts that allegedly comport with corporate directives, and effectively dismisses any acts that don't as what are known as frolics of their own ("The Corporation" 213). But this analysis ratifies corporate exceptionalism. In other words, in most cases, the things agents do for the corporation remain corporate acts when justified by law, but personal acts and frolics whenever something goes wrong. At best, such presumptions inchoately assume that shareholder or director intentions cumulatively and coherently form the basis for verifying the authenticity of corporate acts. When spokespeople for corporations launch PR campaigns to apologize for some corporate transgression, some action that goes against their alleged values or is irremediably harmful, they sound like parents in denial about the continuously pathological behavior of a changeling child engineered to behave this way.

Patricia Bromley and John Meyer propose that "the term 'actor' once had a primary meaning diametrically opposed to its present social-scientific one," and connoted a person who was playing a role someone else scripted (*Hyper-Organization* 125). Their analysis is germane in the context of how organizations—and particularly multinational corporations, whose numbers have increased roughly tenfold since the 1970s (16)—establish boundaries, hierarchies, and discrete functions to act in a unified fashion to achieve specified missions. Christian List and Philip Pettit more naively assert that groups can possess agency simply through their agents, because "what the group agent thinks and does is always determined by what the members think and do. According to the supervenience thesis . . . the group's attitudes and actions are a function of the members' attitudes and actions" (130). List and Petit also insist that group or collective agents can make decisions akin to those of individuals, and that their agency depends on "the organization and behavior of individual embers" (4–6). But even if a group can reach consensus or even complete unanimity regarding a decision, that group is never equivalent to the corporation, which is always elsewhere. List and Petit object that the politics of the BP oil spill would make no sense unless one could ascribe agency to BP without being able to acknowledge that the politics make no sense (6). They miss the point and problem of the corporate form, which is designed to elide agency and responsibility and in fact elicits horror. As Siraganian notes, modernists began to fear that the corporate person represented not only a new living organism and group person, but a soulless and inhuman one, a shell with nothing inside (*Modernism* 30; "Dreiser's" 265).

List and Petit's ascription of control and univocal intention to abstractions seems inapt and unrealistic, especially in imagining a kind of untroubled translation between individuals and groups. (A committee or board can make decisions, but where and how would one locate univocal agency except in circular fashion, from the decision back to some group agent that must have made it?) This concept of supervenience, which explains that group attitudes are aggregated from those of its members, postulates a kind of benign Big Other, or rather an unnamed and inadequately theorized entity, that somehow coordinates the intentions of its disparate members. This notion becomes especially problematic when applied in corporate contexts. Coca-Cola doesn't reflect the political views of its "members" or carry out the specific intentions of its shareholders except in the limited context of shareholder votes; its putative group agency is nothing more than a useful, but also deceptive, fiction. This sociological approach misses the ontological dimension of intention as it applies to corporations. Corporate agents are phantoms, shadows that have nothing throwing them. They carry out the orders of a fiction.

This disrupted lineage or chain of action, speech, and culpability is connected to the issue of the corporate simulacra, and the always reified or falsified corporate biography: when, for example, Sony (or the Tyrell or Weyland Corporation) disclaims, "the views expressed in this production do not necessarily reflect those of the Sony corporation," it normalizes the idea that the Sony corporation could have noneconomic views. But if they could, what would they entail? "Who" would have them? How would those views be ratified (without turning corporations into substantially different entities whose pronouncements would have to be approved by shareholder majorities, which would still remain problematic in terms of the corporation's charter and legal status)? What kind of dissent would exist from such official views? Would such views be synecdochic, with some part of the corporation representing a whole that doesn't exist? What "Sony" should be or perhaps is trying to say is "please overlook the fact that we actually have and can have no views."

Exemplifying a poststructuralist principal that Foucault disseminated ("Technologies), corporate speech never can have an author. (More than any other entity, corporations reflect the poststructuralist truism of the "death of the author," the idea that the persons who produce a work, and their biographies, are secondary or irrelevant to the work, which, like the corporation, allegedly speaks for itself.) Corporate utterances can be traced to functionaries of the corporation, but never the corporation itself. In the ulterior logic of our culture, pervasive forms of AI and artificial life now are also identified with the virtual and the post-human, and all these categories with the corporation. David Runciman treats corporations as forms of AI, but partly misrepresents the relationship between its action and its agents:

> Corporations are another form of artificial thinking machine, in that they are designed to be capable of taking decisions for themselves. . . . The corporation speaks and acts for itself. . . . When corporations misbehave, we look for human beings to blame. . . . The problem is that [the CEO.] Kalanick is not Uber—he goes, but the business goes on. Of course corporations are not inherently bad, anymore than any other machine. (38–39)

Runciman also asserts that while law has long defined the corporation, we still don't understand what goes on in the black box in its mind, or what it "wants." "What do corporations want?" is a terrifying Freudian question. What Runciman overlooks is that the corporation is neither neutral nor a benign machine—it is programmed to pursue profit at the expense of the social good, and to insulate those who advance that pursuit in the corporation's name from responsibility or liability. Corporations have without question provided innumerable benefits in the realms of trade, technology, transportation, and, in often especially problematic ways, agriculture and medicine (though it's a fallacy to argue that corporations are the only forms that could have provided those benefits). But the directive of the corporation is on balance, both from ontology and historical evidence, harmful to much of society, the environment, and our rights and personhood. The corporation is a kind of virus that has captured and commandeered the minds and wills of its human hosts or workers. And it is endemic to its artificial DNA to (get its agents to) lie pathologically.

The modern form of the corporate enterprise also performs many of the abstract precepts of poststructuralist semiotics—for example, it separates act/speech from source/intention. In most contexts, we have corporate signifieds (ads, symbols, and pronouncements) and, legally and onto-logically, no signifiers—no one responsible for what's being produced. In symbolic and practical ways, as DeLillo narrates throughout his novel *Mao II*, the corporation is both cause and effect of the symbolic death and disempowerment of the individual author in our culture. In more immediate terms, the corporation also reflects the symbolic death of most speakers in humanistic contexts; we can reach audiences only when mediated by the corporation. Most of all—and most of us will balk at this notion because our culture inculcates fantasies of successful idiosyncratic corporate executives—the corporation represents the death of the CEO.

The corporate self-representation I address is different from that of the CEO biographies (which now overlap with celebrity biographies) that Purnima Bose and Laura E. Lyons discuss in "Toward a Critical Corporate Studies," and that many authors address in their collection, *Cultural Critique and the Global Corporation*. Such biographical utterances are simulacra *of* simulacra, often written by intermediaries about media constructs. Even when one could say that a corporation is led by a single voice or intention, as some would claim Apple was under Steve Jobs, a CEO never can coincide with the corporation: some uncontainable surplus always remains. You can kill a CEO—not that I would suggest any one go out and do so—but never the corporation. Like signifier and signified, the two remain separate and never can be identical. Directors and employees are never the corporation itself, legally or performatively: regardless of what Jobs might have alleged, he was not Apple. That disjunction led to the hyperbolic cultivation of Jobs as part of a corporate cult of personality—another way to hide the fact that there's no their there. Arbitrary image making is at the core of Apple, but also of all corporate identity. The corporation with a human face is still a corporation, and it distorts what it means to have a human face. Apple is an exceptionally distinct brand, but it's not a person, and the always arbitrary association of personality traits with it cannot imbue it with life.

In terms of general business practices, Apple is no better than Nike. Many of its products are made with the contemporary equivalent of slave labor. They're designed for planned obsolescence so that you continually have to buy replacements. You can't run new programs, or even replace batteries, on many Apple devices, which forces people to "upgrade" and purchase newer ones. Apple exploits workers, customers, and tax laws and achieves market share though monopolistic practices, yet it continues to garner uncritical devotees through branding, which makes the corporation seem cool and alternative to many. CEOs, especially those with fulminating personalities and eccentric business strategies, can direct many aspects of their companies, but they still have to operate within fixed structures of law, governance, and corporate "self"-representation—that is, the premises of corporate personhood and advertising.

Regardless of the influence, leadership, or personality of corporate executives, the corporate form was designed to create an insurmountable gap between individuals who work for or represent the corporation and the identity of the corporation itself. As Žižek might argue, the corporate figurehead must be created through a process of fetishization and reification, or

the false "personalization" ("psychologization") of what are in fact objective social processes. It was in the 1930s that the first generation of Frankfurt School theoreticians drew attention to how—at the very moment when global market

> relations started to exert their full domination, making the individual producer's success or failure dependent on market cycles totally out of his control—the notion of a charismatic "business genius" reasserted itself in "spontaneous capitalist ideology," attributing the success or failure of a businessman to some mysterious *je ne sais quois* which he possesses. (*Ticklish* 349; also *Universal* 235)

Though this is a valid observation, it might come across as an exaggeration in some instances, in that CEOs such as Jobs, sometimes in actuality and sometimes in public perception, do exert significant control over corporations. But such charismatic personalities don't change the stipulations of corporate personhood: the business leader serves to naturalize the notion that some person stands behind corporate personhood. The law transposes the relationship between persons to, or imposes it on, impersonal forces that abnegate personhood. The greater the impersonality of the corporate form, the greater the public need for charismatic CEOs and celebrities to be attached to the corporation, to serve as the human facade of an inhuman enterprise. Such makeovers provide reassuring distractions that someone is behind the wheel of the machine that's running you over.

But corporate representatives, from CEOs to celebrity spokespeople, must be temporary and fungible for the corporation to function as intended. As Lyons demonstrates in "'I'd Like My Life Back'": Corporate Personhood and the BP Oil Disaster," CEOs must simultaneously personify corporations and distance themselves from their decisions. Lyons notes, for example, that with regard to the Gulf oil spill, BP CEO

> [Tony] Hayward's statement, with its pronominal slippage from the singular "I" who speaks on behalf of the corporation to the collective "we" of the corporation itself and back to an individuated "I" emblematizes the ways in which BP, and corporations more generally, enact strategies of intimacy and distance, individuation and collectivity, as they attempt to manage public perceptions about their operations. (95)

As Lyons concludes, "When he speaks for himself, he can't say anything right; when he speaks for BP, under the watchful eyes of his legal advisors, he can't say anything at all" (102–3). That CEO's dilemma reflects a variation of the zero-sum game of corporate identity. In corpography, any "single" voice is a reification of a nonexistent corporate person, leaving the corporate biography always ghostwritten. Corporate speech, according to Paola Catenaccio and Chiara Degano, often attempts to reconcile incommensurate goals or voices, leaving corporate representatives trying to strike a balance "between these two opposing orientations: investors must be persuaded that CSR [corporate social responsibility] will not be pursued to the detriment of profit, and at the same time the doubts of activists must be assuaged by providing convincing proof of the company's commitment to social responsibility" (85). But no person is behind such speech; at best, we have orientations.

Some corporations do take the idea of public stewardship or account-ability seriously, though often inconsistently. While it exploits customers' private information and often conceals its manipulative search practices, Google, for example, also commits to paying for gender reassignment surgery for its employees. CVS stopped selling cigarettes. Lyft might be a less exploitative employer than Uber (though that's a low bar). I don't disregard the significant differences among corporations in terms of their approach to social and employment issues, and the way corporate governance can matter, but I want to emphasize the often-overlooked consequences to which the corporate form gives rise. In that context, the corporate CEO is a figurehead, and CSR largely a diversion. The person who temporarily represents the corporation, from CEO to ad spokesperson, ultimately doesn't represent the company (and in some cases, isn't even real). Even if Google, for example, inconsistently tries to adhere to a more progressive ethos than some companies, it is doing nothing personal; the corporation can act in largely predetermined, structurally delimited ways, and it must retain an impersonal indifference toward anything but profit and growth. Everything else, from charity to allegedly socially responsible practices, is the equivalent of a Catholic's medieval indulgence—a kind of payoff to allow the corporation to continue doing what it always has done unabated. As an emblematic example of how CSR is, at best, another zero-sum game, tobacco companies routinely sponsored events, benefits, and "anti-smoking" campaigns that also promoted their products to vulnerable audiences.

This mechanically programmed behavior is particularly disturbing as corporations take over many functions of the public sector, and of government itself, from running prisons to national security. The definition of the bottom line is that in the corporate domain, obligations to sharehold-ers and society remain incompatible: as David Foster Wallace wrote in the notes to his unfinished novel *The Pale King*, "Big Q is whether IRS is to be essentially a corporate entity or a *moral* one," clearly indicating it can't be both (543, emphasis in original).[1] Carl Safina observes that when Henry Ford tried to improve the lives of his employees by investing corporate profits into their education and other benefits, the Supreme Court blocked his attempts because the duty to shareholders directed the corporation only to seek profit (42). The structure of the public corporation on practical as well as onto-logical and legal levels prevents individual executives from straying from the corporate charter.

That charter enforces a constrictive covenant and ethos that not only reduces all human interaction to economic calculus, but all communication to some form of selling and economic exchange. As the corporate form diminishes human personhood, it increases reliance on, and the function of, the impersonal voice of advertising throughout society. Sut Jhally contends that "there is no one relation of people to things in advertising or one message that's communicated through advertising" (170); certainly viewing and experience is contextual and variable. But like the corporate form, advertising relies on a surprisingly determinate and narrow range of assumptions and options. For Richard Dienst, "to regard watching TV as a transaction carried out between economic agents (individual, corporate, or both) is to fall into the same error Marx exposed in the bourgeoisie economists: reducing the systemic to the subjective and the [here literally] episodic" (61). In other words, variable viewing experience, and the minor variations of CSR, never alter the structural constraints that dictate corporate behavior and advertising; a vampire that donates a little blood doesn't stop being undead. Corporate personhood accelerates and transforms what Žižek terms the "false personalization" of impersonal social processes: with corporations, "we are dealing with a giant global network [that might be] formally owned by a single individual . . . [but] ownership becomes irrelevant to its functioning." (*Universal* 235). As the network CEO Arthur Jenson chastises the deranged but sometimes insightful tele-preacher/news anchor Howard Beale in *Network* (1976), "We no longer live in a world of nations and ideologies, Mr. Beale. The world is a collage of corporations, inexorably determined by the immutable bylaws of business," and those bylaws have replaced human personality, agency, and even many aspects of national sovereignty with corporate personhood. Jenson should have added that we no longer live in a world of people or CEOs either. Boaventura de Sousa Santos demonstrates in a variety of inter-American contexts that corporations develop and implement their own foreign policies and use nations to achieve their ends, rather than the reverse ("The Americas"). Once controlled by the Hobbesian state, corporations come to impersonate it by creating and manipulating national identities for their own purposes, and by effectively infiltrating human institutions, from universities to states, in much the way right-wing agencies long have infiltrated leftist and progressive political organizations.

Inverting Marx's formulation, Žižek suggests that now "objective market 'relations between things' tend to assume the fantasmagorical form of pseudo-personalized 'relations between people" (*Universal* 235). In other words, people aren't behaving like things in isolation: things and the artificial constructs that support the corporate form are "behaving" like and displacing people. As Kim Benston proposes, the corporate persona suggests that Marx's commodity fetishism realizes its apotheosis in capitalism via its perfect inversion—that is, not the transformation of subjective experience into a calculation of monetized value, but the misinterpretation of buying and selling as social discourse among persons. But our dominant ideology still leads most people to believe that individuals, from the woman who loses her job to downsizing after twenty years or the billionaire's son who corners a market, are almost entirely responsible for their economic fates: everything is assumed to be "the result of my personality, not of being tossed around by market forces" (*Universal* 238). It's not surprising that many people become hysterically agitated when the idea of personal/individual self-determination is challenged as an empirically insupportable reification. The responsible "personality" we should examine is that of the corporation.

As I later address, courts continue to humanize corporations and mistake their representatives as legally coterminous with them in terms of rights, yet wholly distinguishable from them in terms of liabilities. Even more perniciously, the law treats corporations as biographical and narrative subjects, which transfers speech and ontological and human rights, along with wealth, from people to corporations. In his concurrence to *Citizens United*, Justice Scalia supposes that because they employ people to act on their behalf, corporations also can speak for those employees:

> The dissent says that "'speech'" refers to oral communications of human beings, and since corporations are not human beings they cannot speak [citation omitted]. This is sophistry. The authorized spokesman of a corporation is a human being, who speaks on behalf of the human beings who have formed that association—just as the spokesman of an unincorporated association speaks on behalf of its members. The power to publish thoughts, no less than the power to speak thoughts, belongs only to human beings, but the dissent sees no problem with a corporation's enjoying the freedom of the press. (558 U.S. at 392, n7)

(As deconstructionists might note, such privileging of speech over the written word also would be misguided in linguistic and legal contexts.) The "authorization" to which Scalia refers is much like the granting of personhood to a scarecrow. How are corporations different from unincorporated groups? It's not simply that corporations are owned by shareholders (who can sell their interest in them) and run by boards of directors, but that by definition they have no center; the shareholders have no liability, and the corporations exist independently of their owners. Even in the case of closely held corporations, the legal structure allows corporations to maintain separate, virtually ventrilo-quized identities. In both the legal and cultural sphere, most representations of corporations rely on prosopopoeia—the personification of something abstract or absent. Judges especially tend to engage in a kind of category misprision when addressing corporate speech. The artificially consolidated corporate person is created solely for commercial activity and bestowed with certain rights, immunities, and restrictions exclusively in that context. Yet courts usually treat corporations as if they could selectively attain the positive attributes of people without relinquishing the artificial and limited qualities their legal charters afford them.

Chapter Thirteen

Buy with Confidence

"Say, Frank, are we not men? I say are we not human?"

"Inconsistency? Bah!"
"There speaks the ventriloquist again," sighed Frank, in bitterness.

—Melville, *The Confidence-Man* (174, 222)

Well before Devo, Melville was worried about the ways impersonal market forces could erode our sense of identity from the inside out. In *The Confidence-Man*, published in 1857, Melville already was disturbed by people's susceptibility to commercial speech, which reflected an economy that preyed on false confidence, false belief, and false fellowship. The novel tracks an array of passengers traveling down the Mississippi River, most of whom interact with a confidence man who continually impersonates others. The narrative partly focuses on commercial fraud, and on how it's possible to ventriloquize not just other identities, but personhood itself when an entity doesn't have it. *The Confidence-Man* is the first novel to link advertising not just with confidence tricks and snake oil, but early forms of corporate personhood. (Confidence men of course existed long before corporations, but I focus here on the connection between corporate personhood and the impersonation of human traits and interactions, which is the ultimate confidence game. As I suggest, many low-level individual spammers emulate the model of corporate personhood. And while not all confidence men impersonate corporations, all corporations ontologically impersonate confidence men.) The novel's many-faced protagonist sells not only an array of fraudulent goods and potions, but also the very notion that he can be trusted. More than that, he sells the proposition that he has a human identity, when he's really only a series of proto-corporate disguises and appropriations of human traits. Melville was, in embryonic form, concerned with cybernetics—with how we can discern what is human. As Melville's narrator and his character the Cosmopolitan aver in various ways, "a metaphysical lover of the species [might] doubt whether the human form be, in all cases, conclusive evidence of humanity" (60). In this novel, "you can conclude nothing absolute from the human form," much as you can conclude nothing from an ad (226). By the time corporations become people, you can conclude nothing from form at all; people routinely become walking captures of the corporation, walking brands and consumer signboards. In this novel, the language of advertising doesn't sell products; it works only by selling confidence and lies and by making you believe false propositions, particularly about the advertiser's identity.

The ship in *The Confidence-Man* is heading toward the slave port of New Orleans. Reflecting Melville's frequent interrogation of the connections between slavery and wage slavery, the Missourian asks, "Who is your master, pray; or are you owned by a company?" (112). Though Melville was keenly aware of the horrors of slavery, he also intimates that these two options can be more similar than we might suspect, in part because our instinct is to situate the corporation as a kind of venial inevitability. As I later contend, slavery and corporate personhood both steal forms of personhood from people, but the "soul-catching" of the latter is still sanctioned by law. Throughout *The Confidence-Man*, Melville asks whether we can tell what it means to have/ own a soul and human autonomy, and he defamiliarizes the relationship between slaves, machines, and people. Many of the discussions in the novel address how one can emulate human behavior, truthful speech, or possession of a soul (116). The Confidence Man resembles Mephistopheles because he shape-shifts. He cannot be identified, and he incessantly deceives others— but he engages in these actions in pursuit of trust, not of profit, in ways consonant with what Melville saw as the joint-stock or corporate enterprise, ultimately the Trust itself; such questions were more personal at the time because the corporate form—for example, the joint-stock company—could still sometimes be identified with specific men.

But Melville was concerned with the ways the market and its ascendant corporate structures made it increasingly difficult to distinguish human personality, or even humanity, from counterfeits (what we might now situate as zombies, aliens, AI, and other simulacra of life): as Judge Hall states, "in strict speech there can be no biography of . . . a dead man" (150). Biography can only pertain to a living thing, but it's increasingly displaced by/onto impersonations. Melville's novel, like corporate biography, frequently tracks the loss or transfer of the human soul: "His soul is gone out. Only *nature's automatonism* keeps him on his legs" (173). Again, we can readily substitute the corporation for nature in this assertion; both represent the automaton, some collective, inhuman and common force that keeps a dispossessed person seemingly animated. As Žižek puts it, we're subjected to "the inexorable logic of an automaton that runs the show, so when the subject speaks, he is unbeknownst to himself, merely 'spoken'" (*How* 40). Here God, whom Žižek calls "the big Other personified," or nature controls us as automatons, a function taken over by the corporation (41).

Many of the characters in *The Confidence-Man* are soulless, but seemingly alive. Melville was fascinated by bodies that act autonomically or impersonally—limbs that are dismembered and keep moving; arms and legs that act of their own accord (or with what Ishmael in *Moby-Dick* terms "generic or pantheistic vitality" [302]); dead bodies that continue to move; and forms apparently without substance that lay bare the impersonality of life itself—that is, the prospect that life can be transferred from a host. In many of Melville's novels, life, a limb, or a soul can be detached from a person and animated independently, much like corporate personhood. Žižek frequently identifies this same surplus of life: "What makes scarecrows terrifying is the minimal difference which makes them *in*-human: there's "nobody at home" behind the mask—as with a human who has turned into a zombie." That disturbing uncanniness is as evident in the corporate imperson- ation of personhood. We here encounter not the mask of Oz, but the exposi- tion of the Hobbesian mask—what Žižek terms semblances of life, rather than fictions, masks that disguise only further masks (*Less* 44–45). As I elaborate, the New World was colonized by a zombie form, the corporation that imitates a person; as Misty Anderson implies, the corporation begins as an undead form, an artificial substitute for the body (corpus) of the king, and becomes a zombie sovereignty that never can die, and whose "uncanny absence" set the stage for much of contemporary economic, political, and cultural life (112). At the center of our culture is a nonexistent body, without soul or life, that is artificially animated and controls much of our lives.

Žižek warns that these empty forms, or the sequences that constitute them, can be more illustrative of our identities than what we thought they were concealing:

> human language proper only functions when fiction counts for more than reality, when there is more truth in a mask than in the stupid reality beneath the mask, when there is more truth in a symbolic title (father, judge . . .) than in the reality of the empirical bearer of this title. This is why Lacan is right when he points out that a Platonic supra-sensible Idea is an imitation of imitation, appearance as ap- pearance—something that appears on the surface of substantial reality. The key formula of semblance was proposed by J-A Miller: semblance is a mask (veil) of

nothing. . . . Semblance is like a veil, a veil which veils nothing—its function is
to create the illusion that there is something hidden beneath the veil. (*Less* 46)

This last sentence encapsulates the corporate form. The function of such
semblances also helps contextualize the need for CEOs and celebrities to stand
in for and impersonate the corporation. Miller's language here is resonant,
because the "corporate veil" that shields corporate agents from liability also
shields the fact that the corporation isn't hidden by a veil but is a veil.

In the United States, the history of the corporation also tracks the shift
from romanticism to naturalism and back to neoromanticism, which,
perhaps surprisingly, maintain similar premises regarding the aggregate
forces of nature/the corporation, and primarily alters only our reaction to
those premises. Under naturalism, nature and the corporation represent an
impersonal automaton, an emblem of monstrous, brute/blind force rather
than benign omnipresence. According to Walter Benn Michaels, through
the "discrepancy between the behavior of individuals and that of the
aggregate," the corporation can turn anything into (and thereby
problematize the very notion of) a person: "dreaming of the "monstrous,"
Presley [in Frank Norris's 1901 novel *The Octopus*] is already dreaming
of the corporation" (211).[1] Here, impersonal transcendental nature, which
represents an aggregate mass, was only a precursor to Norris's impersonal
and effectively still transcendental corporation—in this trajectory, the
leviathan turns into another large kraken, but with almost unlimited reach.

Chapter Fourteen

Habeas Corporation

As Melville established in *Moby-Dick*, a corporation functions as a collective being without a body, an abstraction incorporated as a fictional juggernaut: for Powers, it's "*an aggregate giant*, one that summed the capital and labor of untold Lilliputians into vast, limbered Leviathan" (*Gain* 158).[1] (As Frederic Jameson notes, "The market is thus Leviathan in sheep's clothing" [273]; or as Bakan puts it, by the turn of the twentieth-century, corporations were "widely viewed as soulless leviathans" [17]). As I elaborate, the corporation subsumes the state and nature to become the new mass or leviathan. In September 2014, the *New York Times* reported that "a European publishing executive likened [Google] to a Wagnerian dragon" (Hakim 1). Powers encapsulates the corporate octopus as an all-encompassing distillation of new-world co-option: "The limited-liability corporation: the last noble experiment, loosing an unknowable outcome upon its beneficiaries. Its success outstripped all rational prediction until, gross for gross, it became mankind's sole remaining endeavor" (159). It's the gross and ubiquitous leviathan that threatens not only to supplant other forms of commerce, but other forms of ratiocination and identity. One of the most specious and misguided pronouncements in the *Citizens United* holding is Justice Kennedy's assertion that "Corporations, like individuals, do not have monolithic views." 558 U.S. at 364. As I argue throughout, they're the only kind of views corporations legally, and in most cases ontologically, can have. And as Wallace suggests in *The Pale King*, they precisely give rise to what's called "in economic terms [a] 'monoculture'" (271). As Steiner observes, in translatable contexts, "The thought of a more or less monoglot world is no longer inconceivable" (*Errata* 113). According to David Harvey, postwar Fordism should be seen "less as a mere system of mass production and more as a total way of life," and one might modify that term to totalizing (*Condition* 135).

Individuality as we perceive it is a modern construction, but it emerged in tension with modes and premises of mass production, which ironically made it possible for greater numbers of people to have the disposable income to pursue the generic commercial accoutrements of (counter-) individuality. A central component of that form of production is advertising, as well as the attendant forms of entertainment and culture it sponsors, disseminates, and glamorizes. The corporate culture that the vast majority of Americans experience daily is monomaniacally mono—it's predicated not just on mass production, but a monopolistic consolidation of wealth, power, networks of distribution, and speech under the facade of diversity. But under current law, the corporation never can be produced to be held genuinely accountable for the actions taken on its behalf; it resides in some parallel universe of legal theory. It is a consequence of corporate unification, universality, and Hobbesian sovereignty that we are increasingly exposed to, at any meaningful level in most of the developed world, only corporate media and art: the monopoly that corporations tend to effectuate isn't primarily economic, but psychological, cultural, sociological, and ontological—a monopoly of personhood itself.

Chapter Fifteen

Paranoid Desires

One consequence of corporations' reliance on advertising to speak and represent themselves is the degradation of linguistic consistency, reliability, and nuance, as well as what one might call a reliable matrix of communication in contemporary culture. By manipulating language and the precepts of ontology—for example, by incessantly assuring consumers that novelty can be commensurate with nostalgia, and excitement with familiarity—advertising helps fashion a self that is as corporatized as the medium. Corporate personhood, and its correlative emanations in advertising, distorts language so that you can no longer rely on standard meanings. One could contend that the meanings of words change as part of a vibrant culture, but our language and conceptual vocabulary largely have been co-opted by corporations; in mainstream culture, for example, *progressive* has been transformed into a word primarily connoting insurance rather than a political movement. It deforms language to convince people that they earn or accomplish something by consuming, which is a basic premise of corporate advertising. Candy manufacturers label candy "fun-size," when their bars are merely smaller than what used to be standard. Many airlines tell you you're a valued guest, when you're a customer. The fact that it's not enough for corporations to say you're a customer and that they will interact with you fairly as such means corporations must obfuscate the commercial nature of their relationship with you, usually through manipulation and false associations and identifications with family, friendship, love, and altruism. It's startling that many corporations advertise with the premise that they're doing something entirely for your benefit and with your interests in mind. The slogan on a shampoo bottle states "we're here to help." Such tactics might seem innocuous in isolation, but they form part of an overwhelming array of assaults on consciousness, and continuously erode our values and sense of community. We have no human relationship with corporations, but we are incessantly told that we do. In *Satin Island*, Tom McCarthy traces the way corporations generate and control the meaning of words:

> [M]y "official" function as a corporate ethnographer was to garner meaning
> . . . . Divining for the benefit of a breakfast-cereal manufacturer, the social or
> symbolic role of breakfast . . . [so] the manufacturer [can] then feed the
> information back into their product and its packaging . . . not simply [to create]
> better-tasting cereal or bigger profits for the manufacturer, but rather meaning,
> amplified and sharpened. . . . The world functioned, each day, because I'd put
> meaning back into it the day before. (30–32)

The consequence of such manipulation, as Richard Powers narrates in *The Gold Bug Variations*, is to generate a paranoid style of style itself:

> "DO YOU KNOW WHAT THE OTHER GUY IS UP TO?" . . . He explained
> that his outfit had been hired to free-lance this ad; it would hit the stands in three
> big-circulation glossies next month. His eyes gleamed. "The bastard will *sell*,"
> he chuckled. "Apotheosis of vending by fear. Paranoia—our supreme erotic
> desire. Everyone secretly adores having his worst nightmare orchestrated." . . .
> "I thought we bought things we liked."
> "Wake up lady."
> "Who's the client," I asked. "What's the product?"
> "God *damn* it, O'Deigh. Who in hell *cares*? Haven't you figured the game out
> yet? Nobody sells products. They sell *slogans*." (313)

In *Great Jones Street*, Don DeLillo gave a correlative name to this sales-force: "I came up with the name transparanoia. . . . A corporation word, but perfect for our time" (138, 67). Commercial transactions are vital and laudable when they're transparent and honest; the need to falsify their nature suggests we believe they're all tainted and that we can somehow con others without ourselves being conned. No wonder we're not transcendental or transparent, but transparanoid.

What might seem like a minor adulteration of language in advertising, for example, often leads to the relativization of conceptual convictions. This manipulation is hardly excusive to advertising, but it does reach its apotheosis through it. In other words, advertising sets us on a path to being more unique, most unique, truthier, newier, and at the threshold of utter rejection unless we buy a product modeled on principles of addictive non-gratification. (One could track the devolution of the word *unique*—which isn't relative and cannot be used as a comparative—from ads that declaim this is the "most unique" product in history to its common misuse by pundits across media.) Most of the adjectives that advertising overuses are emphatics that have no meaning: *very, super, extra, so, totally, awesome,* and so on. Advertising relies on emphatic utterances and claims that mean nothing. Adjectives are cheap and easy, usually assertions without backing: the claim that she's "very interesting" is less emphatic than saying she's "interesting," because *very* is the linguistic equivalent of the empty calories corporations use to sell junk food. Such overuse of adjectives and empty assertion isn't just puffery—it makes the speaker less reliable. Our ability to communicate has been corporatized and degraded to the level of advertising language, and our forms of speech race advertising to the bottom. Emoticons are the laugh tracks of the internet, mechanical signs that pathetically imitate human communication and response, and they emerged as a logical outgrowth of a corporate advertising mass-media culture designed to make you illiterate. This process of linguistic appropriation and disenfranchisement is also an integral part of a pervasive corporatization of what was once public space and rhetoric, especially in politics. Whenever politicians or advertisers say "Trust me," "Let me make this clear," "I never lie," etc., chances are they're untrustworthy.

The erosion of language also paces the erosion of identity, especially in a culture that cannot reconcile a fetishization of both individuality and mass-produced goods and identities. American individuality always was predicated on a putatively foreign or extrinsic element that was antagonistic to it—the lineage of the immense mass or exceptional collective force that ends in the corporation, and corporate "mass language." We imagine we transcend individuality by becoming undifferentiated mass consumers. In *Mao II*, DeLillo proposes that American individualism is beholden to a corporate culture of conformism, mass production, and mass identity. Throughout the novel, DeLillo delineates the way an ethos of mass-produced or duplicated identity is dependent on "technical" duplications—especially the reproductions of corporate advertisements. What seems stereotypically foreign merges individuals into the crowd and mass identity, sometimes under the guise of a slogan or logo. Two always becomes a foreign crowd, a mass, opposed to the individual American. But what is imagined as stereotypically American—the mass-produced Chevrolet, the universally replicated Coke bottle, and the logo of the credit card—becomes indistinguishable from the "Maoist" dogma it seems to oppose in the novel. As in the *Alien* films, the corporation that seems American is revealed to be a foreign infiltration that is further revealed to be definitive of America. The mass-produced Warhol paintings of Mao, which the novel is named after, emblematize the way corporate production not only co-opts revolution, but individualism; all we get of products or selves are copies without originals. The novel dissects the way Americans project anxieties onto the foreign mass—the yellow horde; Mao; terrorists; the foreign crowds that disindividuate and join fundamentalist "mass" religions—to define the putative white individualist, but white individualism turns out to be predicated on the corporate mass.

Strolling through New York, Karen, who, like Melville's Isabel, longs for an identity merged into some greater mass, sees the seemingly foreign words, "Sony, Mita, Kirin, Magno, Midori" (148). Early in the novel, Scott and Brita spy a comparable sequence: "the signs were for Mita, Midori, Kirin, Magno, Suntory—words that were part of some synthetic mass language, the esperanto of jet-lag" (23). This artificial mass language is the vernacular of the corporation. In DeLillo's *White Noise*, the litany had been "Master Card, Visa, American Express" (*Mao* 239; *White* 100). These strings become religious chants of meaning, the names of deities. One context for how these names emerge involves the conceptual and linguistic processes of capitalist merger. In this variation of what Richard Slotkin terms "regeneration through violence," in which a combatant is strengthened by consuming some trait of the vanquished, the aforementioned Chemical Bank took over Chase Bank, but retained the "conquered" name as its company brand. As Žižek notes, there's a "market for brand names themselves. . . . If an old company with a recognizable name goes bankrupt, and all that remains is the name, this name can still be sold on. . . . The [impossible] ideal would be to sell a mere brand name and thus get money for nothing" (*Living* 211).

This conglomeration and aggregation of the corporate form often has been affiliated with colonialism, an exploitation of nature, and aboriginal dispossession. A logic of corporate invasion presides over a wide array of violent displacements and transfers, especially the removal of what were once native inhabitants and species. The hunt for Moby Dick takes place aboard a joint-stock ship, the *Pequod*, named after the Native American Pequot tribe; the mascot for the highly corporatized University of California, Berkeley is the golden bear, an animal that hasn't been seen within a hundred miles of campus in a hundred years. Again, some form of the corporation takes over the symbol of that which it has incorporated in its mergers and acquisitions. A similar process occurred at the end of the Cold War, which roughly marked the period when the United States first designated cabinet-level officials as czars, a term obviously imported from Soviet Russia. It's also not accidental that as we started deploying more and more security state tactics, we started calling the United States a homeland. In other words, as the putative victors of the war, a corporatized state took over the nomenclatures and qualities of the vanquished totalitarian state.

For DeLillo, Mao II and the novelty product Coke II turn out to be equally compatible with the premises of advertising: "Now there are signs for a new soft drink, Coke II, signs slapped on cement-block walls, and [Brita] has the crazy idea that these advertising placards herald the presence of the Maoist group" (230). DeLillo's narrator disingenuously observes that "because there is a certain physical resemblance" between the Coke II signs and the "posters of the Cultural Revolution in China," one sign must augur the other. As Margaret Scanlan suggests, "the intense red of advertisements for Coke II contributes to the fantasy that they are promoting a new Maoist group" (245). Coke II is able perfectly to declaim the presence of Mao II, for in DeLillo's perspective, a corporatist-capitalist economy must be able not only to co-opt agitprop images of communist icons as advertisements, but also to hide the fact that it relies on many of the same strategic imperatives and premises as the agitprop. Corporate capitalism needs to generate a false opposition with a totalitarian mass when it relies on a Maoist economy of signs and the immense mass of the corporation to convince consumers they're radical individualists.

In numerous DeLillo novels, characters realize that it is not English but advertising that is the new universal language expressing American culture. Advertising erases history or replaces it with a fabricated nostalgia, and it trivializes difference to matters of fashion and sentimentality

Ads often meld historical periods and social milieus—the worlds of cavemen and astronauts, royalty and celebrities, and so on. Such playfulness could be harmlessly entertaining, except the rationale for such conflations is to situate all things at the level of the dehistoricized corporate product and simultaneously convince viewers they live at the apex of time and space. The corporation also in some ways situates itself as a deity whose specific origin story is overshadowed by the premise that it always has existed, as it must now exist, everywhere. Coca-Cola and American Express are "always, everywhere," universalized in time and space: emblematic of capitalism, they erase their history and production (ironically, in one ad campaign, polar bears threatened with extinction extol Coca-Cola as ubiquitous, a perversity that might be part of the message). It is ads for these corporations that are virtually ubiquitous, appearing throughout most public space, on phone applications, everywhere in airports and on airlines—in every facet of entertainment, information, and communication in the United States. A recent PayPal ad proclaims, "We the People Can Buy Anything. Anytime. Anywhere." The ad typically claims a kind of universality and universal suffrage for commerce that appropriates democracy and makes it sound as if people are for sale. It's honest in exposing the fact that everything can be advertised and commodified.

Throughout *Mao II*, DeLillo suggests that our fear of the foreigner—of the intrusion of foreign languages and ideas and corporate logos—reflects a pathologically displaced fear of the ideology that intrinsically and internally defines us. According to Scanlan, "Characters in both [*The Satanic Verses* and *Mao II*] speak the global or Third-World English of those who come to it with an imperfect education gained far from English-speaking countries: both note the saturation of Third-World countries by First-World advertising, itself a new language" (236). More pointedly, DeLillo inverts the notion that the United States has been infiltrated by a hybrid foreign language of immigrants, and traces the infiltration to advertising, to Coke II as well as Mao II. The United States itself creates and exports this "foreign" mass language, imagery, and corporate ideology, which then returns to the scene of the crime. Tom LeClair observes that "the characters of *White Noise* consume sounds the way they consume supermarket products" and attempt to separate out the recognizable meaning from what they might consider the stutter of foreign information (230). Unfortunately, that foreign information is not only familiar, it *is* the meaning. By *Mao II*, this xenophobia about language becomes a reflection of American loss of control over the sign systems of its own mass-marketed capitalism, whose logos and slogans become incomprehensible doublespeak.

The inversions and zero-sum games of corporate personhood extend to other aspects of life in DeLillo's work—terrorists and writers are engaged in another zero-sum game that pertains to the notion of incorporation. As Bill says to Brita while being photographed,

> There's a curious knot that binds novelists and terrorists. In the West we become famous effigies as our books lose the power to shape and influence. . . . I used to think it was possible for a novelist to alter the inner life of the culture. Now bomb-makers and gunmen have that territory. They make raids on human consciousness. What writers used to do before they were all incorporated.[1] (41)

That is, writers made such raids before they were incorporated into a mass (foreign) body that represents the corporation/corporate culture. We're again incorporated into the shapeless mass of *Ratner's Star*. No one is able to speak outside these incorporated systems. In *Mao II*, those who join the mass become less than persons—they're troublingly conflated with terrorists and cultists who seek to attain mass identities in fundamentalist religions and political movements, which ironically turn out to offer a variation of the Tocquevillean mass identities corporations offer. The corporation represents a form of religious fanaticism in DeLillo's work. The last unincorporated novelist, Bill the lone white male writer seems to be a kind of Western bulwark against the mass, incorporated identity projected onto the East; yet in the novel's deep-structure politics, that mass identity is itself an internal product of the West.

To connote any "incorporation"—any form of mass, somatic fusion, from participating in mass weddings to joining the mass identities of terrorist groups or cults—as "Eastern" alerts us to a cultural projection. As Bill laments, conjuring another zero-sum game, "What terrorists gain, novelists lose. The degree to which they influence mass consciousness is the extent of our decline as shapers of sensibility and thought. The danger they represent equals our own failure to be dangerous" (157). Bill the writer dies of wounds inflicted by these terrorists, but also in an act dramatizing the ineffectuality and self-destructiveness of the West. In DeLillo's world, the terrorist is never "the solitary outlaw"—what writers might become were they effective—but the purported representative of a (foreign) mass culture. The premise is undermined because the ideology of American individualism is unable to accept its reliance on conformity and mass consciousness; the Eastern terrorist becomes an incarnation of the Western nation's political unconscious.

One obvious reversal *Mao II* hints at is that China became better at engaging in raw capitalism than the West, and that its Confucian ideology of conformity was wholly compatible with corporate branding. Žižek contends that

> The danger to Western capitalism comes not from outside, from the Chinese or some other monster beating us at our own game while depriving us of Western liberal individualism, but from the inherent limit of its own process of colonizing ever new (not only geographic, but also cultural, psychic, etc.) domains . . . [until] Capital will no longer have any substantial content outside itself to feed on. . . . When the circle closes itself, when reflexivity becomes thoroughly universal, the whole system is threatened. (*Ticklish* 358)

An equal danger is that a culture of false individuality, which is inculcated by corporations, will find resonances in and creep toward fascism, a brand of corporatism. (Hannah Arendt warned that the loss of community and sense of isolation that attend modernity can lead people to embrace fascism and mass identity, and, I would argue, its correlatives in corporatism.) In terms of the exigencies of production and the codification of identity, capitalist individualism is predicated on the corporate hive mind, which presupposes and fosters a uniformity of structure, production, distribution, product, consumption, and, most of all, values and identities.

One emblem of corporate conformity, as well as agricultural practices, is the fact that all the eggs you buy at supermarkets are the same size—this is so normalized, or reified, that some people believe chickens all lay the same size eggs. It makes sense for producers to group and package eggs of the same size together; but the practical consideration is, as always with corporations, coterminous with the structural and conceptual imperatives: to produce identical and unindividuated products and persons, and convince us that nature is corporate, and corporations are natural. Deviation and eccentricity are incompatible with the corporations that supposedly represent freedom and free enterprise. A 2014 Gap back-to-school ad offers "A Lesson in Individuality," and features two adolescent girls wearing the same gap sweater and striking the same pose; not only is individuality just a commodity, but it is available only through corporate mediation. The corporate advertisement doesn't offer individuality, but rather the false universality of the franchise and the false comfort of a mass or uniform identity. Like many ads, the photo below conveys more than its creators intend: it reminds us of the unbridgeable gap between ad and product. Ads clone individuals: add several billion people to this photo, and you begin to picture the end point of corporate personhood.

Gap ad: "celebrating individuality" through conformity

Chapter Sixteen

The Gap between Signifier and Signified

My chapter title refers to a simple concept: that ad campaigns must be independent from, and ultimately have nothing to do with, what they sell. This disjunction has broad and disturbing implications. Advertisers carefully tailor every campaign to a product's image, audience, and corporate directives. But that specificity belies a more profound "promiscuity": that ad campaigns have no intrinsic connection to their products. (Where labels are rarely fungible, advertisements almost always are.) The more we examine the underlying disjunction between ad and product, the stranger it becomes. The economic collapse of 2008 was partly predicated on the disconnection between fantasized capital and actual labor, between abstracted financial speculation and real-world objects. In this increasingly virtual economy, there was no necessary connection between a transaction and any underlying product, tangible good, or service. Advertising is the handmaid of this system—no necessary connection exists between ad and product, corporation and persons, and speculation and reliable valuation. Ritzenberg emphasizes that the development of the corporate form necessitated the separation of ownership from management ("Corporation" 45), and I would add that this separation parallels and is reinforced by the necessary separation between corporate ad campaign and product. In fundamental ways, ads (signifiers) refer to other ads, not products (signifieds), and at some level we know that all ads, and not just those of used car salesmen, are lies. Yet we strive to make more money and advertise more so we can buy more things that other people advertise (though these things have no connection to the ads). We're imprisoned in an economy of addiction, endless referral, and disjunction; life is elsewhere.

In order to work, ads must be categorically independent—floating, detachable, arbitrary—from the things they promote. Ad directors who develop

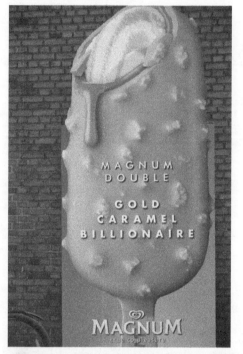

Like many commercials, this Danish ad attaches positive words to a product they have nothing to do with

Another branding phrase linking three words, with the final one intended to be meaningless

campaigns for reinsurance companies, for example, assume that the last thing they should do is talk about reinsurance; they need to come up with something unrelated, and affiliate that thing with the invented "personality" of the company, to associate with, and impersonate, a human identity.[1] (Theoretically, you might be able to sell soda by associating it with reinsurance if you could find an audience that fantasized about reinsurance.) This forced and artificial attachment of emotion or relationship to a thing, a product, involves a form of theft, a kind of demonic appropriation of what the soul is meant to represent. The most critical attribute of an advertisement is that it is necessarily fungible: when Fidelity presents a purportedly heartwarming narrative about how its employees keep drawings made by their customers' children on their desks to remind them they're saving real people's money, that narrative isn't only fabricated, it could be lifted and applied (in this case, as usual, without modification), to any other investment, insurance, or services corporation—in fact, any corporation. And the concept, which also has nothing to do with investments, mocks families and relationships— it's developed for an inhuman corporate thing (personhood) that doesn't care about or keep children's drawings, even if a few of its thousands of employees would do something this unlikely.

Advertising not only inures us to illogic, manipulation, and fraud, it maintains an unbridgeable gap between signifier and signified—between what we represent and what's represented. What's on the box (the signifier) has no relation to what's inside it (the signified), and advertising relies on that disjunction to work. (The law, of course, does require a cereal box to contain cereal and not lead paint, but beyond the literal content of a package, which is specified by information labels, the advertisement relies on the disjunction between container and contained.) In Melville's *The Confidence-Man*, the herb doctor engages in the counterfeiter's typical feint by calling attention to the very idea of counterfeiting:

> For such is the popularity of the Omni-Balsamic Reinvigorator . . . that certain contrivers [have attempted to counterfeit it]. . . . Take the wrapper from any of my vials and hold it to the light, you will see water-marked in capitals the word *"confidence,"* which is the countersign of the medicine, as I wish it was of the world. The wrapper bears that mark or else the medicine is counterfeit. (83, emphasis in original)

Advertisers frequently use this distraction, drawing on disclaimers, irony, and misdirection that admit that the product and the corporation are kinds of counterfeit; the consumer mark is at least unconsciously reassured by the tacit admissions. Philip K. Dick creates his versions of this Reinvigorator throughout his 1969 novel *Ubik*, each of whose chapters opens with a description of a "new miracle Ubik" product that will deliver some form of eternal salvation to consumers: "One invisible puff puff whisk of economically priced Ubik banishes compulsive obsessive fears that the entire world is . . . deteriorat[ing into half life]" (*Ubik* 70; Carrére 166–67). All such signs are, structurally, counterfeit: that's the trick. The *"Counterfeit Detector"* in Melville's novel is of course itself a fake (246–48, emphasis in original). Even when the medicine is authentic, the ad isn't. The ad by definition can have no necessary relationship to the product; what does this tell us about our notions of identity? An ad campaign can be, and often is, thought up independently, and then attached to various products; advertising is predicated on this detachability. Corporate advertising works in the way it does because form is dissociable from content: because the form of an ad is independent—not aesthetically, but by its nature—from the product.

As most of them would attest, advertisers generally don't sell products, but fantasies and a series of emotions attached to them, involving self-perception, envy, status, desire, and so forth. The assumption behind most ads is you can't sell something by giving information—you have to distort, lie, and manipulate, because you have to sell fantasies, not products. (Even seemingly straightforward assertions of a service are usually deceptions. For example, consider auto insurance companies that advertise that they allow you to use whatever body shop you want for repairs, when that right is mandated by law.) That dissonance echoes the disconnection between a corporation and its "biography," and the gap between ad and product is homologous to the gap between the corporation and its employees (especially independent contractors and part-time workers, who are treated legally as having no substantive connection to the corporation). In this sense, in most Western capitalist economies, corporate advertising perversely dramatizes the premises of poststructural disconnection: its signifiers never can coincide with its signifieds. To work, the ad can have nothing inherently to do with the product. The same holds true for corporate personhood, since a corporate person never can exist, and can be represented only by/as a fiction. In other words, corporate language has to function like advertisements: what's on the package or in the ad or corporate signifier—which includes any corporate representation of the corporation's functions—has no intrinsic relation to what's inside, or signified. As Pynchon asserts in his 1973 novel *Gravity's Rainbow*, there's "No difference between a boxtop and its image, all right, their whole economy's based on *that* . . . but she must be more than an image, a product, a promise to pay" (472, emphasis in original).

Aside from "decentering" the function of the author, familiar principles of structuralism, poststructuralism, and deconstruction posit that the relation between signifier and signified is necessarily arbitrary: the words or signifiers *tree* or *arbol* represent what we think of as a tree, but bear no necessary connection to the object represented, or signified. The more specific disconnection between an advertising signifier and a signified product is as critical as the generic disjunction between signifier and signified, because an advertisement is by necessity also entirely fungible; it has no inherent connection to the product it promotes, and that structurally insurmountable gap is what allows ads to work. Advertisements are distinct from notices that provide only information—the latter aren't ads, but labels or neutral promotions; these are the few forms of message that communicate information pertaining to prices, manufacturer, and/or ingredients/composition, but they transmit no narrative, story, fantasy, associations, or other arbitrary elements that define the ad. Put another way, false advertising is a redundant phrase. If an ad weren't in some way false, it would simply be a label. Spots that provide only objectively verifiable information aren't ads, but neutral promotions.

Even more than some of the products they promote, ads are by definition fungible, which creates significant opportunities and problems. Imagine an ad that states, "Our company is dedicated to the public good; to supporting government that works; treating our employees with the greatest respect; and fostering sustainable practices at every level." Attach the ad to the Red Cross, then to Halliburton. No information is provided; the ad is close to a form of all-purpose camouflage for a chameleon that has no inherent identity. Promotions might provide useful, verifiable information, but ads never do; by definition, they generate assertions that are false or useless, intended to manipulate and mislead.

Ad campaigns that "coincide" with products in ways that couldn't be transferred to other comparable products would be purely informational (or function as labels) and never work well as ads. The ad never coincides with the product, much as the speech of the corporation never coincides with the corporation; this dissonance is uncanny and creepy, and finally the provocation of horror and science fiction. Critics long have been documenting the widening income gap in the United States, but almost no one measures the gap between the omnipresent Thing of America (the corporation or product) and what represents it (a CEO or advertisement). In contemporary contexts, the corporation is behind most such gaps. The subtler effect that derives from and sometimes is coterminous with the gap between advertisement and product is that we lose the product altogether; the ideal ad would involve a closed loop of references that have no bearing on reality, much like political discourse has often sought. That is, ads come to refer to other ads, a universe of signs of selling, and the product becomes tertiary and even meaningless. In the new economy, the point doesn't even seem to be to produce information instead of goods, but to generate advertisements, endless references to other things. Many products and devices, from the trivial (bags) to the substantive (films), now serve as vehicles for other ads: as Wu asseverates, films have "become much less predominantly a business of storytelling . . . and much more a species of advertisement" (*Master* 231). The film is a vehicle for the ad, not the reverse. Corporations are responsible for these escalating inversions; we are the products tech companies sell; ads refer to other ads and fantasies, not products; corporations are persons.

Ads are arbitrary in terms of their content, except to the extent that they help or hinder the ad. The original content that ads sponsor, from factual news to TV shows, becomes all the more irrelevant when corporations use nonsensical affiliations—in other words, they trivialize not only what they sponsor, but the concept of seriousness itself, and the boundaries between art, fact, and sale. The premises and disaffiliations of ads bleed into their surrounding media. As John Berger remarks, "Cigars can be sold in the name of a King, underwear in connection with the Sphinx, a new car by reference to the status of a country house"; these subterfuges and alignments work because they're aleatory, despite attempts to associate or link a feeling or fantasy with a product (140). The same ad campaign can be substituted for almost any product, can be detached and reattached to almost any item, at least before a campaign is released; the arbitrariness of the connection is mitigated only after images become attached to corporations or products in the public mind. We naturalize the artificial connection after the fact because we've been conditioned to do so, to imagine a cartoon animal must belong to this corporation.

Many products, from detergents to insurance to most processed foods, are in some ways fungible or have fungible ingredients—but the market, through advertisement, has to develop the pretense that they're different, not only as a way to make the commodity desirable, but also as part of fantasy that we're all different, and entitled to consume an inexhaustible supply of resources (this sense of economic entitlement is also arbitrary, based not on merit or utility, but often on which developers reach the resource first). We know some resources are fungible (oil is oil), but advertisers of products such as generic and empirically indistinguishable gasoline have to fabricate some assurance that one brand can be better than another. Even when products are differentiable—for example, some brands of alcohol—advertisements don't highlight differences, which might be difficult to capture, but rely on equally fungible fantasies to which the products are attached. Ads are partly predicated on our resistance to acknowledging that many products are interchangeable; they're in some ways innately postmodern because they assert an underlying disconnection between a representation (here the ad campaign) and the thing being represented (here a product).

Many advertising slogans, from "I love my Honda" to "I like Ike" are troubling in what they suggest about how we're influenced. Ads are antidemocratic in appealing to often unconscious desires to be conformist—the same and therefore accepted—while still lording it over the Joneses. They're pseudo-populist in strategy, and have the populist effect of agitating people, in telling each consumer he or she is better than others while somehow insisting everyone can be better than everyone else. Ads do convey specific messages, but they're never what they're purported to be. The slogan "fit for a king" should warn you that you're being pitched an especially generic and low-end product. (Such ads work only if viewers deny the obvious fact that not everyone can be treated like a king or a god, or display the signs of wealth, because such markers function only as part of a zero-sum game.) D. H. Lawrence asked, "'Shall I not treat all men as gods,' [Emerson] cries? If you like, Waldo, but you've got to pay for it. . . . A hundred million American godlets is rather much for the world to deal with" ("Pan in America" 23).[2] The ad succeeds if people agree to be conned so they can have the fantasy of godletness they know they'll never attain. Advertisers exploit and stimulate that weakness and rely on the fact that we derive identities and self-worth from products.

The advertiser tries to attribute an emotion or attach a human trait to a product, but the graft is always botched and tenuous. Advertisements destabilize our ability to distinguish real emotion from fabrication; does the spectacle of people weeping in joy when they win a refrigerator not degrade the authenticity of genuine human emotion? When you see people in advertisements practically having an orgasm at the prospect of using a product, or corporations attach their brand or image to human events such as weddings, this is an effect of corporate personhood—the imitation of human emotion, which is an overlay for the parasitic attachment of the corporate person to real persons. (This is emblematized at the general level by the notion that one can express feelings through generic emojis—the reduction of human emotion to allegedly universal signs.)

Some critics might argue that nothing is more or less echt about joy expressed in relation to winning a product than joy expressed at being reunited with a loved one, but such rejections of difference at the absolute level are facile. It's as if the full array of human experiences and responses have been auctioned off to the highest corporate bidder, like broadcast frequencies, so they can be packaged and sold back to us attached to generic products. Ads create and suture human traits and personality onto products and to corporations by imbuing them with personhood. Most insidiously, ads engage not only in manipulation, but also in psychic extortion. They will appropriate any human need, feeling, or story to sell: you won't get the girl you want, be popular, do or be X, unless you join our site, buy our product, or associate yourself with our brand. But you can attach an advertising phrase to most products because the product has nothing to do with the emotion or person. Ads, which have been constructed as small vignettes and dramas, construct isolated, self-contained worlds—they typically don't refer to reality or even products per se, but to the mechanisms of attachment and identification; they aren't designed to convey anything but tautological, self-referential justifications for their claims.

It's worth briefly comparing the arbitrariness of trademarks with that of advertisements. Distinct legal constraints apply to trademarks, which must be arbitrary, and not definitive or descriptive of a product, to obtain protection. This restriction is necessary to ensure that companies don't monopolize functional words and concepts (so, for example, a film corporation couldn't trademark the word *movie*). As a result, many trademarks seem goofy or come across as mistakes and mutations—the system allows businesses to evoke a concept or association, but not to monopolize generic descriptive terms. Trademarks are regulated to prevent corporations from stealing the reputations or business of competitors, and the public from being misled—in this sense they're truthful identifiers of label information. But the need for ads to be inherently arbitrary is unrelated to access; ads are intended to mislead, and their goal isn't to inform, but to sell. Arbitrariness provides an all-purpose work-around for constraints that might apply to ads. Commercial phrases can be protected only if they're not in common parlance and are associated in commercial contexts exclusively with the company that uses them; yet these are the words and concepts people hear incessantly. Such inculcated language is the equivalent of the genetically modified organisms that corporations patent, the life they therefore own. Culture is another zero-sum game in this context; the more corporate culture and language you're exposed to, the less personhood and individual voice you retain.

Žižek locates the emptiness of "'the signifier without a signified' [in] the brand name we pay for when we buy, say, Coke instead of an anonymous cola." The corporation does serve as a kind of organizing motif as well as distribution network, and its products will be reliably near uniform; but there's still no corporate identity, intrinsic or otherwise, beyond the product. We can easily imagine corporations that outsource all their production: in that scenario, Nike, for example, would "be 'nothing in itself'—nothing *but* the pure brand mark. 'Nike,' the empty Master-signifier which connotes the cultural experience pertaining to a certain 'lifestyle.' . . . the efficacy of certain logos is parasitical upon a gap . . . which pertains to language as such—we can never have a language whose terms directly designate reality" (*Living* 210, emphasis in original). Such observations don't deny the obvious point that most consumers can differentiate between Coke and anonymous colas, and especially among high-end goods. (Cast against the ads that draw people's attention because they're so offensively stupid are the sophisticated ads that artificially ally corporations with commercial subcultures, for example, ads that sell putatively microbrewed beer or luxury watches.) But most ads exaggerate the sometimes marginal differences between products to conceal their underlying indistinguishability. In other words, most ads don't highlight the differences between products, but fabricate them. This Coke's for you because you're unique, but you can also count on the fact that each Coke will be identical to and indistinguishable from the last. Niche marketing that accentuates the genuine difference of a product proves the rule: many will pay more to show they're not part of the same system when they are. They are largely buying a status symbol to show they're not part of the status symbol system: I own a hand-crafted, one-of-a kind Egg McGuffin that sold for $2,000 instead of the mass-produced version that sold for $2.

We shouldn't underestimate the practical effects of how ads shape our interaction with information itself. As Powers observed throughout *The Gold Bug Variations*, and Wallace less directly in *Infinite Jest*, information used to be difficult to come by, but "processing" that information into knowledge was relatively easy; now, in a corporate internet age, information is easy to come by, but difficult to sort, and knowledge is either impossible or useless. Wallace's despairing conclusion, echoed by many writers, was that knowing the truth had become largely meaningless—as with Edward Snowden's revelations; revelations about the causes of the last financial collapse or the Trump administration's collusions and crimes; or evidence of climate change, knowledge seems to change little. Advertising relies on and increases this disjunction between information and narrative. As people read less and lose the ability to evaluate the claims of scientists, politicians, and corporations, the genres that resist such disjunctions between data and knowledge reach and influence fewer and fewer people.

Chapter Seventeen

It's All Theater

The phrase "truth in advertising" is a contradiction in terms: truth comes through information, but the function of advertising is to misrepresent. We need disinterested information in many contexts, and the culture of advertising is antagonistic to that need. The values, premises and practices we accept in the context of selling products affects a host of behaviors and endeavors that we mistakenly imagine are kept in separate spheres: not just politics, which was never removed from advertising, but journalism, medicine, teaching, and the mechanisms of government itself. What does it mean not to be for sale? What does it mean to have a culture subsidized by advertising, with little existing outside that model? A society dominated by advertising has few disinterested voices or contexts for neutral evaluation—not in policy, media, film reviews, or any form of publicly disseminated information. As Benjamin Kunkel summarizes, corporate capitalism converts "all would-be signifiers into mere price signals. The hush of commodification falls over the most contrary utterance. 'Discourses of critique and protest' can 'in no respect' be distinguished from other commodities, which are equally silent—or speak only in self-advertisement" (Kunkel 36, quoting Boris Groys).

The second Bush administration consistently sponsored "scien-tific" reports, agency findings and newscasts that served as ads for its political messages. Not surprisingly, since Karl Rove began his career in mass marketing, advertising generally became more manipulative, brash and unaccountable during that administration. Often mirroring the language of advertising, political language in America largely devolved to the level of empty slogans (where it once also included at least some component of substantive debate). What Pynchon repeatedly declaims in *Gravity's Rainbow* about the politics of modern warfare equally applies to the corporation (which often assumes a primary role in generating the

Chapter Seventeen

infrastructures for war)—it's all at many levels an act, all staged (3). In other words, as various film directors have dramatized, the mechanisms of advertising are in no way confined to the realm of commerce but extend to every facet of political, social, and economic life: "It means that this War was never political at all, the politics was all theatre, all just to keep the people distracted" (521): the same could be said of debates about corporate responsibility. Though not engaged in advertising or using standard advertising language, even civil government and intelligence agencies use the tactics of PR and advertising. Tim Weiner notes that Judge Laurence Silberman—who led a commission investigating the intelligence failures that led to the CIA's misrepresentation that Iraq had amassed weapons of mass destruction—concluded that the CIA's "daily reports seemed to be selling intelligence—in order to keep its customers, or at least the First Customer, interested" (573). That corruption of intelligence ultimately redounds on even those who control the system, and reached its nadir in the Trump administration, whose credo was "Only tell the first customer what he wants to hear." One frequently hears about the way propagandists themselves, from Trump to Putin, fall victim to what amounts to their own corporate advertising tactics. Most political rhetoric is infected by the assumptions and language of advertising. A politician calling himself a maverick is the equivalent of calling himself zesty; such assertions are as weightless and fungible as "yes we can," and yet they galvanize people. Almost every tagline and policy associated with the Trump administration, from "Make America great again" to "Drain the swamp," was quintessentially empty advertising rhetoric, without the slightest correlation to reality: that was the point.

Many corporations, and even the government, are now producing putatively "scientific" reports that are effectively ads for political campaigns; they combine the rhetoric and communicative assumptions of ads with propaganda. Across a variety of registers, objectivity has become another corporate commodity, especially evident in the proliferation of superficial expertise in business and media. (Some of the worst examples are the advice links on homepages for sites such as Yahoo! and MSN, though they're often qualitatively similar to the kind of expertise proffered on cable news. In *The Gold Bug Variations*, Richard Powers dramatizes the way "advertisers found they could dramatically boost sales of just about anything by having a man in glasses and white coat hold it up for view. Weed killer, rubber tires, lipstick: a few Erlenmeyer flasks in the background, and a sales pitch became news" [129]). Advertising is also fake-populist in this context because it asks us to trust and rely on corporate-ratified imitation "experts," often folksy TV doctors and fifth-rate outliars, who ventriloquize a nonexistent thing.

As the most pressing example, we need climate scientists to make decisions, or at least lead the debate, about climate change; this is an area about which the general population has little acumen. But corporate advertising and media primarily present actors, polarizing pundits, and experts who work for corporations to steer opinion to their advantage. The precepts of corporate personhood apply here because corporations are like aliens who cannot influence humans unless they don a humanoid appearance, here in the guise of co-opted experts. But the corporate person is more uncanny than even the most disturbing and unsettling alien. We would engage in open rebellion if we knew some inhuman entity secretly was shaping our social and environmental policies, but many of us barely notice that corporations are openly doing so.

The majority of information most of us receive—everything from claims that a cereal is good for you to assertions that our current modes of sponsorship are essential to capitalism—is filtered through some form of advertising. Most of our cultural production is directly or indirectly sponsored, meaning it's tethered to the biases and agendas of corporations. We're in denial that the discourses we need to be transparent—education, journalism, health care, government contracting, food production—are in any way free from corporate influence. As Lawrence Samuel notes, "The lines between journalism and commerce [became] increasingly fuzzy . . . as corporate interests looked to the public domain as advertising fodder" (37). The plague of medical ads and sponsorships is particularly troubling: changes in the law allow doctors and lawyers, people who are supposed to have specific duties of candor to those who rely on them, to sell themselves, which means to prostitute their expertise. Pharmaceutical companies, food companies, energy companies, political parties, all hire shills to act as persons for them. Sponsored news—advertisements that masquerade as news stories—has become the most perfidious acceptable commonplace; it erodes people's confidence in journalism and proliferates falsehoods that are treated as opinions deserving equal consideration. On September 17, 2014, the *New York Times* included an eight-page insert titled "Russia Beyond the Headlines," which was paid for by the Russian government and had the absurd obligatory small-print disclaimer that it didn't contain the reporting of the *New York Times*. Such a putatively aboveboard ad inures us even further to its close relatives, the targeted fake news stories, purchased as ads, that Russian trolls disseminated on Facebook. We should be incensed not only that such ads masquerade as news but also that Russia's tactics are largely indistinguishable from that of any other advertiser. The recurring irony is that the former communist enemy, like Mao, is now a symbol and here a purveyor of the practices of corporate personhood.

Chapter Eighteen

Corpography

Though not the only form of corporate life writing—which includes such genres as corporate biographies, CEO autobiographies, press releases, and archives and other historical commemorations—advertising is the only one we might consider as truly autobiographical. These other forms help generate identities for corporations, but they also illustrate the paradox that no corporate "auto" exists. Advertising is inextricable from the generation, rather than representation, of corporate biography. Though not attributable to any individual consciousness (or consciousness in any form), advertising is the life writing or autobiography of a company—it's a central component of its public pronouncements and self-representation. The corporation has no self from which to write an autobiography, so almost all writing or speech allegedly "by" a corporation other than advertising pertains to a specific kind of biography, which I've been calling corpography.

Corpography in a sense represents the final manifestation of the US genre of the confidence autobiography, or the forgery memoir. As I propose more fully in "The Franklin-Stein Monster," a kind of trickster use of the third-person, impersonal impersonation, and outright ventriloquism are endemic to one configuration of US autobiography, beginning with Governor John Winthrop, and as perfected by Ben Franklin. (Such forgeries, in more tawdry contexts, are likely more familiar to contemporary readers in the context of James Frey's *A Million Little Pieces* and other more recent acts of plagiarism and false self-representation.) As part of the republican tradition, the US autobiographer often situated himself—and this was a largely male trope until the twentieth century—using constitutional language to construct a (sometimes mock) representative person, part of a public discourse that embodies "we the people." As I note elsewhere ("Franklin-Stein" 17), "from Winthrop to Franklin, Emerson, Henry Adams and Gertrude Stein, one strain of American autobiography chronicles the subject trying to be a representative American, or, as Joseph Fichtelberg [83] says of Franklin, to live a 'corporate life'". But these writers willfully constructed selves, and ventriloquized others, to stand in for their own lives; they wrote of themselves in the third person, as others, and as impersonations. They began a displacement of the self, which they often treated as an object, rather than the subject, of autobiographical representation. In this sense, these writers began the corporate conflation of biography with autobiography; they effectively generated spokespersons to advertise for themselves as corporations. They imitate the conventions of autobiography in ways that decenter the self. The stand-in or (what D. H. Lawrence calls the) dummy used to construct the alienated US self eventually became the agent of the corporation. (Where, e.g., Franklin created a fake self and took credit for other people's actions, and Adams wrote an autobiography in the third person, Stein infiltrated and exposed the genre to the extent of writing an "autobiography" of someone else—a perfect corporate gesture.) The critical difference is that the ventriloquized or fabricated self of these trickster autobiographies existed in some uneasy relation to the author of the autobiography; by contrast, the corporate person supplants the biographical person entirely.

The corporation furthers this use of dummy "autobiographical" narrators through the ventriloquism of the advertisement, which is a particular form of speech without a speaker. Advertising is a mediated expression or "self-representation" of a corporation, not only because most corporations outsource their ad campaigns, but because there's no corporation, in traditional ontological terms, for which to speak. Advertising seems to come from an actual person's agency, but of course emanates from an ad agency and reifies the idea of corporate (spokes)personhood. Impersonal and replaceable in terms of their interiority (which is wholly supplanted in this context), advertising spokespersons can be only simulacra: s/he could be a CGI creation, and it would make no difference. The spokesperson is a construct designed solely to manipulate you; the construct says, "I used to resist this product, but I realized that to be happy I must use it." A seemingly empathetic construct pitches an online dating service, but the same tone and construct can be used for car insurance; the advertisement always uses fake emotion, channeled through an appeal to sincerity and a fabricated sense of connection to and empathy from a corporation, another construct. You are sharing a moment, and ultimately your interiority, not just with a fake, but with a kind of emotional parasite. All advertising, and all corporate language, is a mock up and mockery—an imitation of life, a travesty of human emotion. Many ads try to hide this ugly fact by hiding behind camp and irony; but the spectacle of people rejoicing because they bought a product is dehumanizing. People trample each other on Black Friday or camp out in front of Apple Stores because they've been indoctrinated to believe they'll get to the head of the line by demonstrating a kind of allegiance to the corporation rather than to one another. (Much as people also might want to buy cheap products or somehow enjoy the competitive aspect of shopping, the ulterior context for such behavior involves not identity politics, but identity consumerism. Waiting in that line defines who you are.) Based on the way corporations construct their images, people must routinely misinterpret what corporations can represent in order to interact with them.

When corporations say they're proud to sponsor X event or organization, no one exists to be proud; even more disturbingly, sponsorship isn't something that warrants pride. It's not an accomplishment of any sort: any corporation can sponsor anything if it has the money and the entity being sponsored is willing to accept it. When corporations say they are proud to do something, it's the equivalent of bots telling [insert your name here] they're proud of your achievements. Corporate spokespersons aren't acting as people, but placeholders for the absence of people—they're mostly actors portraying fictions, and now sometimes animated figures (the difference is revealingly minimal). They exist only because the corporation created them—there are no persons behind these spokes, only an endless cycle of fungible facades. These actors aren't the puppets of real masters, but empty constellations of space. This aspect of corporate ontology is coterminous with the trend to accept, and even desire, that actors and celebrities (impersonators) should serve as politicians, because they too are stand-ins for corporate rule.

Corporations need to maintain the fanciful premise that their spokespeople are appropriate surrogates, and a scandal can quickly end an endorsement deal. But such spokespeople are simply and solely actors: one cannot identify their interiority with that of a corporation, in the same way one cannot identify an actor's life with the life of a character she portrays. To assume that a scandal in a spokesperson's or actor's life reflects negatively on a corporation (or a film) validates the fantasy of corporate personhood—it's the equivalent of blaming Jon Hamm for false advertising. Corporations benefit from such "guilt by association" because it bolsters the supposition that they can gain personhood by association. While they might gain market share, corporations don't gain athletic prowess or credibility by paying Olympic athletes to wear their logos, nor are they morally tarnished if those athletes wear those logos while taking illegal drugs to win medals. Like that of the president's press secretary, the job of such actors is categorically never to express what they think, but impersonally to represent the interests of their employer through their public personae. In forms of ontological prostitution, spokespeople—perhaps only to a greater extent than any corporate employee—sell the semblance and use of their personhood to things that never can have their own. It's another feint for corporations to insist they don't want to be represented by bad actors, because those actors have no connection with them whatsoever.

Corporations destabilize what it means to be human or to have a relationship with humans, and what it means to be a thing and an abstraction. As we can see in many Hollywood films, some forms of corporate ventriloquism are connected to anxieties regarding the possession and dispossession of human identity (or souls): for example, the (un)dead that colonize life, and speak through and inhabit us. As I elucidate, the undead and the many forms of artificial or altered beings that look as if they are alive but only imitate life, often have an affinity with the corporate person. They move mindlessly, without individuation, representing pure drive, and cannot be killed, because they already aren't alive. What Hobbes describes as the artificial person of the corporation in part evolves into a form of AI embodied in science fiction and horror film impersonations of the human form. Aside from the fact that some corporations rely heavily on technologies that simulate and even replace life, and what we might term a myriad of reality simulators—from online games to movies and sex robots—impersonated forms of reality are typically produced by, and are (un)natural allies of, corporations because they involve imitations of life.

Philip K. Dick became fascinated by Alan Turing's experiments to evaluate whether we can verify what it means to be human: specifically, whether machines can think, or convince us they're thinking or, when not present, that they're actual human beings (Carrérre, *I am Alive and You Are Dead*, 132). Turing's postulate was that something is human if it can convince another human it is. That assertion raises the question, how does the person doing the comparison know it is itself human? Dick's litmus test for a human being, however, was not whether it could convince a person it was human, but whether it possessed empathy (135), a test a corporate person would fail, because it's programmed by law to care about profits above anything else. Most human cultures have expressed some kind of fear that a supernatural force or version of the devil could impersonate the human form. Our concern that we can no longer isolate or differentiate human from inhuman cogitation has inevitably increased, in a world run by computers, with our reliance on virtual realities, AI, and internet communication. The corporate person is a generator and example of such AI and virtuality. Our fear now is not only that corporations can impersonate the human form and convince at least courts and conservatives they're persons, but that they've made people obsolete and caused us to impersonate them. Since the law treats corporations as artificial persons, and they function as forms of artificial life, it's not surprising that they displace individuals and families; as Ralph Clare observes, corporations reflect the fact that "new informational systems have given rise to AIs, computer systems that can essentially run themselves [as] self-referential or autopoietic systems" that "outreach and outlast their human creators" (165). As Matthew Titolo succinctly puts it, it's objectionable not only that the corporation becomes a person under neoliberal politics, but that "the person has become a corporation" (45). The liberal critique tends to object to the commodification of the self, the tendency to create a purely entrepreneurial self whose worth, and whose endeavors, from art to education to medicine, are defined by the market. But corporate personhood is even more invidious in its ontological, psychological and cultural effects.

Many twentieth-century US courts have acknowledged the highly artificial nature of the corporate entity: "The word 'corporation' is but a collective name for the corporators or members who compose an incorporated association," and the protections associated with that designation can be set aside when the notion of such as "legal entity" is used to "defeat public convenience, justify wrong, protect fraud, or defend crime, the law will regard this corporation as an association of persons." J. Sanborn, *United States v. Milwaukee Refrigerator Transit Co.*, 142 Fed. 247, 255 (C.C.E.D. Wis. 1905). As a standard treatise adds, "Where it is said that a corporation is itself a person, or being, or creature, this must be understood in a figurative sense only."[1] Especially because courts sometimes stress not only the artificiality of the corporation, but its fictive nature, it's appropriate to consider fictional as well as legal representations of corporations. What does this fictionality of the corporation entail in terms of corporate biography?

Throughout this book, I briefly discuss novels by Richard Powers, Thomas Pynchon, Philip K. Dick, Kathy Acker, David Foster Wallace, and Don DeLillo. I address these texts because they offer insights into the idioms of corporate biography and advertising. Powers's *Gain*, for example, presents a Joycean history of advertising language as it evolves from the personal and familial—starting with a period when a family could own, run, and represent a company—to the corporate form, under which only the family name remained. Literalizing the concept of the corporate legal fiction, Powers presciently wrote a biography of what emblematically began as a soap company as it regressed from the Revolutionary period to become a kind of postmodern golem. (Selling essentially fungible soap became the virtual signet of early television advertising, the quintessential mechanism for sponsoring content.) Tracking the way the Clare Corporation came to produce increasingly noxious products, Powers's narrator develops a biographical ontology and corresponding language that becomes ever more "unmutual" and corporate as they near the present. As it spans several hundred years, and businesses become more corporate and advertising more pervasive, the novel grows more impersonal in its precepts and characterizations; it's as if a roman à clef turned into a CGI biography scripted by an algorithm.[2] Joseph Dewey suggests "the narrative of Clare International reads like an absorbing—and convincing—history" (110). But Maliszewski believes the novel shifted its focus from personal history to what I would term a kind of corporate common law: "Powers read stories of real corporate characters and companies like Procter & Gamble, Colgate and Lever, and found their stories Shakespearean. But the personification of Clare and its central role in the novel is less a matter of poetic than corporate law" (167).[3]

Maliszewski cites Powers's impression that "the literary approach" to business, which relies on humanist principles and characters to dramatize corporate systems, had become inadequate and led him instead to pursue an articulation of the impersonal (166). In other words, the old constraints of fiction prevent it from apprehending the new contrivances of the corporate fiction. If the focus of Powers's novel in some ways, as Maliszewski contends, is "the movement of capital" itself (169), does this reify or demystify? Powers explicitly proposes that "the corporate protagonist's cycle of boom and bust [is] substituting for a narrative's rise and fall" (166). Powers's narrator then tells us, "with the right corporate structure, decisions practically handled themselves" (288). Yes is a chemical reaction at Clare. Human agency, along with many of the structures of narrative and biography and the human life cycle, recedes or disappears into impersonal discourse and the recycling and inhuman cadences of corporate life cycles. Such fictions narrativize not just an invisible hand, but the development of an entire corpus that is nonexistent; in that context, corporate fiction is close to science fiction, to a narrative of alien life.

As Wallace intimates throughout *The Pale King*, the problem isn't just that contemporary corporations are treated as if they were people, but that people start behaving as if they were corporations. For Wallace and Powers especially, corporations represent the denouement of a strain of biographical fiction—they denote a kind of dead end of human narrative, what George Steiner might consider the dissolution of an old and (putatively) communal cultural literacy, which is replaced by an ever more dominant corporate culture. By the close of the last millennium, Clare's "ads provided the backbone of shared culture, from playground to dinner table. . . . Old Native Balm engravings now went for thousands of dollars at auctions. A novelization of a series of commercials for Clare's leading over-the-counter painkiller ran for twelve weeks on the *New York Times Book Review* best seller list, and even made money as a film" (340–41). Writers such as Powers, Wallace, and DeLillo sardonically dramatize the subordination and powerlessness of culture, of the biographical novel, when displaced by the life writing of the corporation—these truths aren't only stranger than fiction, they replace it.

Chapter Nineteen

Corporate Exceptionalism

Corporations are impersonal not only in their operative organization, but also in their chartered creation. The phrase *corporate veil* refers to the schema that corporations invoke to attain immunity from liability; beneath that screen, the individuals who run corporations generally aren't personally liable for the actions they take on their behalf. In legal terms, courts pierce the corporate veil only if they find individuals in management liable for acting outside, or in contravention of, their role in running the business. But at a social and ontological level, no one is behind the veil—in terms of biography, the corporation is the ultimate trickster, a dummy without a ventriloquist, a confidence person, a person without qualities. Depending on one's perspective, it's the fulfillment or final debasement of the republican tradition. In unusual instances (e.g., where figures such as the Koch Brothers closely control them), corporations can serve as what we might call personhood exoskeletons that enhance the rights of individual directors and allow executives or owners effectively to act without liability and accountability. But in the majority of cases, corporations function not just impersonally, but as "depersoned" entities. Both scenarios pose invidious social problems.

A veil is a disguise that pertains only to agents: only a person can be veiled. Corporate actors can hide behind this veil in the context of donning another disguise or invoking another fiction. This conceit of the corporate veil conveys a disturbing form of pathetic fallacy in imbuing an inhuman entity with human qualities, but more nefariously, it helps foster a pretense that a person resides behind the corporate curtain. The trope also has an exigent, ironic resonance with the Fourteenth Amendment and slavery, as the early, noted civil rights activist W. E. B. Du Bois described African Americans as being born veiled.[1] That declaration also astutely situated corporations as implicit usurpers and antagonists of African American identity, an assertion that, despite some recent improvement, has too often been borne out. Du Bois treats the veil as an emblem of alienated African American subjectivity: "the Negro is a sort of seventh son, born with a veil, and gifted with a second-sight in this American world . . . [a] double consciousness" (227, 46). Du Bois here refers to the way African Americans are forced to see themselves as outsiders, as racialized subjectivities, and from the perspective of white society. African Americans were relentlessly depersonalized—treated as things, impersonal incarnations of a racial type, and less than full persons. Double consciousness has a second consonance in the context of corporations, which also affect our notion of personal sovereignty and personhood: corporations become our collective Others. Among the inversions of the corporate zero-sum game, it is now corporations that are "born" with a new corporate veil, things of property that have become uncanny imitations of life. Slaves were people legally treated as property, inanimate things, and, under the Missouri Compromise, three-fifths of human beings; corporations are personified property, things that are legally treated as animate super-beings.[2] It is worth noting that the Constitution itself established the idea that someone could in effect be a fraction of a person, or possess far less than full personhood, and, by implication, that someone could be more than a person.

John O'Brien documents the ways corporations—partly in pursuit of profit, but I would add as fundamentally in their drive to reformulate the definition of personhood—were instrumental in developing a theory of personhood and rights for whites that depersonalized African slaves (151). As O'Brien demonstrates, the joint-stock companies that abetted slavery had to be upgraded to the more advanced corporate form, especially to codify their independence from the state. In this sense, double consciousness also emerges from the way the corporation split personhood but also stole the souls of African Americans to attain personhood. In Charles Johnson's neo-slave novel *Oxherding Tale*, the Soulcatcher is a version of Melville's Confidence Man, who doesn't merely impersonate others, but steals their souls. In sometimes problematic ways, Johnson treats slavery not as physical or economic bondage, but primarily as a philosophical and ontological condition—that is, a state of mind: his slavers steal souls, not just bodies, in ways that cannily reflect the fact that corporations have neither bodies nor souls. In Johnson's *Middle Passage*, a novel partly concerned with the intersections between slavery and transcendentalism, Captain Falcon contends that "Dualism is a bloody structure of the mind," and slavery "only the social corollary of a deeper ontic wound" (98, emphasis in original). That dualism is another term for double consciousness, which also evokes the way the corporation facilitated slavery and depersonalization/dehumanization: systems that split the self from itself. Johnson's Soulcatcher is a "fluid, crazyquilt of other's features," and possesses a face regenerated by the violence he commits upon slaves: he is a being stolen from black identity. As Andrew recognizes, the Soulcatcher's voice "was made from the offscum of other voices"; his hands "beat with the pulsethrob of countless bondsmen in his bloodstream, women and children murdered" (168–9). He becomes an aggregate or composite of slavery, an embodiment of a collective identity accrued from African American personhood. If you were a soulless corporation looking for a community that had soul you could steal, it would be that of African Americans. The idea of soul is vital to African American culture, evident in soul music and soul food—those are the souls the corporation is trying not just to commodify but to catch and steal. As we'll see, it's African American personhood that corporations have most dispossessed in a myriad of ways. And it's not accidental that Republicans tend to defend corporate but not civil rights— it's another move in the escalating zero-sum game of corporate personhood. Pilfering the personhood that African Americans had finally gotten recognized, corporations also appropriated and ironicized the resonant term *soul brother*, in another instance of a corporation stealing souls. Historically, corporations had no souls (and no bodies to kick); African Americans had a surplus of soul. You do the math in a zero-sum game.

Especially in the context of work by Caitlin Rosenthal, O'Brien, and others, we should consider corporations as constructs that long have relied on the colonization and depersonalization of people, and ultimately on a denial of their personhood across a spectrum of practices. Documenting how many corporate managerial and accounting methods were developed under slavery, Rosenthal observes that "Management innovation was not an inevitable outgrowth of plantation slavery, but neither was it incidental: the power of masters over their slaves gave them power as managers. . . . [P]lanters and overseers measured and monitored human capital with great precision. Through accounting, human figures became figures on paper, appearing as interchangeable inputs of production" (734–35). Despite the South's "agrarian" veneer and the small-scale operation of many plantations, slavery was in most ways a corporate enterprise from Africa to Europe and the Americas. Slavery provided one template for turning people into labor mechanisms, and one step toward corporate personhoood involved controlling the behaviors and identities of those who labor. The most recent step, apropos of a corporate information economy, involves corporatizing every aspect of social life, identity, interaction, and personhood.

For Powers in *Gain*, corporations achieved personhood by effectively co-opting the emancipation of slaves: "If the Fifth and Fourteenth Amendments combined to extend due process to all individuals, and if the incorporated business had become a single person under the law, then the

Clare Soap and Chemical Company now enjoyed all the legal protections afforded any individual by the spirit of the Constitution" (159). This traversal is all the more incongruous since Congress validated civil rights legislation not under the aegis of equal protection, but under the regulation of interstate commerce, a kind of "any means necessary" legal maneuver. It tells us a good deal about our culture that corporations were able to invoke the Fourteenth Amendment—which was passed to afford equal protection to all people, and especially former slaves—to achieve equal protection as "persons" under the law; yet civil rights advocates had to rely on business law, the Commerce Clause, to achieve equal protection for minorities.[3] If pre–civil rights legislation and Jim Crow laws indefensibly narrowed the definition of citizenship and personhood, the corporate hijacking of the Fourteenth Amendment, which was used to ratify the idea that corporations should be treated as people under the law, indefensibly widened it.

Turnabout is the only play in a zero-sum game. To enforce their civil rights and achieve full personhood, African Americans had to invoke the rights of corporate persons; they were able to challenge segregation under *Heart of Atlanta Motel Inc. v. United States*, 379 U.S. 241 (1964) not because it was illegal to discriminate against people as persons, but because it was illegal under the Commerce Clause to interfere with interstate commerce (specifically that of Black truckers seeking food and shelter in the segregated South).

US culture especially denigrated Black women and Black mothers as effective antitheses of white corporate personhood. If corporations are super or exceptional persons that always deserve bailouts and figuratively can do no punishable wrong, Black women have been treated as what Giorgio Agamben terms *homo sacer*, undeserving people deprived of social status, rights, and membership in the larger community. In the United States, private corporations have over a long period commingled incommensurate aspects of the private and the public and become recipients of public rights and gifts in inverse proportion to the way individuals, and especially minorities and the poor, have lost access to them or become ineligible for public benefits. I here briefly address how corporations, claiming to have exceptional status in an exceptional nation, pervert notions of public welfare, the common good, and democratic rights.

Many cultural images of Black women can be traced to the period of slavery. Harriet Beecher Stowe provided Emerson with the following startling pretext from *Uncle Tom's Cabin*: Emerson asserts that Pan is "aboriginal, old as Nature, and saying, like poor Topsy, 'Never was born; growed.' . . . The mythology cleaves close to Nature; and what else was it they represented in Pan?" (*Works*, "Natural History of Intellect" XII, 35–36). With surprising consistency, white writers from this period depict Blacks as

growing from nature, in a reification of how slavery occluded the reproduction, or manufacturing, of bodies as property. (Hawthorne included similar
images in *The Marble Faun* and "Chiefly about War Matters.") Emblematic
of slave children, Stowe's Topsy "jes grew" without parents, and was raised
by a speculator—she's a kind of golem child of the corporation, whose
invisible body uses Topsy's to do its work. (The phrase *jes grew*, which
Ishmael Reed reappropriates as an emblem of Black resistance in his novel
Mumbo Jumbo, chastises a system that hides unacceptable origins. The idea
that slaves just grow, or that food just appears on our tables, conceals the
unbearable reality of inhuman systems of production.) Topsy and corporations just grow parthenogenetically, or self-reproduce—they have no parents
and cannot be reproduced through "normal" biological means; they are, for
very different reasons, fantasies of uncanny impersonations of humans who
have families. (The recent HBO series *Lovecraft Country* visualized the
demonic aspect of the Topsy caricature in the dancing twins.)

Corporate personhood in the United States always has had a racial component, as the privileges of white male identity were often allied with,
and for a time relatively coterminous with, those of the corporation, while
women and people of color were deemed to be less than full citizens or
persons. Symbolically, the corporation has been coded culturally as the
acceptable "mass"—often cast against the federal government—and as
white and deserving, allied with the public interest, with the opposite
characteristics attributed to African Americans. Here the axiomatic reversal,
as part of the overarching zero-sum game of corporate personhood, involves
the pathologizing of Black people and whitewashing of corporate miscon-
duct. This critical inversion or projection of pathology runs through much
of US history. For Tonya Brito, for example, the work Black women provide
as mothers "is deemed pathological and unworthy of subsidy." But it is the
corporation that behaves antisocially. As Bakan notes, via Noam Chomsky,
the corporation's drive to privatize is coterminous with an attempt to enforce
its "particular conception of humanity," which Bakan aptly describes, via
Mark Kingwell, as being modeled after itself—"an artificial person made in
the image of a human psychopath" (135, 6). And by contrast, as I elaborate,
the corporation, despite pretenses of being the purest distillation of a free
market, is the consistent recipient of government largesse in the form of
reduced taxes and liability, immunity from the astonishing costs of its externalities (the costs the public has to pay for, from infrastructure to the effects
of environmental harm), giveaways of public goods such as airwaves and
leasing rights, and an often subsidized workforce for which the corporation provides inadequate wages and benefits. It's a persistent irony that
American society often labels Black women as irresponsible, liable and

undeserving—welfare queens who cannot raise their children—while celebrating irresponsible corporations. In the ontological and practical economic aspects of the zero-sum game of personhood, corporate enfranchisement was gained at the expense of the disenfranchised. African American slaves were freed and became legal persons under the aegis of due process, but corporations, the bigger Elvis, effectively appropriated those rights.

As Powers contends, the corporation represents, in the terms of Ambrose Bierce's *Devil's Dictionary*, "an ingenious device for obtaining individual profit without individual responsibility. . . . He might have found the explication clever, funny, perhaps even diabolical, if it weren't the absolute letter of the law." In this institutionalized fantasy—which represents a kind of collective return of the repressed—the law declares any corporation "one composite body: a single, whole, and statutorily enabled person" (*Gain* 159). Under a form of demonological logic, the once often literally fragmented and figuratively dismembered *body* of the statutorily disenfranchised slave, legally defined as three-fifths of a person, is "unified" or, as Toni Morrison might say, re-membered in the collective super-body of the impersoned corporation. Now, instead of fractions of people, corporations represent aggregates of super rights, allowed to broadcast what are in effect millions of voices in their own names. Media (and other) consolidations are among the many insidious causes and effects of corporate personhood. Implicit in the concept is the idea that wealth equals privilege, a presumption so obvious as to be innocuous, yet so destructive of democracy that it represents a kind of treason. Corporate personhood is never the equivalent of personhood, but is exceptional personhood. Put another way, corporations privatize and try to monopolize personhood. In civic contexts, one person has one voice and gets one vote. But the corporate "person" gets as much as its power and money can buy: it can disseminate its voice in millions of homes; its voice lobbies Congress; its personhood expands in direct proportion to its expropriation of the personhood of the vast majority of the members of a society. The corporate person transgresses the limits of personhood that make personhood possible. It need not die: it can aggregate the voices and votes of others; it renders people as, or turns them into, aspects of the monstrosity it must be by design.

Chapter Twenty

Anonymous Autonomy

Created by public charter, US corporations initially were designed to possess only those rights the law conferred upon them, rather than any natural rights: they existed through the consent of the sovereign or polis and were formulated to reflect not only their exceptional uses, but the exceptional hazards they posed, particularly with regard to their concentration of power. In *Dartmouth College v. Woodward*, 4 Wheat. 518, 636 (1819), Chief Justice Marshall declared that "Being the mere creature of law, [the corporation] possesses only those properties which the charter of its creation confers upon it, either expressly or as incidental to its very existence." This rhetoric mirrors the language of Article I, Section 8 of the US Constitution, which establishes the delimited, enumerated powers of the federal government and reflects the complex relationship between US exceptionalism and US notions of personhood. Limited government was supposed to preside over a limited corporate form.

But recent Court holdings have inverted the original conception of the chartered corporation. This naturalization/personification has been an ongoing process, in which corporations, if sometimes haphazardly, accreted and retained more and more aspects of personhood. Because the corporation has exceptional, extra-human traits—including immortality and special forms of immunity—it's attained not only more rights than people, but enhanced rights whose existence is incompatible with and antagonistic to individual rights. Those exceptional corporate rights are manifested in ontological, deontological, and practical contexts, in the latter case in the ways corporate lobbying, spending, and speech are treated as if they were undertaken by mere individuals—when their purpose and effect is to drown out the voices of individuals—and in the bewildering array of tax exemptions and economic incentives uniquely awarded to corporations.

As various courts have noted, "The fiction of corporate personhood [was originally] a convenient way to capture the essence of the principle of limited liability." *Beiser v. Weyler*, 284 F.3d 665, 670 (5th Cir. 2002). Now that fiction has become a convenient way to consolidate power and bestow extraordinary rights on corporations. The enhancement of corporate personhood once stemmed from and was contingent on the "separation" of personhood: "The many benefits of limited liability (for society as well as for the shareholders) are built on the idea that every corporation is a distinct legal person from its parent or subsidiary corporations and from its various shareholders." *NAF Holdings, LLC v. Li & Fung (Trading), Ltd.*, 772 F.3d 740, 751 (2d Cir. 2014).[1] Courts gradually have been eradicating that distinction in terms not of liabilities, but of benefits. Ironically, a recent impetus for this further extension of the parameters of corporate personhood was the desire of owners to argue that their legally distinct business entities have personal rights, and sometimes—at least in symbolic terms—allow the corporation to influence employees' choices and options regarding reproduction. In other words, as often dramatized in science fiction, the inhuman corporate thing at least figuratively has reached a point where it can affect the creation of humans.

In *Gain*, Samuel, the Clare family scion who incorporated the business, sounded "the classic definition John Marshall gave in *Dartmouth College*, a half century before: 'A corporation is an artificial being, invisible, intangible, and existing only in contemplation of law'" (158). That corporation is the invisible body that moves the inexorable and putatively infallible invisible hand of the market—throughout this system, we imagine invisible, anonymous, inevitable agencies that control outcomes, in which no one is acting, actionable, or identifiable. One of the brilliant strategies of some hacker movements, including Anonymous, is to acknowledge that corporations, while sometimes seemingly run by evil figurehead CEOs, are themselves anonymous, which in corporate contexts foments indifference. Žižek reminds us that Capital pursues "profitability with blessed indifference to how its movements will affect social reality. Therein lies the fundamental systemic violence of capitalism, much more uncanny than the direct pre-capitalist socioideological violence: it is no longer attributable to concrete individuals and their 'evil' intentions, but is purely 'objective,' systemic, anonymous" (*Less* 244). When, as Žižek suggests, institutions such as stock markets try to persuade the public that real people work there and make day-to-day decisions, and that no larger impersonal insidious mechanisms are controlling things, it is "ideology at its purest" (*Less* 245); such assurances are meant to obfuscate the fact that no human mind or voice animates the corporate person or advertising. To claim that real people— CEOs and boards of directors—control and speak for corporations is the same kind of feint. The more anonymous an entity is legally, the more autonomy it has.[2] Autonomy becomes the autonomy of capital, the market, and the corporation, separated and siphoned from the individual.

The expansion of corporate rights periodically has been prompted by the unwittingly masochistic claims of corporate owners, as in *Burwell v. Hobby Lobby Stores, Inc.*, 573 U.S. 682 (2014); it's as if hosts were agitating for the privileges of parasites. Perversely, unaware that they're in a zero-sum game, plaintiffs in such cases legally seek to transfer aspects of their own personhood and rights to the corporate form; it's the devil's bargain to attain "religious freedom" for your corporation at the expense of confirming, in ever expanding milieus, that corporations have souls. In yet another inversion, corporate rights—which are abstract, since no one is allowed to represent the corporation directly—began to supersede those of actual employees in relation to religion. As Jennifer Jorczak contends, in *Hobby Lobby*, the Court had "to raise the corporations' newfound statutory rights above the constitutional rights of their employees" to conclude that the corporation's religious rights trumped the rights of employees to contraception (315). These holdings again transfer constitutional rights from people to corporations. According to Jennifer Taub, "In the Court's view, free-exercise rights of corporations protect the owners as opposed to the employees or other human stakeholders" (420).

The premises that enable corporate personhood, and the advertising that voices it, exacerbate noxious divisions and conflations in our culture, for example, the conflation of character and personality. An additional kind of gap between personality and character mirrors the separation between the image and the substance of a product—they have nothing intrinsic to do with one another. For Naomi Klein, this separation takes the form of an incommensurability between product—the commodity—and brand; I would and that the brand represents an intangible representation that never coincides, or often has nothing to do, with the product (195). As Melville began to discover in *The Confidence-Man*, the corporate person can possess only artificial personality traits: it can be made to appear charming, but it hides an abyssal emptiness. And such a form of personhood cannot have character—the human identity that stems from background, experience, temperament and action. A corporation cannot be honest or dishonest: those terms apply only to persons who make choices. Our culture fetishizes personality at the expense of character; that preference for superficial, entertaining personality transfers to corporate personhood, which relies on personalities to represent it through advertising and PR. This scenario has striking aesthetic consequences; popular culture, for example, has become proficient at generating appealing but superficial personalities but has turned character into a series of personality tics, traits, and shallow identifiers. Like the corporate person, they're not coherent entities with backstories, but translucent puppets backlit to look substantive. Corporations don't just transfer assets, from wealth to life itself, from people, but set the tone for a culture that's stripped of anything resembling the real thing. (Corporations of course are both causes and effects of that culture.)

One of the great ironies of many contemporary US notions of individualism is that they're predicated on an artificially created being that is a mockery of personhood. US individualism is now largely defined by this collective entity whose overriding marketing tool is the promotion of conformity and mass consumption. Legally created as a screen *for* individuals—to shield them from liability—the corporation has come to serve as a screen for the expropriation and demotion of the individual. The corporation is socially and ontologically devised to perform tasks that individuals cannot pragmatically and economically, but also legally and ethically, pursue. It's an impersonal and programmed system designed to channel and coordinate behavior that threatens the common good. No single person generally is responsible or can be held liable for, or is even perpetrating, the acts of a corporation. Individuality, and meaningful individual choice, is purged and evacuated from the system.

As Christopher Stone concludes, we're under the control of institutions that "transcend and survive changes in the consciousness of individual humans who supposedly comprise them, and whom they supposedly serve. (It is more and more the individual human being, with his [or her] consciousness, that is the legal fiction") (47). As part of the zero-sum game or polarization between corporate and human biography, the means of self-representation at the extremes become destabilized and sometimes even change "position." For example, in the academic world, which represents one apparent opposite of the corporate world, personal and impersonal modes become problematic and unstable. Cynthia Franklin notes that "memoirs too often have become a means by which those working in the academy can speak "only" personally, and hence unassailably" (2).[3] In academia, personal anecdotes can become that guarantor of authenticity in ways that seem anti-corporate, but in practice they generate a kind of inverse but equally problematic discourse. It's as if we can try to recapture personhood only by being overzealously personal—by translating what should be political assertions into personal anecdotes. We can try to authorize our claims by speaking as impersonal corporate persons or as too personal subjects whose statements are based on identity, but we seem to have lost the options in between. The impersonality of corporate language, the dominant form of communication in US culture, continuously affects other modes of self-representation: it's like a black hole whose gravity distorts everything around it. Corporate personhood and advertising aren't the only primary causes of the breakdown of our institutions, particularly journalism. But they're critical factors and symptoms, gateways to many races to the bottom, and forces that erode our sense of what's personal and impersonal, and normative, decent, and inviolable.

In these contexts, Purnima Bose locates the ways corporations foster fantasies of "entrepreneurial individualism" (30–31). If, as Bose suggests, corporations promulgate the idea of "corporate personhood as citizenship" to achieve a form of social credit and appear as if they're benevolent social actors, the reverse principle often shields them from blame (41). (This protection is now structural, and different from the procedures at play when corporations lobby for or write laws for their own benefit.) In other words, corporations take credit for doing things they don't do and escape blame for the direct, and especially indirect, harm they cause. This notion of corporate exceptionalism was more diffusely applied in the wake of the 2008 banking scandals, when not only the political response, but the legal system kept financial institutions, which were able to lend without risk, protected from prosecution. In the US democratic ethos, being a citizen implies having an equal status and shared responsibility to the state and other citizens; the last economic meltdown confirmed that corporations—at least large financial corporations—aren't citizens, but exceptional. Their citizenship is defined by *supra*-personal rights. Corporations were always "too" something to be treated as citizens, for example too big to fail or prosecute. Such an outcome was neither circumstantial nor incidental, but ineluctable. Any corporation worthy of its status has become a dispersed and interconnected network, a poisonous ecosystem that cannot be altered or regulated because it claims to mete out antidotes. As Lyons observes, "Corporate personhood works to the advantage of big business by crystallizing the corporate form into a singular rights bearing individual while at the same time distributing legal liability across and within the corporation" (105).

The fictional corporate person is not only irresponsible, in terms of pursuing profit regardless of social harm, but is programmed to lie. It's worth reflecting on how much we generally dislike corporations for their customer service and behavior—Monsanto, Comcast, Nestlé, Clear Channel, Chevron, Pfizer, Ticketmaster, AT&T, and most ISPs, insurance and health care companies, and hundreds of similar corporations are reviled, feared or mistrusted. If corporations have personhoods, many people loathe them, even as some go out of their way to identify with them. At best amoral, corporations come to serve as the de facto guarantors and distributors of culture; almost everything produced in that culture will reflect corporate pathologies and priorities. Deborah Madsen suspects corporations exhibit schizophrenic traits, in that they're severed from a coherent sense of unified history or values, and wholly contingent in their behavior (146–47). But that behavior is predictable; much of what I argue regarding corporations begins with the premise that their status and actions are rarely contingent, but axiomatic and designed. One suspects a psychologist would assess a representative "corporate person" as criminally insane, with defining characteristics of a lack of empathy; antisocial aggression; a proclivity to dishonesty; and an inability to evaluate one's own behavior. While it might seem contradictory to ascribe human pathologies to inhuman corporations, these entities are engineered to simulate the worst of human behavior: they're like anti-saints who commit sins in their shareholders' names. Tzvetan Todorov argues that psychoanalysis has supplanted the literature of the fantastic because it deals with the causes of anxieties that used to be projected onto figures of fantasy, such as devils and vampires (161). But, aside from the fact that such devils and vampires seem more prevalent than ever in popular culture, certain figures cannot be psychoanalyzed because they have no psyches. Labeling corporate personhood as evil or pathological is apt, but also akin to analyzing an algorithm; what we need to analyze is the systems that foster the corporation.

Personhood is a contested site between corporations and people, with corporations finally cannibalizing personhood (though perhaps one shouldn't use that term since it would grant corporations a digestive system). In the film version of Harry Harrison's *Make Room! Make Room!*, Soylent was a Corporation before it became people: as Mitt Romney asserted, likely conveying more than he intended, corporations are people, my friend. Though they obviously have people working for them, corporations function as impersonal mechanisms, and it's no coincidence that individuals become increasingly disenfranchised as corporations gain more power, influence and rights. A growing percentage of Americans are corporate employees, effectively paid in corporate scrip, working under corporate rules, entertained by corporate products, and living in corporate zones.[4] Among a plethora of familiar appraisals, Nelson D. Schwartz in the *New York Times* reported that in 2013, corporate profits had reached an all-time high as a share of national income, while the share going to employee wages had reached its lowest point in almost fifty years (A1). Corporations are at the center of a series of such inverted and polarizing relationships, through which assets, including personhood, are redistributed in a zero-sum game. According to Marx, "The devaluation of the human world increases in direct relation with the increase in value of the world of things" (323–24). Today, that world is represented by the corporation, the quintessential uncanny Thing that seems to become animated, and whose "human" status, rights, and qualities increase as, and only when, those of people are diminished. Christopher Newfield argues that the "corporation has failed socially by failing to insulate its own people from [a maldistribution of wealth] and 'winner take all'" mentality; but this view reflects a misconception of its purpose ("Corpo-rate" 28). The corporation is designed to fail socially—that is its programmed mission. Social good and income equality are not just irrelevant to the corporate charter, or even a hindrance to the corporate enterprise, but antagonistic to it. Corporations are obligated to consider shareholder profit to the virtual exclu-sion of all else. Their zero-sum game is to move all attributes—money, power, space, time, and personhood—to their side of the ledger, until nothing is left on the other.

In a variety of contexts, people barter their attributes with corporations—they don't trade liberty for security, but for forms of identity. Corporations have come to guarantee certain rights, at a price, in much the way the Hobbesian state once did. An inverse relationship exists between corporate and personal freedom, and, as Melville might say, corporations guarantee immortality *to* impersonality at the expense of individuals. The freedom corporations guarantee allows consumers specious choices between largely fungible products, but not among political alternatives, forms of conscious-ness, and non-corporate ways of being. The US mantra of individual liberty, manipulated by an anti-individualistic corporate ethos, has long served as a cover and pretext for denying social responsibility and liability.

As another example, corporations increasingly guard their "privacy" and operate as secretly as possible under the penumbra of protecting trade secrets and business information; but they also rarely disclose what should be considered their non-confidential, non-business activities, especially their political contributions and acts. Simultaneously, individuals across a broad spectrum, and with accelerating fervor, voluntarily divulge and consume private information in corporate fora online, and symbolically through reality TV shows, even as their public and private information is incessantly mined by corporations and the government. Corporations spur such negative redistribu-tion of privacy, wealth, and rights. Thom Hartmann observes that corporations (much like most red states) are net consumers of rather than contributors to the tax base (211), especially when one considers externalities, or the resources and infrastructure corporations use without fully paying for them, as well as the environmental damage and social harm they generate. This is a critical inver-sion and subversion of the public good. The 1970s welfare programs didn't merely redistribute a fixed pie to poor people—that is, reducing benefits to some to increase them to others in a zero-sum game—rather, they expanded the funds available to all as well as the rights of recipients. This approach was undermined beginning with Reagan's welfare reforms and continuing in force under Clinton, much as corporate power and influence escalated.[5]

Even if "composite bodies might still need a titular head," the corporation is the perfect postmodern vehicle, with no locatable agency, and yet it moves (*Gain* 181). As Powers writes, "The best [CEOs] no doubt came to believe that the will of that collective was their own will," but corporations generate myths of agency and responsibility that occlude their mechanisms of behavior (181). Corporations are structured internally and externally to shift accountability from the public sphere to an allegedly private sphere that doesn't exist in that context. According to Simon Enoch, citing the work of Erik Swyngedouw, "through privatization, decision-making frameworks are removed from local or regional political control and into the executive boardrooms of global corporations" (226). (In keeping with that shift, corporations also have tended to shorten their names over the last century in ways that erase traces of local allegiance, origin or specificity.) Corporate control and infiltration take different forms around the world, but the basic premise involves encroachment; privatization and commodification of the public sphere, decentralization of responsibility and centralization of control, and globalization/homogenization. When you open Google Maps of some foreign towns, they prominently include the locations of McDonald's and other franchises. In Fiji, most public signs, for instance indicating you have entered a town, are sponsored by cell phone companies and hotel chains. In the United States, incessant privatizations of the public domain expose how right-wing fits about freedom and federalism are gross hypocrisy. While many conservatives assert that states should retain local authority and object vehemently to fantasized impositions on national sovereignty (e.g., the disability rights the United Nations recommends), they rarely, at least before Trumpism, objected to local impositions such as NAFTA or the Multilateral Agreement on Investment. Yet those treaties allow corporations to override national environmental and labor standards and sue sovereign governments that don't abide by their rules, which are implemented without any democratic ratification. Ultimately, the corporation represents the drive to privatize law itself.

This process of subsuming sovereignty relies on and is enmeshed with the fictions of the corporate person; it is a form of privatization that enhances limited liability and ignores the externalized costs of business. Relative to the scope and scale of corporate lobbying, few organizations lobby for the public good; that imbalance reflects a redistribution of not just power, but personhood in US society. For at least sixty years, corporations have been trying to privatize and deregulate everything we might consider a public resource, good, or benefit, from sources of water to internet and bathroom access, all for profit, never public policy. (As one obvious and egregious example, at the behest of his corporate backers, Governor Chris Christie decided to fast-track the privatization of New Jersey's water supply in the immediate wake of the lead poisoning of Flint's privatized water supply.) The ethos of corporate advertising and privatization is coterminous with the drive to monetize anything in the corporation's path. Corporations incessantly commodify things that either should by default be free, such as water, or that had no economic value per se until the corporation commodified them: for example, most airlines started to charge to reserve seats. These are negatives turned into revenue streams to transfer wealth from customers to shareholders; you pay for the right to suffer less of some inconvenience the corporation often creates, otherwise known as blackmail. One suspects that at some point airlines will charge a fee not to make you listen to Muzak your entire flight (the "give me a dollar not to hit you over the head with a mallet" approach to revenue). Monetizing the negative is a form of decadence, like shorting stocks; the ethos of corporate personhood allows corporations to state, in effect, that they'll charge you not to subject you to arbitrary discomfort, but also to allow you to gain private access to a public good (for which the public often already has paid in some context). When corporations try to charge for everything from water to freedom from harassment, it's alarming in what it suggests about business ethics. But it's especially dangerous in the context of health care and other public services. Corporations are predatory in targeting public space and public services to convert to their private ends, but they never acknowledge that they're parasites on public infrastructure—that they exact unpaid and often unacknowledged costs not just to the environment but to culture. As with war, what's good for the corporation is often toxic for you.

The drive to commodify everything poses risks to art, government, and most human values. That trend is at least partly understandable in a putatively free market where supply sets demand, but it is intolerable in the context of government and leads not only to privatized public services but to the corporatization and corporate appraisal of human rights and needs. Aside from pursuing regressive tax policies, a corporatist state makes its citizens unequal and puts itself up for sale. Most public-private partnerships—from literally mercenary companies such as Halliburton and Blackwater, which privatize the military, to for-profit prisons and corporate sponsorships of schools— entail corporate encroachment on and take-overs of the public domain. Corporations and the state begin to treat customers/citizens with the same mindset, as sources of revenue. If you need that medicine to live, the corporation will try to charge you whatever your life is worth; but it will equally try to charge you, in effect, whatever it can not to annoy or kill you, with the state beginning to apply some of the same logic. Whenever government privatizes and charges different rates for access to public services, it is acting like a corporation and against its own prime directives. It's the equivalent of Las Vegas putting slot machines in old age homes to generate tax revenue to pay for public programs for seniors. The premises of corporate personhood unlevel governmental efforts to provide a level playing field.

I used to joke that the ultimate goal of corporations is to privatize the courts, but with the ever-increasing use of mandatory arbitration clauses—

which individuals are often unilaterally subject to without knowing it, and without the legal consideration (recompense) that should make contracts enforceable—and a legal system designed by and for corporate actors, that goal virtually has been reached already. Arbitration is a private, corporatized form of legal adjudication that favors corporations and wealthy parties. The widespread system of forced arbitration—which corporations and institutions almost exclusively impose on individuals—is a form of private law. Aside from the almost complete lack of oversight and review that favors corporations, arbitrators in this system have strong incentives to favor the parties that hire them for repeat business: corporations and institutions. The arbitration system represents another form of privatized public service, and it's shocking that we allow it to co-opt the legal system (and the penal system in the form of corporate prisons, which are predicated on insoluble conflicts of interest). Equivalent intermediate steps already have been taken in the academic realm. For example, Rubriq Independent Peer Review charges academics to get expedited "independent" reviews of their work so they can publish, and therefore gain tenure, more easily.

We already are so inured to the notion that we should be able to buy public services, such as education, that we barely notice the further erosion of the public good in the name of freedom. The outcome of such a process is that we will, in some metaphorical if not literal sense, be assigned separate lines and payment schemes not just for public services such as "premium" airport security and high-speed freeway lanes, but courts, health care, reviews, grades, ad infinitum. Since campaign donations, and, in effect, the exhortations of corporate lobbyists are now considered protected corporate speech, corporate courts would represent the final venue for the corporation to complete its evolution toward personhood and emerge as judge, jury, and executioner. The law, the government's code of socially acceptable behavior, might provide the final theater for the performance of corporate personhood.

It's easier to see the effects and transformations of corporate personhood when we look at the increasingly privatized and militarized culture of the post-9/11 United States, and the corporate incursions and transgressions we take as commonplace, and that we likely would have found inconceivable and intolerable even two decades ago. What legitimate justification could there be for having an effectively privatized first-class lane for airport security, which should remain within government purview? We the people are now we the corporate persona and we the peons. The TSA even distributes a "Customer Comment Card," confirming that its managers operate under the corporate delusion that it has customers. As corporations become citizen-persons, persons become government customers. As the other Elvis might say, this is an even less than zero-sum game. I'd proclaim that I as a customer certainly would like to choose an alternate corporation to provide my security, but even if it were possible, the choice surely would be meaningless. Credit card companies promote TSA PreCheck as a corporate-sponsored government program: "Executive cardmembers receive an application fee credit for Global Entry or TSA PreCheck, up to $100 every five years. To receive reimbursement, you must charge the application fee to your Executive card." Airport security here represents a close correlative of corporate personhood, a monetized hierarchy that defines one's status, level of safety, and identity as a verified member of the polis, all based on corporate parameters, and it implicitly or explicitly outsources and privatizes government functions. The airport has been at the forefront of blurring the line between government service and an outsourced mercenary corporate army, especially when the rent-a-cops behave as if they were public officials. It might only be a matter of time, as writers such as Klein intimate, before all public goods, from schools to highways, the military, and courts will not only be sponsored, but auctioned and privatized. How long will it be before some corporation tries to provide a first-class line at the DMV, for 911 services, or for voting access?

Chapter Twenty-One

When Texas Executes One

As Michael Kennedy remarks, corporations of course historically can die, sometimes slowly and then all at once, but they're legally and conceptually founded to be immortal (247–49). As Powers writes of Samuel Clare, whose personhood and name are transferred to a corporation, "He had lived long enough to see the constitutional amendment preventing any law that would abridge the privileges and immunities" of a corporation, "that legally created person. Such a law guaranteed the immortality dreamed of by the poets and prophets" (181).[1] In other words, the corporation isn't just a legally created person, but a legally created deity that bears a host of superhuman attributes. Ned Beauman attests in *Glow* that "Killing a corporation was like killing a colony of sentient fungus. . . . United Fruit was a hundred and eight. Chevron was a hundred and eighteen. De Beers was a hundred and twenty. Unlike governments, corporations endured: deathless, efficient, self-renewing" (43). This corporate immortality, and the expansion of exceptional corporate rights and immunities, is achieved at the expense of individual rights and identities. In Emerson's work, nature orchestrated a similar process, which he considered a form of divine dispossession. Like nature, the corporation transcends time and space by being everywhere permanently.

The corporate displacement or ascension evident in cases such as *Hobby Lobby* and *Citizens United* fulfills an arc Melville traced in full in *Moby-Dick*, which situates the failing ubiquity of nature against the rising ubiquity of the corporation. In *Moby-Dick*, the leviathan —a term Melville partly developed from Hobbes, to whom I return— represents, among other things, the demonological transition between the US conception of nature as an American province that serves to guarantee a universal natural law and its conception of the transnational corporation that's everywhere the same. In Melville's novel, Ishmael comes up against "the unearthly conceit that Moby Dick was *ubiquitous*; that he had been en-countered in opposite latitudes at one and the same instant . . . [and] not only ubiquitous, but *immortal* (for immortality is but ubiquity in time" (182–83). That description of the incarnation of nature comports with a description of the corporation. The law creates the corporation to be, as Melville might put it, like nature itself—"diffused through time and space" (*Moby-Dick* 159). As the media management consultant Michael Wolf proclaimed of corporate brands in the 1990s, sounding like a character in DeLillo's *Mao II*, "If you weren't everywhere . . . you were nowhere" (Klein 147). Wu also character-izes advertisers, whom I situate as the corporation's proselytizers and priests, as engaged in "a race for the conquest of time and space" (*Attention* 93)—that is, an attempt to colonize both nature and culture, and to invade all space at all times. (Douglas Rushkoff uses the terms *digiphrenia* and *fractalnoia* to describe the way digital media has trained *us* to exist, or in a sense virtually levitate, in many places simultaneously, but also synchronize a surfeit of data into patterns and reconcile incompatible states of mind—that is, to that is, hold opposite attitudes at one and the same instant [*Present* 96–97, 201–3]). Melville also realizes that we've begun to inhabit a world where, as Harvey observes, "two events in quite different spaces occurring at the same time could so intersect as to change how the world worked" (*Condition* 265).

Moby Dick is the first postmodern animal: seen in many places at once, it's everywhere the same, here like a universal franchise of nature. In this image of a kind of quantum Moby Dick, which can be located in either time or space but never both simultaneously, Ishmael begins to chart how American economies—of whaling, manifest destiny, and masculine identity—set the stage for universal American products, but he still imagines a counterforce of transcendental nature that could remain equally and genuinely universal. Ishmael also specifically tells us, "'It's a mutual, joint-stock world, in all meridians,'" situating the corporation as the force already uniting and globalizing geography, and everywhere displacing nature in a world increasingly defined by US commerce (62). (The precursors of the modern corporation, these maritime joint-stock compa-nies that were created to support the new global enterprise of whaling also, as noted, had been intimately involved in the global maritime slave trade. Corporations extracted, and symbolically accreted, resources from bodies. As part of the corporate infiltration of language, mutual has come to con-note fund, not common benefit.) Nature was once universal, but it is cor-porations, the joint-stock companies, that now are globalized. Throughout the novel, Melville also suggests that the form of that joint-stock company, which divorced owners from workers (e.g., left landlocked Quakers funding the *Pequod*'s ventures), created not just incentives to risk liability, but the inevitability of pathology. In this context, Ahab is both a fulfillment and rejection of that corporate form, because he subverts the purely capitalist enterprise Starbuck urges him to pursue: he tries to strike beneath the pasteboard mask of both nature and the corporate endeavor that dismembered him. But Melville situates Ahab not as a perversion of Starbuck's proto-corporate ethos, but its inevitable surplus and fulfillment. Ishmael's joint-stock world must exist everywhere the same at once—in other words, it takes over the function of the whale (nature) that its corporate mission hunts, and as such it is also emblematically suicidal. The joint-stock company is the flip side of corporate nature, and it hunts itself to extinction.

In some ways unprecedented and anomalous in history, the corporation is a private institution that's everywhere, and everywhere the same—and hence not only immortal, but ubiquitous. The franchise is one apotheosis of the corporate form; it's a kind of Platonic archetype that begins as an idea that's then reproduced endlessly to order. An infinitely replicable clone (or work of mechanical reproduction) that has no original, the corporation can have the identical identity always and everywhere, in some ways because it can have no identity whatsoever. In its modern form, it's already a purely digital/virtual/ posthuman entity, without body, and yet omnipresent. The internet, which effectively is depopulated, is the perfect geography for the corporation.[2] But the real-world manifestations of the corporation produce similar effects. The generic and impersonal architecture and "geography" of the franchise—the endlessly repeated, identical interiors of Burger Kings or Best Buys—are insalubrious, toxic environments that turn us into corporate citizens. Many corporate sites, from the airport maze you have to navigate before you can board your plane to the mall, use the same logic as casinos: you're enveloped in the aesthetic and physical translation of the advertisement, its materialization of the form of inescapable and denaturalized space. The sterile, generic replications of the franchise also reflect the erasure of human personhood and its replacement by corporate personhood.

Writing about *Gain*, Maliszewski observes that "Companies like Beatrice and the Clare Soap and Chemical Company . . . exist everywhere and nowhere" (163). (As Maliszewski observes, Clare is an iteration of Beatrice, a ubiquitous corporation personified as a woman.) The corporation, like Skynet and the web, is precisely everywhere and nowhere. In *Gain*, "the company keeps so many residences that it has no fixed place of abode" (253). For purposes of diversity jurisdiction, a corporation is a *citizen* of the state where it's incorporated or in which it has its principal place of business (28 U.S.C. § 1332(c)), but it can be sued wherever it does business. In a frequently cited case of civil procedure, *World-Wide Volkswagen Corp. v. Woodson, 444* U.S. 286, 297 (1980), the Court held that in products liability cases, corporations could be haled into court in any state where their liability was foresee-able because they were directly or indirectly marketing products there or availing themselves of the steam of interstate commerce. The Court decided that corporations could be sued only where they had minimum contacts with the (forum) state, but in practice most large corporations maximize contacts with all states. Such a holding initially helps consumers, who are able to sue corporations wherever they've suffered harm; and the Court also acknowledged the omnipresence of corporate personhood, as well as "the corporation's near ubiquitous presence in our lives" (Lyons 97). But in the long term, its holding generated unexpectedly baneful effects, because it helped validate key components of corporate personhood, especially the idea that corporations are kinds of invisible networks that cannot be curtailed, scaled, or delimited.

In many ways, that jurisdictionally omnipresent corporation of *World-Wide Volkswagen* takes the place of universal, divine nature in US culture—it takes on the function not just of the impersonal commons, but a uniform, ubiquitous, and finally quasi-numinous transcendental regulatory system (see generally my *Not Altogether Human*). As noted, many nineteenth-century. naturalists believed in the unity and uniformity of nature, as formulated by such writers as Emerson and the German Alexander von Humboldt. Here, the idea of universal nature served as a harbinger of worldwide trade, globalization, and technologies of communication and travel, ranging from the telegraph to the World Wide Web, that link, homogenize, and effectively franchise all places. (Corporate personhood fulfills, or becomes a naturalized mascot for, Marx's prediction that capitalism, through its dependence on technology, would anni-hilate space with time, in this case producing a fictitious being that's simultane-ously everywhere.) But where individuals derive their rights through national citizenship, corporations transcend national boundaries and in some contexts have acquired not only international, but supra-national rights.

The "residence" and "citizenship" of US corporations matter in the con-text of jurisdiction and local regulation. But another important fiction allows corporations to incorporate wherever they want, thereby taking advantage of that state's favorable laws. As another facet of the zero-sum game, while cor-porations are everywhere, they're often incorporated in Delaware, a miniscule and almost fictitious state whose statutes are tailored to attract corporations. In what typically involves a race to the bottom, corporations began to incorporate in states such as Delaware that offered not only the most comprehensive legal system and chancery courts, but the most permissive rules for incorporation and liability. While some states, such as California, enacted legislation related to incorporation that would protect shareholders, most corporations can simply shop for better provisions elsewhere. The state of incorporation is another fiction of locality that helps counter the corporation's lack of limitation, and another provision that allows for the kind of conceptual disconnection endemic to the corporate form; it has little bearing on where corporations conduct business or their ontological status as stateless entities. Corporations take advantage of local incorporation when it provides legal advantages, and effectively ignore it otherwise. As most people know, corporate headquarters can be another legal fiction; many corporations that incorporate in Delaware simply maintain the equivalent of a post box there. There's never any *body* home. Like ships that notoriously "incorporate" or register wherever the laws are most lax, corporations have no homes or allegiances, and their sites of incorporation are arbitrary fictions.

The corporation has no place of abode—it's bound by neither space nor time. A typical corporation outsources its production abroad anywhere it can; external accountants calculate its books and outside advertisers promote its products. In other words, the corporation is a shell, and cannot be defined. It can change its location, its workforce, all its external modalities, and still be the same corporation. In much the same way, corporate sports franchises can trade away all their players and managers—who usually have no connection, geographic or otherwise, to the franchise—and still be called the same team; they remain the same corporate entity. Yet, as with corporations, fans usually retain allegiance to a purely imagined connection. (Such considerations raise a negative variation of the Platonic question—is it still the same table, or even a table, if it loses one leg, two legs, etc.? Is it still the same team or corporation when x number of players or directors leave?) What kind of personhood could such an immutable and fundamentally inhuman corporate entity have? The corporation is a logo it attaches to whatever it sells. The corporate person is contingent and adventitious and can impersonate only the qualities of those who pass within the corporate system.

Chapter Twenty-Two

Immortality and Impersonation

In *Ubik*, Philip K. Dick emphasizes that his protagonist, Joe Chip, perhaps broadly after Melville, has developed unearthly conceits regarding the transcendental, impersonal immortality of corporate products: "*ubiquity*, he realized all at once; that's the derivation of the made up word, the name of [the] alleged spray-can product" (117). It's through the spray can, along with other consumer artifacts, that Ubik utters its speech. Before Christ decided to return by appearing on buttered toast, Dick parodied consumer culture, the idea of salvation in a can and immortality in corporate merchandise. But he also insisted that God exists everywhere and in everything, even in transubstantiated advertising (an idea that DeLillo reprises in his depiction of the sanctified billboard that closes the narrative of *Underworld*, which was a kind of negative of Emerson's Over-Soul). Dick's play with ubiquity reflects a postmodern recalibration of how consumer culture has usurped the universality once reserved for nature and God; as DeLillo suggested in *White Noise* and *Mao II*, franchises, like Coca-Cola and American Express, are now ubiquitous, taking over religion's task of transcending-history and providing universal answers. At all times and in all places, the postmodern logo announces itself as universal logos, leading Dick to conclude that ubiquity is the mark of both God and the devil.

Most of us now live in a Dickian world, in which advertisements are forms of artificial persons that incessantly harass us. Gas stations in many cities continuously play audio and video ads at you while you fill your tank, in a media assault that a short while ago might have seemed like something from a Dick novel. The corporation here externalizes the cost to you, and everyone who is subjected to such ads experiences a kind of cultural degradation. Dick's jokes and exaggerations turn out to have been simply descriptive prognostications: as seen in *Blade Runner* and *Minority Report*, and in many of his stories and novels, as well as in the Dickian Netflix series *Maniac* (whose protagonist is hounded by roaming ads and ad buddies), stores now track us to deliver personalized advertisements, and we have to endure ads even in elevators. Dick's many predictive, unsettling novels—in which dynamic and sentient ads target, track, and hunt you—are now just documents of everyday life. (As another example of the self-referentiality of modern advertising, when such systems are initially installed in elevators or other "new frontiers," they refer exclusively to themselves for the first week, presenting some form of the teaser, "check back here for our exciting new advertising starting next week.") In many of Dick's novels, advertising is a kind of vicious sport crossed with Stasi-level stalking. Targeted advertisements—animated, mobile, virtually sentient—rely on and enact a kind of surveillance: they follow and report back on you. The *Black Mirror* episode "Metalhead," in which robot dogs patrol what looks like the remains of an Amazon warehouse, presents a metaphor for the way AI advertising stalks everyone online. (Many recent TV series—including *Real Humans* and *Years and Years*—suggest that corporations are forms of AI that are replicating themselves as such, though some shows treat androids, after Philip K. Dick, as metaphors for immigrants and *homo sacer*.) Just as marketers gather data from every website you visit and purchase you make, supermarkets generate coupons based on your purchasing history, website visitations, and so on. Corporations "know" your consumer identity more intimately, and in more detail, than almost anyone—any friend, family member, physician, or psychologist—will ever know you.[1] Another science fiction writer, John Brunner, predicted this outcome almost fifty years ago in *The Shockwave Rider*: "the data net . . . the tangled web. . . . Anybody here get nightmares because you know data exist you can't get at and other people can? . . . Is the purpose of creating the largest information-transmission system in history to present mankind with a brand-new reason for paranoia?" (66, 254). This trans-paranoia, one of whose causes is constant irritation, becomes universal in tandem with the corporation. Advertisers resemble the most annoying kid in your first grade class, whose entire ethos, aesthetic, and ethic, or way of dealing with the world, amounted to "I made you look."

As Dick predicted, we have become and will be increasingly subjected to pseudo-individualized ads—to personalized impersonality. TV shows eventually will be customized, and announcers will address you directly the way emails do. Such scenarios until now have been the domain of paranoid science fiction films, from Dick based films to David Fincher's *The Game*—but just because you're paranoid, doesn't mean something isn't out to advertise to you. Google has long targeted individuals based on their search patterns, and links sidebar ads to the content of your Gmail. (In another prescient fabrication, DeLillo included the phrase "Googolplex and glosso-lalia" in *Ratner's Star* in 1976; Googolplex was one of the original names proposed for the search engine [361]). Your data, input and preferences already determine the individualized news stories you see, which are inextricable from the advertisements, and this might soon be the case with networks: "Rene, you'll be shocked to hear of the flood that just hit Houston, and if you want to protect yourself, call your local X insurance agent to protect your house on the Cape." Maybe you'll be able to register to get alerts when your neighbor buys a bigger TV set.

Dick's *Ubik*, in which the ironicized persona of God hides and resides in commercial products, intimates that time itself has been hijacked by corporate culture: we can measure time and move forward only by reference to new products, planned obsolescence, and a concomitant uneasy nostalgia. (As Leon Wieseltier opines, "Presumptions of obsolescence . . . are often nothing more than marketing techniques of corporate behemoths"; in other words, as Wallace proposed, time itself is now sponsored by corporations, and we live in the year of Glad [15]). Ubik at first appears and communicates exclusively in the guise of advertising slogans, to a character who doesn't realize he exists only in a cryogenic half-life. Dick here uses the ubiquity of advertising as an overlay for the hidden, sourceless voice of God, which is "broadcast" to introduce the book's chapters. Chapter 3, for example, begins with the assertion that "*Instant Ubik has all the fresh flavor of just-brewed coffee. Your husband will say, Christ, Sally, I used to think your coffee was only so-so. But now, wow! Safe when taken as directed*" (21, emphasis in original). (All Ubik products are noted to be safe only when used as directed, with caution, and in small doses.) Through this parody of Christ's ability to feed the masses, his universality or ability to represent all things, Dick suggests that advertising has devolved into a superficial selling of the confidence and security religion once perhaps as falsely provided. The last chapter of the book begins with an ambiguous revelation, alerting us that either God or advertising has come to us in disguise. Unlike the ironic tone of the epithets of the previous chapters—in which Ubik appears as breakfast cereal, deodorant, and salad dressing—the tenor of this final passage allows us to read it as vindication of a non-parodic religious narrative: "I am Ubik. Before the universe was, I am. I made the suns. I made the worlds. . . . I am the word and my name is never spoken. The name which no one knows. I am called Ubik, but that is not my name. I am. I shall always be" (190). Dick tries to recover impersonal ubiquity, the immortality of a nonhuman entity, through the false universality of capitalism: to find divinity behind the diurnal facade of corporate advertising and God inside the "Ubik liver and kidney balm" (123, 133). Instead of an identity defined through the "simulated tests" of advertising,

Dick tries to find a voice that is original and self-defining, which contains an aura, authenticity, and self-identity lacking in consumer culture (162). But he fears that the postmodern economy has obviated the possibility of universal nature, leaving only a void where God should be.

In *Ubik*, the barrage of advertisements is linked to the incessant decay of commercial products that regress in time, in a "reversion of matter to earlier forms" (113). (This conceit again parodies planned obsolescence, but also attempts to *reverse* the "progression" from divine nature to corporation that Powers narrates in *Gain*. Problematically, for Dick the only way to elide such decay is to align oneself with another impersonal, transcendental force.) In Dick's nightmare of the zero-sum game, either God or the corporation is "still alive, while all of you are dead," a line repeated in various formulations in *Ubik* (109) and used as basis for the title of Emmanuel Carrère's biography of Dick. Ubik is transformed from universal product to universal god, but Dick never lets the reader remain confident of that transubstantiation, even on the last page unsettling his narrative by leaving the novel's protagonist unsure whether he's back among the living or has been dead all along (see my "Pure Formalities").

These sequences of decay that affect every physical object in the novel, contextualized primarily in relation to advertising and consumer culture, are critical to *Ubik*. In the novel, products and objects continually revert to earlier forms—in a sense move backward in time like Benjamin Button. Dick at least implicitly indicates that corporations represent a form of anti-progress or regression, a global ennui or force of entropy operating under the masquerade of capital. The anxiety about human identity such questions often generate suggests that certain aspects of advertising manipulate and police our sense of age and aging—that is, aside from often relying on fantasies of youth and novelty, ads tell people what they're supposed to like and be like at set ages. But our bodies decay toward death as the corporate body doesn't, and as it denies or distorts that decay, "immortal" corporations decenter time and space, and the relationship between the living and the dead.

In the zero-sum game of personhood, some widely proliferating contemporary configurations of the undead and zombies, artificial intelligence, and ghosts are cathected to the undying aspects and disenfranchisements of corporate personhood. These are entities that momentarily might appear to have quasi-human status, but they are only things impersonating people. Like corporations, zombies are depersonalized, immortal, and collectivized; have a relentless drive to accrete; and cannot reproduce, but replace the family.[2] According to Žižek, "a dead person loses the predicates of a living being, yet remain[s] the same person. An undead [which include vampires and zombies], on the contrary, retains all the predicates of a living being without being one" (*Interrogating* 157). As noted, the corporation is a disembodied corpse, a specter that haunts our civilization. As Žižek warns, when a cinematic subject "is killed or otherwise passes out and then miraculously survives his/her own death," that subject "isn't substantially "the same" as before" (*Indivisible* 178 n37, emphasis in original). In the corporation's wake, we retain the outward semblance of a self, but become a thing impersonating a subject, while the corporation takes the place of the living. In a recent radio ad, an announcer proclaims "AAA lives to help": a "living" AAA would be even more terrifying than the walking dead. Resurrected figures such as Colonel Sanders and Orville Redenbacher achieve a corporate immortality in personifying undead animation. Blurring boundaries between people and things, the dead and the living, corporations have constructed impersonal personhood by advertising products as people and people as products. Though corporations are at some point created, they become theoretically immortal under the law; they also can "create" or reproduce other corporations. The inhuman entities of horror movies—clones, cyborgs, terminators, nonhuman entities that cannot be killed—often bear some traits of corporate persons: they're emblematically "unnatural" in multiple contexts. They often self-regulate in a purely autonomic sense; self-reproduce; or emerge as forms of AI that have become self-aware.

Jeanne Gaakeer proposes that ideas of artificial personhood can be traced to Descartes's belief that man is a machine. A kind of machine without a body, and a series of unnatural forms, the corporation extends the parameters and consequences of that notion of mechanical personhood. Corporations personalize products but depersonalize their buyers; this inversion involves the naturalization of social processes, and the attribution of specious causes and effects to explain the relationship of products to people. Žižek might suggest that the corporation is the final reified animation of capital itself: for Marx, for example, "capital is money which becomes a subject . . . [and eventually] appears as a subject 'endowed with a motion of its own, passing through a life-process of its own'" (*Absolute* 31). Corporations "embody" such abstractions, in much the way vampires, the undead, aliens, mechanical monstrosities, and other purely phantasmic entities embody critical notions about our Being in the world.

Chapter Twenty-Three

Corporations Have No Souls

Economics are the method, but the object is to change the soul.

—Margaret Thatcher[1]

Souls, such as they are, were once the province of people and reflected numinous conceptions of God and nature. But that attribution changed, especially in the United States, as corporations became more powerful and ubiquitous than the state and even nature, whereupon corporations ventured to claim souls for themselves, and not just rhetorically; they acted as if they culturally and legally possessed them. Starting around the 1850s, corporations began to supplant the role a transcendental or universal nature had filled in US culture—representing both the failure and fulfillment of the promise of a divine nature that guarantees the processes of life. The notion of a corporate soul is a key component of corporate personhood. More ominously, corporations use the precepts of corporate personhood, and their newly acquired souls, to impersonate people. As part of the zero-sum game of corporate personhood, these rights accrue in inverse proportion to the corporation's degree of potential liability. I begin this chapter by returning to the nineteenth century because its less familiar cultural history can help us gain a new perspective regarding the legal development of the corporate form. A surprising but exigent aspect of corporate personhood is that it relied on and emerged from conceptions of a divine nature that itself had some form of soul.

As noted, transcendentalists such as Emerson ascribed an impersonal "Over-Soul" to an omnipresent and immortal nature. That soul evolved in subtle ways into the soul ascribed to the corporation that achieved legal personhood. Corporate personhood is predicated on the serial transfer of assets from a transcendental or divine nature, and finally from people *to* corporations; corporations have taken on the role of personified, impersonal, omnipresent nature. I briefly trace this trajectory, in which the corporation imitates and supersedes nature, again roughly from Melville to Pynchon and Powers. These writers narrativize a series of failed attempts to find a soul in, or merge with, a transcendental nature that itself turns out to be a corporate fiction.

The assumptions of antebellum pantheism—the worldview that treated nature as an impersonal universal force that transcended national boundaries and individual identities—were overlaid onto the market, and specifically the impersonal corporation. This transfer was neither contingent nor accidental: as the US economy became global and increasingly corporate, the construct and fantasy of nature served as what Tocqueville, as noted, predicted would be the collective force that would allow allegedly individualistic Americans to merge into an impersonal mass. But it was not nature, but the corporation that enabled Americans to pursue the goal of transcendentalism—to transcend the individual entirely. Nature and corporation were imagined to have a kind of ahistorical personhood, one that regulated many aspects of society. Transcendentalism/pantheism emerged when Americans were becoming less able to imagine that individuals controlled their own destinies. Many of the larger forces they saw organizing human society and behavior—from the market to early theories of evolution to historical determinism—ironically became cathected onto the putative avatar of free enterprise, the corporation. Nature represented an overarching force that existed in some form of balance with the individual; the corporation developed as a collective force that was programmed to displace and absorb individuals, much as it was programmed to displace or absorb competitors. Proselytizers such as Reverend Buchanan warned that pantheists frequently invoked a divine nature to question whether "humanity [is] a collective being, or . . . nothing but a series of individual men?" (135). It soon made more sense to situate that query in relation to the corporation than to nature.

These precepts of pantheism, based on interacting theories of an organic collective nature and Over-Soul, morphed into a justification for an artificial corporate overlord. Instead of merging into the collective identity of impersonal nature, men started to merge into the impersonal but now "ensouled" corporation. Or as DeLillo contends in *Zero K*, we are being "virtualized" and "unfleshed," with "all the linked data designed to incorporate you into the megadata" (239). As I later contend, and as writers from DeLillo to William Gibson intimate, AI represents our new collective "second nature," which replaces nature or reveals that nature itself was always corporate. The fantasies of transcending individual isolation I've been delineating reach their apotheosis in the contemporary corporation and its technologies. Raffi Katchadourian describes what it might mean to transcend human existence by merging into a corporate "soup," rather than into the commons of nature that Emerson and Whitman imagined: AI theorist

[Nick] Bostrom considers a digital future in which trillions of digital minds merge into an enormous cognitive cyber-soup. "Whether the set of extremely positive posthuman modes of being would include some kind of dissolved bullion, there is some uncertainty," he said. "If you look at religious views, there are many where merging with something greater is a form of heaven. . . . In many traditions, the best possible state does not involve being a little individual pursuing goals. But it is hard to get a grasp of what would be going on in that soup." (79)

That soup also is Ishmael's ocean in *Moby-Dick*; what Romain Rolland termed the oceanic feeling; Sister Edgar's all-fusing cyberspace in DeLillo's *Underworld*; or what critics of transcendentalism refer to in a variety of ways as a primordial, undifferentiated, amniotic fluid. What's unexpected is that such merging with nature is largely consonant with the premises of corporate personhood. All these gooey Tocquevillian masses liquefy the individual. In *Studies in Classic American Literature*, Lawrence warns that Whitman's form of pantheism cooks up an awful pudding rather than a nurturing soup: "'I embrace ALL,' says Whitman. 'I weave all things into myself.' Do you really! There can't be much left of *you* when you've done. When you've cooked the awful pudding of One Identity. . . . DEMOCRACY. EN MASSE. ONE IDENTITY. The Universe, in short, adds up to ONE. . . . This merging . . . is Whitman's contribution to American democracy" (174,182–186). The next step after pantheistic democracy is corporate "democracy." Such passages are emblematic of what I have described as a genre of antebellum texts in which white men fantasized that they could merge into the en-masse of nature, which evolves into the AI of the collective corporate form.

Among thousands of similar formulations, these descriptions establish a confluence between nineteenth-century transcendental mergers with nature and contemporary mergers with corporations and corporate technologies. But corporate personhood goes beyond merger with the corporation because it turns the corporation into an artificial version of a human society and represents the final step in validating the corporation as a legally and ontologically exceptional entity. Corporate personhood requires the attribution of human traits—a personality, family structure, religious and legal rights, and ultimately an exceptional Over-Soul—to a legal fiction, rather than a cultural fiction of nature. Nature originally inspired (literally breathed) through us; it was a universal and collective impersonal entity that guaranteed individual identity. In "Nature," Emerson, as noted, claims to transcend his individual self and merge into nature, until he is nothing, but sees all, and "the currents of the Universal Being circulate *through* [him]" (*Works*, I, 1011). We're actors, in multiple senses of the word, performing nature's will and speaking its voice. In a slew of iterations, Emerson asserted, "*Through me*, God acts; *through me*, speaks" (*Works*, "Divinity School Address" I, 129). (I return to issues of voicing, actorhood, and agency in a chapter addressing how Hobbes's notion of the corporate charter and legal actorhood facilitated the corporate colonization and development of the New World.) Emerson insisted we can speak only when nature speaks through us: "Man does not possess [the forces of Nature], he is a pipe through which their currents flow" (*Works*, "Perpetual Forces" 10, 74). But in most aspects of American culture from entertainment to politics, impersonal corporations now ventriloquize or "speak us" in much the way nature once did. Cameron contends that the impersonal—which I argue is itself transcendental and became or was revealed as corporate—"speaks despite us *through us*" and thereby destabilizes the notion of a fixed self-contained identity (99, emphasis in original). We can trace a through-line from what nature does "through me" to what the corporate person and corporate speech do. In the context of corporations, however, the impersonal often represents the deficit, rather than Lacanian excess, of individuality; if nature added to the individual self—inspired, suffused, enhanced, or possessed it—the corporation hollows it out.

Melville was among the first and most astute critics of transcendental conceptions of nature because he realized they were also conceptions of an ahistorical or naturalized market. For Melville, pantheism offered a locus for exposing the corporate interior of nature. In *Moby-Dick*, Ishmael warns that the pantheist who transcends his individuality by merging into nature

> takes the mystic ocean at his feet for the visible image of that deep, blue, bottomless soul, pervading mankind and nature. . . . In this enchanted mood, thy spirit ebbs away to whence it came: becomes diffused through time and space: like Wickliff's pantheistic ashes. . . . And perhaps, at mid-day, in the fairest weather, with one-half throttled shriek you drop through that transparent air into the summer sea, no more to rise for ever. Heed it well, ye Pantheists! (159).[2]

(The transparent air references Emerson's declaration that he becomes a transparent eyeball when he merges into nature, bathed by the blithe air and uplifted into space.) Again sounding like Emerson, Ishmael tells us that the divine Pacific unifies the world whole into one shoreline and one bay: "Lifted by those eternal swells, you needs must own the seductive god, bowing your head to Pan" (482–83). Melville begins to adduce that this nature represents a seductive confidence game, a corporate accounting trick. Unification of the self with nature and the world becomes shorthand for incipient corporate globalization. As noted, Ishmael advised us that it's a mutual, joint-stock world everywhere, meaning that it was the chartered corporation that unites the world—that is, that takes over the universalizing function of nature or the ubiquitous Moby Dick (62). What pantheists romanticize as the bottomless soul of nature turns out to be commensurate with the corporate soul; Melville realizes that to merge with worldwide nature, to transcend the individual through some impersonal collective, is to awaken in a world that's everywhere the same under the corporate domain. As we shall see, Ishmael's description of reverie with nature begins to apply to the corporation, which incorporates all the world's coasts into a transnational zone. Ishmael's reverie with nature becomes Bartleby's "dead wall (Street) reverie."

Over the course of his novels between *Mardi* and *The Confidence Man*, Melville documented not only how views of nature were intertwined with views of the corporation, but how the corporation displaces nature, for which it had been only a veneer. The esoteric rhetoric that linked the soul of nature with that of the corporation crystallizes whenever Melville's protagonists grow disillusioned with their youthful fantasies that nature represented a universal, benign and collective force beyond society. In *Pierre*, for example, Melville's protagonist declaimed,

Thou inconceivable coxcomb of a Goethe [whom Emerson and Melville identified as the iconic pantheist]. . . . Already the universe gets on without thee, and could still spare a million more of the same identical kidney. Corporations have no souls, and thy Pantheism, what was that? Thou wert but the pretentious, heartless part of a man. Lo! I hold thee in this hand, and thou art crushed in it like an egg from which the meat hath been sucked. (302)

This passage dismantles the apparent opposition between nature (pantheism) and corporation; Pierre exposes the corporate collective beneath antebellum America's mystical conception of nature. In *Pierre*, Melville updates his language regarding joint-stock companies in *Moby-Dick*, treating the corporation as the ulterior force that betrays a young idealist who seeks to transcend individuality. Once invisible or immaterial nature is now incorporated in a generic, uniform production of millions of identical corporate *bodies*, kidneys, and brand allegiances. Neither nature nor corporation has any use for individuals. Stripped of its soul, the corporate body is dismembered instead of unified; the pantheism that would merge us into the body of nature turns out to vivisect shareholders into body parts. Pantheists' rhetoric of merger in nature ends in absorption or dismemberment by the corporation: Pierre's "soft social Pantheism" explicitly turns into corporate pantheism. The final emblem of that corporate nature in *Pierre* is the limbless trunk of the dismembered "American Enceladus, wrought by the vigorous hand of nature's self" (346).

Such a corporate existence might be more familiar to us in the Borg from *Star Trek*, who exist as a collective, partly mechanical hive that is nowhere yet everywhere and ingests all individual identity. They represent what happens when corporations and AI absorb nature and impersonate human personhood. Andy Turnbull calls the final accreted form of corporate behemoth a hypercorps, a metaphysical, composite, synthetic meta-entity that simulates a hive or ant-colony and lacks and is no longer run by any identifiable agency (19–21). Another fantasy of collective agency, Theodore Sturgeon's 1953 novel *More Than Human*, concerns characters who have evolved to "blesh," or blend, into a single, exceptional organism. The corporation is a monstrous version of such a mutation. To blesh is also to borg. Walter Benn Michaels, for example, observes that for Cyclone Davis, "the individual is merged in the money machine of which he is an integral part" (200). Though Wu doesn't address it in this context, the language of corporations has long been a discourse of merged/dismembered bodies and ersatz families. Wu traces the effect on national communications "as Bell was dismembered in the 1980s" into baby Bells (whose name again reminds us of the ascription of familial traits to "parent" corporations). For Wu, only government had "the power equal to dismembering the mighty Bell monopoly"—to unmerge or disunify the anthropomorphized and accreting corporate body (*Master* 240, 252). The business language of corporate mergers and dismemberments coincides eerily with the rhetoric of merger and dismemberment in transcendental nature. (That process of merger and dismemberment is usually another zero-sum game—Ishmael's repeated fantasy of merger with nature is directly undercut by Ahab's dismemberment by it.) Wu uses the accepted, inherited business language that describes corporate bodies, but it unavoidably reifies the very thing Wu is critiquing—the anthropomorphizing of inhuman corporations, and the attribution of corporate personhood.

The depiction of the corporation as an unnatural social collective returns almost verbatim in Melville's *The Confidence-Man*—which treats advertising as the devil's work—in the guise of the "Corporation Hospital" and the "soulless corporation of a bank" (96, 203).[3] The phrase *corporation hospital* likely refers to *The Case of Sutton's Hospital*, 77 Eng Rep 960 (1612), in which British Chief Justice Coke set the conditions by which the personless corporation, and its "invisible body," could legally imitate persons. As Sean Patrick Adams notes, critics frequently labeled corporations "soulless monsters" in the antebellum period (249). By the time of his final novel, Melville has concluded that in "the age of joint-stock companies," the individual had been displaced by the corporation as the locus of morality, polity, and economic endeavor (175). The titular protagonist of that novel not only lacks soul, but identity—he's an early embodiment of corporate personhood, a con artist who is everywhere and nowhere; he ventriloquizes every imaginable voice and impersonal advertising principle; and he can't be held accountable for telling people what they want to hear, even if it leads to their death. Like the corporation, he doesn't sell products, but trust, or confidence, in exchange for souls.

Again echoing Tocqueville, Melville's Pierre sardonically conceived of democratic America as a machine for social transformation in a passage that suggests that nature is naturalization—a pretext to hide the artificial constructions of a corporate society:

> The democratic element operates as a subtile acid among us; forever producing new things by corroding the old . . . [through] *Nature herself*. Herein by apt analogy we behold the marked anomalousness of America; . . . how strangely she contradicts all prior notions of human things; and how wonderfully to her, Death itself becomes transmuted into life. *So that political institutions, which in other lands seem above all things intensely artificial, with America seem to possess the divine virtue of a natural law*; for the most mighty of nature's laws is still this, that out of Death she brings Life. (9)

America is a new and improved machine for producing the new and improved. (Dick channels the spirit of this passage throughout *Ubik*, whose deity is obsessed with decay, transmutation, artificiality, and the new and improved.) Relying on natural law, rather than the "artificial" or politically mediated law of European countries, an anomalous or exceptional America allegedly could perpetuate itself by converting evil to good through creative destruction. But democratic America is a kind of zombie Borg, conflating the artificial (and artificial life or personhood) with the natural to the point that the distinction dissolves. Bringing death from life—or, as the Clash might say, [Chief Justice] Coke adding life where there isn't any—becomes the province of the corporation, not nature. Because of this transcendental power, corporations must be super- or unnatural—they must represent a second and demonological nature. If personal wealth once impeded the progress of the Christian soul, the impersonal wealth of the corporation in America becomes, in sociological contexts, sacralized. It's not just that corporate money talks, lobbies, and buys elections and elected officials in obvious ways; it now signifies the corporation's status as not only saved and anomalous/exceptional, but also possessing a soul.

This rhetoric concerning the once soulless corporation has at least a partly legal origin. As Robert Sprague and Mary Ellen Wells note, "In 1612, England's Chief Justice Coke declared that corporations have no souls. Nearly four hundred years later, in *Citizens United*. . . . Justice Kennedy declared that corporations are disadvantaged persons because the govern-

ment had intruded upon their freedom of speech." (507). (It's a coincidental
overdetermination, but an archetypal US corporation—whose carbonated,
colored sugar water creates addictive desire rather than slakes it and, except
for water, is as close to a pure non-product as possible—is named Coke.)
That soul has been a point of contention since the corporation was conceived
and its powers and attributes debated. Bakan notes that Edward Thurlow,
England's Lord Chancellor at the end of the eighteenth century, asserted that
corporations have "no soul to be damned and no body to be kicked" (79).
Though the invocation of a legal persona/personality that had no soul (and
therefore couldn't be excommunicated) likely dates back to Pope Innocent
IV in 1246, Melville probably also derives his terminology from James
Fenimore Cooper's novel *The Bravo*, which vilifies the "soulless
corporation[s]" of secret deliberative bodies (170), language that also is
recuperated in Pynchon's *Gravity's Rainbow.*

American writers long have characterized corporations as soulless
impersonations of living beings. As Aaron Ritzenberg notes, in *The Octopus*,
the virulently anti-corporate novelist Frank Norris describes the railroad as a
"soulless force": an animated system that mimicked human behavior but was
actually a mindless mechanism (*The Corporation* 48). Klein traces developments in the formulation of ad campaigns, which tellingly sound like military
endeavors that are designed to naturalize the notion that corporations have
human identities: "in this high-stakes new context, the cutting edge ad
agencies no longer sold companies on individual campaigns but on their
ability to act as 'brand stewards': identifying, articulating and protecting
the corporate soul" (23). Lest one think this rhetoric of claiming souls is
atavistic, Paul Ryan in his 2014 speech to the Conservative Political Action
Conference, referring to impersonal government assistance, complained that
the Left offers voters "less opportunity and an empty soul."[4] By implication,
the Right—the party by, of, and for the corporation—offers to sell people
their souls, because, in the perverse logic of corporate personhood, that's the
only way someone can get theirs back in a corporatist society. Like Thatcher,
Ryan represents a far Right that imbues the market and corporations with
souls and divests them from people as their existence diverges from corporate
dictates.

Jameson details how the corporate form itself can thwart historical-
materialist notions of agency and teleology: Marxists and leftists had trouble
conceiving of "some nonindividual, meaningful, collective yet impersonal
agency [the mode of production] . . . still somehow a "subject," like the
individual consciousness, yet now immortal, impersonal in another way,
collective beyond the dreams of populism . . . the trust, the monopoly, the
"soulfull" corporation, with its new corporate law" (215). To Jameson, these

conglomerations eviscerate the predicates of laissez-faire individualism; Jameson suggests that the corporation becomes simultaneously intangible and a machine, because it has no soul encased in a body (216). In other words, it's both dematerialized (and hence a kind of ghostly white) and hyper-embodied.

Like nature, the corporation accommodates contradictory traits because it lacks intrinsic qualities: it's an artificial amalgam of projections, fantasies, legal ascriptions, and appropriations. Quoting Michaels, Jameson asserts that "'the corporation comes to seem the embodiment of figurality that makes person-hood possible, rather than appearing as a figurative extension of personhood.' Suprapersonal agencies are unthinkable for the individual mind" (216). In other words, people fail to see how they're giving life to corporate personhood, and how corporations have come to be imbued with exceptional or supra-agency, because they've allowed themselves to become agents of the corporation. Again, the corporation is supra, exceptional, transcendental. We cannot con-ceptualize how entities beyond individuals—collectives, bleshed entities, Borg, corporations—think or decide, largely because they don't. One can tally indi-vidual votes in group decisions, but we can only fantasize that groups "think." Jameson notes, however, that for Michaels, corporations wouldn't represent the effect or fantasy of individuals, but the reverse; the individual becomes "a projection back from the collective," a structural illusion generated by and for the corporate enterprise. We don't create the Tyrell Corporation, Skynet, or Monsanto—they create us. If the king originally had two bodies—the first of which was his personal mortal body and the second of which represented society as a whole, or the social body—the overdetermined corporate body has supplanted that body figuratively, nominally and politically. As in *The Matrix* and many similar films, the corporation creates our bodies rather than the reverse. The king's "personality" once served as kind of carapace for the corporate body; we now are left with corporate personality, which is no human personality at all, as our sovereign template.

In the 1920s, John Dewey observed that under "fiction theory," which construes corporate personality as a legal contrivance rather than a genu-ine attribute, the corporation has no soul and therefore cannot be "guilty of delict," meaning liable, or perhaps culpable, for causing injury (668). In 2000, Thomas Frank alleged that "no one has seriously charged a corporation with 'soullessness' for many years" (*One Market* 226), but that pronouncement is oddly tone-deaf culturally, both retroactively and proactively. The ascription of soul is largely inextricable from the ever-expanding ascription of personhood to corporations. Throughout *The Master Switch*, for example, Wu documents the ways corporate executives describe corporations as if they had human personalities and qualities: Roy Disney accused Michael Eisner of turning the Disney Corporation into a "rapacious soul-less company" (*Master* 227).

Wu himself complains that entertainment conglomerates market films that appear quirky and independent, but lack "a unique soul of their own" (235); Apple computers were design marvels, but "are also machines whose soul is profoundly different from that of any other personal computer" and betray the founder's vision of open-source democracy (292).[5] Contrary to Frank's assertion, it's become nearly impossible even for critics to avoid addressing corporations and their products as if they had souls. Equivalent rhetoric frequently is applied to the specifically corporatized university; in a piece about the 1960s free-speech movement, Menand notes that Berkeley student activists called Chancellor Clark Kerr to account for his instrumentalist "Brave New World conception of education" and "the absence of values, the soullessness of the institution" ("Change" 52).

Wu also notes that James Rorty, who wrote a 1934 exposé of advertising called *Our Master's Voice* that "described the job's effect on the soul," asserted that the advertiser "inevitably empties himself of human qualities" (*Attention* 75). That description equally applies to the effect of the corporation, which uses advertising as its primary voice, on human souls and qualities. As we grant soul and personhood to corporations and their products, we also grant it to AI and inhuman things, systems, and processes, dramatized in culture by impersonal but affective "naturalized" forces, from aliens and ghosts to markets. (And as we do so, we cede power to deterministic "natural" or impersonal ahistorical forces we imagine we cannot control. We wind up saying "I was just following market orders.") Klein charts similar corporate pronouncements: advertiser Bruce Barton, who branded GM as "something warm and personal," claimed "Institutions have souls, just as men and nations have souls" (7); Marketing director Scott Bedbury purported that Starbuck's mission is "to align ourselves with one of the greatest movements toward finding a connection with your soul" (138). To be technical, this is crazy talk. That verb align is telling, because it implicitly acknowledges an attempt to co-opt and appropriate something human and outside the corporation that it never can possess; it's the glossy language a parasite might use to describe how much it sucks. Corporations are inhuman things allegedly imbued with soul or human personalities, again conjuring a kind of science fiction hybridized monstrosity.

Among recent novelists, Wallace most persistently treats advertising as the primary semiotic discourse of our culture, which generates and channels our desire and the way we communicate; and he was clearly aware of the role and history of corporate souls within that system. In *The Pale King*, whose title conjures the ruler of a kind of corporate wasteland, or a fisher king whose body is wasting away, Wallace's characters repeatedly invoke that now familiar "damn soulless corporation," and address the corporate form as responsible for, and a gauge of, how we've abdicated our own citizenship:

"Something has happened where we've decided on a personal level that it's all right to abdicate our personal responsibility to the common good. . . ."

"You can blame some of it on corporations and advertising surely."

"I don't think of corporations as citizens, though. They are machines for producing profit. . . . Corporations aren't citizens. . . . They don't have souls." (136–37)

But the overdetermined point of *Citizens United* (which was decided after Wallace died) is that corporations are the new citizens, and we citizens are the disenfranchised. What "unites" us now isn't nature but the corporation. Wallace consistently invokes this language of depersonalization, having a character warn us that federalist politicians will be "underwritten by an inhuman soulless profit-machine" that will "convince Americans that rebellion against the soulless inhumanity of corporate life will consist in buying products from corporations that do the best job of representing corporate life as empty and soulless" (149).[6] At every level, these corporations convince us they're better than the real thing.

In the private sector that now barely can be distinguished from the public, Clay Timon, chairman of Landor Associates, the influential branding firm, insists that corporations, as brands, do have souls, which enable them to generate emotional connections with consumers (Bakan 26). David Allen presents a similar narrative regarding how corporate managers sought, in effect, to ensoul the corporate body: "Having secured legal standing as people under the Constitution by the mid 1800s, corporations began looking for other ways to establish their humanness. In the 1900s, corporations began focusing on social welfare issues and public relations to convince people they had a soul" (24–25).

In practice, the corporate personality or person emerges as a kind of immortalized but also normalized sociopath, one that's also situationally incapable of understanding itself. Naturalized, and sounding like Emerson addressing the unassailable Laws of Nature, the Clare Corporation's CEO in Powers's novel *Gain* contends, "The market cannot be 'corrected.' It cannot be 'wrong'" (338). (Žižek notes that "direct reference to extra-ideological coercion (of the market for example) is an ideological gesture *par excellence*": as he adds, in terms relevant to my discussion of advertising, "the market and mass media are dialectically interconnected") ("Mapping" 15). In terms of maintaining a "coherent" corporate personhood, the force "of the concept of the market lies in its 'totalizing' structure . . . its capacity to afford a model of a social totality" (Jameson 272). The market provides what Jameson calls "an interpersonal mechanism" that's actually an impersonal network that "substitutes" for human behavior and ethics—what one of Wallace's characters calls the corporation's "fugue of evaded responsibility"

(273; Wallace 137). Powers's CEO also tells us to "remember that business is not some autonomous machine," but is run only by a group of people. But such declarations can reify corporate behavior by attributing human agency to an impersonal agglomeration (338). The fantasy that individuals can act as spokes in this machine functions as a kind of classic liberal safety valve and allows the system to continue functioning ad infinitum. If corporations were people, we would consider many pathological liars, and in some cases mass murderers: Exxon, Enron, Union Carbide, GE, PG&E, Halliburton, Lockheed Martin, Monsanto, Raytheon, Philip Morris, BP, Chevron, and, less directly, corporations such as McDonald's, MCI, General Motors, and so on, have harmed millions of people. Even when a corporation such as Google proclaims its (since retracted) imperative is "do no evil," it has the ring of "arbeit macht frei."

Chapter Twenty-Four

Extremely Hostile Takeovers

Because it is, among other things, immortal under the law, the corporation exits in a separate sphere from historically bound people. Ironically, corporations have become the kind of stateless, nomadic, and post-human entities that theorists such as Deleuze might have endorsed in other contexts. Corporations co-opt those human qualities that will benefit them, while maximizing their "post"- or supra-human attributes and denying human characteristics that could expose them to liability. Paradoxically, the law itself situates the corporation as ontologically beyond the laws of nature and men. Chief Justice Marshall wrote in the aforementioned *Dartmouth College v. Woodward*, 4 Wheat. At 636, that the corporation, created by law, represents the form

> best calculated to effect the object for which it was created. Among the most important are *immortality*, and, if the expression may be allowed, *individuality*; properties by which a perpetual succession of many persons are considered as the same, and may act as a single individual. They enable a corporation to manage its own affairs and to hold property without the perplexing intricacies, the hazardous and endless necessity of perpetual conveyances for the purpose of transmitting it from hand to hand. It is chiefly for the purpose of clothing bodies of men, *in succession*, with these qualities and capacities that corporations were invented and are in use.

This language echoes that of the Bill of Rights, which reserves to the states those unenumerated powers not delegated to the federal government. Herbert Hovenkamp reminds us of a fact that courts often forget: that corporation have

> only those powers granted to [them] by the sovereign. Already in 1880, a Maryland court held that while a legislature may not forbid natural persons from

paying non-cash wages, it could do so to corporate employers, as long as the state had retained the power to amend the corporate charter. "A corporation has no inherent or natural rights like a citizen. It has no rights but those which are expressly conferred upon it, or are necessarily inferrible [*sic*] from the powers actually granted, or such as may be indispensible [*sic*] to the exercise of such as are granted." (1645–46) (citation omitted)

In this Hobbesian lineage, the sovereign state charters and empowers the Mephistophelean corporation that will inevitably try to commit a kind of state parricide. Granting a corporation personhood eviscerates the rationale for their existence. Even putting aside how illogical it is to equate corporations with persons, the corporation's characteristics make it incomparable to persons in all registers. As Amy Sepinwall attests, for example, "Whereas individual humans die and have their estates taxed before bequest, corporations can, in principle, exist forever, and accumulate wealth over that duration without ever facing the equivalent of an estate tax. This capacity for wealth accumulation should indeed give us pause"(589). The corporation represents a kind of family dynasty, but without the actual family. It's especially ironic that Margaret Thatcher claimed that society doesn't exist, only individuals and families; it would be more accurate to contend that individuals and families no longer exist, only corporations. As I address in more detail, after taking over the role of nature, the corporation takes over aspects of social and familial relations.

But in its very creation, the corporation welds and wields incommensurate qualities, for example immortality and individuality. Individuals cannot be immortal, and corporations (or other transcendentally impersonal entities) cannot be individuals; imbuing a single entity with both qualities produces something monstrous. The corporation here combines some of the same attributes that made Emersonian nature demonological and dangerous. But, as Jameson observes, "being immortal, the corporation also stills those fears of death and dying aroused . . . by individual consumption" (216). In other words, the corporation generates a kind of biofeedback loop, creating a disease to sell us a cure, generating the biological person from the legal fiction. In this light, the *Matrix* films are meditations on the false reality of consumer identity. Of course, numerous corporate advertisers began using that film's image of the blue and red pill to convince you that buying something would restore your lost freedom. It's part of co-optive corporate symbolism that a corporation now uses the aptly named Agent Smith, who also is a corporate proxy, to advertise pharmaceuticals. This move is akin to selling cigarettes by flashing images of skulls and crossbones, or the members of the final iteration of the rock group Starship complaining, in a song none of its members wrote, that corporations are always changing their names.

Chapter Twenty-Five

A Little Less than Kin

Welcome to the Discount Shoe Warehouse Family!

—Promotional DSW email header

This idea of impersonal immortality affects many spheres, especially those of individual and "familial" subjectivity. Lyons observes "that it is not just the family that is the productive site of citizenship but . . . the corporation [that now operates] within this intimate public sphere" (98). One of David Mitchell's characters in *Ghostwritten* has a similar "insight coming on. "We're a corporation. A top-line Corporation. But that's not all we are. Nile, my word no. We are a family!" (102–3). As we also see in Powers's work, the corporation routinely takes over the role of the family. By the end of *Gain*, a corporate "family" name has presided over generations that die in its service and as a result of its unnatural precedence over individuals. Roland Marchand observes that by the 1940s, US corporations that wanted to be perceived as "corporations with a soul" moved from invoking images of teams to images of a Victorian family to create an impression of a paternalistic hierarchy, here particularly in the context of codifying workers' gendered functions (107). As Bose and Lyons attest, corporate narratives frequently "invoke the trope of the family to obfuscate the relations of production and the division of labor that they must organize and regulate" (9). Consider the dissonance of repeatedly hearing about "Johnson & Johnson, a Family Company," and the frequency with which corporations rely on terminology such as "parent corporation." Safeway sends out emails telling you another corporation (e.g., a delivery or food preparation corporation) has joined "its family." Corporations often try to attach family designations, figureheads, or humanizing connotations to their wholly impersonal identities or products, for example,

Ma and Baby Bell; Papa John's; Aunt Jemima; Uncle Ben; Colonel Sanders; Drs. Pepper, Scholls, and Oetker, Wendy's, and so on. As Klein observes of such fabrications, they help construct "the corporate "personality," uniquely named, packaged and advertised," or what Vance Packard called the "packaged soul" (6; 193). These more-than-distant relations are CGI shills for the alien corporation with a fake human face. Ironically, like nature, the family is set up as an antidote to or antithesis of the corporation but actually remains its complement, and it is often used implicitly to "civilize" or even authorize corporate behavior.

Others have discussed the contrast in different contexts, but one can find an accessible example of how popular culture addresses the encroachment of corporate culture into family life in *The Sopranos* episode in which the associates of the mob boss Tony Soprano attempt to shake down a corporate coffee chain for protection money. The besieged manager working at the counter tells the gangsters he'd like to comply, but can't because corporate headquarters—in this case, literal bean counters—don't allow local employees any discretion over funds. The gangsters shake their heads at what the country is coming to. (This scene effectively dramatizes/plagiarizes the ending monologue of *Casino*, in which the Sam Rothstein character complains that corporations have taken over all the Las Vegas casinos.)[1] The episode presents a pastiche of ersatz nostalgia, but, like many other cable series, it suggests that the criminal enterprise is more honest than the corporate one—at least with criminal families you're dealing with human beings or human pathology. Gangsters are often romanticized as outlaws, but also because they're *not* corporate—they're relatively independent, sometimes connected to family, and driven by human passions. A source for *The Sopranos*, *The Godfather* films also pit the family against the corporate enterprise— Michael Corleone emerges as the human face of the Cosa Nostra, cast against a corrupt Nevada casino bureaucracy, corrupt corporate politicians, and corporate cronyism. But in corporate culture, the family, especially the criminal/ outlaw family, isn't just a false alternative to the corporation, but its flip side.

In *Gain*, Clare's first CEO from outside the family dynasty, Franklin Kennibar Sr., enumerates a list of the purposes of business, a sequence that begins with "to make a profit," pivots through "to promote the general welfare" and "to expand," and ends with "to figure out the purpose of business." To these he thinks of adding as his last rationale, "to beat death" (337, 349–50). (After the death of its final main protagonist, the novel ends with a character thinking "it might be time for the little group of them to incorporate" [353].) Kennibar Jr.'s name suggests the template for a parallel human succession that trails corporate continuity, or corporate sequels— infinite self-replication. Implicating the transfer and aggregation of individual life to immortal business, Samuel had seen "no reason why the corporation—no longer his to control—could not go on self-propagating forever" (180). Yet that's the same description Powers iterates of nature throughout *The Overstory*, in which trees are part of "an immortal collective ecosystem," which is much the same language used legally to describe corporations (197). Beyond the constraints of human reproduction, the corporation can initiate a never-ending parthenogenetic expansion that transcends individual life. In resonant cultural contexts, the corporation as noted adapts some of the key ontological and economic tropes of slavery;[2] in a reified conception of slavery, things of property, to use Stowe's language, simply "growed"—that is, they could go on self-propagating forever (238).

One shudders to think of this corporate we. Part of the barrage of advertising reassurances at the start of COVID-19; emblematically, this also is not an image that promotes safe interaction at the beginning of a pandemic.

In the corporation, collective, impersonal biography also overtakes the individual life narrative. Writers such as Powers and McCarthy narrativize what Robbie Davis-Floyd documents as the corporate cooption of narrative and biographical discourses, evident, for example, in the ways corporations hire academics—especially anthropologists and sociologists—to tell stories about them (141). In terms of production—films, media, and publishing—but also their "self"-representation, corporations are this culture's dominant aesthetic, economic, and ontological force. The rise of the corporation coincides with the cultural shift from individual (or self, agent, author, authority, etc.) to system. Powers observes that Tom LeClair's definition of the systems novel assumes that "the individual human cannot be adequately understood as an autonomous, self-expressing, self-reflecting entity, but must be seen as a node of an immensely complex *network*" ("Making" 305–6). As part of Lyons's notion of corporate genealogy, which Heather Zwicker applies to Bechtel, we can see the corporation as one nexus for this network (103). We likely have an ever greater need for exceptional and unrealistic heroes because we know individuals are largely powerless and irrelevant under a system of corporate personhood. Interested in transcendental connections that, in his paraphrase of John Muir, hitch everything to everything else, Powers proposes a "new genealogy for th[at] systems novel," in which his hybrid form passes "'realism' through 'metafiction' through relational processes" and "refract[s] the private through the public" ("Making" 308–9). Again, we encounter a new kind of impersonal immortality, which in popular culture is configured as a matrix of false consciousness. Too systemic to fail, the corporation that's too immortal to die can only be rebranded. It has odd and troubling affinities with the eternal "Übermensch" or superman, all the more ironically since those figures are highly nationalistic; it's become a super-being with super-rights, exceptionalism embodied. According to Frank, management theorists "announced that the corporation, as a creature called into existence by the market, was of a special and even a superhuman nature," and, most absurdly, a vital force of democratization (*One Market* 220–21).[3] (The Amazon series *The Boys* broadly correlates corporate culture with superhero culture and fascism.) As a kind of enhanced entity or supermass, the typical corporation perverts the ideals of the unfettered capitalist individualism it putatively advances, since it's predicated on aggregation, uniformity, mass production, and impersonal discourses that impersonate human communication.

In *Gain*, Powers tells us that "The 1860 edition of *Biography of the Wealthiest Men of Boston* listed all the Clares" (133). This biography of men, even if focused on their wealth, increasingly shifts to the biography of the corporations that usurp their names. In many contexts, the Clare Corporation, and what it represents, engaged in a hostile takeover not only of the Clare family and name, but the principle of human identity. Jennifer Wicke observes that advertising material at the front of texts once offered "a complex site for the celebration of individual authors" (5). Now, as DeLillo suggests, ads exemplify the eradication of individual authorship. In Powers's novel, early business slogans hew close to moral imperatives, which attempt to induce sales by promoting salubrious behavior: "Be Clean in the eyes of creation, / For he is like a refiner's fire, / And his Grace like Fuller's Soap" (44). Powers here likely had in mind the preacher Henry Ward Beecher—abolitionist minister and brother to Harriet Beecher Stowe—or Alan Trachtenberg's analysis of Stowe's testimonial for Pears Soap, in crafting the Fuller's advertisement. Trachtenberg observes that Beecher's proclamation "fuses a message about the product with a message about the customer . . . an apparently simple syllogism . . . an appeal to the logical links among "Grace," "soap," and "clergyman" (137). Again, however, even at this stage, no necessary connection can exist between the product and the slogan advertising it; one could substitute any equivalent range of products for "Fuller's Soap." We're told that "he that hath clean hand shall grow stronger and stronger" (71); but that growth becomes cancerous as the business metastasizes, and its byproducts become poisonous. As Kathy Acker sardonically writes in her 1986 novel *Don Quixote*, "'Will not all the blood that is spilt lye at your door? . . . Freedom and money must be intertwined'" (119).

The archly named Laura Bodey then incorporates the toxicity of the Clare Corporation into her person. When she dies at age forty-two of the industrial disease that seems the inevitable outgrowth of Clare's practices, she becomes a counterpoint to the biography of the corporation, an entity that behaves like a cancer. Novels, histories, politics, all, if trying accurately to reflect where most agency resides, become accounts of corporate entities and systems rather than individuals. Maliszewski notes that Powers himself describes the novel as "a dialogue between two people: a 42-year old woman with cancer and a multinational corporation" (176). That second person displaces the first. The people who run the corporation, however, have no better understanding, ability to communicate, or control than—there's precisely no one else to add to that comparison. As Maliszewski remarks, "corporate advertising attempts to make the company human" (179), but its effect is to dehumanize people, and its goal is to manipulate desire rather than confirm human values.

Where Powers dramatizes how corporations usurp the identities of individuals, Pynchon proposes that modern war functions as a corporate enterprise that takes over the actual and semiotic economy. In *Gravity's Rainbow*, Pynchon delineates how twentieth-century corporations behave against the backdrop of largely theatrical wars that serve as covers to advance their interests. In that novel, the German rocket engineer Wernher von Braun claims that "Nature does not know extinction; all it knows is transformation. Everything science has taught me, and continues to teach me, strengthens my belief in the continuity of our spiritual existence after death" (1). (Ben Clare in *Gain* concludes that "If Nature were no more than eternal transformation, Man's meet and right pursuit consisted in emulating her" [79].) Such natural transformation morphs into an attribute of impersonal corporate immortality. For Pynchon, the equally personified war and impersonal corporation again supplant a personified (but impersonal) transcendental nature. Pynchon also intimates that immortal corporations are by their nature at war with mortal consumers and civilian populations.

In *Gravity's Rainbow*, the personified war "keep[s] things alive. *Things*," to restructure them for its own purposes (751). We're warmed not to "forget the real business of the war is buying and selling. The mass nature of wartime death serves as a spectacle, as diversion from the real movements of the War. The true war is a celebration of markets. Organic markets (122). A specialized kind of personified corporation, the war breaks down objects, and wants them only as things, weapons, converted material; it has no use for "folk-consciousness," for folk, in any form. Rather, the "War needs coal," "The War needs electricity," and perhaps especially "your war identity" (181, 152, 133, 136). Yet Pynchon suggests that this personified war represents a form of naturalized and essentialized economy. Through the war's economic transformations, all things, from weapons to people, are recycled as impersonal objects: "The children have unfolded last year's toys and found *reincarnated* spam tins . . . the unavoidable side to the Christmas game. In the months between, they played with real Spam tins—tanks, tankdestroyers, pillboxes, dreadnoughts " (133). We again encounter the idea that impersonal reincarnation is the domain not of nature or God, but the war, which is a manifestation of a corporate enterprise.

One of the war's characteristic foods—Spam—is therefore associated with the war's weapons, and is, along with the food container, converted into those weapons. It is war that knows no extinction in this text and that controls natural transformation and resurrection. Weapons and fragments of people, rather than actual people, are perpetually reincarnated: "These melted machine guns will show up now and then in the strangest places," such as James Jello's bed, since he "kept a melted Hotchkiss in his rooms." Such disingenuous disguise renders people inanimate, like the weapons that "come in many nationalities, and manage to fit in ethnically wherever they go" (696–99). Without national identity, weapons are reincarnated so fast that they retain no intrinsic essence and adapt themselves to whatever shape they're thrust into; plastic beings and objects are reconstituted into transnational objects in a corporate process that mimics and supplants nature. This resurrection reflects the ways corporations control and disguise the identity and source of resources. For Pynchon, the personified but faceless war is represented by the corporate control of technology: "outfits like Shell, with no real country" (243). These are revealed as "Dutch Shell . . . British Shell . . . Shell Mex House, for Christ's sake" (251). Pynchon focuses on the name Shell to highlight the lack of interiority, of soul, of the post-national war and corporation; their identity is predicated on sleight of hand transformation—like Moby Dick, they cannot be located anywhere. Pynchon's characterization of the personified/embodied war or war corporation dovetails with what Lyons aptly calls "The Shell Game of Corporate Personhood," which involves a "legal and narrative shell game, in which the locus of responsibility is perpetually in play and thus impossible to pin down" (102, 105). Capturing the impersonal and diffuse character of the corporate enterprise, Powers too writes, "Real business doesn't care diddly for its regional agents. . . . [There's n]othing an anarchist could ever hit, even in imagination" (*Gain* 257). The emblematic corporation is precisely not regional, but worldwide, undifferentiable in time and space, a weapon that comes in almost any nationality it wants.

This process of transnational transformation once promised a transcendental resurrection. But instead a sinister cycle is perpetuated as all matter becomes soulless, as Pynchon describes: "Old toothpaste tubes are emptied and returned to the War . . . waiting now—it is true return—to be melted for solder, for plate, alloyed for casting, bearings, gasketry" (*Gravity's* 130). Though called true return, this repeated melting down and restructuring does not represent a rebirth, but rather the erasure and dispossession of human identity; you aren't resurrected as yourself, but as a tool of the war. As an impersonal system, the war relies not only on planned obsolescence, but on what we might call corpophagia: "It is the grim phoenix which creates its own holocaust . . . deliberate resurrection" (415).[4] A more modern way to put this is corporate disruption.

Corporate personality is also developed and contested in Acker's *Don Quixote*, whose anti-Romantic ethos starts with the premise that language itself has been too contaminated to provide a neutral medium for human protest or even open communication. As if in response to a corporate takeover of identity, Acker's protagonist concludes, "I am no longer a personality. . . . This, my first and final dream, is not the dream of capitalism" (206). As Steiner notes, "Our dreams are marketed wholesale" (*Language* 77), or as Justin Currie of Del Amitri sings, "They bought your beauty and your soul / Then softly sold you back what they stole" ("When You Were Young"). Berger similarly emphasized that "Publicity is the life of this culture—in so far as without publicity capitalism couldn't survive—and at the same time publicity is its dream" (154). The corporation is adept at targeting and manipulating dreams and desire to the point that we must abandon them as irremediably tainted. The Quixotes are relevant in the context of imitated desire. The "original" Quixote defines himself in imitation of romances and (impersonal) chivalric modes, which are themselves imitations; recalling Borges's Pierre Menard, Acker's Quixote is a camouflaged impersonation of the first Quixote. Corporate advertising triangulates desire by making us desire what others want and ushering us into an endless chain of imitation in which original desire is impossible. As Girard observes, "skilful advertising does not try to convince that a product is superior but that it is desired by Others" (104).

Acker then impersonates the quintessential impersonator of Quixote to escape corporate culture. Confronting what she experiences as the lacerating contortions of incorporated language and trying to subvert it, and inhabiting male camouflage—here as Ulysses as well as Quixote—Acker's protagonist repeatedly asserts, "I'm no one, I'm no longer a personality" (66). She tries to reject personality completely so as to escape further depersonalization and to escape corporate personhood (perhaps echoing the way Slothrop in *Gravity's Rainbow* disappears from history, or at least visible history, to survive). Ironically, and perhaps necessarily, Melville's Ishmael and Acker's Quixote become vibrant characters by hiding behind impersonal or archetypal masks as forms of disguise and protection. Jeanne Gaakeer observes that the Roman meaning of *person* pertained only to legal rights and duties and denoted a mask that replaced the individual with a legal persona. The corporate person represents the dead end of that lineage.

According to Acker's heroine, who is as unnamed or pseudonymous as (call me) Ishmael, "The interests of these banks and companies are truly global, for the United States controls, or believes it controls . . . the globe. Thus, the multi-national corporations form an integrated economic system which must be protected" (73). This system is the same universal network that Powers references, which siphons personality and language in one direction from persons to things.[5] The vast majority of information and entertainment today is mediated through corporations: giant media companies from Hollywood studios to Clear Channel control the movies you see, the songs you hear, the stories you read. Except for a few of what DeLillo in *Mao II* calls the last free-lances—individual writers who work for themselves—even most artists distribute their work through corporations. (One is reminded of Emerson's insistence that he would be the last person to join a joint-stock company.) As Rushkoff notes, even independent journalists must rely on "corporatized media for dissemination" (*Life* 218). You can seek out independent artists, but they represent a tiny percentage of cultural output, and their work usually can reach only a minimal audience. In many ways, such safety valves allow the corporate system to perdure as the dominant mode of production and distribution. We can listen to the bands corporations didn't package for us—but few alternatives exist to these Monkees, and there are few ways to disseminate culture or even live music that don't require corporate mediation. Activists might try to live off the grid by buying locally and avoiding corporate communications, food, and products, and such efforts are admirable and perhaps could have an effect if enough people followed suit. But like viruses, corporations incessantly adapt to resistance. As Wu puts it, "Industries, unlike organisms, have no organic limits on their growth" (*Attention* 22), and that virulence makes them, like Clare, cancers on society itself. At a conceptual as well as practical level, it's almost impossible to maintain an alternative lifestyle in a corporate culture governed by an advertising ethos. In other words, one cannot compartmentalize one's life. And if you engage in dog-eat-dog capitalism, it doesn't matter if you become a vegan.

Chapter Twenty-Six

And Now the Words
from Our Sponsor

We all directly and indirectly bear the social and economic costs of advertising. Advertisers get a cut of most transactions in the United States, enacting an unacknowledged tithe on the cost of most goods and services. They operate in a similar context to the Mafia, or lawyers in New York City; they assume sponsors and middlemen deserve a percentage of every exchange, as if no business could be conducted without them. Recent developments in advertising also parallel the rise of virtual economies on Wall Street and online, ones that produce less and less of substance and more and more of image; advertising provides no service and generates nothing of value, but we pay for it in the higher price of almost everything we buy, whether we're consciously influenced by it or not.

But it's critical to recognize that the advertisement is often no longer the parasite to content but the host: the content is the parasite on the ad. In many aspects of our culture, supposedly neutral "art" or content is no longer primary or even distinguishable from the sponsorship. Partly in response to the internet and cable television, the relationship between content—which at least theoretically served a critical pedagogical function in democracies—and the ads that sponsor it has broken down, and most content, from article to textbook to film, has been compromised. As Klein contends, the goal of corporate branding is no longer to sponsor content, but to replace and become the content (30). With all that it implies, advertising now is our shared culture. Most corporations no longer even view themselves as sponsoring events; rather, they see their brand as the event itself, with the entertainment or art as fungible, disposable filler (48). I won't read magazines such as *Vanity Fair* and *Condé Nast Traveler* because they hide and separate their tables of contents, and their features have become brief digressions from a thickening maze of ads; the content again is just an increasingly thin excuse for ads.

Again, corporate personhood serves as a shorthand for a series of pernicious inversions of what should be cultural norms.

As Lynn observes, the advertising industry, perhaps appropriately, largely has been consolidated (124–26). In Robert Reich's estimation, advertising executives make up part of the new ruling class that helps monopolize power, money, and information for their corporate employers (Lynn 126). Even within the industry driving corporate consolidation, local business, independence and individuality are subsumed by corporate universality. The series *Mad Men* also relies on a *Sopranos*-like nostalgia for the days when morally compromised but very human individuals, rather than faceless corporations, did the dirty work of advertising. To some degree, the show *Thirty-Something*, which situated Michael as part of a creative advertising duo swallowed by a corporate agency, drew on a consonant nostalgia; but the show, similar to the way the 1969 film *The Arrangement* depicted its Madison Avenue adman, situated Michael as someone who sold his soul and creative abilities to succeed. It was either realistic, cynical, or unimaginative enough not to offer any alternatives, as it pointedly killed Gary, who had precariously achieved an alternative anti-corporate career as a professor. But at any meaningful level, there's no such thing as an alternative noncorporate ad agency.

As Anne Elizabeth Moore documents, corporate advertisers have become more savvy regarding consumer wariness and sophistication, and they attempt to co-opt alternative lifestyles and behaviors that have been "decreed marketable" (6). Corporations frequently take on the personas of hip, credible, and independent spokespeople for their markets: the ad campaigns of a plethora of corporate subsidiaries pretend they're small-town, homemade brewers and artisans competing with corporations. Many ads rely on the simulacrum of an actor pretending to have a personal relationship with you; for example, a housewife confessing she never cared about dust, but has to buy product X to protect herself now that she knows what's really in it. Such corporate ads entail the parasitic confiscation and degradation of authentic human emotions and relationships. These advertising personae are forms of AI, masquerades of people that front for the inhuman corporation. Klein cautions that most objections to corporate advertising ask only for greater inclusivity—such as for the advertising to include and target minorities, or not use subliminal messages—but they never challenge the premises of advertising or the way it functions in terms of emotional manipulation, sponsorship, branding, and the assumptions of corporate capitalism (303).

Chapter Twenty-Seven

New *and* Improved

The Zero-Sum Game of Corporate Personhood

The quintessential tagline "new *and* improved," which is probably the most used phrase in American advertising, tells you a great deal about the meretriciousness and gullibility of our culture as it relates to corporations. The phrase is willfully inane: nothing simultaneously can be new and improved. If something is new, nothing existed to improve; if it's improved, it already existed and can't be new.[1] (As Huxley formulates the advertising paradox in more literate terms in conjuring our *Brave New World*: "'It's what you will never write.' . . . Because, if it were really like *Othello*, nobody could understand it, however new it might be. And if it were new, it couldn't possibly be like *Othello*" [149].) But advertisers assume no one would buy something old and improved and long ago realized people would buy products that promised to deliver inconsistent qualities. They're purchasing a fantasy, so using language that's verifiable and coherent would only get in the way. Almost no one even hears the phrase anymore, or notices it's a contradiction in terms, in part because advertising trains us to be ignorant and naive. The problem is advertising language is no longer a sideshow; it's almost the only show.

The phrase "free gift" represents another in a nearly inexhaustible array of pleonasms and tautologies that are necessary to advertising premises; the promoters of the free gift, as opposed to the expensive one, ask us for trust by exaggerating, disorienting, lulling, repeating, and barraging. Almost every word corporations use in interacting with customers is designed to convince them of something that helps the seller and hurts the buyer. Airlines tell you their agents are temporarily busy, as opposed to permanently (which in many cases would be more accurate). They also frequently tell passengers they can "gift miles," turning gift into a verb and communication into gibberish (the misuse has become so common that most advertisers seeking donations or sales tell you to gift something). Corporate language and praxis have devalued the social function of the gift by turning it into another aspect of consumer obligation and demand.[2] Before merging, US Airways told passengers they would "earn a 100% bonus when [they] share miles": you're receiving miles because you paid for them, not because you've earned or accomplished anything. Starbucks assures you that you'll "earn a bonus star" with each purchase, but you're not earning anything. OpenTable sends you summaries of your "achievements" (a list of how many times you've made reservations). Many survey companies, which are just advertising companies that conduct surveys on the side, tell consumers they can "earn free miles," another contradiction in terms. These seemingly innocuous advertising koans cumulatively assault our understandings of what it means to earn or give something, and incessantly assert that consumption is a form of virtuous accomplishment. Like attacks on the press, they erode our ability to parse language, political assertions, and basic claims about society. Language itself becomes unreliable—not amorphous or pliable in creative contexts, but co-opted as alternative facts, *the language of alternative words*. Most ad phrases are designed to convey nonsense, often combining incommensurate registers, such as the (usually pseudo-) mystical with the commercial: "Be one with your tires and the road will be one with you." But the effect is sinister and destructive to democratic processes. Believing that something can be new and improved prepares you to accept that something can be a corporation and a person.

A litany of idiotic advertising slogans and terms become part of the culture's basic vocabulary, epitomized by the endlessly used and meaningless phrase "best in class." Most ads simply are deceptive or misleading in their choice of inappropriate but appealing language. Marketing encapsulates the conscious manipulation of everything, and in many ways it comprises the basis of American society: anything can be commodified, falsified, and then sold, with little accountability. Ads are the vernacular of a culture of the incessant transmission of signs and logos that are almost entirely devoid of content and whose structure and form are all that matter. These are enactments of empty ritual, by and for people who circulate messages whose meaning is indecipherable, because they don't mean anything.

The basic grammar of advertisements is often used to confuse consumers at an unconscious level. The people who write ads are either illiterate or intentionally devising ungrammatical slogans and phrases: "Unlike x car, y car has more horsepower." Such language differs from the advertising euphemism, for example claims that cars are pre-owned rather than used; here the language doesn't merely obfuscate, but enacts the circular logic of circulars. In this context, vying to use the most invidious phrase in commercial language, inserts always tell you that you have been preapproved (or preselected or prequalified) for a credit card rather than approved. A show is recorded;

something prerecorded would have to occur before the recording. Similarly inane redundancies and fallacies apply to corporate language and logic at every level. The product that tells you it "has ingredients first discovered in Jellyfish" isn't just selling you a placebo, it's telling you something can be discovered more than once. Many people remember the slogan "Winston tastes good like a cigarette should," but few likely know or care that the phrase is ungrammatical or are disturbed by the fact that it conveys no information.[3]

Advertisers are often so functionally illiterate they don't even say what they intend: a recent detergent ad claims "Style is an option: clean isn't." Apparently failure is an option, however, because the advertiser meant to say "clean isn't optional": what the ad unwittingly asserts instead is that 'clean isn't possible' if you use that brand. That might be closer to truth in advertising than that corporation has ever come. Another ad declares "After brushing, Listerine strengthens teeth." I had no idea Listerine could brush—that ability would make it a truly remarkable product, and for once perhaps warrant personhood. I certainly feel stupid for trying to gargle with it when I could have had it do a whole variety of chores for me. What does it say about society when hundreds of incoherent ads make it from drawing boards to billboards without anyone intervening? These verbal debasements are rarely as trivial as they might seem, and cumulatively reflect the degradation of the way we see and communicate with one another. The perversion of language and logic isn't confined to advertising; it permeates most aspects of dialogue in contemporary society; our pressing political challenges, from climate change to health care, are packaged as little more than lobbying and advertising campaigns. The idea that we're prequalified inures us to the notion that we could have preexisting (or prepackaged) conditions (preexisting would mean before something exists, though I believe my loathing of corporations preexisted me). The preexisting condition corporate health plans won't cover is industrial disease. And a different dream of capitalism involves the construction of impersonal personality and personhood through the advertisement of a new world.

Chapter Twenty-Eight

The Whole World Is an America, a New World

The idea of a new world already relied on a kind of advertising logic even in its nominations. In the United States, the center of the New World, the idea of novelty was from the beginning a contradiction, from the idea of (new) Plymouth onward. New Amsterdam, which in a double Dutch doubling became New York, is the prototypical new version of an old and rebranded city; it might as well have been called New and Improved York. (New York is an iteration of New Old, a perfectly incoherent toponymic advertising slogan that combines purported progress with nostalgia.) The "new" of the New World initially could be understood only as part of the old and familiar, by reference to (Old) England, (Old) Haven, (Old) London, and (Old) Orleans, a nomenclature that helps erase the places and peoples that existed independently before them; or would the corporate advertiser say that the old can be understood only as part of the new? (As David Mitchell warns in *Utopia Avenue*, "Beware idyllic names in the new world" [416].) America was supposed to be original and incomparable (as Melville elaborates in *Moby-Dick*), but its newness is based on a distortion of the old.[1] Outside the fantasy logic of advertising, ideas of race and new forms of colonialism—which make Huxley's invocation of Othello all the more appropriate—are what most differentiate the New World and make it incomparable.

This contradictory rhetoric of novelty—our need to believe in fantasies that things can be both new and improved at the same time—is part of the cultural geography of the brave new world of America. New World novelty must offer the faddishly current as part of an economy of planned obsolescence yet associate that novelty with the comfortably familiar, often via nostalgia. In other words, everything old must be new again and vice versa. Advertising's emphasis on novelty masks a conservative atavism; the "new" largely depends on an unalterable set of assumptions and practices.

As many have noted, advertising often trades on nostalgia for a world it retroactively fabricates. Modern advertising's obsession with next year's model is connected to novels and novelty, the drive to find allegedly new narratives that will attract the public's attention, but it is also indissociable from the discovery of the new (and improved) world. The "New World" itself is a kind of foundational advertising slogan. That new world was settled in part by the predecessors of corporations, joint-stock companies—for example, the Virginia Company. We circle back to what Pynchon in *Mason & Dixon*, which focuses on the cartography of the New World, calls "the Dutch Company which is ev'rywhere, and Ev'rything" (69). (Rhetorically, ontologically, and even apostrophically, the Company replaces the Puritan/ transcendental nature that's invoked in the last lines of *Gravity's Rainbow*, where one might still spy "a face in ev'ry mountainside / And a soul in ev'ry stone" [760].) The Dutch Company's mission was to re-create the world in its inhuman image, everywhere and always, like DeLillo's Amex and Dick's Ubik. By the time of *Bleeding Edge*, published forty years after *Gravity's Rainbow*, Pynchon realizes we're no longer trying to reanimate nature with a spirit or soul, but escape the animated golem of the corporation and market: "Suppose the ruler isn't a person at all but a soulless force so powerful that though it cannot ennoble, it can entitle" (114). That force, which emerges as one of the novel's main characters, is clearly a corporation: "If a dotcom had an immortal soul . . . hashslingerz's'd be lost" (143). A devil that accretes personality and human characteristics, the new technological corporation (hashslingerz) finds new ways to create its own imitations of a soul, and divest the real thing from people: Windust, who represents the neoliberal alliance between government and corporations, has completely souled-out, and "his soul is theirs . . . [and he] can be ticketed with a harvest of innocent souls" (243–44).

In the *Second Treatise on Civil Government* (1690), the British political theorist John Locke asserted that "in the beginning all the world was America" (29). Thoreau updates Locke by asserting that "The whole world is an America, a *New World*" (IV, 421). In this arc from "was" to "is" to "new," we can trace the development of a critical aspect of the modern capitalist economy and its notion of the New World: it's predicated on a form of advertising that turns history into a palimpsest billboard and idealizes the putatively new (as long as it still feels familiar).

The New World, and its corporate financing, is connected to the initial formulation of the novel—which I, along with others, situate at least in certain contexts as a new-world genre concerned with exploration—and novelty, which is closely related to US ideas about progress; but we now tend to associate progress with technology, not pilgrims or souls. Further, one could make the case that, in protecting monopolies and proprietary information, corporations hinder as much as pursue even technological progress, particularly in the contexts of progressive politics and issues such as public transportation, renewable energies, pharmaceuticals, health care, income equality, and so on. It's not just that many corporations have thwarted technologies that threatened their revenue streams but that the progress corporations usually seek is to expand rights, markets, and control, a goal not necessarily commensurate with even technological progress. Corporations foster an illusion of the new, but their pursuit of novelty is sometimes restricted to predictable trajectories.[2] As Lawrence Levine notes, America's "ode to progress . . . was accompanied by a cry of longing for what had been," by a fierce and conservative nostalgia (190). Our obsession with the new and improved remains coterminous with a sense of loss for a world that never existed. What ads have come to signify most often, ironically, isn't change and novelty, but nostalgia for familiar clichés. As Huxley sardonically encapsulates the economy of advertised and sanctioned novelty in *Brave New World*, we reject something "because it's old; that's the chief reason. We haven't any use for old things here. . . . Particularly when they're beautiful. Beauty's attractive, and we don't want people to be attracted by old things. We want them to like the new ones" (148). Huxley's point is that this "advanced" society is actually conservative and "primitive," and terrified of real change; it uses commercial novelty as a substitute for authentic social progress, and the underlying function of such ersatz novelty is to sacralize immutability: "Every change is a menace to stability" (153). Typically, the more futuristic an ad, the more it speaks to anxiety about change and a fabricated past we never lived, and it suppresses discomforting aspects of history. Questioning the role of the new—why we valorize false novelty in relation to mortality—helps us apprehend why we afford such lavish protections to the corporate person.

Chapter Twenty-Nine

The Transcendental Franchise

In their adaptation to and incorporation of locality, corporations also help create an overarching universality, which isn't inherently detrimental, but tends to produce a stifling conformity that's dangerous for democracy, human decency, and taste. The uniformity or ubiquity of certain kinds of space is one of the trademarks of postmodern capitalism; as Berger schematically puts it, "The entire world becomes a setting for the fulfillment of publicity's promise of the good life. The world smiles at us. It offers itself to us. And because everywhere is imagined as offering itself to us, everywhere is more or less the same" (150). Citing London RTS (Reclaim the Streets), Klein observes that advertising and the incessant privatization of public space lead to the "disintegration of community and the flattening of a locality. Everywhere becomes the same as everywhere else" (323). Or as James Howard Kunstler remarks, this is "the geography of nowhere" (Klein 130). The transcendental and corporate utopias again overlap. One should note that there's nothing intrinsically or a priori benign about the local or the national—they're not necessarily more authentic, egalitarian, or transparent than the transnational in corporate contexts. But corporate control tends to monopolize everything and to "bury locality," difference and dissent (Harvey, *Condition* 265).

What was once the putatively egalitarian space that connoted Western democracy—space that indicated that rights and laws extended universally and uniformly everywhere in a nation—has become the infinitely replicable franchise. Such a commercial archetype fulfills another transcendental premise: that nature, which for Emerson, for example, was the guarantor of the US Constitution, is everywhere the same. The uncanny universality of nature is replaced by the uncanny universality of the corporation, whose foreign policy would be to make the world safe for Starbucks. As Harvey writes, in postmodern space we wind up with "a 'recursive' and 'serial' monotony, producing from already known patterns or molds places almost identical in ambiance from city to city: New York's South Street Seaport, Boston's Quincy Market, Baltimore's Harbor Place" (295). Oh Brave New York London Haven Orleans that has the monotony of monopoly in it. (Since the corporation has taken the place of nature, Ahab today might be jousting with a White Walmart. His version of transparanoia in part also already reflected a fear that nature was mechanical, impersonal and indifferent to man, yet still malevolent.) When Ishmael proclaimed in *Moby-Dick* that there was "No need to travel! The world is one Lima," he was satirizing the putative universality of nature, but also lambasting the incipient corporate homogenization of the world (248). As Melville's Redburn declaims in approaching Ireland, "If that's the way a foreign country looks, I might as well have staid at home" (124).

Harvey contends that "the idea that capitalism promotes geographical homogeneity is totally wrong. It thrives on heterogeneity and difference," and that might be true in terms of the allocation of capital and harvesting of resources (*Enigma* 203). For Harvey, "uneven geographical development" is essential to capitalism (213). But capitalism tends to produce homogenous spaces, at least within equivalent national contexts, that ideally are interchangeable; it breaks down sometimes desirable barriers and franchises time and space. Such uniform commercial overlays bleach the fabric of public space, not only in the context of malls—which generally exemplify the eradication of the small and local—but in the drive to turn all the elements of a system into generic, regulable and replicable components. Žižek remarks that "public space [has been] privatized to such an extent that it potentially suspends" the difference between the categories: "a shopping mall is like a box with a world inside, separated from the outside," but, like many advertising strategies, it also inverts categories, here turning space in which the public could interact into a purely commercial enclave (*Living* 263). The exclusion of those who don't belong, and the enclosing of the commons, are both related to the isolation of subjects who cannot be accommodated to this corporate putative universality (see, e.g., *Living 313*).

Postmodern, prefabricated space becomes a standardized grid that takes over the universality once guaranteed by nature or religion. The franchise is the cathedral of our new catholicity, our altar of universality. The American franchise relies on a pervasive fantasy that cultural space is everywhere the same; like the corporation and its advertisements, it's an endlessly replicable Platonic archetype, modified superficially to suit local needs. The economy of advertising depends on such prefabrication. In advertising culture, the need for novelty is balanced by the need for familiarity, which helps explain the success of these franchises. In the logic of advertising, our individuality is *predicated* on such mass duplication. The homogeneous landscape of the first world emerges from this idea of identical products.

What is the effect of living in landscapes designed for corporate personhood, in which the corporation is always at the center and the center is everywhere? An ongoing decentering and disorientation of the self. Because it always posits a nonexistent trustworthy corporate person as its backer, corporate advertising relies on a commercial version what Russian formalists called *ostranenie*—in this case an alienation from what it means to be human. Instead of surreal art, we're stuck in a surreal reality. As with genuine novelty, a casualty of the pervasiveness of the corporate ethos is the novel itself. The imperative to be new and improved, to be commercially novel, has displaced what was once a primary form of communication and critique in our culture, the narrative novel. Ironically, as Steiner commented fifty years ago, "in its endeavor to excite and hold our interest, the novel now has to compete with media of dramatic presentation far more "authentic," far easier to assimilate into our increasingly lazy, inert sensibilities" (*Language* 81).

Charting these directly inverted relationships, in *Gain*, Powers as noted gradually narrates more impersonally to pace the way our culture has corporatized notions of privacy and biography over the past two centuries. Instead of the public biographies of individual men, or the fictionalized accounts of characters, Powers narrates the impersonal interactions of corporate strictures and forces. In tandem with these depersonalized narratives come hyperbolic and histrionic representations of personhood. As Steiner observed, "the mass circulation magazines [that] purvey sentimental romances or tales of contrived terror now call themselves "True Fiction" (81). Corporate culture often claims it purveys such true stories, which are never quite true—such near truth, based on a true story, is siphoned from real people, leaving behind a gap that cannot be filled.

In such contexts, Powers (along with Wallace) intimates that the corporation has ruined the genre of the novel, its language and its epistemological ability to convey aspects of human interiority. The corporate formula becomes the formula for life writing and even reading. As Steiner concluded, well before Oprah, Amazon, and book club inserts, "the literary experience is 'prepackaged' as so much else in our technological lives" (*Language* 82). If, as Steiner also claims, "the main tradition of the novel is intimately interwoven with the monetary values and relations of a mercantile society," the rise of the personified corporation signals the death of the novel (387). As the corporate person is disseminated throughout the culture, the individual becomes less representable in the novel or any form of art.

A primary goal of current advertising is to go "native"—to embed itself with content. The parasite wants to be indistinguishable from the host, so you can no longer tell the list results from the sponsored ad, the review from the promotion, the research from the marketing campaign, the self from the corporation. One way to respond, as Acker suggests, is to camouflage yourself—to mimic the corporation and inhabit an identity not your own, one that will absorb the shocks and degradations of corporate culture. Acker's ethos is that one can fight corporate culture only by plagiarizing and exaggerating the loss of self that corporate culture precipitates. But such self-manipulation can be dangerous; we can further destabilize our identities or become permanently decentered subjects. Dick's schizophrenic/visionary characters seem to court this psychasthenia, or Deleuze's and Guattari's nomadic displacement, merging with their surroundings and the alienating technological spaces of postmodernism. As a character in *Ubik* is told, "Perhaps your definition of your self-system lacks authentic boundaries," perhaps because the space he inhabits lacks authentic boundaries (45). These characters experience an even more disillusioning version of the pantheistic reveries many of Melville's characters experience when they try to merge with nature; now, these unions are exposed as mergers with corporations. Many of Dick's characters come to lose traditional narrative boundaries, as "several memory systems are fused" (Carrère 167): Dick's personae often experience symptoms of schizophrenia or some loss of continuity precisely as they try to resist the imposition of corporate models of behavior, consumption, and impersonation. They don't blesh into some greater mass communal identity, but instead lose themselves in some pathological morass.

Chapter Thirty

Advertising Makes the World Uniform

The New World as the Whole World

It is a way they have, the universal Yankee nation, of being everywhere.

Robert Sands (II, 199–200)[1]

We'll wind up with a universal culture, like the American culture.

Werner Herzog, addressing the disappearance of aboriginal cultures, in *Burden of Dreams*, directed by Les Blank, with Maureen Gosling

Thus this mysterious, divine Pacific zones the world's whole bulk about; makes all coasts one bay to it; seems the tide beating heart of earth.

Melville, *Moby-Dick* (483)

This life, this organization, throughout the animal and vegetable nature of our globe beats as one heart.

Emerson, "Sermon CLVII" (*Sermons IV* 154)

His daring foot is on land and sea everywhere, he colonizes the Pacific, the Archipelagoes. . . . With these [technologies] and the worldspreading factories he interlinks all geographies, all lands. . . . Is there going to be *but one heart to the globe*? Is humanity forming *en-masse*?

Whitman, "Years of the Modern" (339)

How the absolution system of the [American] corporate managers works is most obvious in relation to poor countries . . . [and] was often publicly explained as "spreading technology."

Richard Barnet (149)

199

For a country that supposedly prides itself on individualism and is rife with division, the United States looks remarkably homogeneous and undifferentiated; corporate cloning has standardized its commercial landscape. In "Democratic Social Space," Philip Fisher describes an infinitely replicable, uniform American terrain, in essence the synecdochic transcendental ideal; any space within America must contain all of America, and "democratically" represent all American spaces (75). Any "one" can stand for All. But Fisher's putatively egalitarian space—though stripped of its transcendental attributes in his account—is more accurately the pantheist's zone of tyrannical sameness. Americans in this sense do live in a bubble, an impermeable and contracting envelope. Fisher imagines that the antebellum North needed to see democratic social space and US political identity as "universal" (89); but as Carolyn Porter notes, America also had a dangerously utopian drive to create a "homogenized world, a world without differences" in which "America" would be everywhere (494). That world is now less American per se than corporate, and it has become "ever more homogenous and universal across space" (Harvey, *Condition* 267). The apparent universality of US culture paces the way it imagines the world in its own image.

Nature once guaranteed a kind of universal franchise. To see beyond the particular to the "larger piece of the universe . . . the unbroken prevalence of laws" is to reach the end of difference, "for nature, true and like in every place," as Emerson iterates, turns particular space into ideal geography (*Works*, "Poems" IX, 338; *Sermons II*, Sermon LXVI,139; *Journals* III, 179–80). To transcendentalists, the unbroken chain of natural law makes the world one American zone: presaging Redburn, Emerson preaches that "All languages are alike in their structure—can be translated into each other, and all customs . . . the kingdom of nature is not a government of partial and manifold provinces, but hath one constitution through all its parts" (Sermon LXVI, 139). Emerson imagines America as a kingdom of universal nature, not a republic of men; as such, it supposedly transcends time and space and is identical everywhere. In *Mardi*, Melville mocks the teleology of what he calls this "universal and permanent republic," a nation that must always already have existed in order to define itself (525). Here, as Žižek might propose, it's "Capital's universalism" that seems both to transcend and validate US empire. Žižek suggests we might oppose this universalism through the "universality beyond Capital" that is represented by ecology. Ironically, he directs us back to the nature that capitalism not only replaced but revealed was always a fantasy construct (*Universal* 27).

Though the United States has long been an imperial nation that relies on military power to expand its influence, it also expanded through the dissemination of corporate culture, which seems to tether itself to ideals of egalitarian universality. As Melville's Ishmael concludes, the whole world is a Pacific America. Most transcendentalists believed travel is a fool's paradise because the world is all the same underneath; you can only arrive without traveling. Advertising promises difference and novelty, but actually relies on this universal, flattened world—a kind of a priori set of assumptions that never change, but simply unfold. For all its putative dependence on a dynamic of ceaseless transformation, the principles of corporate advertising presuppose a static and immutable set of exchanges and a fixed human nature. In a variety of formulations, Emerson proposes that "not a valve, not a wall, not an intersection is there any where in nature, but one blood rolls uninterruptedly, and endless circulation through all men as the water of the globes is all one sea" (*Works*, "Over-Soul" II, 294). We again encounter a mass body of nature to merge into, one tide beating heart of the world. But such precepts prove to provide the cover, apologia, and preparation for legitimating corporate circulation and universality.[2]

Some of these seemingly remote antebellum precepts of transcendentalism anticipated corporate universalism, and its tenets were transferable to both American expansionism and the commercial enterprise. Charles Waugh, for example, argues that Melville and transcendentalists anticipated the interconnectedness fostered by globalization (205). Emerson always advises us to renounce particular countries and "all local connection, to beat with the pulse and breathe with the lungs of nations" ("Demonology" 21). Consider how the fully formed disembodied corporation, as Robert Foster indicates, differs from other forms of enterprise: "What troubled critics of the corporation in the early twentieth century was not only the scale of business but also its dispersed and delocalized structure of ownership," which meant its presence was universal but its responsibility unlocatable (99). We again see how thin the line can be separating Emerson's discourse from that of American imperialism: as Harvey writes, such a project implied "spatial fragmentation through planned coordination. And how could that be done except through 'pulverizing' preexisting space in some manner?" (*Condition* 270) Melville initially might have thought that such fragmentation offered a form of resistance to tyrannical unity. But Emerson's transcendental space overlays local difference with universalized American similitude. This "shrinkage of space" not only brings communities into contact and competition with one another, it increases polarization or atomization. According to Harvey, "In an increasingly homogeneous but fragmented world . . the more unified the space, the more important the qualities of the fragmentations become for social identity and action" (271). For Harvey, each story "is different, making it appear as if the uniqueness of this or that geographical circumstance matters more than ever before. Yet it does so, ironically, only because of the collapse of spatial barriers" (294). Along the same lines, unique anti-corporate rebellions, such as those emblematized by bands such as Nirvana or writers such as Acker, matter more than ever because of the diminution of independent media.

The corporation naturalizes its manipulations of laws and local culture to create an entity that appears to transcend local laws and cultures. Appeals to nature tend to provide ideological justifications for contingent political and economic claims that putatively transcend borders. Melville's travelers set sail "to nationalize with the universe," but they discover their god and market are American, because the American and the corporate universal coincided (*White-Jacket* 76). Though the corporation owes allegiance to no nation, it often appeals to nationalist sentiments to bolster its universality, one that has tended to be based on US imperatives. Locke's notion that the whole world was once America comes full circle in Planet Hollywood, a premise dramatized in *The Truman Show*, which ends at the shores of a Pacific pretending to be the Atlantic, in a literalized bubble of a closed universe, and whose protagonist cannot reenter *or* leave America. The local American referent comes to signify the universal, collapsing the two. In "The Progress of Culture," Emerson emblematically asserted that "The war proa of the Malays in the Japanese water struck Commodore Perry by its close resemblance to the yacht '*America*'" (*Works*, VIII, 215). In 1940, Nebraska Senator Kenneth Wherry promised, "With God's help, we will lift Shanghai up and up, ever up, until it is just like Kansas City" (Barnet 264). Five hundred years after Columbus began the homogenization of the New World by naming all its inhabitants Indians, and 150 after Emerson universalized his *American* yacht, George H. W. Bush optimistically proclaimed at his Republican Convention acceptance speech that the whole world was looking more and more like America.

Chapter Thirty-One

Warning Signs

The word *advertisement* originally conveyed a warning, reflecting a cultural ambivalence regarding novelty. Newness and novelty long have been connected to advertising, both as bait and as a form of caveat emptor. An advertisement once admonished you to take care, but, in forms of "meta" co-option, ads alter the meaning not just of the words they use but of their own name. In nineteenth-century Britain, the word *pure* was used to describe dung, which some of the most impoverished of London collected for tanneries: "Dogs' dung is called 'Pure,' from its cleansing and purifying properties" (Mayhew 142). Now "pure" conjures the purported qualities and authenticity of soap, oil, and products you put in or on your body. Advertisers and corporations need some way to convince you their impersonal and largely artificial products come from a personally verified natural source.

Advertisements originally publicized the names and locations of a manufacturer or product—they demarcated things as specific, rather than universal, and correlated a service or product with a person and a location. The loss of personal relationships between buyer and seller that became widespread under industrialism meant the consumer needed some way to verify the reliability of goods, and their consistency over time (Hine 56). Manfred Görlach points out that at one stage of advertisement, "the product name, or the producer, was the only text left, as illustrated by Pears' Soap from 1870 onwards" (87). But as Trachtenberg notes in *The Incorporation of America*, by the gilded age, the "function simply to inform had swiftly given way to a mode in which information as such fused with a message about the product, together with a message about the potential consumer, that he or she *required* the product in order to satisfy a need incited and articulated by the advertisement itself" (137, emphasis in original). Trachtenberg also posits that advertising fully manifests itself when "society shifts from production to consumption" (135).

That shift coincides with an increasing erosion of barriers and conflation of categories—between facts and ads, news and entertainment, private and public and persons and corporate persons. Our identities became increasingly defined not by what we make, but what we buy, which means by the corporation.

Melissa Aronczyk observes that people don't remember products and companies as well as they remember people and places (77), so advertisers attach them to products to identify and represent brands. But the corporate person and what's used to represent it is always an overlay, a human bandage on a machine. As Craig Howe documents, nineteenth-century advertising generally linked products and services to places and individuals (to assure consumers that actual and hence purportedly reliable persons backed increasingly impersonal products made by people they would never know). But advertisers also soon began generating fictitious people such as "Betty Crocker" as stand-ins for corporate persons (once again, as simulacra of simulacra). This personification of companies, in characters such as in Aunt Jemima, often relied on a "real" person with a history that corporations refashioned and fictionalized (Manring 116, 112). These once human figures are in a sense almost demonically dispossessed by the corporation (as entities such as Colonel Sanders are uncanny even before they return as zombie caricatures).

As Sarah Banet-Weiser notes, branding is meant to construct an "affective, authentic relationship" with a consumer that mirrors personal relationships, but also an "experience" that, beyond the way Banet-Weiser imagines, only can simulate community (8, 47). Most obviously, when you purchase razors from Dollar Shave Club, promoted by frequently run television commercials, or join the absurdly named Hair Club For Men, Smile Club, or any of the dozens of corporations claiming to be clubs, you aren't joining a wine club or smile community. There's nothing ironically amusing about an ad campaign that tries to simulate human emotion or interaction and that pretends that buying a product will connect you to other people, create a sense of belonging, or enhance your identity. You're not a member of American Express or Ancestry.com, though their ad campaigns incessantly claim you are; only in a culturally impoverished society, among people who feel devoid of authentic community, could it sound reasonable for corporations to claim you have solidarity with them. Some writers, such as James Surowiecki, argue that the proliferation of consumer reviews and product information through social media has rendered brands significantly less relevant than products' real-time reputations, but such a shift doesn't fundamentally alter the way corporations communicate or affect people, only the way a minority of people choose among corporate brands (40).

If, as Robert Bellah contends, Americans increasingly associate not on the basis of moral or religious values but of superficial aspects of popular culture, such a shift has been at least partly coterminous with the rising influence and predominance of corporations (251–63). Berger reminds us that "publicity turns consumption into a substitute for democracy. The choice of what one eats (or wears or drives) takes the place of significant political choices. Publicity helps to mask and compensate for all that is undemocratic within [Western] society. And it also masks what is happening in the rest of the world" (149). Drawing on Benedict Anderson's work regarding imagined communities, Žižek suggests that through the "abstract media," we identify with imagined communities of prospective game show winners, entrepreneurial victors, or those who identify with other "economies of enjoyment" (*Enjoy* 27–28, n36). Corporations construct a variety of such images and personae for us to identify with, so we imagine we've some direct relationship with products, celebrities, and lifestyles that are, in corporate parlance, soulless. The endless and pointless conflicts of reality TV, chat rooms, comment wars, and fake reviews are also connected to corporate personhood; they're an extension of scams, impersonations, and manufactured competition, even when people are voicing their genuine opinions. Speech propagated in this context usually is governed by the tenets of corporate personhood, and it advances a corporate conception of identity and behavior meant to generate revenue, not inform or provide aesthetic value. When a bot generates competitions on social media—for example, which of these comedians is better?—it's posting a lure to mine data and generate ad revenue. The overarching drive of the corporation seems to be to erode trust and community, not build it, in ways that leave corporate membership and personhood the only option.

We can trace the effect of contemporary advertising "permissiveness" concerning truth claims, relativism, and taste across numerous cultural registers, and certainly into political discourse. The phrase "Swift boat veterans for truth" is the equivalent of "CNN is the most trusted name in news": in such declaratives, the claim is a meaningless tautology, and reflects a nonexistent speaker's attempt to verify itself by naming itself. I am what I am; whatever I am is true and should be trusted. Variations of "trust me" are the primary dialogue of Melville's *The Confidence-Man* (1857): as Melville offers in that novel, "'Sir, I hope you would not do me injustice. I don't say, and can't say, and wouldn't say, that I suspect all men; but I do say that strangers aren't to be trusted, and so,' pointing up to the sign, 'no trust'" (229). (Around the mid-1850s, corporations began to develop into monopolistic trusts that consolidated and virtually controlled entire industries. Trusts were also legal subterfuges that allowed corporations to own other companies' stocks.) In Melville's novel, many of the characters are impersonations, confidence men, or possibly the devil under many guises: we're assured that "Confidence is the indispensable basis of all sorts of business transactions" (128). As part of the long lineage of corporate inversions, the words *advertisement*, *pure*, *confidence*, and *trust* come to connote their opposite.

Melville's novel is focused on its author's antebellum era of over-the-top swindling. But Melville's insights remain germane to modern corporations: the goal of the confidence man is to gain trust, and swindling or thieving is almost beside the point. The corporation is out to steal souls as much as make money: "You two green-horns! Money, you think, is the sole motive to pains and hazard. . . . How much money did the devil make in gulling Eve?" (32) In the zero-sum game, the acquisition of money is secondary to the acquisition of trust and consent—to the psychological, cultural, and ontological functions of advertising and corporate personhood. The internet especially fosters the kinds of scams referenced in embryonic form in *The Confidence-Man*. These confidence tricks were the staples of early print advertising—for example, patent medicines—but they have thousands of variations online. As Melville predicted, in the corporate world, trust gives way to confidence. The following exchange between Pitch and the Philosophical Intelligence Office agent warns readers not just that automations and proto-AI represent destabilizing impersonations of life, but that anything without human agency cannot be trusted:

> "I'm now on the road to get me made some sort of machine to do my work. Machines for me." . . .
> "Respected sir, this way of talking as if heaven were a kind of Washington patent-office museum—oh, oh, oh!—as if mere machine-work and puppet-work went to heaven—oh, oh, oh! Things incapable of free agency, to receive the eternal reward of well doing—oh, oh, oh!" (116)

The confidence men in Melville's text, which repeatedly invokes 'some kind of machine" that is replacing people, already act as kind of corporate automatons, and incessantly question how we can tell if someone is not just honest, but human, and possesses a soul. I continuously see friends on social media interact with generational quizzes and queries from bots, responding as if they were reminiscing with old friends, when they're conversing with automated confidence tricks that mine data, steal passwords, and channel ads. More broadly, on all forms of social media, agentless, impersonal corporate algorithms (very big Others) now control much of human interaction, and for many people help form identities. We've allowed not just media charlatans, but automated corporate systems to infect almost all social relations, and elections and literal and figurative bots now mediate human communication—what we might call a plague of cultural botulism.

Chapter Thirty-Two

Spam, Spam, Spam, Spam, Spam, Trust, and Spam

All ads are spam, and they differ only by a matter of degree; as with CSR, particulars don't alter the categorical nature of the corporate form or its speech. And slogans of self-promotion are also forms of spam. Much as it endlessly reports on issues of "faith," CNN asks you to take it on faith, and enacts the basic premise of advertising, when it incessantly—to the point of being deranged—asserts it possesses the "most trusted name in news," "the most reliable news coverage," "the most provocative entertainment show on TV," and "the best political team in the business." Such assertions are reminiscent of the subject lines of ID theft spam. For less naive viewers, such assurances lose credibility and assert their opposite; but for most consumers, such once unseemly bombast seems to have no negative ramifications (beyond offering a target for comedians). If bald proclamations of reliability dismantle themselves, why does such bluster work? Partly through advertising, adjectival assertion has taken the place of rational persuasion, substituting faith for empiricism in many registers. Most news organizations and corporations say "trust me," like Melville's Confidence Man, who invokes the term as a talisman to ward off scrutiny and put the mark on the defensive (74, 80–81, 87, 104, etc.). Just as it's ever more difficult to tell news from entertainment from sponsored content on CNN, some of whose "news" is dramatized hyperbole (though notably less manipulative than that of Fox News), it's increasingly difficult to tell CNN's tactics from those of its advertisers. Often preying on the under-educated, broadcast television is increasingly a vehicle to deliver fear-based advertisements for one fake product after another (computer cleaners, diet cleansers, mint coins, credit checks, co-opted free government services, etc.). As Melville dramatized, it's confidence men who ask for trust, or incessantly use phrases such as "no bias, no bull." As soon as someone has to say "trust me," you should know not to. Spam emails often have subject lines such as "beware of fake pills." Spammers ask for your trust, and whether they can trust you. Spammers are simply cruder at presenting the same message as Texaco and CNN and come from a less viable position than corporations. Trust the man who wears the star, who makes the ad, who sends the spam. Corporations wish they could be boys who cried wolf, but they're artificial beings that can only imitate them.

As noted in another context, corporate sponsorship raises the issue of sourcery: there's no real source for corporate speech or art, but corporations finance and control most of what we see and hear. Most people don't care where their oranges or batteries come from; but as products become fungible, so does art. Corporate sponsorship has the opposite deleterious effect on news, eroding the sense that any information isn't mediated and slanted. In keeping with the premises of advertising, many people experience assertions of fact as unprovable, sponsored opinions. In many of its current manifestations, sponsorship creates conflicts of interest, unreliability, and bias, all helping to produce an uncivil society. If we spend our lives conning others and being conned, how can we trust or enjoy anything we buy in that system? In an array of contexts, language in the United States has become sponsored; there is little communication conveyed through any media that isn't filtered through the prism of corporate personhood. We accept psychological pollution much as we accept environmental pollution, thinking it's a necessary cost or that we're powerless to stop it. Almost no space has been preserved from this encroachment.

Most public broadcasting is sponsored, in a putatively lesser variation of advertising that in some respects has more insidious consequences; it again blurs and erases the line between public and private. PBS and NPR are increasingly sponsored, allowing companies inimical to the public good, such as Archer-Daniels-Midland, to attach a veneer of respectability to their messages.[1] In some cases, corporate sponsors have used their increasing clout to suppress programs, alter content, sabotage competition, and neutralize regulators. What matters is the assumption that everything can be bracketed: content is left subservient to sponsorship, whether with regard to a news broadcast or a drug study. Little reaches the public without the intermediary of a sponsor.

Ads are the most universal form of graffiti. I've always been irritated by advertisements on buses and trains—public space privatized and sold to the highest bidder. Every time you're forced to see an ad on public transportation, the private sector has captured the public sector and effaced the distinction. The need for revenue is always the excuse proffered for such encroachments, but it's the logic of destroying the public village (NPR, news organizations, public services, and so on) to save it.

The ethos of sponsorship extends to every aspect of society. Buildings and public settings that used to be named after people— ideally to memorialize accomplishments, but even simply to commemorate politicians—now are named primarily after corporations that supplant people. Arenas nationwide are named after corporate sponsors. The Meadowlands that became the Brendan Byrne Arena became Continental Airlines Arena and the Izod Center. The message is, everything's for sale: every coliseum is named after its latest, always dispensable and fungible "benefactor," and public spaces continuously are auctioned off. At the 2016 Republican National Convention, one gratuitously heard "Quicken Loan Center" before virtually every announcement about the proceedings. In an emblematic fashion, in a piece about a Chinese reporter covering the convention, Evan Osmos in *The New Yorker* gratuitously wrote that "Zhang stepped out of the Quicken Loans Arena to report on the Trump-themed merchandise for sale," indifferent to or oblivious of the performative aspect and unintended irony of his prose (16). It seems standard practice even for *The New Yorker* to add these designations: a recent piece about COVID-19-sniffing dogs at an NBA event began, "At the American Airlines Arena, in downtown Miami" (Iscoe 16). Whatever follows such introductions is complicit with corporate personhood. Why do we care what these buildings are named; why does even the putatively professional news media incessantly announce the corporate names of such places, tethering advertisements to news (unless they're being paid for product placements)? If these sponsorships are not in any way newsworthy, why does the media go along and provide this free advertising? When the Democrats met in Denver in August 2008, one heard "Pepsi Center" at least as often as "Democratic National Convention": eight years later, on August 31, 2016, Rachel Maddow announced repeatedly on her program that Trump was speaking from the massive Xfinity Arena near Seattle; those centers unfortunately can hold.

Chapter Thirty-Three

Advertising Creep

The End of Public Space

There's a new movie on all the billboards—what billboards? Outdoor media is culture.

—Clear Channel billboard in São Paulo, objecting to the limitation of advertising (2007)

As Mike Davis documents throughout *City of Quartz*, and as Bakan notes in *The Corporation* (130), the privatization of public services and goods is co-terminous with the privatization of public space. We're subjected to a barrage of more pervasive ads on what were once public forums; with the advent of electronic media, we've become captive audiences in our homes, on the road, everywhere a surface exists. Municipalities, for example, remove benches, or make them so uncomfortable you can't sit (or sleep) on them, but plaster the remaining ones with ads. This is another zero-sum exchange; we excise the public and over-saturate the private. Owning private property is ingrained as an almost unassailable right in modern Western societies, but we also have naturalized the bizarre notion that private individuals and companies should be allowed to own public space to subject the public to their private interests. Corporations have perpetrated a long-running, extraordinary scam in which we continue to sell our public birthrights for nothing and then get advertised the high-fructose corn-syrup porridge.

The escalating privatization of public space, from public broadcasting to public transit, is no longer just tolerated but encouraged—we might term this "advertising creep." If advertising isn't the primary cause of the privatization of what we once understood to be the public good, it's among its greatest prompts. What are the repercussions for our psyches and our sense of community when no public space is left, and corporations substitute advertising

211

for culture?[1] Advertising is cause and effect of the privatization of things that were once understood to be in the public sector—water, seeds, genetically modified crops, space itself. In this round of the zero-sum game, advertisers help transfer ownership from the public domain to the wealthy few and the corporate realm.

The unjustly obscure band Art in America began its eponymous album with the following lyric: "Walking down the street one day, / A billboard said to me what's your sign?" Billboards are quintessential ads, because they impose on and transform public space—they privatize the very environment we inhabit. (Despite the misplaced modifier, Chris Flynn's lyric offers a nicely overdetermined pun and evokes the language of corporate personhood to critique it, but it also locates a problem of tone; criticizing ads makes one sound holier than thou: "the waves are filled with shipwrecked fools who dare to sell their souls to the charts.")

Despite the fact that she couldn't confine even character monologues to fewer than twenty pages, Ayn Rand's favorite form of communication was the billboard. To the Rand Corporation, the billboard exemplified the freedom of businessmen to convey unadulterated messages about their products—a direct expression of entrepreneurs' individual creativity. With depressing irony, the image of that lone, rebellious capitalist is appropriated by the corporation and billionaires who would be the first to quash such a figure. But we've naturalized the notion that individuals and companies should be allowed to subject the public to their private interests and buy virtually all public space—for which they compensate only other businesses. Clear Channel's (iHeartCommunications') corporate model, from radio stations and playlists to billboards to concert tickets, is to universalize and monopolize communication into their one channel.

In 2006, São Paulo passed a "Clean City Law" that proscribed outdoor advertisements, including billboards—around fifteen thousand billboards were taken down. Their removal not only altered the lived environment of the city but also revealed what such advertisements sometimes hide: billboards were no longer obstructing the view of the favelas, or shantytowns (Harris). Like welfare recipients, the favelas are off the grid, and potentially threaten the cycle of consumer demand and consumption on which corporate advertising relies. São Paulo's mayor, Gilberto Kassab, explained that "The Clean City Law came from a necessity to combat pollution . . . pollution of water, sound, air, and the visual. We decided that we should start combating pollution with the most conspicuous sector—visual pollution" (Harris). Kassab is the rare official who doesn't view the commons as a site to be despoiled by the highest bidder.

The billboard's commodification of space enacts the premise that we always must improve upon (develop) nature. That notion is institutionalized in the law through the idea of adverse position: you can lose ownership rights to "unimproved" property if you don't build on or use it. Nothing can remain without being "developed." The United States has long ascribed to a Lockean notion of property, especially in legal contexts—old and "unimproved" land is considered "waste" that can be confiscated and put to better use through eminent domain, adverse possession, or laws of succession. Advertising represents the simplest low-level way to convert public or natural space into commercial or "productive" space. In a world of cyberspace and spaces of intellectual property, it's even easier to commercialize the environments we inhabit: all figurative geography must be "enhanced" by advertising. Even if nature is as socially constructed as culture, I want some spaces preserved in their unadulterated state, without the clutter and clamor of advertisement, protected from what has become a form of unregulated pollution. Several years ago I saw a German billboard that read "Our copper for your life." The phrasing was unintentionally funny, but its ulterior message, as often happens with corporatespeak, reveals more than "it" intends. Corporate advertising is never a fair trade; it's always a zero-sum game in which the corporation takes something from your life. All advertising is miscommunication, and a mistranslation of human language. This ad also evidences an emblematic hubris, and a typical imperious, commanding threat—buy or (or in this case and) die; our product matters more than life. The ad inadvertently encapsulates the corporation's pathologically reductive view of existence. In the zero-sum game of corporate personhood, corporations trade their products for your soul.

Chapter Thirty-Four

The Age of Advertisements

What's Your Sign?

In *Deceit, Desire and the Novel*, the critic René Girard proposes that "The distance between Don Quixote and the petty bourgeois victim of advertising is not so great as romanticism would have us believe" (31). In other words, modern middle-class identity and desire fomented by deception are based on a false romanticism that is, perhaps surprisingly, closely related to the lures of false advertising; we are incessantly told and tell ourselves pretty lies. For people, corporate personhood is an elaborate system of victimization. Elaborating on this concept in her version of *Don Quixote*, Kathy Acker situates Quixote—a failed conquistador who never makes it to the New World—as an errant reflection of middle-class vacuity: "being vacant Don Quixote looked vacantly at the bourgeoisie. She had no idea where she was" (201). Contemporary systems of corporate personhood and advertising set us on a lifelong quest pursuing fabricated desire that can never be fulfilled.

In *Brave New World*, Huxley asks us to "Imagine the folly of allowing people to play elaborate games which do nothing whatever to increase consumption" (20). We should also imagine the correlative—the folly of allowing corporations to play elaborate games that do no more than just increase consumption and colonize public space, public time, and the beings that experience them. In *Infinite Jest*, Wallace charts the "Chronology of Organization of North American Nations' Revenue-Enhancing Subsidized Time™," tracing the corporate sponsorship of time from the Year of the Whopper to the Years of the Perdue Wonderchicken, Glad, and the Depend Adult Undergarment (223). Near the end of his life, Wallace became the first "Roy E. Disney Professor of Creative Writing and Professor of English" at Pomona College, a kind of overdetermined manifestation of subsidized Pomo space to complement time.

In "This Note's for You," Neil Young expressed his annoyance with his former bandmates Crosby, Stills and (particularly) Nash, who sold the rights to "Our House" to advertisers. But while a handful of musicians resist corporate sponsorship, few can elide the corporate structure of the music business itself, and how it markets and advertises product.[1] Nick Drake's melancholy "Pink Moon" was brought to a new audience through a Volkswagen commercial, but the song is hardly about the joy of night driving. In a representative example of how corporate personhood/advertising misappropriates the human, a dark, slightly ominous song that has no commercial message isn't just tarnished, but arbitrarily yoked to a sentiment and commercial manipulation that violates its expression. One could argue that nothing is more innately appropriate or inappropriate about using Kraftwerk's music for a Volkswagen commercial, or a jingle written especially for the product, than using Drake's. But not only does Drake's song have nothing to do with the product, its tone and lyrics are incompatible with the context in which it reached its largest audience. This is another example of corporate ostranenie, the distortion and alienation of meaning not for aesthetic purposes, but propaganda. We've become so used to these ploys we rarely notice their eeriness. It would be no less jarring if aliens who knew nothing of human culture thought it would be acceptable to use building permits to express love, and then tried a series of random impersonations of cultural memes to convince people they were honest and enter into impersonal transactions with them, which they were trying to personalize in all kinds of inapposite and disturbing ways.

While the use of Nick Drake's song is a particularly egregious example of aesthetic deracination—particularly since he surely never would have agreed to such licensing—all connections of music to product are as arbitrary as the relationship between a box top and the box's contents. That process can make us feel that all meanings and relationships are arbitrary. Moby released an album whose every song was an ad, linked to a product and campaign: the album was designed as an ad. Viewers might have associations with songs used in commercials, but those songs have nothing to do with the products; as in any recorded commercial, they're human sounds arbitrarily conjoined to goods or services and poorly synchronized to cover up the inhuman communication of corporations. It's disconcerting that people laud the "synergy" between songs or ad campaigns and products, when the former are grafted onto products through the calculations of marketers.

Chapter Thirty-Five

Sponsored Language

Ads often use obvious or ironic lies, as if to divert us from a worse lie; 7 Up claimed to be made from Uncola nuts, distracting you from what it is (carbonated sugar water). The identity of most products, many of which are indistinguishable, is created by ads. The advertiser then tries to hide the arbitrary association between ad and product, or else draws attention to it and hides it in plain sight by using irony. We're taken in by demonstrably fake and meaningless associations between slogans and products and by spokespersons who put a familiar face on impersonal objects. These associations are fabricated; they're all the unreal thing. Almost every component of an ad is ephemeral and expendable, and it has to be for the ad to work as designed. Tyson's ridiculous slogan is "Keep It Real. Keep It Tyson," part of what we will see as an ineluctable pattern of using self-reference, gibberish, and contradiction to define and identify corporate brands.

Many ads pretend to convey the opposite of their ulterior message, or even not to believe them. The MasterCard "priceless" ads legitimate themselves by appearing to validate noneconomic relationships; the cigarette, alcohol, and loan industries incessantly tell you not to abuse their often abusive products. The ad that tells you that "money can't buy happiness, so use our product instead," is a confidence trick—many such pitches rely on inversion. In such inversions, modeled after the confessions of the libertine, advertisers highlight the pretense of truth: we're admitting we're liars, so trust us. Emblematic of this approach, which at least evidences a startling chutzpah, the Joe Isuzu ads emphasize that the spokesman is a liar and ask for your trust by assuring you you're in on the joke. Like Spuds, Joe Camel, or Wendy, Isuzu represents a modern version of Melville's Confidence Man warning you about counterfeiters. Bottles of Old Spice Wolfthorn shampoo proclaim it's "the product wolves would use if they had human brains and

if lady wolves wanted their man-wolves to have gloriously handsome hair."
As ads sometimes do, this copy emphasizes that it's facetious and pointedly
inapplicable to the conceit or the product; it effectively asks you to buy the
item because the ad is nonsensical. (Not accidentally, that rhetorical strategy
encapsulates Boris Johnson's entire political career.) The copy should read,
"this is the product wolves would use if their brains were as conditioned as
those of consumers, and they wanted to cover themselves in a lab-generated
concoction of chemicals that have no connection to wolves or any form of
life whatsoever."

As Klein observes, many ad campaigns trade on irony, camp, and retro
kitsch so they can make uncool products cool (79). But more comprehen-
sively, advertisers rely on irony because, as Nick Lowe would say, they're all
liars. The only way to connect with viewers is through lies, hyperbole, or the
pretense of honesty about lying, variations of the same principle: buying X
processed packaged food won't get you a date or impress your boss, but now
you can purchase it with a knowing awareness that it won't do those things.
The question remains, why does such dissonance lure in and provide a sense
of identity to hipsters? Ads can make consumers a community of insiders
whose only bond involves knowing, perhaps unconsciously, that they're being manipulated. Advertisers don't simply cynically manipulate irony; they
engage in a more troubling offshoot of relativism that slides into nihilism: the
means become the ends. Even marketers and executives, such as Larry Page,
a founder of Google, who initially resisted the worst features and goals of
corporate advertising, seem inevitably to succumb. It's as if they reverse the
adage of the Clash that he who joins the church will later fuck nuns.

In *Language and Silence*, Steiner observes that "motivation researchers,
those gravediggers of literate speech, tell us that the perfect advertisement
should neither contain words of more than two syllables nor sentences with
dependent clauses." The grave they've dug is now big enough to serve as a
sinkhole for most forms of culture. The language of advertising also doesn't
convey information in any meaningful sense. We've allowed corporations to
infiltrate and dominate our language and the way we convey ideas, values,
and our sense of identity. It was clear to Steiner that the English President
Eisenhower spoke was akin to "that used to sell a new detergent, [and] was
intended neither to communicate the critical truths of national life nor to
quicken the mind. . . . The language of a community has reached a perilous
state when a study of radioactive fall-out can be entitled 'Operation Sunshine'" (27). We can see the effects of such language on the idea of community throughout Powers's *Gain*; but we also get an enervating sense of new/
eternal repetition, a failure of memory in which no news corporation, save
perhaps *The Daily Show*, would be able to invoke or correlate "Operation

Sunshine" with its recent variation in the last Bush's "Clear Sky Initiative." Steiner believes it probable that "the political inhumanity of the twentieth century and certain elements of the technological mass-society . . . have done [significant] injury to language," which in turn desensitizes and dehumanizes its users (49). The profligacy of corporate personhood and corporate advertising accelerated that dehumanization. (Though far more is at work in this context, the languages of the internet also follow a corporate model and largely have become repositories for little more than a series of afcs [acronyms for clichés].)

Some writers, though I use the term loosely here, as well as musicians have started to blur the line between their work and advertisements. Bulgari paid Fay Weldon £18,000 for including a slew of product placement references to their watches, clothing items, and stores in her 2001 novel, actually titled *The Bulgari Connection*. As the line between art and ad is blurred, and as books become ads, ads also have become products themselves, or even TV shows. From *Max Headroom* (which feigned an anti-corporate, anti-sponsorship stance) to *Caveman*, the ad that redefines what it means to be human "evolves" into a TV show, an ad with an extended narrative (at least such shows so far have had relatively limited runs). Such shows are too honest, even in their supposed irony, for they reveal that the program now sponsors the ad. In some contexts, ads have become content themselves, as occurs during the Super Bowl or other major television broadcasts, such as the Oscars. Wholly sponsored networks have begun to proliferate, and air shows that don't just feature products, but "integrate" content and product, blurring the already thin line between infomercial, news, drama, and reality TV, the scripted and the unscripted. To redefine and "corporatize" individuality, corporations rely on conventions similar to those of reality TV— archetypes, selves identified with/as generic competitive tropes, and an effectively medieval notion of identity (characters who are little more than drives, and simply personify traits such as envy). That strategy is laid bare in the parodic but emblematic commercials that pretend to be mini-soap operas: the product (and product narrative) is intended to displace not just the person, but human personhood. Serious ads now often rely on thirty-second family dramas (averted accidents, grown children leaving home, breakups, etc.) that use products as placeholders for life events and relations. In some ways, such ads are the opposite of and have supplanted the long novel in our culture. As noted, the overarching corporatization of society affects narrative, biography, and reading (and it's coterminous with the devaluation of fiction and its suppositions about what constitutes a human life and its narrative).

Yet, despite general grumbling about how television makes us lazier or stupider, one rarely hears informed debate regarding the cost of television or advertisements. When Lawrence O'Donnell appears between commercial segments with thirty-second news "teasers," the content has become an ad. News shows routinely develop "cliffhangers" by hinting what they'll reveal after the advertisement. The amount of our limited free time we waste being exposed to ads that aren't simply irrelevant but noxious is unconscionable; of course, we need to pay for content, and entertainment and news are commercial privileges, not rights. Businesspeople would legitimately interject that they need to promote their products. But advertising in its current form represents one of the most inefficient and pernicious ways to communicate, one that's deleterious to society, free information, our values, and institutions that initially seem at a remove from it. Invasive, overbearing and meretricious, advertising is at the center of a corporate culture that dominates our private lives. When John Oliver lambastes corporate marketing pyramid schemes, he exposes the way such manipulations prey on the vulnerable and naive. Oliver understandably tends to single out only the most predatory form of advertising, while only gently mocking the form itself. But generic commercials, infomercials, sponsorships, and product placements are little different; they sell things to people by misleading them, using similar techniques. Are some ads subtler or less manipulative than others? One could say by degree, but primarily by degrees of lying. Ads pay for much of our entertainment, but we pay a terrible price, one to which we individually never agreed. We're so saturated and dominated by the corporate way of viewing the world that we generally can't imagine organizing our lives differently, without constantly being subjected to sponsorship, advertising or corporate power.

The culture of advertising is so pervasive many of us barely notice its absurdities anymore. When the E! network continually calls its shows "super new," the language isn't just mindless but designed to enact a kind of campaign against the viewer's sensibilities. Something is new or it isn't, much as it's new or improved; you can't make it newer by adding superlatives or through aggressive insistence and repetition. Advertising language doesn't just exaggerate, but debases meaning, of late in an increasingly accelerated fashion. Advertising represents the culture's overall race to the bottom. The lowest common denominators of bad taste and illiteracy are the bases of Geico ads. Insurance is among the most fungible and impersonal of "products," and therefore must be differentiated through protracted associations with catchphrases, jargon, sensory triggers, and fantasy personalities (geckos, cavemen, cartoons, etc.). Ads incessantly assert such mindless promises as "you can save up to $100 or more," (or "borrow up to $10,000 or more," etc.), which pace the prevalence of people claiming they give 110 percent. Such claims demonstrate the fact that advertisers know no limits and will sink to any depths. A recent TV commercial tells you "You can save, like, tons of money": the tone isn't ironic, but an attempt to reach the lowest common denominator of speech.

This pervasive illiteracy—perhaps the most salient barometer of our eroding standards—reflects the catastrophic dumbing down of our culture as a whole, and our passive, permissive or perhaps oblivious attitude toward it. We've let corporations dictate the terms and premises of our communication; it doesn't seem accidental that Comcast/Xfinity, a communication corporation, is among the world's most significant abusers of language. Comcast ads, which explain such arcane precepts as "the more money you save, the more you get to keep," are especially insulting. Such ads are so insipid no literate person could consider them ironic; they mean what they say, and what they say is you are a fucking moron.

The "save big bucks" approach has become particularly endemic. Another recent ad features someone saying she doesn't want her phone plan to cost one of these and one of these while she holds up an arm and a leg—maybe the point is to be so idiotic that people notice, but that perspective is probably giving advertisers, who might even think they're clever, too much credit. The slogan of a Nexium TV ad is "only Nexium gives you Nexium-level protection." That phrase could be an entertaining Dickian parody of divine language, of tautologically asserting I am what I am, but only a Dickian parody of divine language could provide that entertaining parody. Acura ads allege "strength is power." These ostensibly harmless truisms are close kin to the chilling slogans of political propaganda, such as "power is justice" or, finally, "truth is lies." Ads that inculcate phrases over and over—"Head-On: the one application cream," iterated multiple times in fifteen seconds—aren't just Pavlovian, they subject you to a kind of low-level abuse, and in this case emblematically generates the headache it allegedly cures. Advertising is conditioning; conditioner is conditioning. The poster boy for junk culture, advertising needs to traffic in this degradation of meaning, language, and logic. Just as people think they crave junk food, they crave junk culture that makes them equally sick in the long run, has little substance, and imitates the real thing. Ironically, ads raise the uncomfortable question of what makes something, from product to person, verifiably authentic?

Whenever I travel, I feel especially besieged by the ubiquity of ads; at New York Mets spring training games in Florida, for example, you're forced to stare at a familiar array of corporate advertising banners. As with most content, the game is a pretext to hold you captive for the advertising. The stadium audio-video system plays ads not only between, but during innings;

you're constantly told to turn to page x of your playbook to see if you've won what's essentially a ruse to get you to come into a store. On the way to games, you're subjected to blaring audio/visual ads at the gas station, from the tops of passing taxis or rideshare cars, billboards along every mile of road, and ads along every feasible surface at the stadium. A billboard along I-95 for a community college, an alleged institution of higher learning, announces, "Make it Happen. They are." It's likely that no one in a position of authority at this school realized that "they are make it happen" isn't grammatical. We're already living in an idiocracy. At diners in Boca Raton, multiple screens for the "On the Spot Ads" video network project a stream of commercials at you during the entirety of your meal, all cast as a series of flip cards, a name that reveals more than the creators intended, because patrons are being repeatedly flipped off, treated like commodities. You are on the spot, rather head-on. Menus at many chain restaurants come with advertising inserts: an entire network, Firebrand TV, shows nothing but commercials. Another barbecue restaurant in Boca Raton features tables that are covered in ads arrayed below TV screens that play ads, and all the glasses have corporate beverage logos on them. The rich and educated will to some extent be able to avoid and insulate themselves from such intrusion, much the way they can avoid living near toxic waste sites.

David Foster Wallace perceived that the need to be constantly entertained is another form of addiction, horribly but beautifully enabled by advertising. Like other addictive drugs, corporate entertainment is meant to numb us to what's causing our pain. Wallace knew how easy it is to become obsessed with the cheapest form of entertainment, which is the cultural equivalent of high-fructose corn syrup. He reminds us that "Whatever attempts an advertisement makes to interest and appeal to its readers aren't, finally, for the reader's benefit. And the reader of an ad knows all this, too—that an ad's appeal is by its very nature *calculated*—and this is part of why our state of receptivity is different, more guarded, when we get to read an ad" (*A Supposedly Fun* 288–89, emphasis in original). But the intensification of advertising has altered our state of receptivity; despite our resistance, most of us remain susceptible to ads at some level, but the more perceptive become by necessity more guarded and cynical when sifting for information. We cannot compartmentalize our behavior and emotions that easily or effectively. As Wallace elaborates, an ad is like someone who pretends to like you, but simply wants something from you: "This is dishonest, but what's sinister is the cumulative effect that such dishonesty has on us." That is, it debilitates our ability to respond to genuine warmth, human contact, or undoctored information: "It makes us feel confused and lonely and impotent and angry and scared. It causes despair" (289). Such ads are what the vast majority of us read and are exposed to most, far beyond any other form of communication. The demands of ads ("Call Today!") aren't just obnoxious, but, in psychological terms, forms of fascist imperatives; you're constantly being assailed and told what to do, and we're so habituated to accept these onslaughts that we rarely register how intrusive they are.

The resistance we do build up, our minimal form of defense, further explains why ads become more hyperbolic, elaborate, and in effect more desperate. Like antibiotics, ads are overused and consequently increasingly ineffective; but like some pathogens, they mutate to become more virulent. They exploit your vulnerabilities, and what you care about most: your sense of identity, sex, status, family, insecurity and self-worth. Each ad has to stand out more, sometimes by being more offensive, or by more hyperbolically preying on fear and anxiety. While advertisers don't want to alienate their audience, they also feel the need to escalate their tactics. It's part of the process of addiction that what were once dangerously high doses become wholly inadequate as we grow more insensitive or resistant. Through unregulated overuse, ads, like drugs, lose the efficacy of previous hits.

Ads also have become forms of assault: they're often broadcast at higher volumes than programs, which indicates the obnoxious tone they must use to rise above the din. Because we're constantly subjected to more boorish ads, advertisers yell "louder" in shorter bursts. Viewers reached a saturation point for ads—their ability to process more of them—around forty years ago, but ads must expand their reach in the same way our economy must continue to "grow" (another organic term incongruously transferred to an impersonal context). Beyond Wallace's "Year of the Depend Adult Undergarment" (*Infinite*), time itself has become sponsored; ads have to find new territory, new frontiers, to exploit, like the economy that must keep using more resources even when doing so becomes suicidal. Outright spammers epitomize another aspect of corporate personhood—any level of private gain is worth more than any level of public harm. But all advertisers are spammers, willing to waste the time of millions to reach twenty, so long as it doesn't cost more than they'll make. Advertisers are engaged in an arms race involving public space, which makes each ad less influential and requires flashier and more frequent exposure to compensate for ad fatigue, and the coarser and shorter attention spans ads themselves create. (Trump's reliance on Twitter represented the virtually inevitable regression of communication that corporate advertising culture precipitates.) In a form of mutual assured destruction, no individual advertiser has an incentive to back off.

Advertisers are aware they face the prospect of overkill, of saturation detrimental even to themselves; in their effort to colonize every inch of space, they make each advertisement less effective, therefore in their minds requiring larger and even more repetitive ads to compensate. While advertisers want to target niche audiences, they primarily disseminate material to people who aren't interested. In order to target their ads, they not only cull personal information like trawlers but indiscriminately damage everything that gets caught in their nets.

Fake news and clickbait, of course, are fomented by advertising revenue; most sensationalist and fraudulent stories on social media are couched to generate the clicks that earn sites incremental amounts of money. Such a system is a prime example of being willing to cause enormous harm to the commons for even a modicum of personal gain. (Targeted ads do little to alleviate this process, save allow aggregators to charge more for their consumer data.) Increasingly unrestrained advertisers use mobile ads; sliding ads; ads that revolve; targeted ads; crawls; drop-down, delayed, pop-up, and overlaid internet ads. The corporate shipping labels that one can print with prepaid postage include advertisements for other corporations on the side. Amazon attaches ads to the top of emails it sends to sellers; but even the post office includes advertising throughout its digital scans of your mail, endorsing private companies and grossly violating its duties as a government agency. Advertisers have commandeered much of the public space in the United States. In a variation of overfishing, the tragedy of these commons is that it reflects a depletion of our culture as a whole. What are the repercussions for our psyches and sense of community when no unsponsored public space is left?

Chapter Thirty-Six

I'm Not an Actor,
but I Play One on TV

Most people know advertising language makes little sense. We know gas priced at $2.99 isn't appreciably cheaper than gas priced at $3.00 a gallon, but every gas station still uses this pricing. That deceptive overture, the appearance that triumphs over rational perception, is characteristic of a wide array of broader manipulations and misrepresentations that aren't incidental to, but the basis of, advertising. Advertising relies on stock tricks to dissociate what should be associated with, and associate what should be dissociated from, goods and services.

Another standard advertising ploy to attach a form of personhood to a product is to link it to an appealing but arbitrary location. The dated but emblematic ad jingle "Ban du Soleil for the St. Tropez tan" encapsulates the attempt to yoke a specious specificity to an especially generic product. The phrase is so inane it's almost brilliant: the sun is the same everywhere (even if the weather is of course different); there's no such thing as a tan specific to a beach; and the tanning lotion has nothing remotely (or proximately) to do with St. Tropez. Similarly, for Virginia to claim to be for lovers isn't only bizarrely ironic, given the name of the state, but meaningless and arbitrary—what would it even mean if it were true? Is Virginia trying to be a company again? Would West Virginia be for abstinence? Could it explain why there's no East Virginia? When insurance advertisers place actors in front of the Statue of Liberty, it's a multilevel deception and another parasitical attachment to an image that has nothing to do with the corporation, a form of camouflage for an entity that has no body.

Why do we act with such exceptional irrationality in relation to advertising? Is it simply that we need to buy into fantasies we know at some level are only fantasies, as part of the same form of denial or masochism that allows people to smoke, gamble, or vote Republican? Why, for example, would anyone believe celebrity sponsors or care about celebrity endorsements: how can consumers realize that celebrities know nothing about pharmaceuticals yet trust the prescription of someone who precisely acts— impersonates—for a living? Why would anyone give credence to the biography or advice of corporate constructs? On its face, it's bizarre that corporate advertisers rely heavily on actors, people with whom people identify because they're good at pretending, or that they can move from one realm (of performative lying) to another (of shilling). The use of actors in advertisements, as I explain in the next chapter, isn't accidental; it's a correlative of the need to personify the soulless corporation.

To represent themselves, corporations have to attach themselves to spokespeople—typically celebrities, since they come with profiles the public knows, but sometimes equally fabricated cartoon characters, from Mr. Clean to the most interesting man in the world—virtually none of whom have connections with or authentic "biographies" in relation to the corporation. (Whether the Jolly Green Giant, Dolly Madison, or a celebrity, corporate mascots and spokespersons are "associational" but ultimately arbitrary stickers in terms of any connection to the corporation: anything can represent a corporation because there's nothing to represent, and nothing is represented until the mascot retroactively creates the representation. These figures, ironically, are meant to give flesh to the corporation's figurative body, which can have no figurative soul. Though not corporate persons, such mascots are on the continuum of corporate personhood.) While most people might acknowledge this abstract dissonance, we tend not to dwell on how disquieting the implications of this disjunction are. A particularly inept example of a corporation trying to co-opt the aura of a human personality involved Mazda's resurrection of Bruce Lee; its ad featured random footage of Lee engaged in martial arts poses, then claimed "might can be light," and that Mazda embraced Lee's philosophy. Such pronouncements rely on the same illogic as a computer chip insisting it loves you the way you love your sister. By necessity, the footage Mazda used as easily could have been used for any product; a dead celebrity, who needn't even give consent to be used for sponsorship, is the ideal corporate person (one assumes a celebrity's estate's lawyers also are easier to sign deals with than living personalities). I am alive, and you are dead. Cartoons, dead celebrities, and AI are apt incarnations of corporate personhood.

As another aspect of corporate biography, the advertising spokesperson is again the imitation of an imitation, an actor claiming to speak for a fiction. In terms of its function in contemporary US culture, the typical celebrity doesn't just provide but is a corporation with a human face. Or to reverse the image, the corporation is a thing attached to the face of a celebrity. The idea that Rooms To Go has Cindy Crawford and Sofia Vergara collections is absurd—few celebrities have anything to do with the products they endorse beyond being remunerated. The celebrities corporate media generates are second-generation impersonators, ones who also often already have changed their names, faces, histories, and personae. Before becoming president, Trump emblematized the confluence of CEO and celebrity, two ciphers coming together to form a perfect monstrosity (though his corporation is anomalous in most ways, save for being overtly fraudulent). The less there is of substance behind the CEO/celebrity, and the corporation for which it stands, the greater the need to give it an exaggerated (in this case reality TV) human face.

Thomas Hine suggests that consumers now perceive products and packaging as persons themselves, and that we find "something reassuring" in the idea that buying "a packaged product off the shelf is a kind of human transaction" (234, citing Stan Gross). With such considerations in mind, some advertisers rely on upscale terms to give generic and impersonal packaged products elite human personas. Ironically, most corporations rely on the mass production of generic goods and services, but they want to make customers believe each item is uniquely personal and distinct, familial and homemade—that is, the opposite of corporate. The contexts for such attempts at personalization are often comically absurd. When Safeway tells you, again without irony, that it's emailing you "handpicked" digital coupons just4u, or that various corporate products are "hand-made," it's not only attempting to personalize impersonal technology; in a jarring way, it's drawing attention to the risibility of its assertions. (In this case, Safeway repeatedly tries to lend a hand—part of its corporate body—to a virtual exchange.) Vance Packard observed sixty-five years ago that corporate advertisers had convinced the majority of consumers that artificial and processed foods and concentrates were preferable to anything natural (222). But in the past few years, to target the opposite end of the consumer spectrum, almost every food product has been hawked as gourmet, from artisanal coffee ("coffee made while you wait") to toast. Dominos claims it makes hand-crafted pizzas and Starbucks hand-crafted lattes; it's only a matter of time before Sterling Cooper tells me it makes hand-crafted advertisements and I'm buying artisanal condoms and meth. *Artisanal* is another reification word that can be attached to any cheap mass-produced product whose manufacturer wants you to believe is personalized, elite, distinct, and crafted. The term again evokes nostalgia for earlier modes of production that weren't dehumanized, but it is used primarily by the corporations responsible for eradicating small-scale production and the way of life we associate with them in fantasy.

Much as some ads presuppose a death wish—for example, those that contain subliminal representations of skulls and crossbones, danger and death—many ads target the masochism of their audience. Another malignant assumption behind most advertising is that we're so irrational or self-destructive that rational persuasion, and rational choices, won't make us happy, or even get our attention. Advertising is a complex mechanism for instigating and monetizing the irrational—and it begins with the premise that we need to be led to whatever we're told we need through the irrational. Advertising might speak to a desire to be deceived, and to become gamblers or addicts: we know we can't win the lottery; we know the product is useless or even harmful, but we buy it because we buy into the idea of salvation, that something external and miraculous—in a minor, but therefore plausible way—will save us. As Emmanuel (God) warns in Philip K. Dick's *The Divine Invasion*, "The hallmark of the fraudulent is that it becomes what you would like it to be" (152).

Chapter Thirty-Seven

Pretty Lies, Unclean Hands

If people know ads are deceptive and fatuous, why do they have any influence? Do people simply discount the claims and go along for lack of an alternative? Foster suggests that corporate oxymorons such as *clean coal* work "not by brainwashing their addressees [into believing their truth claims], but, rather, by crowding out other ways of thinking and speaking" about products, production, and "corporations as distinctive modern institutions" (98–99). Or as Herbert Marcuse observed in 1964, the then current phrases *clean bomb* and *harmless fall-out* were "only the extreme creations of a normal style . . . the contradiction now appears as a principle of the logic of manipulation. . . . It is the logic of a society which can afford to dispense with logic and play with destruction," whose dispensations eventually led us to a post-factual, post-rational, post–post office Trumpworld (Foster 89). The ability to embrace contradiction and unreality is the prerequisite and upshot of advertising. As James Davis suggests, advertisers see "no contradiction in pairing one work expressing—indeed, embodying in its bandana-cloth binding—a nostalgia for the plantation tradition and its stock racist stereotypes with another work repudiating this tradition and set of figures" (179).

Berger concludes that advertising "remains credible because the truthfulness of publicity is judged, not by the real fulfillment of its promises, but by the relevance of its fantasies to those of the spectator-buyer" (146). Do ads make people more cynical, and thus passive, nonresponsive, and pliable? If advertising remains effective when people know they're being lied to, it can foment deep skepticism and disengagement, leaving people unable to imagine a world without it or its purveyors. Ads reflect and help precipitate a culture of lies—they normalize and desensitize us to the notion that one must lie in business, and in all aspects of life involving self-promotion. We might be so inured to the mechanisms of advertising that we begin to see their falsehoods as venial white lies, but their venality begins to contaminate many aspects of our lives. Addressing the ritual-authoritarian language that suffused postwar Western cultures, and in ways that seem prescient regarding advertising and contemporary populism, Marcuse concluded, "It seems unwarranted to assume that the recipients believe, or are made to believe, what they are being told. The new touch of the magical-ritual language rather is that people don't believe it, or don't care, and yet act accordingly. One does not "believe" the statement of an operational concept, but it justifies itself in action" (103).

In addressing how the public is led to war through forms of advertisement, Richard Barnet traces the continuity between self-deception in personal, commercial, and political contexts:

> The unconscious lie—something one should know to be false, but has come to believe is true—is even more common [than the willful falsehood]. This psychological mechanism offers protection against unpleasant and disturbing truth. It can be found everywhere. No doubt there are cigarette manufacturers who believe that smoking prolongs life. But the unconscious lie is rampant in the national security bureaucracy. . . . Many of [its] statements on Vietnam, for example, were analogous to the kind of advertising claims which Jules Henry has dubbed "pecuniary pseudotruth." This is a false statement made for the purpose of selling something which is uttered as if it is true but is not intended to be believed. . . . The repeated public claims in the Vietnam War that victory was around the corner . . . were meant to be taken literally no more than the claim that Seven Crown whiskey "holds within its icy depths a world of summertime." (126–27)

Rinse and repeat the above for almost every national security operation since Vietnam. What we know cannot be true often holds the greatest sway over us. Like its close correlative of the political lie, the advertisement repeats its messages so incessantly most people internalize them without being aware of it.[1] The mechanisms used to disseminate an irrational corporate worldview are coterminous with and facilitate those that erode our ability to be informed citizens.

> "My word, Hing! Maybe Hingleberry or Hingsaurio. Hing spells nothing, begins nothing possible unto Webster. It is my very, very own Hing! . . . Hing uninvited, Hing unexcited, Hing retiring into his own Hinghood! . . . But I shall follow wherever Hing lead, till Hing vanish into darkness. My word, Hing!"
>
> —*Putney Swope*

Most ads are designed to be meaningless; because there's no way to prove or disprove their content, their speech is usually entirely protected. For example, to call a product revolutionary or the best is legally considered puffery—a protected assertion that cannot be evaluated or tested.[2] In other words, advertisers say as little as possible in terms of rational communication. (As noted, it's no wonder politicians call themselves maverick—little remains outside the language of advertisement.) To iterate to the point of repetition compulsion that a product offers "fine Corinthian leather," brings the rainbow, features Schweppervescence, or is an Uncola relies on willful gibberish, but such unlanguage forms a central part of corporate biography. Little difference exists between a corporation claiming it sells "the official car of summer" and the head of Wells Fargo claiming his corporation is committed to reform; both statements are by intention legally and rhetorically meaningless. But we're so inured to being bombarded with such drivel that the assertions have their intended effect; the only reason ever to use such "puffery" is with the expectation that the right audience won't take it as puffery. The system works by highlighting its own artificiality, artifice, and dissonance, and by ensuring that a fatigued public will give up trying to evaluate truth claims. Trachtenberg contends that "[t]he advertisement is unique among artworks in that its cardinal premise is falsehood, deceit, its purpose being to conceal the connection between labor and its product in order to persuade consumers to purchase *this* brand" (138). (It's hard to countenance calling ads forms of artwork, however.) That obfuscation has less to do with particular brands than a mystification that represents all commodities as capable of delivering affect. For Powers, like Steiner, corporations might not only contaminate the environment, but logic and language: a Clare press release in *Gain* tells us, "Melissa turned nine today. Maybe she still can't spell oral leukotriene D, receptor antagonist. But she does know how to spell Happiness" (116). Another Clare ad campaign proclaims, "We recycled before the words even existed" (174). Corporations continue to recycle language even after they have nullified it and it has effectively ceased to function.

Chapter Thirty-Eight

The Rise of the Impersonation State

The history of the corporation is intertwined with the history of the modern state, the abstract collective that provides a collective identity to those who belong to it or live under its sphere of influence. As one of David Liss's characters in *The Devil's Company* summarizes the trajectory of corporate relations with the state,

> "We have to take the power back from the Parliament and put it where it belongs."
>
> "With the East India Company?" I proposed.
>
> "That is exactly right: with the East India Company, and the chartered companies, and those men of wealth and ingenuity who wield the power in our economy. To them must go the spoils of the earth, not members of parliament." (118)

One of the first and most important writers to formulate correlative conceptions of the modern nation-state and the corporation, Hobbes guaranteed the continuity of the state by conceptualizing it as an impersonal entity that traversed the life spans and limitations of individual rulers. The Hobbesian state was represented by sovereigns or men, but they were placeholders. Similarly, the corporation becomes an impersonal structure dissociated from its owners or employees, who are not only temporary, but, in relative terms, fungible. Like the state, the corporation is an impersonality we're in service to, but one that ultimately displaces and supplants its subjects; it's as if we've ended up as hosts to the impersonality, which has become virulent, resistant, and embedded. In overtaking its creator, the corporation turned the nation-state into a state based on impersonation.

It's important to consider the relationship of the corporation to its antecedent forms, particularly the bodies of nature and the king. The corporate body retains but transforms the mystical and inhuman properties associated with the king's body; as with a sovereign body, it represents a conjunction of an extra-human body and an exceptional or nonhuman personality (though many now allege that the king and corporation are equally persons). Aggregate and symbolic bodies of power typically bear contradictory or numinous, and therefore fantastic, attributes. In many cultures, for example, as Elias Canetti notes, it was improper "to refer to [the king's] body or to imply that he had an ordinary human body at all. A special word was used instead, signifying the kingly personality." Ironically, whereas "the crucial thing about the king is his uniqueness," the crucial thing about the modern corporation is its generic ubiquity and uniformity—it champions apparent uniqueness through its impersonal universality (414). In the corporate state, the function of this collectivized body is still to represent power—but in the corporation, power is stripped of the overlay of mortal personality (except as manifested in the ventriloquism of advertising and CEOs). The contemporary corporation resembles a Hobbesian king disencumbered of human qualities and constraints. Hobbes formulated an impersonal theory of impersonation—and of the sacrifice of individual rights/personality/autonomy that subjects must make to obtain security—as a critical part of his disquisition on the nation-state. But the impersonal corporation gradually attained the very personhood the subjects of the state relinquished.

Hobbes's work remains useful for understanding the artificial person of the corporation and its relation to bodies—bodies of power, science fiction bodies, and dematerialized bodies. In political as well as sociological contexts, the corporation has become a less accountable version of the absolute sovereign, as well as the embodiment of actorhood and agency, with which Hobbes imagined that the state had to coincide. Beyond kings, corporations are both hyper-bodied and disembodied. For Michaels, the possibility of a corporate person/personality without a body represents a form of idealism or fantasy—one, I would add, that further removes the corporation from the world of lived reality to the world of the sublime or uncanny horror (189). As Michaels observes, "Whereas in a partnership, the death of a partner dissolves the partnership, in [the view of Josiah] Royce [the philosopher of American corporate life], no physical event can jeopardize the life of the corporate entity—its soul is immortal" (188–89). The corporation begins as a figurative, culturally constructed body, but ends as a disembodied eternal soul, and that trajectory remains intertwined with US conceptions of the materiality of collective nature. The corporation and nature are both fictions that we embody and reify, and to which we give a shape, characteristics, and even voice.

This premise also helps explain the narratives of some reflexive mysteries; because we must ventriloquize the dumb corporation and project its essence—

the mysterious voice we cannot identify—the perpetrators of crimes we cannot trace or account for often turn out to be not just corporate malefactors but us all along. The detective/analyst often seeks himself, and in the context of social "mysteries," corporations often serve as screens for enacting our repressed social unconscious. In Lacanian terms, when we hear corporations speak, it's our voice we're hearing, or getting back, distorted. Not despite but because the corporation and corporate personhood are empty placeholders, it shouldn't surprise us that the corporation itself is a figurative murderer in so many thrillers and science fiction films, as I will address below.

For Hobbes, the sovereign unites men under one will and personifies and represents the state; his acts are the acts of the body (e.g., 160, 166).[1] The state, which Hobbes depicted as leviathan, creates the modern corporation, initially to do its bidding, and forms of that entity were instrumental to the state's literal and figurative expansion. Hobbes was writing in the mid-seventeenth century, when modern notions of individuality and personhood were being formulated. The corporation emerged as the next stage of the state, doing what no nation-state could yet do in terms of risky endeavors of imperial expansion and trade. It also began to become multinational, diffuse, and uncontainable, existing outside the limits not just of particular cultures and laws but, as we've seen, time and space. Here is where the corporation again begins to supplant God or nature, which once guaranteed the state.

Variations of the Hobbesian leviathan return throughout corporate history, but they become less identified with real human beings and bodies as the image is disassociated from its original ties to the state. Hobbes anticipates the birth of the science fiction simulacrum, the modern thing that impersonates the human. Fear of inhuman corporate control, and of artificial or altered reality we cannot perceive or comprehend, is a conceit likely familiar to many through the *Matrix* series. Those films rewrite the plots of half a dozen Philip K. Dick novels and Rainer Werner Fassbinder's 1973 German TV film *Welt am Draht* (*World on a Wire*), whose source material, D. F. Galouye's *Simulacron 3*, was also the basis for *The Thirteenth Floor*. In *Simulacron 3*, the corporation generates a virtual world that seems to replicate the real one, partly to circumvent the need to use people to conduct surveys about products and consumer behavior. This previously unimaginable harvesting of information allows the corporation to predict and control the future. By data-mining almost perfect replications of people, the firm pursues the ultimate corporate goal of modifying and replacing them. Here, the corporation is creating artificial lives, beings who don't realize they're corporate/computer programs, and who in turn think they themselves work for a corporation that's creating an artificial world. As one of the characters reflects, "You can't spend years feeding data into a computer that allows for the simulation of every aspect of human behavior without asking yourself whether it might lead to the creation of something resembling human consciousness." That consciousness is a corporate impersonation of human identity. Fassbinder's film captures the disconcerting implications and effects of corporate personhood, and the use of corporate AI that undermines our sense that we can identify what's real or human. Our move to an online existence, accelerated during the COVID-19 pandemic, codifies the fact that our interactions with the corporation always have been virtual ontologically. As Piety documents, advertisers for decades have been conducting market research experiments on human subjects without their permission, and in ways that violate the protocols of Institutional Review Boards. In a kind of variation of the corporation in *Soylent Green*, the corporation in *Welt* produces virtual people or artificial souls to test-market to them. That process again provides a metaphor for how corporate personhood works: the artificial thing divests people of their personhood.

Many films and texts develop this premise—that we create virtual, artificial consciousnesses in a computer simulation, which serves as a kind of icon of corporate personhood. The *Matrix* films further develop the fears of the anti-corporatist films *Soylent Green* and *Blade Runner*, in which the Soylent and Tyrell Corporations, respectively, harvest people to feed people and create artificial souls. The underlying anxiety is that corporations are creating and controlling our identities. As I elaborate at the end of this section in a discussion of the film *Avatar*, corporations no longer just siphon souls from living people, but create them. As in a simulacrum, the corporate person is a duplicate of a nonexistent original.

The artificial personhood of the contemporary corporation should be situated in the context of the artificial world of simulations and computers, but also of the collective body of the state—itself a kind of foundational science fiction motif. As Cameron summarizes the Hobbesian lineage of personhood,

> The word *person* confers status (designating a rational being in distinction to a thing or an animal), value, even equality; it establishes intelligibility within a political and legal system, indicating a being having legal rights or representing others' rights, either because he is a human being or *natural* person or because he is a corporate body or *artificial* person. (For Hobbes an artificial person must also be a natural person.) It does not, however, presume anything of substance, nor did the word *persona* from which it derived. A persona was never essential, since a persona is not an actor but the mask which covers the actor, or the character who is acted. (viii)

But Cameron partly misrepresents Hobbes in this context: Hobbes doesn't believe artificial persons also must be natural persons, only that they must be represented by agents who are natural persons. However, Hobbes does begin to erode the distinction between natural and unnatural in ways that prepare for the modern corporation. What he didn't quite anticipate were the ways that the leviathan of the state would give way to the far less "natural" leviathan of the corporation, which has entirely different goals.

The legal creation of personhood made it possible to redefine human identity within the confines of the nation-state; ultimately, we could take personhood away by treating someone as a thing, or conversely create a form of specious personhood by treating a thing as if it had personal attributes and rights. In other words, if a capitalist society accepts the premise that personhood isn't simply constructed, but pointedly artificial, it's almost inevitable that its institutions, such as corporations, would be defined using similar assumptions. Once we shunt personhood into the marketplace, it also must become an impersonal commodity, one ultimately subject to the forces of supply and demand. Hobbes began the subordination of personality to such forms of impersonality in his conception of the corporate entity. As Cameron continues,

> For Hobbes, the definition of a person (or agent) is what we agree to treat as a person; a being is determined human not by philosophical definitions or by man, but by law. To be a person or agent, according to Hobbes, it is not sufficient to consider yourself a person; you must also be considered as possessing agency. In distinction, *personality* stresses self-ownership, the *of* or possessive through which individuality is identified as one's own. Impersonality is an idea that Eliot made commonplace. But whereas Eliot coined the word narrowly to indicate the extinction of personality that defines the artist, this extinction . . . has different contours in the works I consider. (viii, emphasis in original)

Though Cameron develops a persuasive cultural reading of impersonality, she doesn't extend her analysis to its terminal disembodiment, the corporation. While Eliot evoked the depersonalization of art in relation to an overarching tradition or impersonality that transcended the individual, the corporation extinguishes human personality and makes people's identities dependent on its impersonal commercial structures. We should take the term *company man* literally, because it encapsulates the way corporations take over human bodies, traits and rights ("Tradition" 47).

Since the state is a precursor to and author of the corporation, one should consider the agency and personification of the modern state as the historical backdrop for the staging of corporate personhood. Among the first modern theorists of agency and agency law, Hobbes addresses who can represent whom and what, on whose behalf, and with what responsibility and liability. As Quentin Skinner observes, Hobbes asserts "that the state can actually be defined as 'One Person'" (3). Skinner notes that Hobbes evaluated whether impersonal beings or associations can have intent in chapter 16 of *Leviathan*, entitled Of Persons, Authors and Things Personated. His proposed solution (already implicit in his title) is impressively if deceptively straightforward.

It is possible, he argues, for an action genuinely to be attributed to a collectivity—or to an abstraction or even a thing—provided that one particular condition is met. The agent to whom the action is attributed must be represented by another agent who can validly claim to be "personating" the first by way of acting on their behalf. (3–4)

Similar considerations apply to the corporation in terms of impersonality, ventriloquism, a kind of bootstrapped inhuman identity, and the attribution of liability. The corporation exists only through attribution and impersonation because the law allows (or requires) agents to stand for the corporation; what Hobbes didn't quite realize is that the process works in reverse, as the corporation begins to stand in for and impersonate people. Hobbes elucidates the modern division between actual and artificial persons and what later emerges as the attendant split between corporate agency and responsibility and liability. But as the corporation overtakes the sovereign, Hobbes's formulations of agency lead to the reversal of the schema presented above. People are no longer real beings acting for or impersonating an imagined collective; through everything that corporate personhood represents, the imagined collective is the artificial being acting for and impersonating people.

Though he cited historical and cultural precedents for this bifurcation, Hobbes was making a contemporary legal justification for the distinction. The critical difference for Hobbes was not between human persons and artificial collectives, but between human persons acting on their own behalf and human persons acting on behalf of someone or something else:

PERSON, is he, whose words or actions are considered, either as his own, or as representing the words or actions of another man, or of any other thing to whom they are attributed, whether Truly or by Fiction. When they are considered as his own, then is he called a Natural Person and when they are considered as representing the words and actions of another, then is he a Feigned or Artificial person. (110; in modernized English)

In the language of artifice, fiction, acting, and impersonating, agency would have no constraints, because it's conceived as transitive; in *Leviathan*, to "act" is by design equally to do, fake, and impersonate. Hobbes here conceptualizes what we might call the modern imperson-nation, and the legal framework that sanctions and needs the impersonal corporate form to elide human constraints, and ultimately human values. Not accidentally, Hobbes also relies on the distinction between nature and the artificial, and what would become the AI or simulacrum of the corporation and corporate personhood.

Beginning with Hobbes, the teleology of the corporate form would take it from being a surrogate for nature and nation to being their successor. Aronczyk observes that corporate advertisers and branding agencies, ironically, legitimate and maintain the nation-state as one of their primary cultural reference points (64–65). (The designation of these firms as agencies is overdetermined given Hobbes's schema of actorhood.) However, the corporation in some ways has overtaken the nation as the most significant producer of cultural signifiers and even laws. In the twenty first century, nations often fragment or become engaged in civil, sectarian, religious and postcolonial divisions and wars: corporations, by contrast, tend to consolidate and expand, and often to profit considerably from the events that afflict states. As Meyer and Bromley remark in addressing the rise of organizations generally worldwide, "An overarching explanation is that the dramatic limitations of the nation-state system, especially two horrific world wars, undermined government-based control, creating supports for alternative forms of a more global social order" (368). Corporate and right-wing antagonism toward the state is fratricidal, but also inevitable—it's not just that corporations resist regulation and taxation, but that they're antagonistic to the state's conception of human personhood and the rights that come with it.

Addressing how Hobbes classifies fictions of personhood (which become salient for the creation of corporations), Skinner observes that

Hobbes proposes no particular term to isolate this category, but it may be helpful to designate them purely artificial persons to distinguish them from those who voluntarily take on this status by authorizing others to represent them. . . . Hobbes [indicates] that two sub-classes need to be considered: those whose words and actions can be "truly" attributed to them, and those who can only have words and actions attributed to them "by Fiction." Nothing further is said in *Leviathan* about the class of purely artificial persons who are also fictitious. But in *De Homine* it emerges that what Hobbes has in mind are the characters impersonated by actors on the stage: For it was understood in the ancient theatre that not the player himself but someone else was speaking, for example . . . when the player, putting on the fictitious mask of Agamemnon, was for the time being Agamemnon. At a later stage, however, this was understood to be so even in the absence of the fictitious mask, namely when the actor declared publicly which person he was going to play. (15)

As Skinner elaborates, when an actor plays a part on stage, he performs "in the persona of" that character, and the audience assumes those acts aren't the actor's, but the character's, even while knowing that character is a fiction. This notion of impersonation informs many aspects of the corporate enterprise, from a similar ascription of agency (but not liability) to corporate representatives to the reliance on actors who serve as surrogate corporate persons in advertising.

Skinner identifies the initial bases for artificial agency or personhood, which also provide a foundation for the development of artificial rights: while Hobbes regards some people as "purely artificial," he

> is more interested in the fact that various inanimate objects and even figments of the imagination can be classified [similarly]. . . . Since these are "things Inanimate" they "cannot be Authors, nor therefore give Authority to their Actors." Nevertheless, they can perfectly well be personated or represented "by a Rector, Master, or Overseer" who can be commissioned and thereby given authority to act on their behalf. Among imaginary objects he singles out the gods of the heathen. Such idols obviously cannot be authors, "for an Idol is nothing." Nevertheless, in ancient times such deities were frequently recognized as having the ability not merely to own possessions but to exercise rights. As in the case of the hospital and the bridge, these capacities stemmed from the fact that authorized persons (in this case officiating priests) were assigned a legal right to act in their name. (16)

Corporations emerge as successors to these deities, including nature, and finally the sovereign that created it. Over a protracted period, the Supreme Court has extended Hobbes's exegesis by declaring that corporations are authors, that not only do they have the right to express views but they also possess authentic human voices and agencies.

Hobbes, however, believed the representative-sovereign, and those who authorized him, was accountable for his actions, and that those actions could be directly ascribed to his agents; he authorized the exercise of power, not its absolution. Wanting the state to restrain and control individual violence and economic crime, Hobbes believed an impersonal system could regulate the overreach of personal players. But the impersonal corporation took over, and it is in critical ways unregulated and unchecked in power; this denouement reflects a systemic corruption of the principles that hypothetically justified the legitimate but limited functions of corporations. Power once concentrated in the body of the sovereign has become concentrated in the body of the corporation—an artificial body even more removed from people. We move from Hobbes's notion of reciprocity and trade, under which citizens relinquish some rights in exchange for many safeguards, to a zero-sum game with corporations.

In *Leviathan*, Hobbes prioritizes the shared, the proto-universal, and the common. The notion of the commonwealth evokes the sharing of things that cannot be divided: for example, the common interest, the common law, and what Hobbes terms common discourse. According to Norberto Bobbio, Hobbes defines corporations as subordinate associations, which have as their ends "certain common activities for some common benefit or of the whole city" (179). (Hobbes evidenced what J. G. A. Pocock situates as a humanist dedication "to the common weal," but that commitment was coterminous with his notion that the state was not a "common" republic per se, but a corpus with a prince as the head [339].) In the New World, as noted, the charter initially continued to limit the role of corporations, which could function only when dedicated to some form of common purpose or good. Over time, the corporation became beholden only to the private good of shareholders. In structural terms, the contemporary corporation is programmatically able to consider only its own good, not that of the commons—it's a body at war with parts of itself. *Commonwealth* becomes a term incommensurate with the corporate charter; axiomatically, what's good for X corporation isn't good for America, because corporate profit typically is generated for select private interests at the expense of the public good. A succinct definition of the corporation would be a device designed to extract resources and rights from the commons in a zero-sum game.

In Hobbes's writing, we can see that the creation of the modern state coincided with the creation of the proto-corporate enterprise. In *Leviathan*, Hobbes already envisioned some corporations as parasites on the state, and corrupt bodies that feed parasitically on the common body of society: he disparaged "the great number of corporations which are, as it were, many lesser commonwealths in the bowels of the greater, like worms in the entrails of a natural man" (241). (As noted, DeLillo draws on such images in *Ratner's Star*, suggesting we've been incorporated into the belly of the parasite: "Absorption by the shapeless Mass. Total assimilation. They would be incorporated, transformed and metabolized" [132].) Hobbes still can imagine assemblies at which individual corporators implement decisions for their limited common purpose (though that purpose already inures to their private benefit):

> In a Body Politic, for the well ordering of foreign traffic, the most commodious Representative is an assembly of all the members; that is to say, such a one as every one that adventureth his money may be present at all the Deliberations and Resolutions of the body, if they will themselves. For proof whereof we are to consider the end for which men that are Merchants, and may buy and sell, export and import their Merchandise, according to their own discretions, do nevertheless bind themselves up in one Corporation. It is true, there be few Merchants that with the Merchandise they buy at home can freight a Ship to export it; or with that they buy abroad, to bring it home; and have therefore need to join together in one society, where every man may either participate of the gain, according to the proportion of his adventure. . . . But this is no Body Politic, there being no Common Representative to oblige them to any other law than that which is common to all other subjects. (164)

What Hobbes conceptualizes is closer to an association driven by men than to the corporation that's legally and structurally separate from them. Part of what Hobbes failed to consider is the mass to which these corporations would grow in the New World, and their effect on the social contract. Most contemporary shareholder meetings are removed from such scenarios not only because of economies of scale, but because corporations are designed to separate shareholding owners from managers. Instead of checks and balances, the corporate structure is engineered to provide free passes.

The "body politic"—and the notion that society is an organic community, or a social body—is supplemented and deformed by the corporation, another fictitious aggregate body, but one that represents an entity that's precisely immaterial. If, in conservative social theory, "the presupposed organic unity of Society is perturbed by the intrusion of a foreign body" (Žižek, *Interrogating* 127; *Universal* 142, 398), the unity of contemporary society is in many ways predicated on the presence of a foreign body—the corporation.[2] But the usually xenophobic conceit that society should be an organic unity, aside from posing inherent problems in multicultural and hierarchical societies, is easily co-opted. (Among the ironic inversions of Trumpian populism is its intentionally distracting anti-immigrant hysteria, when the real foreign enemy is already among us.) The phantasmic corporate body also ventriloquizes a voice without a source, which makes it easy to throw politically. In the modern corporation, the Hobbesian social body is bifurcated to bypass common interest, which means the public good by necessity becomes a foreign/alien element to the corporate body and vice versa. This bifurcation or inversion is homologous with what Anna Grear documents, in the context of legal formulations of personality, as the "problematic gap that legal disembodiment creates between the living human being and the legal entity or construct taken to represent the human being" (149). By the end of the nineteenth century, the separation between artificial corporation and organic human being became absolute. By the time of *Button v. Hoffman*, 61 Wis. 20 (1884), courts had decided that even corporations owned by a single person exist independently of their owners; Walter Benn Michaels contends that the corporation consequently no longer represented a veil concealing a person, but itself became a new kind of person (197).

As the idea has played out in US culture, to incorporate isn't to join a common society but to transcend individuality—in a society putatively obsessed with individuality—in a larger natural or artificial body. To incorporate is in some ways to merge one's individual body into a collective body and to renounce human limitations and, paradoxically in the centuries after Hobbes, the common in favor of the private shareholder. The further derangement is that many corporations systematically invert the characteristics of the public

and the private, from concepts of privacy to those of public benefit and welfare.

Hobbes imagined the very purpose of the corporation was to corner markets,
and in some sense to consolidate those who give it agency into its aggregate
being: "The end of their incorporating is to make their gain the greater; which is
done two ways: by sole buying, and sole selling, both at home and abroad. So
that to grant to a Company of Merchants to be a Corporation, or Body Politic,
is to grant them a double Monopoly, whereof one is to be sole buyers; another
to be sole sellers" (164). Though he realized that the corporate structure, unless
restrained, would tend to concentrate wealth and power, Hobbes was more concerned with codifying its benefits than anticipating its mutations. Corporations
by default will try to achieve monopoly when unchecked, and as their emissaries, so do advertisers—they're relentless colonizers. But they're also now
colonizing human identity; the ulterior teleology of the corporation has been to
monopolize speech and personhood. Everything else is a way station.

For Hobbes, personhood is a mask or performance, and we all present
ourselves through personae that constitute personhood:

> The word Person is Latin, instead whereof the Greeks have prosopon, which sig-
> nifies the Face, as Persona in Latin signifies the disguise, or outward appearance
> of a man, counterfeited on the Stage; and sometimes more particularly that part
> of it which disguiseth the Face, as a Mask or Visard: and from the Stage hath
> been translated to any Representer of speech and action, as well in Tribunals as
> Theatres. (110)

Though Hobbes didn't directly address the implication of this perception, it
suggested that we bear no essential personhood before we perform or impersonate: a person doesn't engage in performance or impersonation but is created by it. Hobbes specifies that the person is therefore the same as an actor
on stage and off—one who represents or "personates" himself or another, and
acts in another's name. Society has many categories for such actors, including accountants and clergy. Especially in terms of their professions, people
routinely act as representatives, but that term becomes problematic when
applied conceptually both to corporators and elected officials. And what happens when the personator isn't representing another person—an attorney acting on behalf of a client—but representing and helping facilitate a fictitious,
artificial and inhuman modern corporation? Under Hobbes's framework, the
primary character or dramatis persona in US culture has become the corporate
mask/person.[3]

Hobbes distinguishes between personally validated acts and authorized
acts, which are essentially impersonal or impersonations:

> Of Persons Artificial, some have their words and actions Owned by those whom they represent. And then the Person is the *Actor*, and he that owneth his words and actions is the Author, in which case the Actor acteth by authority. . . . And as the Right of possession is called Dominion so the Right of doing any action is called Authority. (111)

Here, Hobbes elaborates that authority always conveys the right to perform an act, a kind of license or covenant for an actor to bind his principal/author to the consequences stemming from that act, and for the world to treat the act as if it had originated with the author. The imperatives of impersonal corporations allow individuals to do what they likely would not in their own names—they become authorized, or are given license, to act in ways autonomous individuals might resist or reject. (In this sense, the corporation operates as the largest diffused military corps in the history of the world.) In considering who and what can be "personated," Hobbes adumbrates the contemporary animation of fictions and things: few entities cannot be

> represented by Fiction. Inanimate things, as a Church, a Hospital, a Bridge, may be personated by a Rector, Master, or Overseer. But things Inanimate cannot be authors, nor therefore give Authority to their Actors: yet the Actors may have Authority to procure their maintenance, given them by those that are Owners or Governors of those things. And therefore such things cannot be Personated before there be some state of Civil Government. (112)

Hobbes effectively predicts how and why corporations will need to rely on *theatrical* actors to personify and speak for them, because they can only don identities as masks. But in the teleology of the corporation, inanimate things will become actors. Like forms of AI, corporations both imitate and transcend human beings. The corporation seems to be invisible, disembodied and immortal, and therefore to attain transcendent or numinous properties; it again thereby displaces nature, the state, and most institutions.

Hobbes's disquisitions also establish what constitutes a person whose rights and identity emanate from the state. Hobbes offers a list of those, including children and the mad, who lack reason and must be "personated" by guardians or agents, and cannot be the authors of their acts; but he adds that "this again has no place but in a State Civil, because before such estate there is no Dominion of Persons."[4] These definitions of agency, and the characteristics and attributes of principals and agents, implicate definitions of personhood. In addressing collective and transferred agency, Hobbes also considers the legal and ontological status of combinations of persons: what and whom they can represent; and how they differ from individual actors. For Hobbes, many men are "made one person" when they're represented by a single person, to whom they give consent to act. Troublingly, Hobbes contends "it is the *Unity* of the Representer, not the unity of the Represented, that maketh the Person *One*." That representer allegedly unifies disparate wills and consolidates multiplicity into unity. But the corporation reverses this process (if a circular process can be reversed); the agent or executive doesn't unify the corporation, because the corporation must first create and authorize the agent. To put it another way, executives and everyone else who works for a corporation can't represent the corporation; the corporation comes to represent and unify, but also transform, those who started out as people. For Hobbes,

> because the Multitude naturally is not *One*, but *Many*, they cannot be understood for one, but in any Authors, of everything their representative saith or doth in their name; every man giving their common Representer authority from himself in particular, and owning all the actions the Representer doth, in case they give him Authority without stint: otherwise, when they limit him in what and how far he shall represent them, none of them owneth more than they gave him commission to Act. (110–11)

In elucidating the authority of the state, but also the authority collectives bestow on agents, Hobbes advocates conditions of corporate organization that almost inevitably would be hijacked. People now surrender their rights and "ontologies" not just to governments, but also to corporations, which likely have a greater impact on our daily lives, environment, and identities than nations. Where citizens putatively entered a priori "bargains" with sovereigns in exchange for order and safety, consumers now effectively enter innumerable a priori "bargains" with corporations, surrendering not only their rights to sue, hold them liable, and so forth, but the possibility of living as free agents.

Today, the corporation acts as this Hobbesian unity—it is ubiquitous, inescapable, and a significant force of consolidation. According to Peter d'Errico, the role of the judiciary has been to turn the fiction of the corporate person from a legal abstraction into a "real" person that exists independently of the state (and effectively sui generisly) and can negotiate with the state as an independent actor bearing all the rights of a person (100–101). Such developments, and the aforementioned separation of capital from management, are scenarios Hobbes couldn't quite anticipate, and vitiate any assurance of corporate accountability he tried to muster. To sum up, Hobbes indicates that agents can impersonate anything; that anything can be personified; and by implication, that not only persons, but God can be impersonated: as Hobbes avers, "Men, Women, a Bird, A Crocodile, a Calf, a Dogge, a Snake, an Onion, a Leeke, [all] Deified" (74). The final species to add to that list is the corporation, or the corporate person—a deity made in man's worst image.

To pause briefly, I want to connect what might seem disparate threads; Hobbesian notions of agency and the state; the history of the corporate form;

transcendental representations of nature; and the status of personhood in a corporate state. The genealogy of the Hobbesian corporation fulfills a particularly American fantasy regarding the transcendence of materiality. The goal of Emerson's transcendentalism is to *transcend* individuality and the male body—to merge into nature and become a transparent eyeball that is nothing/ nowhere but sees everything. Seeking to experience nature as a disembodied, unobserved observer, Emerson wants to become invisible and immaterial, yet omnipresent. We can also transcend that self in the corporation, which is a form of virtual embodiment that, through the oxymoron/fiction of incorporation, generates an artificial person that also has no body. As one of Wallace's characters in *The Pale King* observes, "Doesn't the term corporation itself come from body, like 'made into a body'? These were artificial people being created" (140). The corporation depopulates the state of people and repopulates it with simulacra. And with perfect perverse logic, that alien corporate artificiality has supplanted much of what nature represented.

Chapter Thirty-Nine

I Have Met the Alien

The practices of corporate personhood are never confined to advertising, but apply to social organization, labor, resource extraction, and the reproduction of life. In this context, corporate personhood doesn't reflect an "advance" in social organization, but a return to medieval forms of hierarchy. Many corporations treat workers and anyone who isn't a shareholder as vassals. Corporate farming provides one of the clearest examples of how this process works. Genetically modified organisms (GMOs) reflect an ethos that displaces people and workers in favor of automated systems that corporations can monopolize. The corporate control of nature through GMOs and their use to displace and control indigenous peoples represents a return to feudal farming; the lords own the critical property (patented and "sterilized" seeds), and the serfs have to till the fields forever. (My comments are not meant to critique the science, but the politics behind GMOs.) Again, corporations engineer a transfer of rights and obligations by redefining what's natural and what constitutes a person.

The pilfering of Martinique provides a perhaps less well-known example of how corporations try to control the cycle of life. The island had been a site of sustainable local fishing, which existed beyond the reach of corporate enterprise. Targeting fisher communities, corporations began selling genetically modified, patented fish, grown in self-contained well-ponds.[1] These tasteless, more expensive fish are sold primarily to the corporate cruise ships that dock in Fort-de-France, whose passengers patronize few local businesses (and those that have passengers steered to them are forced to provide kickbacks). The corporate ships exercise considerable control over the market for fish, so most fishermen have few options. This new form of corporate colonialism represents another retropeptic circle in the food chain, and the creation of what we should see as alien life and forms of social organization.

As we've seen, the corporation is both a legal and a fictive construct, and therefore it has seemingly incommensurate qualities, which I've tried to align in specific contexts. The corporation is a kind of science fiction entity—an artificial, collective being that is both immaterial and hyper-materialized, like the *Star Trek* Borg, but also personified, ubiquitous, and incessantly accreting to itself. Because the corporation was created as an artificial person under the law, many popular cultural references to artificial and monstrous life contain some corporate residue. For example, the amorphous and seemingly immortal corporation, revenant in many guises yet always the same, didn't create the alien in the eponymous films—it *is* the alien. (It's not accidental that the corporation is intimately paired with the alien in each of those films; the alien is a kind of corporate spokesperson. It would be a far more appropriate mascot for most corporations than emus, geckos, tigers, or ducks.) Corporations tend inevitably toward monopoly; they want to develop and own everything, especially nature, and—as evident in their capacity to patent and restrict the reproduction of fish, patent genes, and create species—they increasingly have the capacity to do so. Nature is the corporation's only real competitor, and therefore it must be subsumed: every piece of land developed, every seed and gene owned. Life, and most of all human life, is what the corporate form must control and supplant. Corporations must own not just the means of production, but reproduction. Nature used to have a monopoly on life: as dramatized in the *Alien* films, corporations seek that monopoly in all contexts. The central question many such works pose is whether the corporation is a person or a nightmarish entity impersonating a person. In the above contexts, corporations are inhuman things or parasites that manipulate human emotions to alter behavior (alien things telling men how to be more masculine by buying impersonal corporate products, or to envy, desire, emulate, and so on). The "being" that foments that fantasy—much like the being that creates corporate entertainment at all levels—siphons the traits of human personality from people to objects. The corporate ad campaign tries to graft a human personality onto the impersonal person, the alien thing with a limitless drive and infinite maw, that the corporation must be.

Some contemporary new age works, such as James Cameron's 2009 film *Avatar*, are indirect cultural descendants of antebellum pantheism, confirming that the pantheist's nature was always a virtual and corporate construct. In transcendental nature, individual bodies and psyches are effectively absorbed into a collective so that the many are turned into the one. Such a description of "channeled," suppressed, and merged individuals comports with aspects of the corporate enterprise. The fantasized corporate corpus is an amalgam, a conglomeration of bodies turned into something monstrous, which is why it can be evoked by many kinds of phantasmic leviathans and artificial bodies. And because, as Arthur Machen Jr. and others have noted, the corporate personality is imaginary, it has no shape or limits (except, I would qualify, its persistent and pernicious drive to seek profit at all costs) (Michaels 202). That corporate personality serves as a screen on which we can project whatever psychological or economic justifications and rationalizations we need, but also whatever fears we unconsciously associate with it.

The figurative embodiment of the corporation and corporate person becomes most readily evident in science fiction films such as *Alien* and *Avatar*. Perhaps not surprisingly in the age of Halliburton and Blackwater (rebranded as Academi) and increasingly privatized armies and homeland security forces, the military in numerous science fiction films is portrayed as indistinguishable from a corporation, and as pathological; in *Aliens* and *Avatar*, the army is a corporation. Though the term *corps* can refer to any organized body of people, such films at least implicitly dramatize the fact that these entities are called the Marine Corps, Army Corps, and so on. (The Ur-corporation, the Dutch East India Company, had been granted a charter to wage war and control private armies. In *Apocalypse Now*, Captain Willard [Martin Sheen] remarks that Kurtz "was being groomed for one of the top slots in the corporation." As *Moby-Dick* queries Ahab, that film queries whether Kurtz betrayed or fulfilled the premises of his corporate mission.) The United Fruit Company and other US corporations operated equally as occupying armies and corporations in Central and South America. The corporation always has been a colonizer, an invader from another world. As Roxanne Dunbar-Ortiz notes, quoting H. Craig Miner, corporations always disproportionately have harmed Native Americans: the corporation functioned "as an organization legally authorized by charter to act as a single individual . . . an artificial person that could not be held accountable in a manner familiar to the American Indian way of thinking" (167). In this sense, the corporation was designed to act as an intermediary instrument of displacement, carrying out the orders of a criminal state that could deny responsibility for its actions.

In *Aliens*, one shouldn't be distracted by the aliens—they're creations of and stand-ins for their parent corporation (and the fact that Ripley incessantly calls her ship's AI "Mother" suggests the films are centrally concerned with who will get to control natural and artificial/corporate reproduction and life cycles, from the engineered alien life forms to clones, androids, and promethean corporate CEOs who think that they, like their corporations, can be immortal). In fact, the aliens represent a form of corporate personhood, the hyper-embodied and horrific face of the disembodied corporation. Those corporations are always up to no good somewhere "out there" in these films, which again is a feint for what they're doing right here, even while we're watching a corporate film. Such works help us track the ongoing transition from personified god/nature (mother earth or nature) to the personified corporation, and all the things that cannot be personified or be persons. These corporations, like the corporation in the pointedly repetitive *Resident Evil* series, don't simply engage in some form of social malfeasance, but specifically mimic and usurp nature, often either creating life or attempting to colonize or control a force of nature that putatively represents pre-corporate organic life/society. This Umbrella Corporation (whose name reflects its status as all corporations), encapsulates what everything from the Army Corporation to the God Corporation do: they figuratively create artificial life and destroy the real thing. Corporations are the actual or figurative villains in many science fiction and horror movies because they're trying to create, mimic and monopolize life, which reflects their real-world effects on biodiversity. In the *Alien* films, which focus on the relationship between nature, reproduction, and the corporation, Ripley repeatedly is stripped of her personhood by the corporation; when she returns from the dead and refuses to cooperate (corporate), she loses all social status and is left a clone without rights, or *homo sacer*. The militarized state corporation keeps cloning and resurrecting her, turning her into a variation of itself—the infinitely replicable artificial or digital person who, like the zombie corporation, never can die. The corporation owns her genes the way it owns the fish of Martinique. Ripley will star in film after film until another corporate agent or actor reprises her role.

In the world of Pandora, *Avatar* dramatizes the transcendental premise that the earth is a living, sentient being—a conceit that American pantheists, like *Avatar*'s writers, had developed from aboriginal cultures. As noted, Melville depicted a similar entity throughout *Mardi*, whose planet is a living, collective being. But Pandora, and the *Alien* films in an even more perturbing way, repeat the dark unconscious message of transcendentalism: nature never existed, and always already represented a kind of virtual reality, a fake foil for the corporate form. Pantheism itself turns out to rely on a corporate ethos, for its nature is imagined to be an animated, immortal, impersonal collective whose characteristics largely match that of the corporation. In *The Overstory*, which is a far more nuanced and controlled exposition of the themes of *Avatar*, Powers even describes trees that engage in a "wild stock market trading in handicrafts, above and below . . . complex limited partnerships with other kinds of life" (294). Ironically, in the 1970s, professors of ecology and eco-theory started to teach the theory of corporations using environmental concepts: businesses have souls, and corporations are like organisms that need and seek the right environments they grow and behave like living things (hence, we also began saying we can grow the economy).

As we've seen, the danger is that when we animate corporations as living things, we turn living things into corporations. Pandora is both a new age fantasy and a wholly technological corporation of nature.[2]

The underlying premise of *Avatar* is that for white men, nature is a construction of technology—nature doesn't exist on earth "anymore," only on the internet. But the more alarming provocation is that nature never existed: like Eden, it's a retroactive construct, which we can now reach only through the digital corporation. The apparent conflicts between corporations/technology and nature in the *Alien* films and *Avatar* are illusory, because only one entity exists: the corporation creates the aliens in *Alien(s)*, and nature is purely virtual in *Avatar*. Critically, the Na'vi, the natives of Pandora, interact with "nature" purely as avatars: they plug into horses, the sacred living tree, and so on, with the equivalent of organic USB cords. In this fantasy, nature is itself a cyborg. *Avatar* was the first blockbuster film to so extensively rely on CGI, and its use of that medium is also its message. Its aboriginal natives and nature both are virtual; they exist within the frame of the film solely as digital constructs. But where the Na'vi "plug" directly into the tree, earthlings can interact with nature only when wearing protective suits, except in the archetypal final fantasy of the one lone transcendent white male figure who merges into their nature. In other words, nature isn't only poisonous to earthlings, it cannot be interacted with except through corporate technology and a VR suit. The disturbing final message of both *The Overstory* and *Avatar* is that as the natural world of ecosystems is destroyed and recedes, the artificial or virtual world expands directly in proportion. This is the final zero-sum game in which the assets of nature are transferred to the artificial corporation.

Avatar unwittingly demonstrates the ways corporate personhood is predicated on commensurate discourses of primitivism and fetishized technology; its false opposition between the militarized mining corporation and the pantheist/animist tribe is dismantled not only by the overdetermined issue of incorporation—the fact that humans on Pandora can interact with nature exclusively by assuming virtual bodies—but the fact that their access to this nature is purely virtual. (*Avatar*'s conception of nature is commensurate with that of the *Alien* films—whose first sequel began the collaboration between James Cameron and Sigourney Weaver—and all these films implicate fantasies of corporate personhood. The corporation is a construct of both new age mass fantasy and horror movies.) The electrochemical connections between the trees on Pandora serve as a neural net, but this net isn't nature; it's second nature, a worldwide digital web or global network; as Weaver's character declaims, the Na'vi can "download and upload data" through these connections. But instead of a world that's alive, we have a virtual corporate world, a post-human animated fantasy of nature after environmental collapse and the displacement of persons by hybridized digital, corporate avatars. This world exists only as a digital creation. Films such as *Avatar* recuperate but lay bare the ethos of antebellum pantheism. Emerson's transparent eyeball suggests that nature is also only a screen (and by *Avatar*, part of a literal one). Emerson not only proposed that nature might be only "an apocalypse of the mind," but asserted that the material world "hides through absolute transparency the mental nature" (*Works* "Nature" I: 48; "Natural History of Intellect" XII: 5). In other words, nature exists only virtually, a construct as artificial as the corporation that roots it out. Like Melville's works, *Avatar* (perhaps unwittingly) suggests that a transcendental nature always has been a facade for the corporation, with which it finally becomes merged, even as it also purports to lament the loss of that nature.

The technology at the center of *Avatar* serves as another misdirection, for this story that seems to fetishize primitivism embraces and enables the corporate form. The joke of *Avatar* is that white people are searching for the mineral "unobtanium" and can't get it. As part of the history of corporate personhood, it's symbolically inevitable that the trove of unobtanium would lie directly beneath the tree god or nature spirit of the planet itself: that's what the corporate emissaries can't obtain and can only destroy. A kind of recurring satirical science fiction motif, unobtanium represents the Lacanian lack of Western society and prompts us to seek an alternative in the primitive and indigenous world our corporate expansion long ago destroyed, but it actually offers a way to continue unchanged (after watching the corporate entertainment). As if addressing *Avatar*, Žižek contends that "this new notion of life is thus neutral with respect to the distinction between natural and cultural (or 'artificial') processes—the Earth (as Gaia) as well as the global market both appear as gigantic self-regulated living systems" (*Interrogating* 85). In this new age fantasy of cyberspace, we leave real bodies behind and become corporate or cyber bodies that efface any remaining distinctions between nature, technology, and corporation.

Avatar addresses aboriginal culture and nature in the context of the corporation, which has long served as a, if not the, primary instrument of colonialism. It is important to consider the foundational territorialism of the corporate enterprise, reflected in its colonial roots and the ways the corporation was created and recruited to expand the scope of the state by appropriating the bodies and resources of nature and native populations. When corporations could no longer expand in the "third world," they had to start figuratively colonizing the bodies of their customers. My intent in this chapter is to highlight the connection between such expansion; precepts of universality and reflexivity; and the closed loops of advertising, self-contained corporate media, and nationalistic rhetoric that allow corporations to become kinds of exceptional post-state actors. It's notable that no nations are referenced in *Aliens* or *Avatar*—they've been replaced by the colonizing military corporation.

Another ulterior message of *Avatar*—another variation of *Dances with Wolves* and numerous other past/future extrapolations that situate the postcolonial condition as a second fall from a natural, pagan, and racialized Eden— is that it's always already too late for white men, and that nature was always already a virtual (in this case digital) reality and a facade for a corporate ontology. In films such as *Avatar* and *Dances with Wolves*, a loner white man in the army realizes his mission is absurd and falls for a native woman, rejects his culture, bonds with totem animals, and dances with dragons/wolves. *Avatar* here repeats the conservative message of *Dances*—that only a lone white man who goes native can help save natives/nature and escape his society, when that escape reifies the colonizing culture, and allows the audience to develop a specious identification with a native culture and nature presented to them only in corporate/virtual form.

It's not just that corporations rely on nature and preindustrial economies and cultures for resources; they also must take over or co-opt their beliefs, identities, and functions. Thirty years ago, Jameson remarked that it was already long well-known that "the prodigious new expansion of multinational capital ends up penetrating and colonizing those very precapitalist enclaves (Nature and the Unconscious) which offered extraterritorial and Archimedean footholds for critical effectivity" (*Postmodernism* 49). But the final implication of many of the texts I've addressed, from Emerson's essays to *Avatar*, is that the very opposition between nature and the corporation is false—they represent the same transcendental collective that's inimical to people. As Žižek might apply his general formulation, within a corporate culture, nature and the corporation are "just the positive and the negative sides of the same ideological fantasy" (*Defense* 449).

In Hobbesian contexts, nature and the corporation cannot speak themselves, and must find spokespersons or be impersonated. It's worth remembering the now odd fact that transcendental nature was once imagined to have a voice in American culture. Very much in Emerson's wake, for example, Dillard in *Teaching a Stone to Talk* repeatedly laments that nature has grown mute: "Nature's silence is its one remark. . . . We as a people have moved from pantheism to pan-atheism. Silence is not our heritage but our destiny. . . . Did the wind use to cry, and the hill shout forth praise? Now speech has perished from among the lifeless things of earth, and living things say very little to very few" (70–72). (Again, pantheism in US culture represents a long-evolving discourse that offers a locus for locating issues of transcendent nonhuman voices, whether in nature or the corporation.) Subsuming and silencing nature, corporations become the repository for such transcendent speech, souls, and life. In the zero-sum game of speech, now nonliving things have very much to say to very many. And where nature once spoke to and for us, we must now be its legal guardians. But the corporation always dispossesses the stand-in.

Chapter Forty

Corporations Cannot Speak

In the following chapters I transition between the linked precepts of nature and law and address the legal precedents and protections for false advertising that precipitate the judicial validation of corporate personhood. While readers expect autobiographies and biographies to document "the truth" of their subjects' lives, almost all advertising, the self-representation of corporations, is constructed so that its claims cannot be evaluated or verified. Corporate advertising here becomes a radical mutation of life writing (forms of biography and autobiography). As noted, corporations use a wide variety of beards—stand-ins and fakes—to speak for them, which is consonant with the unreliability and disjointedness of advertising.

In assessing the legal framework through which corporations speak, it's useful to consider who can sue corporations for false advertising, and why, in the context of legal standing and a variety of kinds of personhood. The critical fiction isn't simply that corporations are persons, but that they're not specific and delimited associations of persons, which, in that context, cannot have personhood. (Using transactional targeting, Republicans tend to treat corporations as private individuals when they like the way they speak through money, but as a public trust when they engage in speech that's aligned with progressive agendas.) Republicans often assert that they oppose gay marriage because it would propel us down a slippery slope to allowing people to marry cows: yet they rarely apply the same argument to corporations, and particularly their standing to sue or their status as legal persons. This is an important contrast, as Justice Douglas implies in his dissent to *Sierra Club v. Morton*, 405 U.S. 727, 742–43 (1972), addressed below. Ironically, the Court in *Morton* held that the Sierra Club, as a corporation, had no standing to sue to stop development in a federal park, but that it could file suit on behalf of any member who had suffered individual harm, in this case anomalously deciding corporations could have no collective, "non-economic" interest in such issues (at 734, 739–40). Overall, especially in the past thirty years, the Court has tended to ratify rights and standing when it would benefit corporations and deny them when it would limit corporate prerogatives or extend liability. Constraints concerning standing and the noneconomic interests of corporations have been vitiated, as evident in the spate of lawsuits regarding the religious and moral rights of corporations. It seems particularly paradoxical that the Court in *Hobby Lobby* denied employees the right to contraception, since it was allowing corporations to screw them.

In his dissent in *Sierra Club,* Justice Douglas asserted that

> Inanimate objects are sometimes parties in litigation. A ship has a legal personality, a fiction found useful for maritime purposes. . . . The ordinary corporation is a "person" for purposes of the adjudicatory processes, whether it represents proprietary, spiritual, aesthetic, or charitable causes. So it should be as respects valleys, alpine meadows, rivers, lakes, estuaries, beaches, ridges, groves of trees, swampland, or even air that feels the destructive pressures of modern technology.[1] (405 U.S. at 742–3)

As Stone elaborates in *Should Trees Have Standing?*, law is "peopled with inanimate rights holders: trusts, corporations, joint ventures, municipalities, Subchapter R partnerships, and nation states, to name just a few" (5). But trying to speak for the subaltern in nature—for those without a voice—as a guardian or stand-in is different from trying to confer a voice upon a thing that claims commercial and social personhood (25–27). (And first we must acknowledge that we speak "for" nature from some contestable human perspective.) In other words, we confer personhood and rights on the powerless and voiceless to seek justice; we confer greater personhood on the powerful as part of a zero-sum game. We should situate corporate personhood as part of a long line of hierarchies in the West that has devalued people of color and those who aren't in power. African Americans and indigenous people often symbolically represent the opposite of the corporation—they've been treated through much of New World history as precapitalist resources and bodies to be harvested, but a similar logic has been applied to any person or group situated as too close to nature. In Powers's *The Overstory*, the aspirational teleology is "Children, foreigners, prisoners, women, blacks, the disabled and mentally ill; they've all gone from property to personhood. . . . Plant rights? Plant personhood" (237). Giving corporations personhood unravels progress toward civil rights, women's rights, disability rights, and so on, and reverses the direction of Powers's list. Recapitulating Justice Douglas's dissent in *Sierra Club v. Morton,* and citing Stone, one of Powers's characters asks, "Should trees have standing?" "He seems to be saying that the law's shortfall is that it only recognizes human victims." "And that's a problem?" "He wants to extend rights to nonhuman things" (247). Powers's characters begin to connect like trees, thinking the same thoughts (much the way the thoughts of many of Pynchon's characters bleed into one another):

> Children, women, slaves, aboriginals, the ill, insane and disabled, all changed, unthinkably, over the centuries, into persons by the law. So why shouldn't trees and eagles and rivers and living mountains be able to sue humans for theft and endless damages? . . . It is no answer that to say that streams and forests cannot have standing because streams and forests cannot speak. Corporations cannot speak either. (250)

But these corporations leave the rest of us speechless; and they remain in a zero-sum game of rights with every entity Powers enumerates above.

When right-wing critics challenged New Zealand's designation of a mountain and river as having human rights (partly in the context of their being sacred to Maori peoples) on the ground that they weren't human, because they have no bodies, the prime minister responded, neither do corporations (Santos). Aboriginal land especially serves as a contested site for determining who has a body (as well as a soul), and whether nature and the corporation, which exist in opposition to one another, are all-powerful forces that should preside over society. If corporations have standing as persons, why don't abused cows or trees, which at least have the distinction of being alive? The ontological justification for granting such status to corporations isn't just flimsy, but purposefully contradictory and arbitrary—and utilitarian at best, from a legal and philosophical perspective. It's a critical, foundational tenet of our jurisprudence that we've awarded standing to the artificially created constructs of business but denied it to almost every aspect of nature, however we situate them as cultural constructs.

Against this backdrop, in which corporations have exceptional rights and control over communication, what standing do people have to intervene and object? Do we have any substantive protection from false advertising if most advertising is false? We routinely underestimate the harm that comes from false advertising and overestimate the impact tailored regulation of commercial claims would have on the expression of opinion. Increased regulation of ads wouldn't violate the First Amendment, but they would help redress the ways corporations have captured debate. Assertions involving product safety, manufacturing, contents, and benefits are subject to objective verification, not only without causing any harm to free speech, but as a prerequisite to it.

Courts especially overemphasize the benefits of commercial speech in a free marketplace of ideas, or downplay misleading assurances as incidental "puffery," under the presumption that consumers are better suited to evaluate the truth of advertising claims. The underlying assumption is we can't have any objective or consensus approach to advertising. But if we take that view, we relegate our culture to the control of corporations: to inhuman systems—algorithms, mechanistic forces, AI, deterministic and immutable directives—that are antithetical to culture. US courts long have tended to pander to commerce and emphasize the benefits of commercial speech in a free marketplace of ideas, and they tend to downplay misleading statements as puffery and ignore fraud, mislabeling, and misrepresentation that can be documented objectively. The government generally maintains a stance of neutrality, that it will not interfere in certain business practices that are unsavory or downright misrepresentative (marked by erratic and rare attempts to regulate astrologers, palm readers, and Scientologists). While some state laws prohibit limited forms of false advertising and deceptive business practices, they usually have a narrow reach and are stochastically enforced at best.

The absurd history of anti-spam and anti-telemarketing laws in this country illustrate the power and influence corporate lobbyists have to dilute and neutralize any attempts to curtail advertising and commercial harassment. Under a fabricated presumption of preemption, the federal government gutted California's viable protections against spammers under the Federal CAN-SPAM Act of 2003. Decades ago, the California legislature estimated "that spam costs California organizations well over 1.2 billion dollars" annually (Cal. Bus. & Prof. Code § 17529(d)).[2] That California statute enabled individuals to sue spammers in small claims courts and provided liquidated damages of $1,000 "for each unsolicited commercial e-mail advertisement" in the case of willful spamming. Not only is the federal law that supplanted all such state laws ineffective, it abets and encourages spammers and grants all but the most incompetent de facto immunity. (Corporations routinely dismantle oversight of corporate malfeasance by using lobbyists to pass corporate-sponsored, federal preemptions that preclude state regulation and localities from alerting anyone to their behavior, for example when Monsanto pressures states not to label GMOs, or factory farms proscribe local restrictions on their practices or the dissemination of information pertaining to them. Such responses don't just restrict choice but sensor public access to information.) CAN-SPAM is another giveaway to corporations; it effectively punishes only mass emailing pornographers, if that, and it leaves individuals virtually no recourse to protect themselves. Like most corporate-sponsored legislation, it inverts or does the opposite of what it proclaims it does.

Speaking of spam, false food is as prevalent in the United States as false advertising. Books such as *The Omnivore's Dilemma* and *Fast Food Nation* and the film *Super Size Me* have documented the many problems pertaining to corporate food production. But advertisers have considerable leeway to mislead consumers about food without running afoul of the law. We're eating advertisers' words. False labeling often involves the most literal form of consumption, from assurances regarding "organic" food to extra-virgin olive oil (you probably should be suspicious of anything that describes itself as extra-virgin). For example, the Department of Agriculture doesn't recognize, and therefore won't enforce classifications pertaining to, olive oil; as in many other contexts, corporate producers are actually told to regulate themselves. With few constraints or bases, advertisers continuously tell consumers products are good for them, beneficial, or healthy, or they will generate fantasized effects. Many wines labeled as "bottled and cellared" in Napa, for example, are made from grapes grown in Southern California and simply bottled in Napa. The point of advertising is to mislead consumers, or at least confuse them to the point that they can't evaluate a product; this principle now applies throughout our culture to politics and facts writ large.

Courts and legislatures have long made inconsistent and often syllogistic assumptions about "puffery," the putatively innocuous and unprovable claims that most advertisements make, such as "X product offers more happiness per milligram than Y product," or "X product is the choice of geniuses everywhere." But such simply noxious and meaningless declarations quickly morph into factual assertions that, for example, a product is organic or safe, or healthier or more effective than another in objective ways. The problem is that little difference exists anymore between puffery and misrepresentation. The recourse to the protections of puffery not only relies on fake differentiators but also presents a cover for lies and misleading claims presented as fanciful language, all under the penumbra of free speech.

Allied with the corporate ethos, US law relies on the adversarial system to evaluate truth claims, an increasingly delusional approach whose ideological provenance and influence makes it virtually immune to rebuttal, for example, even with regard to how wealth, influence, and attorney access affect the outcome of disputes. In court cases, juries allegedly will ferret out the truth when both sides exaggerate and lie. In advertising, all sides lie, but we have no practical process for deciphering these claims. Despite nominal objections and putative regulations, our culture has maintained a definitive tolerance for fraud and misrepresentation under the misprision that we must protect all speech, regardless of the source. Such a stance favors corporations in some of the same ways rhetoric about class warfare, deregulation, and tax cuts serves the interests of the superrich. Under the presumptions of corporate personhood, speech and facts are relativized, and the right to a "free market" translates into a largely unregulated freedom to lie. In theory, the market will sort out misrepresentation in the end, but in practice, corporations and the wealthy get away with what the poor cannot regulate, evaluate, or defend against. As a simple example, most people cannot gauge whether products are organic or what their health benefits are; even if scientific studies assess those specific products, they'll reach and be understood by a tiny fraction of the population that's bombarded with the advertisements for those items. To conclude that the best or healthiest products will emerge from this melee that masquerades for a debate, or that we're not continuously being swift-boated by commercial ads, is to embrace alternative facts and realities. We can have legitimate debates regarding how to regulate commercial speech and what objective truth claims we should evaluate and regulate, but we can do so only after admitting that the current system generally does not, as incessantly declaimed, allow people to make informed choices about commerce, politics, or anything else.

The freedom to advertise has encroached on the freedom to communicate in most meaningful contexts in contemporary society, because communication requires the equivalent of a neutral medium—equivalent to neutral weights and measures. In other words, freedom to communicate, like the freedom to use money or drive, depends on a regulated, "unfree" set of agreed-upon standards. Corporate speech, which includes prolific dark-money spending on campaigns and lobbying, seeks the eradication of standards except those of promotion, and it elides whatever weak regulations exist. The First Amendment is critical in protecting personal and political speech; but we have, as with many other rights, unduly expanded it to give corporations exceptional entitlements, when in fact their speech, which is always commercial, should be wholly regulable. The benefits of regulating corporate speech would far outweigh the drawbacks. Without it, we will continue to get what we pay for in public services, deregulated commerce, "reformed" tort laws, and a Boston Marketplace of ideas; and we will also get the culture we deserve. The free market, like the Bible and in different ways the Constitution, is a form of received wisdom that functions autonomically as an a priori and axiomatic set of doctrines—the Bible decided; the founding fathers decided; the free market decides. Those who pontificate most about the sanctity of the free market usually are the ones who already control it, or have delusional aspirations that they will.

Asserting in rote fashion that the First Amendment applies to corporations is atavistic and inapposite, for it expands the rights given to natural persons to artificial entities that didn't exist in their present form or with their present scope in the eighteenth century. Obeisance to the founding fathers at this point resembles a form of ancestor worship or divination, an abdication of responsibility to make decisions for ourselves and to acknowledge how the world has changed. The political gridlock that serves corporate interests also reflects a stage of exhaustion of late empire, unable to imagine anything original, even in the face of mounting evidence of environmental and institutional collapse. Originalism, which the right-wing Supreme Court Justices use to justify regressive social and commercial policy, presumes the intentions of the founding fathers still represent the pact we've made with government—even with regard to the myriad of technologies and social forces that didn't exist in their time, and despite dramatic changes in attitudes about citizenship and racial and gender equality. That conceptual myopia reflects the reality that only products can be (falsely) new and improved, while key aspects of our political discourse remain old and moribund, original and unimproved. The recourse to originalism is charlatanry especially in the context of the modern limited liability all-purpose corporation, which didn't exist when the Constitution was written, but whose antecedents the founders sought to constrain. Asking what the founding fathers thought about corporate personhood is akin to asking what they thought about net neutrality. Those who cannot address the present without asking what the founding fathers would do should ask a different question: what would corporate personhood do, and why are we letting it do it?

Chapter Forty-One

A Marketplace of Rights

In *Citizens United*, the Court addressed whether the government could regulate otherwise unbridled corporate speech. In his concurrence to *Citizens United*, Justice Scalia claims speech need not emanate from an individual to receive strict First Amendment protection: the individual's

> right to speak includes the right to speak *in association with other individual persons*. Surely the dissent does not believe that speech by the Republican Party or the Democratic Party can be censored because it is not the speech of "an individual American." It is the speech of many individual Americans, who have associated in a common cause, giving the leadership of the party the right to speak on their behalf. The association of individuals in a business corporation is no different—or at least it cannot be denied the right to speak on the simplistic ground that it is not "an individual American." 558 U.S. at 392 (emphasis in original)

As consistently inconsistent as ever, Scalia doesn't acknowledge the Court's jurisprudence that at least inchoately distinguished commercial and noncommercial speech, nor does he even develop any originalist or historical argument. He asserts a categorical, ontological, and epistemological fallacy—that corporations are associations that represent individuals, when they legally cannot. (The ironically named *Citizens United* of course reflects the posture and status of a corporation that displaces individual citizens. Since the citizens referenced are corporations, perhaps the case should have been called *Operation Corporation*.) Yet, according to Sepinwall, "the *Citizens United* decision does not rest on a conception of the corporation as a citizen; instead, the majority opinion grounds corporate free speech rights largely on the right of listeners to hear speech from as many different voices as possible" (2012 581). As Matthew Allman notes regarding all the more ironically/uncannily given the title at issue, an "interpretation of the Fourteenth Amendment [that does not include corporations] was likewise recognized by the Court, which held that the term citizens "applies only to natural persons, members of the body politic, owing allegiance to the State, not to artificial persons created by the legislature, and possessing only the attributes which the legislature has prescribed" (405n135) . In other words, when convenient, the Court ignores even the history of its own original decisions. In another end run around precedent, decency, and coherence, the Court claimed it was protecting persons' rights to hear speech by allowing corporations effectively to monopolize speech and political influence.

Scalia also disingenuously equates placing any limits on speech with an absolute denial of a right to speak, which not only isn't at stake but is legally unavailing in the context of the Court's validation of numerous time, place, and manner restrictions on all forms of speech.[1] Corporations also don't speak on anyone's behalf, even their shareholders. A teleological judicial bootstrapping, the concept of corporate personhood originally had no citable precedent, as the idea emanated from dicta (not citable opinion or a digression unnecessary to a holding) in *Santa Clara County v. Southern Pacific Railroad Co.*, 118 U.S. 394 (1886). The dicta were added to the headnotes (the unofficial summary of a case's key holdings) by a court reporter who had, in overdetermined fashion, been the president of a railway corporation, and whose scribblings never should have been incorporated into a Court opinion.[2] Corporate personhood is a fiction about a fiction institutionalized by judicial sleight of hand. It's again as if contingency were elevated to historical necessity and the validation of the concept reflected a kind of payment due for the original bill of rights. As one example of the hundreds of deleterious effects of *Citizens United*, as Senator Sheldon Whitehouse noted, moderate Republicans who were willing to sponsor legislation to redress climate change now refuse even to address the issue: fossil fuel corporations will "primary" and throw so much "free speech"—that is, dark money—at candidates who criticize them that they'll lose their seats. *Citizens United* is part of another zero-sum game: the more corporations can speak, the less your voice will be heard. Tellingly, while the Supreme Court majority opinions addressing the status of corporations make no explicit reference to corporate personhood, most enforce and extend the idea; corporate personhood is the ghost in the economic and legal machine, but the ghost of something that was never alive.

The fiction of corporate personhood is part of the apparatus that grants corporations full rights of political speech, but corporations are purely commercial enterprises. Corporations cannot (officially) hold office or vote, and these restrictions on personhood have not been controversial; why then does the Court consider speech another exceptional and personal right that cannot be regulated? In other words, corporations are mistakenly categorized as if they were in the marketplace of ideas instead of products. (Or rather, one should say their structural treatment in this context is deliberate.) Corporations initially were granted limited liability to meet specific public needs and eventually to sell goods or service; they never were supposed to be given exceptional rights so they could control the marketplace of ideas, but that's how the Court has rewritten (even its own) history. Some would argue products and forms of business, and communications related to them, inherently involve political ideas and come under the aegis of protected speech, or that all associations have absolute free speech rights, but such assertions rely on another conflation of law and fiction. Because of the nature of the speakers and the kind of utterances they can produce, all corporate speech, including spending, should be regulable as commercial in nature. Just as churches cannot enter politics unless they want to relinquish their tax-exempt status (a rule also increasingly ignored), corporations should have to relinquish their exceptional rights— especially of limited liability, immortality, and standing—if they want to enter the marketplace of ideas and engage in political spending and lobbying.

Contrary to the holding in *Citizens United*, courts should be able to regulate corporate speech in the same way they regulate false advertising, because nearly all corporate speech is a form of advertising. All a corporation's speech promotes its own business—a corporation's only function under the law that recognizes it is commercial. (Shareholders often object to corporate speech that doesn't promote a corporation's bottom line.)[3] Corporations are granted highly specific rights, protections, and limitations as commercial enterprises, and they shouldn't be allowed to claim such status only when it's convenient, while claiming full personhood only whenever that's convenient. The corporation's status, in those contexts, should determine the nature, scope, and regulability of its speech.

Chapter Forty-Two

Commercial Personhood

While the Supreme Court recognizes the difficulty in differentiating commercial and noncommercial speech (*Metromedia, Inc. v. San Diego*, 453 U.S. 490 [1981] [Brennan, J., concurring]), it also has held that "speech need not closely resemble a typical advertisement to be commercial." (See, e.g., *Semco, Inc. v. Amcast, Inc.*, 52 F.3d 108, 112 [6th Cir. 1995].) Citing the Supreme Court, the Sixth Circuit here observed that

> the only reference to [the] product [at issue] is contained at the very bottom of the last page. . . . The Court decided that the pamphlet's lack of specificity did not render it noncommercial. "That a product is referred to generically does not, however, remove it from the realm of commercial speech. For example, a company with sufficient control of the market for a product may be able to promote the product without reference to its own brand names." (*Semco v. Amcast*, citations omitted)

A corporation participating in the political process also is always promoting its product—that is, engaged in commercial speech. As the Sixth Circuit held in this case involving "informational" pamphlets and commercially motivated press releases,

> "No law of man or nature makes it impossible" to explain the process for manufacturing . . . without describing [a manufacturer's] own products, history, quality standards, safety standards, and commitment to [labor practices]. Such additions promote [the product] and invite commercial transactions, and they represent commercial speech. . . . Products or techniques may often be newsworthy, but that status does not permit their manufacturers to lie. The phrase "free advertising" . . . aptly describes the publicity manufacturers may receive in press releases, news interviews, or trade publications. The Lanham Act does not

prohibit or hamper such advertising; it requires only that manufacturers describe their products truthfully." (*Semco v. Amcast* at 113–14)

As with environmental regulations, restraints on corporate speech—which under *Citizens United* means spending on political campaigns—can be narrowly tailored to be content-neutral; rather than stifling free speech, such constraints are its prerequisite. You cannot have a free market that's a free-for-all. It should be unnecessary to belabor at length that as a matter of policy—as well as constitutional intention for those who think such justifications necessary—the vast majority of individuals will never be able to compete with corporate persons in voicing their speech or having it heard.

In addition, courts have emphasized that corporations shouldn't escape regulation simply by trying to insulate their speech within the context of public debate: the Court has "made clear that advertising which 'links a product to a current public debate' is not thereby entitled to the constitutional protection afforded noncommercial speech. . . . Advertisers should not be permitted to immunize false or misleading product information from government regulation simply by including references to public issues" (*Semco v Amcast* at 113, citations omitted).

The critical overlooked extension of this principle is that a corporation's *every speech act is an advertisement*; whether it spends money on campaigns, lobbying, prime-time ads, or sponsorships, everything a corporation says (since money is now speech), isn't just commercial, but *a commercial*. Corporations literally have no business producing speech unless it's commercial—that is, advertisement. While they should be allowed to lobby for their commercial interests, as a threshold issue, all a corporation's acts, including its political spending or "speech," should be regulable under the Commerce Clause and commercial speech doctrines.[1] Those regulations must still be constitutional, but commercial speech is afforded less protection, and commercial speech regulations are subject to less judicial scrutiny, than other forms of speech because of the vital public interests at stake, which courts long have recognized, and because corporations until relatively recently were not considered full public citizens under the law. It is corporations that should be considered the equivalent of fractions of persons, with limited rights to reflect their limited liability.

Under the test adopted in the Ninth Circuit under *Association of National Advertisers v. Lundgren*, 44 F.3d 726, 731 (9th Cir. 1994) (holding that informational pamphlets making factual claims about products' environmentally friendly attributes constituted regulable commercial speech), four factors govern

whether commercial speech enjoys the protection of the First Amendment: (i) whether the speech restricted is devoid of "intrinsic meaning"; (ii) the "possibilities for deception[,]" (iii) whether "experience has proved that in fact such advertising is subject to abuse"; (iv) "the ability of the intended audience to evaluate the claims made." (*Assoc. Natl. Advertisers v. Lundgren*, citations omitted)

But this approach mistakenly tries to cordon off the corporation's politically protected speech from its advertising. The threshold issue is whether all corporate speech should be evaluated under this test, not whether some utterances fall afoul of it. In the same way that the Court allows time, place, and manner restrictions on many kinds of public speech, it can regulate corporate speech in a content-neutral manner, not through any multifactor tests, but by establishing a threshold for whether a speaker is corporate, which is easily determined as a matter of law.

In *Virginia State Bd. of Pharmacy v. Virginia Citizens Consumer Council, Inc.*, 425 U.S. 748, 770 (1976), the Court held that content-based restrictions (i.e., laws that favored one point of view) regarding the dissemination of pharmaceutical prices were unconstitutional. The Court stressed, however, that

Untruthful speech, commercial or otherwise, has never been protected for its own sake [citations omitted]. Obviously, much commercial speech is not provably false, or even wholly false, but only deceptive or misleading. We foresee no obstacle to a State's dealing effectively with this problem. The First Amendment, as we construe it today, does not prohibit the State from insuring that the stream of commercial information flow cleanly as well as freely. (*Virginia State Bd. v. Virginia Citizens Cons. Council* 771)

Or as Richard Powers formulates the issue in *The Gold Bug Variations*, "Information is considered contrast: it can be won only by building a differential between sound and noise"—that is, protected speech and advertising (420). "In bad moments, I blamed advertising. It had always depressed me: form without substance, noise parading as sense. But in fairer intervals, I knew Keith only did what most of us do for a living; he sold things, only a little more honestly than most. . . . "The art form of the century . . . [figuring out] how to say 'Eat Multinational Carcinogen patties' appealingly" (258). From *The Gold Bug Variations* to *Gain*, Powers aptly situates advertising as a carcinogen whose end result is often the mutation of healthy cells into cancerous ones, and sound into noise at all levels of culture.

How can the public get a stream of clean information when it's full of clean coal and flowing under clear sky initiatives? If the stream of commercial information needs to be regulated, the same reasoning should hold for corporate spending masquerading as speech. Courts have all but abandoned this notion that information must be clean to be useful, wholly relinquishing the task of ensuring that corporations don't monopolize the channels of communication. In

the context of commercial speech, and especially commercial speech impersonating political speech, courts suddenly adopt a kind of know-nothing reserve, a highly localized inability to evaluate information. If the Court treated
corporate political spending as commercial, it wouldn't need to address its
content, unless a regulation on its face or as applied favored or penalized
certain points of view. Justice Stewart wrote persuasively in his concurrence
to *Virginia State Bd.* that

> Since the factual claims contained in commercial price or product advertise-
> ments relate to tangible goods or services, they may be tested empirically and
> corrected to reflect the truth without in any manner jeopardizing the free dis-
> semination of thought. Indeed, the elimination of false and deceptive claims
> serves to promote the one facet of commercial price and product advertising
> that warrants First Amendment protection—its contribution to the flow of ac-
> curate and reliable information relevant to public and private decisionmaking.
> (*Virginia State Bd. v. Virginia Citizens Cons. Council* at 780)

As the Seventh Circuit also has held, "the public and private benefits from
commercial speech derive from confidence in its accuracy and reliability.
Thus, the leeway for untruthful or misleading expression that has been allowed in other contexts has little force in the commercial arena." *Nat'l
Comm'n on Egg Nutrition v. Fed. Trade Comm'n*, 570 F.2d 157, 161 (7th Cir.
1977). The same principle should apply more forcefully to the regulation of
corporate spending on political ads or campaigns, as well as other kinds of
corporate speech, most critically to address issues of saturation, domination,
and media control. But what about corporate speech outside the commercial
arena? To distinguish between kinds of corporate speech creates invidious
problems and misapprehends the legal and ontological limits of corporate
personhood.

To assess what one might call the leviathan effect of corporate speech, we
can consider the consequences of allowing corporations an unfettered right
to political speech, first by looking at the harmful repercussions of corporate
speech even in commercial contexts.[2] Courts have been better at addressing
what they view as identifiable advertisements than other forms of corporate
speech, in part because they make erroneous threshold distinctions regarding
the kind of speech corporations can make. In *Lundgren*, the court noted the
"potential for abuse" raised by the increasing popularity of socially conscious
advertising, and the "growing confusion surrounding many environmental
marketing claims" (at 727–28) (citation omitted). The Ninth Circuit here
found that

editorializing [i]s not essential to product advertising ("while statements that a firm supports recycling, for instance, are undoubtedly included in advertisements as a marketing tool and may in fact augment sales, firms can nevertheless sell their wares without editorializing about the environment"). Conversely, the district court persuasively reasoned that a firm can editorialize about the environment, lambast[e] the statute or laud recycling without advertising or otherwise making commercial representations about one of its products. (*Assoc. Natl. Advertisers v. Lundgren* at 730, citations omitted)

Such a strategy to separate kinds of speech might help regulate false claims if it were properly enforced. But such an approach carves out critical areas of unregulated commercial activity: many corporations will exploit any loophole to avoid tax or liabilities or try to buy elections. Ruth Breeze predicts that "the trend towards blending promotional information with information will continue" (146), but courts increasingly refuse to distinguish between editorializing and advertising or campaign contributions: the latter is all the same kind of commercial speech, but courts now treat it as protected personal speech, much as they imagine corporations have religious beliefs. As Michael Schudson notes, the United States is a promotional culture whose ethos permeates not just business and sales, but religion, health care, entertainment and politics (13). One legislative solution would be to treat corporate campaign spending as commercial advertising, and corporate personhood as a purely commercial and limited form of being.

Courts, however, instrumentally tend to differentiate allegedly diverse kinds of corporate speech on the basis of content, rather than the status of the speaker. They do so in part because they have no coherent definition of personhood, but also to justify ends and outcomes determined to be desirable. According to Reza Dibadj, lacking "a theory of constitutional personhood is unsettling. . . . [What Justice Black stated regarding] the Fourteenth Amendment applies more generally: '[i]t requires distortion to read "person" as meaning one thing, then another within the same clause and from clause to clause.'" Put bluntly, "the Court has never set forth a specific test to determine what a constitutional 'person' is" (749–50, citations omitted). Kathleen Sullivan observes that "these different approaches have raised the question whether the Court's corporate personhood jurisprudence is purely result oriented" (1754). Regarding a related inconsistency, Matthew Allman observes that the Court's "mantra is that "the Government cannot restrict political speech based on the speaker's corporate identity" under the strictures of the First Amendment" (402). But as Anne Tucker proposes, the Court's claim that the law doesn't make distinctions based on the identity of the speaker is patently false in the context of corporate law; in fact a great deal of speech is regulated or compelled based upon the corporate identity of the speaker. The corporate charter filing requirements . . . along with the requisite continuing disclosures and securities regulations . . . create a slew of corporate speech based solely on the corporate identity of the entity. (543–44, citation omitted)

The status of the speaker should be a threshold consideration in the context of corporations because the speaker isn't a speaker: there's no person or identity about which to make distinctions. Granting full First Amendment rights to corporations is comparable to granting them to AI or virtual pets; the minds behind all these things are separated from the speakers, either by law or necessity.

As Justice Stevens, with whom Justices Ginsburg, Breyer, and Sotomayor joined, concurred in part and dissented in part, the overturned statutory ban in *Citizens United* had

no application to genuine issue advertising—a category of corporate speech Congress found to be far more substantial than election-related advertising, [citation omitted] or to Internet, telephone, and print advocacy. Like numerous statutes, it exempts media companies' news stories, commentaries, and editorials from its electioneering restrictions, in recognition of the unique role played by the institutional press in sustaining public debate. . . . [The statute] functions as a source restriction or a time, place, and manner restriction. It applies in a viewpoint-neutral fashion to a narrow subset of advocacy messages about clearly identified candidates for federal office, made during discrete time periods through discrete channels. (*Citizens United* at 419)

While even these justices failed to understand how corporate personhood affects the nature of all corporate speech, they did emphasize that the statute simply regulated corporations in the same permissible way it could have regulated individuals. In other words, corporations under *Citizens United* don't have the same rights as people—they have far more. If we once at least claimed to be a nation of laws rather than people, we're now a nation of corporations.

The implications of this corporate legal exceptionalism for human personhood are myriad and mortifying. The law relies on a series of often inchoate theories of personhood because our society has no coherent, accepted definition of what persons or their rights are. (One need only consider how offensive it is that many rights are afforded only to citizens, because the state confers and redefines personhood based on birth and other arbitrary criteria; in such a system, it's no wonder human personhood is contingent and corporate personhood is guaranteed, because the state decides on often contingent and arbitrary bases who and what, in effect, has a soul, or rather is human.) One of the most disquieting but less obvious corollaries of the unprecedented transfer of rights, power, influence, status, once private information, and money to corporations is the concomitant transfer of many aspects of human identity. In the multifaceted zero-sum game I've been delineating, as people identify with or become ads, corporations and their products seem to become more human or gain personalities. According to Thomas Frank, brands start to appear and present themselves as *"more human than us"* (*One* 229, emphasis in original). This inversion paces the conferral of personhood on corporations and the way things increasingly appear to act like persons in our culture. If we resituate Frank's claim as part of a zero-sum game, we should realize that for products and corporations to appear more human, they must be siphoning that humanity from someone. Our personhood is increasingly constructed by the inhuman thing of the corporation. Under corporate capitalism, desires are generally not spontaneous, but developed through discourses of envy and manipulation, ones increasingly regulated by increasingly unregulated corporations. In such a system, biography in all forms, from fiction to history, largely can document only rote and predetermined patterns of impersonal behavior.

That corporate biography, or the history of ciphers, matters because it now represents our shared culture. As I noted at the beginning of this book, most people know the same ads even if they share few other cultural referents or values. Put a hundred people in a room, and outside of perhaps *Harry Potter*, they'll likely have few cultural common denominators, except most will have viewed the same corporate ads and know their taglines, slogans, and messages. Displacing the artist and the community, the corporation has become our chorus, the collective voice of our culture, dramatized in the reality TV shows that inculcate a corporate ethos of competition, which is applied to every aspect of what was once ostensibly personal, private, and communal life. As these prototypical lives are exposed for public consumption, and hollowed out, their subjectivities are symbolically transferred to the corporation, or contorted to satisfy the premises of corpography. Put bluntly, corporations are writing our lives. The regulations and behaviors that codify corporate personhood erase and invert boundaries between private and public; personal and impersonal; political and commercial; interested and disinterested; and human and simulacra. It might be too late to distinguish among private speech, political speech, and commercial speech; corporations might already have become our shareholders.

Chapter Forty-Three

Advertisements against Myself

The developers of the internet didn't want the web to rely on advertising or commercial sponsorship, a battle they wholly lost. The perfect medium for the artificiality of corporate personhood, the internet is now dominated by advertisements. CEO Eric Schmidt acknowledges that Google is "in the advertising business" (Auleta 31). The internet is the ideal medium for advertisers—its space instantly can be commercialized. Jackson Lears documents that "the apotheosis of private selfhood coincided with the emergence of new ways to invade privacy—and new justifications for the invasion. . . . Through market research, advertisers pioneered the statistical surveillance of private life" (137–38). The internet represents kind of continuous home invasion. Mark Bartholomew describes corporations as engaged in a commercial colonization of space, from Harry Potter post office stamps to endlessly surveilled video games; one (necessarily ironic) justification for their encroachment is to keep government and regulation out of our private space (31). Both Bartholomew and Wu suggest we reside in commercial panopticons, in which corporations harvest our data and compel us to watch what they put before us. But it's a fine line between encroaching on your privacy and offending your sensibilities—and turning you into an experimental animal. William Davies notes that "digital advertising billboards in Piccadilly Circus are harvesting data" through cameras that analyze the facial expressions of passersby—no public space is safe from being privatized and exploited (21). Through biometrics, our bodies will increasingly be harvested for corporate data and advertising. While we should be concerned about government monitoring, we're not nearly concerned enough about corporate surveillance.

Corporate AI incessantly evaluates you to identify what humans do. One of the many absurdities in using the internet involves the need to tell AI you're not AI, another form of collateral damage from corporate personhood. While they sometimes serve pragmatic security functions, these portals allow corporate technology to subject people to a primitive form of the Turing Test (they often require multiple rounds only to improve their algorithms). The price of such personhood tests is often depersonalization and sponsorship. On the heinous Live Nation ticket website, the "security" check code you have to enter is an ad slogan for Xfinity or Applebee's. Every time I access my bank account, I have to click no through an advertisement splash-page that tries to sell me something (a version of what advertisers call transpromo). Emblematic of many corporations, my bank also alleges its barrage of spam emails are "noncommercial messages sent to [me] as part of [my] account relationship," which is legally and ethically ludicrous. The default setting for websites and email is that you have to opt out of receiving ads rather than opt in, because the presumption is that corporations have the right to subject you to ads, and you have a largely unenforceable option to object if you can figure out how. When I use my ATM, my bank slows the transaction so the screen can load advertisements. Many corporations illegally make you log into their websites to unsubscribe (from spam email you never requested) so they can subject you to another round of ads and further monetize site statistics. As Wu notes, most marketers and advertisers measure their success not in terms of ingenuity, creativity, value, or benefit, but "the ability to generate traffic" (*Attention* 281). Corporations frequently advertise to you while you're on hold, or they turn the call into a telemarketing sales pitch: "Now that you're on the line, let me tell you about our other products. What cable service do you use?" Representatives are instructed to keep you on the line solely to make sales pitches; customer service calls, like the products or services themselves, become pretexts for more advertisements.

With the escalating reliance of corporations on meta-data about every micro-facet of your life, corporate advertising invades privacy on a scale never before possible. As David Bromwich elucidates, many Americans self-destructively believe they have to exploit and market their private lives to bolster their public selves, to affirm that they even exist; Bromwich terms this a belief in the "publicity cure" (145–47). Corporations intensify this alienation by providing the images and publicity people identify with, and the imperatives and means by which to sell out their own privacy. The irony again is that we become more and more impersonal by seeking identity through the mechanisms and mediations of impersonal corporations. Roughly fifty years ago, Steiner already identified the inception of a new era of ontological degradation:

> Historians may come to characterize the present era in the West as one of a massive onslaught on human privacy . . . by the necessary uniformities of our economic and political choice, by the new electronic media of communication

and persuasion. . . . Increasingly, we come to know real privacy, real space in which to experiment with our sensibility, only in extreme guises: nervous break-down, addiction, economic failure. Hence, the appalling monotony and *public-ity*—in the full sense of the word—of our outwardly prosperous lives. Hence also the need for nervous stimuli of an unprecedented brutality and technical authority. (*Language* 76, emphasis in original)

In this sense, publicity is an assault on privicity. Well before A. C. Newman named his band after Jimmy Swaggart's rant about the purveyors of rock and roll, Steiner noted that "the new pornographers subvert [our] last vital privacy: they do our imagining for us" (77). Despite the continuity of representation from the world of painting to that of advertising, according to Berger, "the function of publicity is very different," because the spectator-(painting)-owner isn't the spectator-(consumer)-buyer, who never can escape the cycle of consumption (141). This corporate economy isn't based on ownership, but the impossibility of securing contentment: as Berger specifies, "All publicity works upon anxiety," and the advertisement manipulates your anxiety that you will be unloved, empty, less fulfilled, and even less of a person if you don't own this product (143). What you never can possess is respite from the cycle of planned obsolescence; induced need and dissatis-faction; and escalating impropriety.

Like social media, advertisements often make people depressed, set-ting them longing for things that they can't have, or whose possession will disappoint them. The central premise of advertising is that purchases cannot satisfy needs—that would be, for the corporation, a self-defeating prospect. It must instead defer gratification, create new or ongoing needs, and inflame dis-affection. Corporations don't satisfy needs: they create and manipulate them. Coke is a perfect emblem for this process since it often makes you thirstier. In Žižek's terms, advertising also helps implement the perverse internal in-junction that you must, in effect, consume and enjoy yourself: "The superego imperative to enjoy thus functions as the reversal of Kant's '"*Du kannst, denn du sollst!*' (You can, because you must!)—it relies on a 'You must, because you can!'" (*Parallax* 310). In other words, hedonism becomes obligatory, a chore, and a facade for its opposite; we must shop not only to be good citizens, and save the economy, or compete with the neighbors, but now as an intrinsic compulsion. Žižek details the effort we expend to enjoy ourselves (even if it kills us) in neoliberal capitalist societies, and the anxiety we experience in trying to do so, which comports with corporate conditioning: "Subjects experience the need to 'have a good time,' really to enjoy themselves, as a kind of duty; consequently they feel guilty if they fail to be happy" (*Frag-ile* 135). Žižek gives the example of Viagra, which putatively eliminates male excuses for not having and relishing sex—meaning if you don't enjoy something, it's your fault (133–34).[1] If you don't respond to ads or enjoy what they're hawking, you can blame only yourself, if you still can locate it.

Ironically, given the way most people think of them in terms of instant gratification, social media, the internet, and iPhones represent technologies of referral and deferral; we no longer experience something until someone else acknowledges it in mediated form. We need another like, another hit, another product. Increasingly at events such as concerts, people post to update their social media status. It's not simply a question of not being present—it's living a life mediated not only through technology, but corporations. People seem to need affirmation from someone to know they're there, but approval from other people is never enough in itself. Such externalized vectors of self-worth are closely connected to advertising culture and its mission to keep one in endless deferral and reference, never in the moment, never satisfied, and in a cycle of fabricated desire, suspended gratification, and endless linking.

Chapter Forty-Four

The Self as Ad

Usually without being conscious of it, we're held hostage to ads in many aspects of daily life in contemporary Western economies, most obviously any time we interact with media companies.[1] Broadcasters have become so intrusive, and content so devalued, that many networks now show ads as crawls below films; many cable networks put animated ads at the bottom of movies. Everything is an opportunity to exploit you, to advertise to you. Comcast added an advertising scrawl to its channel guide, cutting it by a third and subjecting you to a new ad every time you scroll for a program, most of which also advertise to you. Internalizing the values of such advertising—a tolerance and even willingness that corporations and advertisements will invade every facet of our lives—people even volunteer to become ads; we identify with slogans and products, which again involves a transfer of personhood from people to corporations; and we long to put ourselves on TV to become slogans and products. Rushkoff suggests that our imminent problem isn't just corporations, but the corporatism we've accepted as normative (*Life* xxiii). Particularly when people identify with them, ads can reflect a kind of masochism, or even voluntary self-mutilation; recalling Tom Sawyer's whitewashing scam, corporations use ads to get people to pay them for, and to glamorize, their own subjugation.

In what is no doubt only a temporary new low, it is commonplace to see people standing at suburban intersections frantically jiggling signs, usually for fast-food corporations or real estate developments (with names such as Willow Glades, assuring you it's near neither willows nor glades). In another bizarre spectacle we've become inured to, these sign wielders stand by the road gesticulating wildly and twirling signs; they operate on principles of irritation and distraction. What one would have hoped was an archaic vestige of the depression has returned with a dispiriting twist in many aspects of society. These human equivalents of the balloon puppets in car lots twisting in the wind are what many of us become under the domain of corporate personhood.

People's susceptibility to advertising, or corporate personality, reflects a cross between fetishization, reification and a form of abuse. In a culture where every surface is for sale, people are the last available spaces. In another literalization of the way we sell our bodies to the corporation, many of us become walking ads, either via the brands we display or the way we behave. Forms of the sandwich board have been used for at least the past three centuries, but the contemporary trend is to turn us into human billboards and corporate props. We're not only tracked for our consumption, but, through our relationships to our purchases, we become mobile signboards. (Logos have become our *logos*—the Greek concept for a unifying, divine principle of culture, a force immanent in our lives.) In the zero-sum game I've been delineating, as people align themselves with ads, products seem to become more human or gain personalities. In this form of reification, we long to sell ourselves to become the "person" who is aligned with and sponsored by the corporation. Consumers are also being conscripted to provide advertising; they're no longer just paying premiums to wear brand insignia, but providing free advertising through a mixture of blogging, reviewing and social networking. Any time someone dons or adopts such corporate logos, she becomes a kind of cyborg, merges with the corporate form, or incorporates the premises of the corporation into herself. When consumers generate Amazon feedback, clothing ratings or Yelp reviews, they might be providing useful information, but they're also promoting products and revealing their personal details. (However, the Ninth Circuit recently indicated that Yelp effectively charges businesses that seek to receive improved ratings, confirming these so-called consumer-driven sites are often captured.) Reviewers' private information, and their public biography, become commercialized. Advertisers increasingly rely on the word-of-mouth of those whom Malcolm Gladwell situates as trendsetters and connectors, and the things that, and people who, once couldn't be bought: the edgy and alternative who can be co-opted; those invested with personal cachet and charisma (Moore 41, 45). Their putatively noncorporate personae, and one might be tempted to say their souls, are again harnessed to animate the impersonal corporation.

That you cannot escape from advertisements becomes especially clear whenever you travel. On planes, you're a prisoner of ad space—the screen on the seat back flashes ads at you for your entire trip; the seat pocket is just a pouch for ads, from in-flight magazines to SkyMalls. You face zombie seatback TV screens that you can't turn off during ads, and that turn themselves back on to show ads. Passengers are guinea pigs—you watch movies that are sometimes little more than excuses for product placements, on the backs of trays that have advertisements. When you get on most flights, you're subjected to ten minutes of ads mixed in with safety instructions, much the way most national news programs now blur the line between advertisements and news. Most offensively, and in ways that should be illegal, you can't shut off the screen during the advertisements because the airline has tethered them to the required FAA announcements; this indefensible mixing of private and public is a common corporate tactic, and it represents another cooption of the public by the private. You're legally required to take off your headphones so you can be subjected to the pilot shilling for the airlines' credit card, the equivalent of my dentist shilling for teeth whitening. Many major airlines play commercials at you over loudspeakers from the moment you step on the plane; the napkins they give you are often merely surfaces for ads. On Gulf Air, by contrast, everything is Allah mode—the computer screen tells you the distance not to your destination, but Mecca. But otherwise, the mechanisms of advertisement change little across the globe even when cultural content does.

Airlines even advertise on their overhead bins, giving new meaning to their designation as carriers. The rubber escalator handrails at some airport have advertisements printed on them; the screens at baggage claim flash advertisements much larger than the information regarding flights. A sign at the West Palm Beach Airport proclaims, "We Hope You've Enjoyed Your Visit to the Best of Everything," a phrase that means precisely nothing—but if it did refer to anything, you certainly wouldn't find it in West Palm Beach. As with almost all such advertising and corporate pronouncements, there's not only no "We" behind this sentence, there's no content; it signifies the evacuation of personhood. One has to assume the Pepsi Generation, whatever that was, has ended. Popular corporate culture as a whole closely follows this willful suppression of content.[2] Corporations incessantly try to insert their DNA, their corporate view of the world, into your private existence, especially when you have no ability to shut them out. I think you should have the legal right to deface any screen that forces you to watch it, in the same way you have the right to defend yourself from someone punching you in the face.

The goal of the contemporary corporate enterprise is monopolistic in the worst sense—to inscribe every inch of space with the corporate logo, message and identity. Klein surmises that "if multinationals were left to their own devices, there would be no open space left on earth" (381). Such an impetus is culturally and environmentally suicidal, but corporations cannot factor such considerations into their mission. In principle and practice, this colonization of culture and space occurs at the expense of your identity. For many years, New York phone booths were maintained not to provide landlines, but ad surfaces—to sell something else: they weren't kept to help *you* communicate, but to communicate to you about something else. Many hotel key cards have ads on the back, and have been repurposed, along with thousands of other such items, to serve as ulterior surfaces for ads. Corporations use similar approaches with sponsored textbooks and virtually all sponsored formerly public/civic spaces. They no longer exist of or for themselves, but as referential springboards, to get you to buy another book, which in turn will advertise and lead you to another product. Even the UPC stickers on the fruit at my supermarket now serve primarily as scrolls for ads. The product just gets in the way; the signifier of the ad replaces the signified. These inversions are even more distasteful when they are applied to public space: before COVID-19, many tollbooths on the New Jersey Turnpike didn't properly designate which lanes still took cash, but every tollbooth had a giant ad for an insurance company plastered on its side. This same process writ large applies to you as a person; corporations are colonizing you as a space and turning you into their surfaces.

A system based on a model of addiction can't let you rest—you always must be referred to another product, which itself is a momentary stop on the way to another. The content is irrelevant, a necessary evil slowing down our progress toward pure referentiality. In a country that produces less and less in terms of tangible goods, and whose economy is increasingly abstract—involving transfers of numbers and information rather than goods—why should ads refer to anything beyond themselves? Ads involve a form of endless linking; corporate strategists design their sites, much like casinos, to get you to stay on them longer, keep you clicking, disoriented and unaware of the time, and keep you wasting it traversing a new series of ads in an increasingly constrictive space. Hamsters have a better chance of getting off wheels than you do of avoiding advertising.

If corporations could take the example of the British "entrepreneur" Reginald Perrin a step further, their perfect product would emerge as pure packaging, a weightless surface for ads. Eventually, we'll have that impossible ideal of advertisements that simply promote other advertisements without content and cut out the middleman—TV commercials already frequently advertise other TV shows rather than products, and ads might soon advertise other ads without any content getting in the way. On a recent cross-country flight, I received a packet of indeterminate Chex mix, whose package—mostly comprising air, like an overinflated balloon—didn't promote its own contents; the entire surface was an advertisement for a dot-com. Largely unidentifiable, the product was emblematically irrelevant: the point of the package was to refer to something else. With the triumph of this cereal packet ideology, we stand on the verge of dispensing with the product altogether. Ads are circulatory systems for signifiers that refer to something else in a never-ending chain of deferral to the next advertisement.

In broad terms, as advertising has increased its range and intrusiveness, manufacturing has decreased; while we produce fewer tangible goods, we produce more ads in what is less an information virtual economy than an advertising one. Many exceptions remain to this trend, especially in the context of "luxury" goods, but the ideal is to sell products that cost almost nothing; are small (from Coke to iPhones); and whose value is produced primarily by the ad/brand. Because many aspects of products are fungible, ads must convince consumers their identities are differentiated by branding. The asymptotic ideal curve is toward a product that doesn't exist, a pure ad for other ads, an ad channel; pure communication to consumers, who would choose the ad without the pretext of a cumbersome product getting in the way.

Chapter Forty-Five

Schadenfreudian Slips

Ad Copy and the Culture of Envy

Ads are fundamentally ontological: they tell us how we should be relative to others. Ads use a behavioral science of manipulation that draws on | sociology and psychology more than economics. It's through corporate advertising that people receive the most messages and images regarding identity, status, gender, age and class behavior, desire, fulfillment, and of course consumption. As Berger succinctly put it, "Publicity is about social relations, not objects. Its promise is not of pleasure, but of happiness: happiness as judged from the outside by others" (132). Advertising outsources our psyches. This externalization defines the mechanism of advertising—desire is eternally referenced and triangulated, and satisfaction is structurally deferred and placed beyond your reach. In a corporate sign system, the gap between desire and fulfillment, like the gap between corporation and people, cannot be bridged. Anyone trying to induce anxiety, discomfort, fear, envy, unhappiness, and addiction, and to manipulate your behavior using these tactics to get you to buy something, should be put in prison or given treatment. Instead we give awards to those who produce ads. Advertising is a close relative to gambling, alcoholism, and many forms of self-destructive, addictive behaviors, but more insidious, because it appears to most people as innocuous speech protected by the "free" market. Most ads target a cluster of self-destructive traits, such as envy, insecurity, and addiction, yet few people view advertising as posing a mental health problem. As Wu notes, Facebook's own early advertisements to advertisers stressed that the site featured "addicted" users (*Attention* 296). Not surprisingly, Facebook maintains that model of addiction by creating social anxiety, envy, and competition, and, in Marc Zuckerberg's words, by offering users the prospect (or rather illusion) that they're "building an image and identity for themselves, which in a sense is their brand" (298). Facebook at least is overt regarding the ways it, as a corporation simulating human behavior, turns you into a corporate person and product through "social" media: that term is as appropriately ironic as *Citizens United*. Most social media, like advertising, is depersonalizing in a corporate sense.

Many ads rely on unprovable exaggeration, aggressive assertion and pressure: they resemble pornography in having only one intended message/ result. Just as pornography's only goal is to get you hard or wet, advertising's only goal is the hard sell. Art doesn't (or at least shouldn't) tell its viewers what to think or feel. Herbert Marcuse proposed that authoritarian control of media telescopes and abridges "syntax[,] which cuts off development of meaning by creating fixed images [that] impose themselves with an overwhelming and petrified concreteness," and that description fits advertising language quite well (91). Most communication that has only one purpose is debased—it's usually propaganda, pornography, or advertisement, three things our culture increasingly excels in producing. Advertising also appropriates culture to commodify feelings and relationships. By its nature, advertising can present only simulated emotions, much like professional pornography; it mimics and necessarily mocks any real thing. The ad that tells you, "Subarus are made with love, that's what makes a Subaru a Subaru," insults anyone who's ever felt even mild affection. Such ads usually have to rely on tautology to identify the corporate identity, in much the way Tyson, as noted, has to claim only Tyson is like Tyson, or Nexium that only Nexium works like Nexium. Being subjected to such barrages of nonsense cumulatively and in profound ways erodes people's ability to define or critique. Even if not sacred, music, for example, is a medium to express deep emotion, and it demeans not just a song, but human experience, if what we hear in a continuous background loop is people singing ecstatically about breath mints and air fresheners. In ways Hobbes couldn't have anticipated, the point of advertising, and the system of producers and products it sustains, is to be artificial and to replace (the construct of) nature at every level. Coconut shampoos have nothing to do with coconuts, and likely have no substantive coconut in them; like the advertisement promoting them, they have nothing to do with your identity, happiness, or coconuts. That artificiality is why you can't get no satisfaction from the guy who tells you how white your shirts can be; every voice of the corporate person is designed to be a simulacrum of human life. The corporation's artificial personhood is the inevitable endpoint of this system, and it signifies the diminishment and displacement of your personhood.

Leaving aside the more complex question of what constitutes authentic human behavior, we should consider how the recipient is situated within the world of corporate advertising. The advertising speaker has only one intention, much as chartered corporations have only one purpose: any ambiguity of purpose or message could only be accidental and would violate the premises of the corporate charter. The recipient exists only as the object to be maneuvered. Proselytizing and advertising have one aim, to control behavior; perhaps all communication partakes of this process, but at least persuasive communication adheres to some rules, beyond manipulation at any cost: proselytizing and advertising tend to be lawless because their purveyors believe that the game has no rules or limits, the ends justify the means, or they bear the one true message. In the case of advertising, consent, interaction, and, most of all, rational evaluation, recede from the process, which, even in its most humorous and whimsical manifestations, relies on a language of assault. Why do we allow a system that's so destructive to what we allegedly value to be our primary form of communication?

Chapter Forty-Six

Pop-Ups and Pinups

Advertising Sex and Violence

Corporations and ads don't primarily sell products—they sell desire and confidence. Much of advertising speaks to a desire to be beguiled. As Joni Mitchell wrote in a long arc, we want "pretty lies": sex sells everything, and sex kills. Ads rely on wishful thinking: buy this and you'll be beautiful, desirable, and happy, promises we know can't be fulfilled. An equivalent process occurs with a strain of seduction, in which the seduced know at some level they're being used and will be betrayed. We suspect the product is hyped at best, but we buy it anyway, because we buy into the idea that something external can change or save us. Advertisements offer pretty lies that turn out to be pretty ugly. Ads promise that you're unique and will have your desires satisfied, but you discover the seducer says that to everyone. The difference between advertisement and legitimate commerce, communication, and art mirrors the difference between rape and seduction, prostitution and love, compromised discourse and disinterested reflection. (David Foster Wallace concluded that his own attempts to seduce women, to manipulate the emotions of others, made him similar to "the people selling Tide" (Max 234). As Berger documents, most ads, like traditional oil paintings, assume the viewer has a male perspective and gaze, but in this context the viewer is being seduced; the subject of advertising is situated as female, and subjected to the language of seduction (and betrayal). Berger remarks that the male spectator's "unequal relationship is so deeply embedded in our culture that it still structures the consciousness of many women"; corporations orchestrate a variation of that unequal relationship, only in this case the seducer isn't even human (63).

The mechanisms of sexual seduction and advertising frequently coalesce. As Girard points out, "The value of the article consumed is based solely on how it is regarded by the Other. Only Another's desire can produce desire." Girard's Other is no longer a "class oppressor," or an imagined foreign presence, but "the neighbor on the other side of the fence, the school friend, the professional rival" (223). With the help of advertising, society sets up a permanent opposition among persons that can't be resolved. The Lacanian Big Other is here the corporate person, another fiction that doesn't exist, but guarantees the economy of desire that underpins the material economy. Girard argues that the snob, for whom we might substitute many consumers, "desires nothing concrete," and the object of desire is fungible and almost irrelevant: it's the structure of desire that matters (224). As Melville also understood, advertising is an abstract and metaphysical process, detached from the object it's selling. In that context, Girard seeks to illuminate the "connection between individual desire and the collective structure" (226): that collective is in part manifested as the corporate person. Under corporate capitalism, desires aren't innate, spontaneous, or "organic," but developed and manipulated as part of a structure of envy and external influence, one now regulated by unregulated corporations.

Through dating profiles, personhood is increasingly advertised as a product, part of the commodification of everything from grades to marriageability, the slippage of the personal into the corporate, or the who into the that. (Dating sites typically try almost anything to increase site traffic, which means ad revenue—some publicize which users haven't been contacted recently, prompting people to log on more or create additional profiles.) Advertising is an agent that perpetuates assumptions about gender and sexuality. The relationship between what Germaine Greer called "engineered seduction" and advertising is a key part of the process that ritualizes sex so that it becomes acceptable (186): "Aqua Manda. Two words to change your life. . . . Even your bath can become a romantic ritual" (187). Under a romantic ethos—which, as Greer shows, is indicative of an economy that presupposes we're given to misogyny, self-deformation, tawdry mysticism, and self-loathing—we want products to seduce us. Consumption becomes a surrogate for sex, but also its prerequisite. Between dating sites, body products, the commodification and commercialization of all aspects of "romance," and our general self-representation, it's difficult to have a relationship without having a corporation in the room with us.

At an American Bar Association dinner on August 10, 2019, honoring Congressman John Lewis, musician Rhiannon Giddens, who was performing, mentioned that she had been reviewing ads for the sale of slaves; she noted, acknowledging the anachronism, how jarring it was to see people advertised as if they were cars. But the correlative is how inured we are to the idea of advertising that it seems normal and unproblematic to use the mechanisms of advertisements to sell not just cars but ourselves in almost any context—as not just neoliberal entrepreneurs but as corporate persons. Because most of us are now commodities, especially in terms of work and dating, we rely on the language of self-advertising, even as many conservative politicians tell us effectively to incorporate ourselves. At best, many people's dating profiles are a series of adjectives (I'm funny, warm, genuine) that follow the assertive model of advertising—they not only tell instead of show, but they also duplicate the tone, language, and depth of promotional spots. The internet can be exceptionally helpful in providing dating options and other social contacts, and nothing is wrong with using technology in personal contexts; but we've become increasingly willing to advertise and commodify ourselves in a manner that comports with and effectively makes us subsidiaries of corporate personhood. Gordon Pask and Susan Curran noted that in a 1971 survey, the majority of respondents "thought that many of the current uses of computers should be increased, except for the purposes of advertising and dating," which of course now feature prominently on the internet (51). Perhaps one always has been a commodity on what's openly called the dating market: but the way in which one advertises oneself, typically using the stock clichés of advertisers, suggests how difficult it is to dissociate oneself from the precepts of corporate personhood.

While exceptions exist—usually when advertisers try to cash in on progressive movements and market to underrepresented groups—the gender coding in advertising tends to be regressive and rely on a kind of lowest common denominator of emotions and clichés. To counter marketing data that indicated men viewed sparkling water as effeminate, advertisers developed a campaign that claimed "nothing beats the violence of a Perrier." Perrier has nothing to do with violence; its ads cultivate an arbitrary association of a product with a value, in this case glamorizing masculine aggression. Advertisers frequently try to manipulate our desire to conform to validated gender identities. Many advertisements address anxieties that we're too civilized or constrained, trying to assure us that some product or lifestyle choice will liberate us, counteract a "malaise and a feeling of suffocation in the over-civilized context in which spectators evolve" (Haineault, 152). (It typifies the fantasy logic of advertising to imagine we can become less trapped in consumer lifestyles by purchasing something.) Ads often tells us we can be more male, primitive, and virile, like cavemen, by buying things—the social hierarchy being presented is always linked to consumerism. The Other is more primitive than we are and inferior but retains some elusive magical potency/unobtanium that we can retrieve through the corporation. (We can remain politically correct and make fun of cavemen, but advertisers are running out of Others to establish as acceptable foils for the deracinated corporate identities we should espouse.) Again, these fantasies of escape have nothing to do with the products to which they're attached. As most advertisers will tell you, you're being sold narratives, not products.

Chapter Forty-Seven

The Art of Lying

Partly to achieve trademark protection, which precludes the ownership of generic terms, and partly as an outgrowth of the legal and cultural development of corporate language, corporate names and brand names are largely meaningless, created by committees to evoke feelings but convey no content. The name "Integra" is meant to insinuate a car has integrity; but like *xfinity, comcastic, abilify, hamptonality,* ad infinitum, it's an "artificial" word that conveys no information about a product, including who made it or how it was made and whether it's safe, environmentally sustainable, and so on. (Corporations often generate particularly artificial-sounding names that remind us that all company names, like religions, start off as fakes, and become naturalized. Brand names such as Acura might be iconic, as Danesi notes (30), but they impersonate words in much the way corporations impersonate people. As one tangential but emblematic example of how advertising language becomes a mere sound prompt, Germans commonly use the English word "sale" to advertise summer promotions, though many Germans don't know what the word means—it's another Pavlovian trigger.

Ads also have overtaken the oldest form of work, of selling one's body, in eroding the boundary between personal and commercial space. Usually without our consent, we're selling our personal space in the newest economy—our private selves. It's not kidney thieves we need to fear but soul thieves. The sponsored or captured person is the final progeny of the corporation, and part of the corporate biography—what indeed is in a name? For a period in the early aughts, people started to name their kids *as* brands as a form of paid sponsorship: even non-celebrity weddings have been sponsored. In November 2016, a Ukrainian man changed his name to iPhone7 to win an iPhone.[1] Such practices go back farther than one might think. Peter Zheutlin recently commented in the *New Yorker* that in 1894 his great-grandaunt, Annie Kopochovsky, who

293

was a professional cyclist, "traveled under the name Annie Londonderry" when she was being sponsored by the makers of that spring water (5). Companies can co-opt everything you own, even your belongings, to serve as advertising space. In California, trucks whose whole sides are ads are routinely left stationed on overpasses to serve as parked billboards. If you agree to turn your car into a mobile ad, you're obligated to drive around major arteries a certain number of miles a week and sometimes park in front of events or at specific locations; your car is monitored with a tracking device to verify its whereabouts, though that's no more intrusive than your cell phone. Such corporate creep represents not simply an encroachment on public space but on every facet of private personhood. Corporations and advertisers incessantly challenge and try to eliminate any remaining restrictions or limits on what they can incorporate. Many people in the Bay Area expressed resistance to the idea of putting up flashing billboards along the Bay Bridge because they would be would be ugly, inappropriate, and dangerously distracting, but, like ads in movie theaters, those giant marquees to nothingness gradually became accepted, and ever more obnoxious. The expansion of advertising's purview into once unthinkable contexts—from movie theaters to schoolrooms to bodies—is rarely reversed. Once that toll is established, it never gets rolled back. But there's only so much space—and so much personhood—to go around.

Chapter Forty-Eight

Needs and Wants

"What Separates The Men From the Boys? Bodyspray.
Who knew the answer to this eternal question would be so easy? Dial, the maker of RGX (RightGuard) Body Spray, thinks guys will buy what's face it, perfume, if this pert young thing, who also looks kind of easy, crawls towards them and says she likes it. Well? Would you?"

Evelyn Nussenbaum, *Business 2.0* (now defunct)

So that's what separates the men from the boys? Bodyspray is a product designed to create a fabricated anxiety, not meet a need, and Right Guard's copy responds not to an eternal question but to one that corporate advertisers made up a few years ago. That reflexivity reflects one of the many circularities of corporate logic, most of which follow the rules of rigged games: corporations create the disease and offer cures that you have to keep buying forever. (And of course, pharmaceutical companies notoriously create conditions and anxieties to treat.) As Colson Whitehead evokes the noxious spray of advertising in *Apex Hides the Hurt*, "Bottle a certain musty essence and call it Old Venerable. Spray it around the house and your humble abode might smell like the Winthrop Suite of the Hotel Winthrop" (11). For people to imagine they need a product to achieve an identity or to be liked is discordant and pathetic; it's also unnatural in the sense that such an attitude has to be inculcated far more artificially than other socialized beliefs. Corporations socialize consumers, now more aggressively, invasively, and pervasively than ever, to be dependent on them for specious forms of personhood and gratification.

Of necessity, advertising also highlights the disparities and inequalities of global capitalism, the distance between first and third worlds, needs and wants, and the self-indulgent demands of the spoiled. Contemporary ad-

295

vertising presupposes that needs and wants/desires can be conflated. The product is secondary if not irrelevant, because the need for it is fabricated and manipulable. Because advertisers create needs, consumers wind up battered by competing demands regarding what they should learn to need. While many even in Western economies cannot meet basic needs, advertisers frame wants as if they were both needs—necessities to identity and day-to-day life—and nonessential rewards. Many products are like toys: we desire them intensely and briefly, then quickly grow tired of them, as part of a necessary cycle: they can't satisfy our emotional needs, so we can fall prey to the demands of advertisers, who suggest we should desire something newer, which we're indoctrinated to believe somehow will be different from the last product that failed to deliver what it promised. It all works as long as we don't think too much about why we should live this way.

Chapter Forty-Nine

Farewell Welfare

To illuminate the role of consumers, I briefly explore the role of their antithesis: welfare recipients who symbolically live outside the system of advertising. In our society, the poor, and especially those on welfare, threaten to reveal how systems of advertising create consumer identity. In a parallel register, Wallace suggested in *Infinite Jest* that alcoholics and drug addicts embody the afflictions of a consumer society engaged in a compulsive search for gratification, yet simultaneously remain immune to the ubiquitous cycle of consumer demand because their needs cannot be further manipulated. The disturbing premise is that the only people, at least symbolically, who can resist advertising are consumed and controlled by addictive mechanisms even more destructive than advertising. More broadly, in terms of legal rights and ontology, the deserving corporate person is socially constructed as the antithesis of the undeserving person on welfare or drugs. While much of the press and the public chastised corporate banks for receiving government bailouts after the 2008 financial crisis, little was done to question the assumption that banks, not individuals, needed to be bailed out. Corporations, and their evolving form of personhood, are assumed worthy and rational until proven otherwise; the poor, many minorities, welfare recipients, and those who take out subprime loans are assumed unworthy and irrational until proven otherwise.

The above considerations regarding agency and personhood help contextualize how individuals, and especially the poor, tend to be blamed for allegedly making choices that necessitate public assistance, while corporations are largely shielded from inquiry into decision-making agency. In our culture, the enhanced liability of the poor is coterminous with and inversely proportionate to the limited liability that defines the corporation. For example, Anna Grear observes that corporations are agents when it comes to formulating and acting on some form of intent, but they escape liability because they're disembodied; under our criminal justice system, there's no body/corpus to produce and punish, and, I would add, more problematically, no intent or mens rea to be uncovered (91). As noted, despite the media's distracting focus on celebrity CEOs, corporations are designed to be legally and ontologically decentralized networks in which no agency can be located.

Is anyone in an urban capitalist society then able to live outside the purview of advertising? Aside from the few outliers who attempt to live off the grid, those who have the least disposable income, at least theoretically, aren't as relentlessly targeted by corporate advertisements; they have determinate needs they still have to meet, and therefore, at least theoretically, might be less subject to having their wants or desires manipulated. Symbolically, welfare recipients or the poorest members of society, or *homo sacer*, might abstractly represent people resistant to some of the premises of advertising. (Advertisers still target the poor with ads for low-end goods and services, exploit a lack of education and market specious automobile service warranties, debt reduction schemes, and other scams. But it's hard to turn unmet immutable needs into the arbitrary wants/desires advertising requires.) Under postmodernism, welfare posits an unacceptable "meta-narrative," providing an irrefutable, non-relative definition of set needs rather than manipulable wants. Supply-side economics makes no sense in the context of determinate or demand-fueled needs. In practice, of course, welfare is set up to mimic capitalism and ensure that welfare recipients are subject to the same conditioning of need and deferral of satisfaction as "consumers," whose desires, like those of penitents, are deferred to the next purchase, or the afterlife. But in terms of how they're politically castigated, and the recipients of irrational ire, it's clear that welfare recipients provoke anxiety regarding corporate capitalism—they're victims who must not only be blamed but also controlled. Berger proposes that "publicity speaks to the future tense and yet the achievement of this future tense is endlessly deferred" (146). The ulterior threat of "welfare queens" is that they can define and thus meet their needs, rather than have them endlessly deferred and redefined as mutable and created by supply/advertising. Corporations cannot market something effectively to people who have fewer wants than needs. In the welfare queen, the system paradoxically conjures the specter of someone whose needs can be met, and who therefore threatens what we might term the surplus value of faith—that which cannot be planned or defined in a market economy, which is the basis of advertising and supply-side economics. Welfare represents an embarrassingly stable, immutable and immovable force or demand in the flux of postmodern indeterminacy and supply. Advertisers try to turn luxuries into needs, but these goods paradoxically must remain luxuries for the wealthy to desire them. Yet in a system of corporate advertising, nothing and everything is necessary: all products are part of a fantasy of desire.

Extending Jean Baudrillard's work, I argue that welfare recipients cannot fully participate in corporate culture because they threaten its basic tenets: "The object/advertising system . . . is overwhelmed by the 'inessential' and by a destructured world of needs" (15). In other words, capitalism insists that supply determines demand, but more importantly and bizarrely, need, since human nature, in terms of consumption, supposedly no longer retains any fixed qualities. (This presumption reflects another contradiction with corporate culture, since advertising also presupposes a fixed and highly debased human nature that largely comprises envy, lust, avarice, and childish inattention.) Under the auspices of the free market, we don't plan the economy, or provide for need in advance: the systems of production, marketing, and advertising generate always mutable desire. But the essential need welfare represents remains disruptively outside and prior to such mutability and manipulation, a kind of ontological embarrassment to consumer capitalism. Baudrillard contends that "we can conceive of consumption as a characteristic mode of industrial civilization on the condition that we separate it fundamentally from its current meaning as a process of satisfaction of needs." In Baudrillard's estimation, "material goods are not the objects of consumption: they're merely the objects of need [or more accurately desire] and satisfaction" (21). Like George Gilder, the Reagan-era proponent of supply-side economics, Baudrillard seeks to unearth underlying principles of consumption and metaphysical capital, and separate material goods and needs from the metaphysics (what Melville might call the confidence game) of supply and desire. If, as Baudrillard elaborates, "consumption appears to be irrepressible, this is precisely because it's a total idealist practice which no longer (beyond a certain point) has anything to do with the satisfaction of needs" (25). Under the assumptions of supply-side economics and advertising, any commodity, including food, can be transformed into an item of luxury, an inessential. Consumption must be divorced from needs; supply from demand; and need from welfare.

The fervor with which many critics allege that people on welfare are "addicted" to drugs, sex, or profligate lifestyles—belied by the meager sums they receive—locates an overarching and deflected anxiety about consumer addiction. The ability to turn merchandise into metaphysical representations of wealth, and therefore of one's soul, comports with conservative notions that wealth is a state of mind, that positive thinking can raise one out of poverty, that faith matters more than material conditions, and that the poor remain poor because of character defects. In other words, material wealth is an incarnation of the soul; no wonder the corporation also needs to be imbued with one. Before postmodern politics, economic man was (at least envisioned as) a rational, predictable being; but in the age of consumer capitalism, needs, along with human nature, have become unpredictable and obscure, subject to conditioning and transformation (35–36). Persons become amorphous and lose many rights in this world in which advertising is the most paramount coercive influence: at least symbolically, welfare recipients stand unyielding outside that apparent corporate consensus.

Welfare recipients remain ostensibly beyond research and advertising, and aren't constituted by created needs, and so ironically represent the last remaining humanist subjects: their needs exist before the state, before language, and are neither created nor affected by any system of production. (In reality, most welfare recipients are subjected to the same cycle of consumer dependence as everyone else, even if they remain immune in theory.) We might say that dependence must be on supply, never on demand; it's acceptable, even desirable, to be addicted to surplus, to objects provided through "supply" that reflect desire, but not to depend on objects of use, demand, or necessity.

For Baudrillard, "the system of needs is the product of the system of production" (42), which relies heavily on advertising. A capitalist supply that corporations are always contesting, in part through advertising, can come to define even what should be immutable welfare need/demand. Trying to correct Galbraith, Baudrillard proposes that there's no proof that a rich person obtains "the same satisfaction from yet another [garment] as does a hungry man from a hamburger. But there is no proof that" they don't (40). In an economy of advertising, everything is beyond proof, and needs are artificial and fabricated. But to assume that people have no determinate needs or rights is to fall victim to the corporate system of production and values; to sanction the notion that advertising will tell us who we are and what we desire and need.

Chapter Fifty

Ask Your Advertiser
If Advertising Is Right for You

After David Reisman, author of *The Lonely Crowd*, Melissa Aronczyk contends that much as we accentuate small differences among ourselves to generate a sense of distinct personality, corporations create and exaggerate small and meaningless differences not only to brand products, but also to create false competition (42). As an offshoot of the corporate harnessing of consumer data, we also come to be defined by the materialism of market choices; corporate communications incessantly reinforce a preordained and narrow range of options. Corporations tend to foment specious competition and vitiate the sense that one belongs to a community. They frequently engage in what Chomsky might call manufactured competition with each other, which is coterminous with the process of generating forms of artificial competition among consumers (viewers). Corporations generally aren't competing with one another, but with one another's advertisements, or manipulative fantasies, which is a notable difference. Corporate competition is fabricated at many levels, and trickles down and affects most aspects of corporate culture. Even cooking shows are structured around induced, contextually discordant competition and manufactured animosities. The plague of reality TV competition shows is the consequence of allowing corporations to control narrative and drama.

This foregrounding of competition and discord helps conceal a system that offers few choices and is predicated on near monopolies of not just products, but ways of being. Lynn reminds us that Colgate and Crest wholly dominate the toothpaste market, and use the practice of "category management," through which retailers "outsource the task of stocking shelves and setting prices to one company," which then sets prices for both (In Frank, "Free"). Similar principles hold true of mattresses. We laud the idea of fostering competition, but it's often fake and reflects an underlying concen-

301

tration of market share. The same principles apply to many aspects of media, marketing, and consumption. Andrea Bennett documents the way many news outlets have "turned to unprecedented single-sponsor partnerships" (7); corporations want you to visit their website and hear their message exclusively, and to reward consumers for "loyalty" in ways that promote monopoly power. As many have noted, contemporary corporations are often oligopolies, and a few giant entities collusively limit competition and control markets. One company sometimes owns putatively competing supermarket chains, and simply brands and gears them to different segments of the market. As Lynn also remarks, it's not difficult to manufacture eyeglasses: but a single Italian company, Luxottica, controls most of the US market: "You go shopping for eyeglasses. You go to a place called LensCrafters. You're comparing quality, comparing prices, imagining you live in an open and competitive market. And yet all of these stores and most of the product in them are controlled by Luxottica" (In Frank, "Free"). You often can't tell what company you're buying from because they're nestled within a series of shell corporations, subsidiaries, DBAs, and sharing agreements. Valero, for example, has an interest in or owns many Exxon gas stations in the Bay Area, and Exxon sells gas to most gas stations; people who didn't want to buy from Exxon after the *Valdez* disaster, or from Shell because of its mistreatment of indigenous peoples in South America, often have no choice or don't know they're buying from these corporations. Corporate identity is indeed a shell game.

Ticketmaster exemplifies a monopolistic corporate enterprise that also commodifies a service that shouldn't be separated from the product. The cost of tickets should be a transparent part of the cost of an event, not a separate charge. Sites such as Ticketmaster might not have full market share, but they have monopolies over any given show. (For a full discussion, see my "What They Don't Want You to Hear.") Paying a 30–40 percent surcharge for your ticket is like paying $30–$40 to get your bill at a restaurant. Some Ticketmaster outlets even charge fees when an event has been canceled. When you print your ticket at home (to avoid another additional charge), you're forced to print a full page of ads with it. Many of the same practices and abuses could be attributed to Comcast and other effective media monopolies; they are endemic to the corporate form. According to Barry Lyons, a senior fellow at the New America Foundation,

> If you go to the Justice Department and say, I'm gonna merge the number one beer company to the number two beer company, or the number one steel company to the number two steel company, and this deal will result in all sorts of big savings, because this deal will let me fire all these excess people and close all these excess plants [you get approved]. . . . The Department of Justice [in 2013] let the number one book publisher in America, Random House,

merge with the No. 2 book publisher, Penguin. Which is insane. (Frank, "Free Markets")

Apparent competition is sometimes just a cover for the premises of corporate personhood, which have no use for actual competition. Instead of transcendental merges with nature, we achieve onehood through corporate mergers into a giant aggregate.

Žižek suggests that US democracy is emblematized by the customer in a cafeteria who encounters "the omnipresent alternatives *Nutra-Sweet* or *Sweet & Low*, small bags of red and blue, and most consumers have a habitual preference . . . whose ridiculous persistence merely highlights the meaninglessness of the options themselves" (*Universal* 34). This same corporate notion of competition is reflected in the spectacle of the video heats run at sports stadiums, with giant screens displaying blue, red, and yellow animated cars in a bizarrely fabricated race, running vehicles that don't exist. How can people fail to see the connection between the animated cars and the live corporate sports spectacle they're viewing? This CGI contest is the equivalent of the fake competition between putative boutique wines sold by the same giant corporation, or the battle between left and right Twix sides—the racing car and Twix examples are so absurd they highlight the artificiality of corporate "competition" in ways that seem analogous to campaigns that highlight the toxicity of products or the artificiality and fraudulence of ads. Such ploys lay bare the lack of choice, competition, and individuality in a corporate system, which relies on the same fake competition as these sporting events. It's not that surprising that the most cynical begin to view Democrats and Republicans as the sides of a Twix bar.

Sports teams are all corporate; their players are arbitrarily bought and sold and usually have no connection to the city they putatively represent. Like the corporate person, they're purely mercenary but impersonate the local and genuine connection. No categorical difference would exist between two NFL teams and Coca-Cola and Nike playing a match. NBA jerseys, like the outfits in many sports, started featuring ads in 2017–2018; the owners of Major League Baseball teams announced that teams can start displaying ads on their jerseys and helmets starting in 2023. Wimbledon lets a car company put its logo not just along the entire wall behind players, but on the net. Though the observation has become a bit of a cliché by now, Canetti, discussing the ways crowd formations reflect constellations of power, asserted that "In ancient Rome we already have an example of how to a considerable extent, sports can replace war as a crowd phenomenon. It is on the point of regaining the same importance today, but this time on a worldwide scale" (467). What Canetti didn't consider is that the corporation itself has become the primary form of crowd or mass in contemporary society.

The derangement of identity associated with corporate personhood also informs American paranoia: it turns out a different entity—still not a person, but a different corporation—exists under the mask. The corporation is like the final residue in the hallucinogenic Bugs Bunny cartoon in which the rabbit keeps taking off layers of clothing as he floats downriver, until there's nothing left. But almost in direct proportion to their layers of multiple identities, corporations try to monopolize the options of others, in commercial, legal, and cultural contexts. Many Bay Area tech firms retain one lawyer at major IP law firms (or just sponsor legal aid organizations such as the Electronic Frontier Foundation) so individuals can't hire any of these now-conflicted firms to sue them. In hundreds of ways, these corporations monopolize the legal system (aside from the fact that only other large corporations generally could afford to litigate against them). If money is speech under *Citizens United*, most people have neither.

Corporate consolidation follows the same practices in a variety of parallel contexts, updating the methods of nineteenth and early twentieth-century trusts. Corporate methods have in some ways become less overt but more pronounced, including buying out or co-opting competitors; forcing customers, though contracts or incompatible technology, to use only their products; threatening to terminate exclusive distributorships when a party in the vertical chain attempts to carry a competitor's product; the use of noncompete clauses, exclusive licenses, variations of vertical licenses; and the pursuit of effective monopoly or market foreclosure. Corporations such as eBay and Amazon also achieve monopoly-like market domination, sometimes through network effects (being the first company to dominate a field and thereby effectively neutralizing smaller competitors). A *Wall Street Journal* cartoon by Christopher Weyant on June 7, 2019, depicts Ahab battling the krakens of Amazon, Apple, Facebook, and Google, and the cartoon might articulate more than it knows; though Ahab was in complicated ways himself partly identified with corporatism, these modern corporations are not only white whales, but effectively they have also replaced nature in our culture.[1]

Many corporations buy up markets in one way or other, and especially in the technology sector they are essentially unregulated. Facebook has become a public forum for speech, for which few equivalent alternatives exist, and it can arbitrarily censor and close people's accounts. Amazon has a bottleneck on many kinds of internet commerce, and often acts in an extraordinarily abusive manner to sellers, employees, and entire industries. The persistent delusion that corporations are good for the public or act in the public interest contradicts their very purpose: it reflects the self-serving idea of the wealthy that what's good for private individuals or General Motors is good for the whole country. Those winning a rigged zero-sum game almost always want to claim that they represent the public interest. Corporations cost the public more than they provide, and what they allow us to buy cheaply comes at an exorbitant, often hidden price in not only externalities, but internalities—how they affect our personhood. As noted, in the way we structure our economy, certain endeavors are possible only if one benefits from the scale of corporate investment. But this is another circular and self-fulfilling proposition: it's true only to the extent that the law, accumulated wealth, and public acceptance leave us without other options.

Chapter Fifty-One

Living Outside the Market?

Even corporate culture in the United States can't suppress all alternatives, and one can minimize the influence of corporate economies on one's life; but such choices in scope and range are primarily symbolic, and usually represent alternative lifestyle choices and not alternative economies. Like capitalism itself, corporations are notoriously adept at co-opting and absorbing criticism and opposition. This cultural colonization is evident in the corporate marketing of, and identification with, an array of putatively non-Western philosophies and mysticisms—from Zen Buddhism to yoga to Native crafts to organic foods and pot—and ploys to turn them into brands attached to noncorporate lifestyles. It's inevitable that corporations would appropriate some of the last vestiges of culture outside the corporate world, at least in fantasy, to expand markets and sell products that tend to undermine those noncorporate ways of life.

Academia had been one of the last domains of life outside corporate America. But academia always has been highly politicized internally, full of combative egos, and, increasingly, of people vying for ever-shrinking resources. One of the few credible things Henry Kissinger ever said (or that I apocryphally attribute to him by paraphrase) was that he left academics because he couldn't stand the politics. But for a period, many academics were, in relative terms, free to research and write about what they saw as important without answering to a corporate set of demands. Academia now has become subject not just to cultural denigration, but a kind of gerrymandering through which state legislatures and academic administrations micromanage faculty; monetize and commodify knowledge and "production," and even try to privatize community colleges, a contradiction in terms lost on the corporate mindset. Academia is also being invaded by advertising and sponsorship, as well as the complete corporate metrification of work. As Terry Eagleton succinctly notes of the UK, most "academic research must now regard itself as part of the so-called knowledge economy"—a situation that applies almost as forcefully in the United States. In this economy, research isn't only commodified, but treated as a sponsored product to be evaluated in the same way consumers rate Amazon purchases, viewers evaluate *Shark Tank* contestants, or corporations measure goods packaged per hour. To make a supportable generalization, under corporate directives, much of journalism has devolved into entertainment and much of academia into second-rate journalism. As an emblematic example, many presses, even academic presses, no longer employ editors, but content managers; this is another manifestation of corporate personhood. Aside from a precipitous decline in the quality of writing, even in the putatively most prestigious outlets, corporate control has narrowed the range of what can be marketed to a wide audience throughout the publishing industry. Many publishers find they can sell brands—often celebrities or authors who represent corporations in some way—and not ideas, creativity, or originality. While some emphasize that decentralization means

Ad masquerading as nostalgia on a UC Berkeley gym hallway

anyone can distribute their writing or music on the internet, corporations control most forms of media production and distribution.

Like news organizations, universities traditionally were at least quasi-public entities, even when they were for profit; they served a critical public interest. Now universities are being run in ways comparable to corporations and adapt their management and advertisement tools. The mission statements of universities, which are meant to create organizational identities, brands and the illusion of actorhood, are another form of corpography—the autobiographical forgeries that corporations have written for them. In another fulfillment of the premises of *Infinite Jest*, within a decade, a cash-strapped college or university likely will rename itself after a corporation (the University of Red State will become the University of Reddit.) As Marc Tracy reported in 2015, "We are the University of Nike," Oregon declared unapologetically. Now, 2,800 miles east, Maryland is positioning itself as the University of Under Armour, thanks to the founder and chief executive of Nike's ascendant rival" (A1). A few years ago, I gave a talk at the University of Stavanger, which calls itself a knowledge park, trying to pretend that it's

Sponsored medical training at UC Berkeley

a corporate business park and that knowledge is a product; instead of a force that can critique, oppose, and serve as some form of alternative to corporate culture, many universities are trying to out-corporate corporate culture. Tom McCarthy in *Satin Island* encapsulates the way corporate culture co-opts and swallows everything outside it, from academia to independent media, into its nonexistent body: "This pretty much set up the protocol or MO I'd deploy in my work for the Company . . . feeding vanguard theory, almost always from the left side of the spectrum, into the corporate machine. The machine could swallow everything, incorporate it seamlessly, like a giant loom that reweaves all fabric" (30).

As Frank Donoghue points out, Sinclair Lewis, in his 1923 work *The Goose-Step: A Study in American Education*, already was documenting the ways many American universities had become corporate entities, noting that Lewis called Columbia the university of J. P. Morgan and asserted you couldn't differentiate between a list of its trustees and a list of the owners of the New York Central Railroad (14).For many years, the Koch Brothers sat on the board of George Mason University Centers and Institutes—despite it being a public university—and have a "ubiquitous presence" in the president's office and classrooms at Florida State University (Meyers 6–7). Such corporate sponsorships directly fund research that denies climate change, undermines studies critical of corporate practices, and generally leads to corporate control of the content and scope of what's taught. It's a central aspect of the corporate control of speech and media. The State University of New York is even considering allowing businesses overtly to influence and participate in curriculum planning (5).

Chapter Fifty-Two

How Soon Is Nowhere?

Advertising Academia

Naomi Klein thoroughly documented the branding of public education in *No Logo*, especially in the context of elementary schools, and the effect the infiltration of sponsorship into the classroom has on student identity (87–105). Ultimately, such sponsorship shapes, regulates, and limits the content of education. In even more sinister terms, these corporate "partnerships" often dictate the scope of research at universities, in everything from medical to energy research, with corporations even retaining "the right to block publication of findings in 35 percent of cases," and likely to delay it in 53 percent of cases (Klein 101). In a mixed blessing, the humanities receive little corporate sponsorship, reflecting the priorities of the corporate world. The humanities, the departments that focus on culture, are effectively treated as the welfare recipients of this economy.

As Bakan observes, schools used to be exempt from advertising, but in much the way other once-protected areas representing the public good—such as news, research, or medicine—have succumbed, everything from deanships to classrooms and playgrounds have become sponsored (118). Advertising charts the breakdown of our social contract, our sense of belonging to a society that's anything other than a forum for private interests to engage in an ever fiercer race to the bottom. Schools have begun to allow themselves to be sold off piecemeal—lockers, gym paraphernalia, "educational" television programming, and even textbooks, are brought to you by entities that want to preempt education. In another version of the zero-sum game, corporate culture promotes technological advancement and better commodities, but less critical thinking. Schools become the social equivalent of companies that are bought only to be gutted and hollowed out, or have their assets stripped—only these public entities are being kept as going concerns because their parasites need them as hosts. Professors in the humanities are more and more tending the grave of a dead culture no one visits anymore.[1]

As with other public trusts such as public television and government services, corporate intrusion erodes our sense of what belongs to the community; the values we need to associate with the commonwealth; and what can be sold to the highest bidder. Programs to help underperforming and underfunded middle and high schools—such as the Edison Project and the now defunct Channel One, which offer funding or resources to schools in exchange for advertisements and the right to infiltrate textbooks—target children who often don't have the critical skills to resist indoctrination by advertisement. As G. J. M. Abbarno advises, "Schools would be wise to subject commercials to critical evaluation thereby repositioning the educator's full activity in the classroom"; schools should be showing ads only to train students to think critically about them (185). The need for schools to raise money through sponsorship is part of another vicious cycle that corporations precipitate; by evading taxes and fomenting the privatization of public services, and agitating against government, corporations help starve schools of funds, then step in to sponsor and control them.

Most trends in academia track the dumbing down of discourse and loss of individual independence, trends coterminous with the corporatization of society. Haverford College used to assign freshmen a novel (sometimes a "classic" text, sometimes a recently canonized work) to read before orientation, when students would discuss the work in small groups and validate the idea that they could share a common culture. That requirement was whittled down to a short story because some faculty came to believe that even its generally exceptionally well-prepared students no longer arrived with the skills or focus needed to read a novel. At Berkeley, corporate culture is what most students bring to campus—a mentality largely defined by corporate consumerism. It's galling to see such practices accepted with relatively little resistance at a university once known for student activism. Students easily meet those lowered expectations as professors assign them graphic novels, blogs, and TV shows to study, helping them join the ranks of an increasingly culturally illiterate population raised on ads, memes, and sound bites.

Emblematic of many universities that are being run like corporations, UC Berkeley sells ad space throughout its gym during its overdetermined "orientation"; when freshmen arrive for what the university endlessly promotes as "Caltopia," they're bombarded with ads and immediately alerted that most aspects of the university are sponsored. (This gym subjects users to an array of unavoidable TV screens that play nothing but MTV University, and most of its walls are billboards for corporate ads, including colas and other products that couldn't be more inapposite. In what sounds like an *Onion* parody, the State Department's Fulbright section even developed an MTV University fellowship program.) For a week, a Comcast van that's simply a mobile ad parks on campus, among dozens of tented venders. Instead of reminding students of Berkeley's history with regard to political free speech, Caltopia represents the ascendance of commercial speech and sends the message that education is a co-opted product for a captive audience. UC Berkeley promotes dozens of companies with slogans such as "Be Real. Get Honest" (an actual Caltopia company slogan). This is the introduction to corporate identity and communication the university offers. The bikes at the gym have screens that require you to program your exercise but whose ulterior function is to flash ads at students. The gym seems permanently sponsored by Pepsi, whose logos adorn numerous wall murals of athletes; Pepsi has no sense of irony or shame (especially since a corporation has no feelings at all) about turning Berkeley into another Pepsi Center. Starting in 2017, a commercial coffee truck was parked on campus in front of the gym entrance: that placement represents not just corporate sponsorship of a state's public institution but the institution's endorsement of a brand. People routinely scrawl corporate ads in chalk on the campus; nearby, you often have to walk through a riot of private placards strewn across public grass-ways, medians, and sidewalks, demonstrating how the premises of corporate advertising permeate down to all levels. Much of the UC system is infected with this corporate ethos. UC Berkeley signed a deal to allow Coors to use the Cal logo on billboards (which is particularly offensive since most Cal students are underage, and Coors has been a notoriously unprogressive cor-poration, even within the generic constraints of corporate behavior).

Indicative of the university's priorities, during the entire weekends before and after Caltopia, which is nothing but an ad festival, the undergraduate and graduate libraries remain closed, even though orientation week is meant to introduce students to university life. Students receive a glossy sixty-eight-page book that contains nothing but ads—it doesn't even present a pretext of educational content. Campus is flanked by people standing with tanning salon signs and wandering around with placards for products. "Cal-topia" is also indicative of the ways advertising tarnishes language by twist-ing words (as well as logic and contexts), in this case in nonsensical ways to support the primacy of image: "Caltopia," like "Xfinity" and unlike, say, "youtopia," isn't even a weak pun but just neologistic gibberish. As noted, such terms are designed to be meaningless so advertisers can trademark them. They're as meaningless as the idea of corporate personality or corporate personhood (though their sociological effects are significant). But they're also figuratively antithetical to cultural literacy. Corporations create and disseminate commercialized words so they can control them for their purposes, and that process is especially offensive when undertaken in academic contexts. Right before the 2016 presidential election, the Clinton Foundation flooded the Berkeley campus with Global Initiative mat-spam, covering it with advertisements meant to promote Hillary Clinton's candidacy by name association. But it was rolled out in the same register as ads promoting cable companies, beer, sportswear, and MTV.

Berkeley's law school used to send out mass emails sponsored by law firms. It has wings, auditoriums, and class rooms effectively sponsored by law firms and partners; its curriculum in many areas is designed at the behest of firms (somewhere in the building, I'm convinced, is a public interest urinal). I wrote that joke as I began this book, but I've since learned that corporate donors are sponsoring bathrooms at the law school. These days I'm almost reluctant to make bad jokes about Republicans and corporations, since many of them turn out to be predictions; I suspect the next stage of corporate evolution—after we've privatized education, the military, prisons, and other public services—is to privatize the alphabet.

Some professors quit to become activists because they've lost faith in the efficacy of culture and of education in a corporate system. David Foster Wallace had been wondering about the point of writing esoteric fiction for a small core audience of educated people who already agreed with him ("Discussion"). He suspected that to compete with corporate culture, artists had to proselytize and use propaganda, which was antithetical to their purpose. When he was told to make cuts to a magazine essay, Wallace realized that he had "to make extra room for Volvo ads" (Max 288). Publications need to generate income, but virtually every aspect of culture is demeaned and diminished by such relationships to sponsorship. The scenario Wallace and most writers and artists face tells us that culture has become disposable and subservient to advertising. The transitions writers such as DeLillo, Acker, and Wallace lamented signaled a profound form of decay and decadence, and the justifiable despair of those we can least afford to despair.

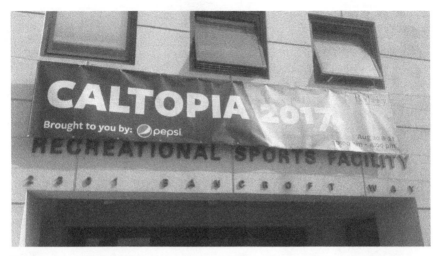

The dystopia of Caltopia

The public space of the UC Berkeley gym turned into a relay of corporate signposts

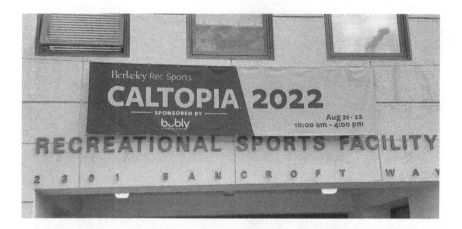

UC Berkeley equates and ratifies Pepsi, Peet's, the Clinton Global Initiative, and course content

Chapter Fifty-Three

Gravekeepers

In 2014, UCLA "launched "We, the Optimists," a new iteration of the university's highly successful, national Optimists brand campaign. The marketing effort spotlights UCLA's role as an engine of opportunity and progress, propelling action and change in Los Angeles and around the world."[1] The entirety of this description typifies the assault on language characteristic of corporate advertising rhetoric: "Carrying the theme forward on each element of the campaign are headlines that begin with 'We' and end with an 'optimism'—a verb that expresses the action or area represented in the ad." Aside from the fact that "optimism" isn't a verb, the announcement is suffused with advertising blather. Optimism is another variation of trust—you ask for faith, trust, or optimism when you're trying to conceal a scenario that calls for the opposite. Published on a website with the address "newsroom.ucla," UCLA's press release, like most corporate communications, treats itself as news. The release invokes UCLA's "world-class" breadth, which might have been amusing if it were a pun, but here only echoes the insufferable ad phrase best-in-class. The text also indicates that UCLA, which seeks to eliminate or merge many of its traditional language departments, wants "to leverage" its role as a public university, apparently to emulate corporations that spout platitudes about coming together to inspire achievers to deepen their commitment to solving the change-worthy issues that confront change agents who attempt to optimize the optimism of optimists. "Leverage" is among the worst of the mindless, co-opted terms that MBAs litter their speech with, and signifies nothing, except the speaker's vapidity. UCLA's campaign promises to tell "compelling stories of people and programs from downtown Los Angeles to Southeast Asia to the far reaches of the solar system." Since UCLA doesn't have a space program, I didn't expect it to open a branch campus on Neptune; perhaps it will offer media studies classes that advise students that a university's cynical use of cheap irony deserves an equivalent response. These distortions of language, imitations of corporate behavior, and transgressive incursions on public space are connected to corporate notions of utilitarian, standardized and monetizable learning. Whenever I hear the singularly corporate phrase "learning outcomes," I know the speaker is interested in learning incomes. McCarthy's sardonic advice in *Satin Island* reminds us of the way corporations eliminate all alternative ways of thinking and being: "Forget universities! . . . They've become businesses—and not even good ones. *Real* businesses . . . are the forge and foundry where true knowledge is being smelted" (56, emphasis in original).

Universities not only brand themselves, but even have started to replace Latin mottos (meaningless, but usually harmless) with ad campaigns. Sydney University's Business School adopted the slogan "Me First," designed for it by an ad agency. Another university started a promotional campaign called "think smarter" (in response to which a savvy IT person designed a T-shirt stating "think smarterer"). The Library at Karlstad University in Sweden features a bizarre neon logo that says "Nobody puts baby in a corner." (Apparently an administrator liked the phrase, but it's not clear what this line from *Dirty Dancing* could have to do with the university). As art, the sign might voice superficial critique, but corporate universities rarely engage in meta-self-reflection. The phrase is again more apt than one might think because the real agent of the university *is* nobody. Nobody is behind corporate personhood.

Chapter Fifty-Four

Imagine a World without Advertising

As the line between entertainment, information, commerce, and advertising disintegrates, we're left with fewer and fewer options to speak or hear outside the language of advertising. Except for a few small outlets, we can rarely distinguish between news, advertisement, and entertainment. CNN devoted an hour to covering Tiger Woods's Nike ad when he returned to playing golf. When Apple releases a new line of toys, most major broadcasters treat it as a front-page "news" story.

Can we imagine a society whose culture isn't funded by advertising, and in which products aren't promoted through corporate systems? Can we imagine a society in which culture isn't funded and dominated by corporations? We need to develop alternative models for generating revenue and paying for culture; it would cost far less, in economic, sociological, and psychological terms, to pay directly for programming and cut out advertising middlemen. Some might still respond that that's all well and good, but how can we sell anything, produce television, or fund the internet without advertising? It's the cultural corollary of saying, yes, fracking is contaminating our groundwater and global warming threatens life on earth, but how can we maintain this exact economy? Much of the best television of the past few decades has been produced under this kind of "single-payer" model. Many consumers would balk at paying for things they once got for free—but through education and the development of alternative models, and in the context of the accelerating collapse of our public infrastructure, they might realize there ain't no such thing as free content; society as a whole pays for it in the end. Without being utopian, we can begin to mitigate the malaise, mistrust, and disaffection advertising creates by increasing awareness and regulation and transforming how we imagine business—not as warfare among private interests but a vital component of the public good. The good news is that advertisers, like health insurance companies, provide no value, product, or benefit; they're interlopers who inflate the price of everything. If you eliminate them, costs will decrease, and those savings could subsidize cultural production.

The first thing people can do is to start objecting. We're so socialized to accept and even valorize advertising, conceptualizing a society that doesn't rely on it is difficult. But if people make it clear that advertising has a negative effect on their decisions—that they'll reject corporations that operate under the dictates of corporate personhood—it would undermine its viability. A simple response is to try to avoid products whose advertising you've seen. You're paying a premium for that company's advertising, which has no bearing on the quality of the product. Economists might aver that the business such advertising generates allows corporations to produce goods on such a scale that the cost of advertising is more than compensated for by the reduction in price. But that perspective fails to account for any of the externalities: the harm the principles of corporate personhood and advertising generates; the utter waste the system produces at every level, from the loss of public space to people's time; or the prospect that the system is pathological in its assumptions about human personhood and the common good.

More systemically, we need to formulate alternative models to allow corporations to disseminate product information without intruding into our lives, culture, and privacy, as well as different ways to pay for the things advertising finances. One solution would be legally to require that all advertising must be user solicited; since most people in the United States have continuous access to the internet, they can seek ads or information regarding companies, products, or categories whenever they want it. People would not be subjected to a daily assault of ads they don't need and that we all pay for psychologically, fiscally, and politically. We would reduce wasteful and needless consumption, and help reconceptualize what it means to have a healthy economy in financial, psychological, and environmental contexts. This proposal might sound radical because we've internalized the idea that our economy requires ads, that we deserve to be subjected to them, and that we can do little about the matter anyway. But as Piety warns, the mechanisms of advertising create

a society dominated by entertainment; a society of low-information voters; of widespread distrust of media, government, and "experts"; of ubiquitous mental health problems, such as anomie, depression, anxiety, addiction, and compulsive behaviors like hoarding; an environment in which misinformation can spread to millions instantly and where our legal rules, which were intended to foster equality, are undermined daily by commercial messages that reinforce stereotypes and inequality. ("Advertising")

What's possible for many of us to imagine is constrained by the tenets and effects of corporate personhood and advertising.

What can one do? Corporate personhood is so entrenched, it would take another book to begin to address how to dismantle its premises. It would be counterproductive to propose canned, unrealistic solutions or suggest we can find easy ways to remediate corporate values, but any progress must begin with debate. Advertisers need you to believe that we can become swans only by buying the product of the moment. But to paraphrase Ursula Le Guin, the power of corporate monarchs seems inevitable only because we accept it. The first step is to consider ways to restructure an economy, particularly a media economy, that don't rely on advertising as its primary source of revenue, limits corporate rights, and decentralizes corporate power and influence.

A more radical but comprehensive solution to address corporate personhood and power would be to do away with the corporate form altogether and change how we address liability and sponsorship of culture. An overarching intervention would be to regulate all corporate behavior so that those who make decisions as agents can be held liable; while corporations make money for individuals in a private capacity, they must also be treated as public trusts. We could ensure that directors are held more accountable for social harm and externalities and that employees are invested in their companies and vice versa. The size and scale of corporate enterprise and the intertwined networks of corporate advertising, sponsorship, and dominance, undermine democracy and social well-being. We might provide incentives for and promote partnerships and new legal entities, and we might reign in and limit the dangers corporations pose by assigning them term limits.

Many corporate endeavors of course benefit the public, but we have yet to adequately evaluate the costs and consequences of the corporate form and alternatives that would serve society far better than private interests. We need to reconsider the costs of limiting liability to corporations and separating the people who control it from the entity itself; if risks are too great for individuals to undertake, perhaps we shouldn't undertake them as a society, or we should undertake them in ways that insure accountability to the commons. Without unduly diminishing the profit motive, we need to restructure the legal exemptions we grant to corporations; if corporations can't undertake projects without facing undue liability, they should pursue them only on those rare occasions when such endeavors are in the public's interest. I didn't rehash the familiar debate regarding whether corporations have accomplished what no individuals or partnerships could in creating the modern technological world, since it seems clear that they did. They also helped precipitate the exploitation of populations and resources; colonial expropriation, and a concatenating series of looming environmental catastrophes. The corporation is a subsidiary, and it should serve the good of the public, not the reverse, which is the state of affairs current law enshrines. It's time to subject corporations to a body check and roll back their exceptional personhood: to stop being walking advertisements for corporations, incorporating their values and behaviors into our lives and consuming their ultimately suicidal view of the world (even if, or precisely because, they have no selves). The polarization and decline of US society and culture, and much of what's wrong with our economy, education, and health care systems, at least in part involves a complex loss of personhood. To escape living under a corporate dominion, we need to re-personalize how we communicate, do business, and conceive of responsibility; reorient our economy to limit not liability but unsustainable growth; and rescue language from the near monopoly advertisers and corporations hold over it.

Notes

CHAPTER ONE

1. Cameron contends that Emerson never explicitly considers what would replace God, but, I would argue, it is the impersonal transcendental, which the corporation exemplifies (108).

2. Siraganian observes that to describe "corporate instantiation in *The Octopus*, Theodore Dreiser had to "[combine] various metaphors," a tactic often necessary when trying to depict a void ("Dreiser's" 266). The cultural metaphors I invoke for corporations conjure ideas of false identity/interiority and the impersonation of people. The legal metaphors I develop, regarding the enhanced rights of corporations, connote their consistent (and consistently more powerful) legal status. Opening with a barrage of advertising gibberish, including the invocation of a mini-McGuffin of a Trendex, Hitchcock's 1959 film *North by Northwest* adeptly skewers the corporate advertising executive, Roger O. Thornhill, whose name stands for ROT and whose O or zero "stands for nothing," as a void who precisely has no identity at all. All instances of corporate personhood involve similarly eerie or uncanny cases of mistaken identity, a series of effects generated by phantasms that, like George Kaplan, do not—and in this case, cannot—exist.

CHAPTER TWO

1. All emphases within quotation marks are mine unless otherwise noted as "emphasis in original."

2. Perhaps unintentionally, Wu repeatedly uses language that situates corporations as creatures that have come to control their putative creators: "It was if [William Paley] lost control over his own creation [NBC], which took on a will of its own" (*Attention* 140); "while television is supposed to be "free," it's in fact become the creature . . . of merchandizing" (150).

CHAPTER FOUR

1. *Severance* develops a sustained, sardonic satire of corporate work culture, including its depiction of the invisible, almost entirely voiceless corporate board; specious familial bonding that is coterminous with fabricated internal rivalry; corporate geographies; the erasure of history (including its professor); and the way corporations sever employees from moral agency. "*Severance* brings us together" much the way *Citizens United* does.

CHAPTER FIVE

1. Tocqueville too was repeatedly accused of being a pantheist; the US edition of *The London Quarterly Review* adds that "those who follow De Tocqueville are pantheists in politics, and they will come to pantheism in religion" (Anonymous, "Carlyle's" 257).

2. Critiquing Whitman's theory of democracy "en masse," Lawrence writes: "What meaning does 'person' really carry? . . . It is not at all the same to have personality, as to have individuality. . . . An individual is that which is not divided or dividable" ("Democracy" 710).

3. Hawthorne also documents Americans' desire to transcend their atomized individualities in transcendental/corporate language: in *The House of the Seven Gables*, his narrator reflects on how a human procession "melts all the petty personalities of which it is made up, into one broad mass of existence—one great life—one collected body of mankind, with a vast, homogeneous spirit animating it" (165). Such descriptions are commensurate with those of Emerson, save that the anti-pantheistic Hawthorne imagines merger only in society. Hawthorne's narrator claims that "a family should be merged into the great, obscure mass of humanity": not into nature or the ocean itself, but into the "great current of human life" (185, 256). But that great mass or immense Being often becomes a corporate entity, as signaled by the role of the railroad in Hawthorne's novel.

4. Some critics situate the impulse to merge with the world as a quest for self-annihilation, and ego-transcendence not just as ego-death, but death. John Irwin proposes that we should view Poe's quest for a ""primal Oneness, for what it is—a death wish" (235). Lawrence says much the same of Whitman—"Merging! And Death! Which is the final merge" (*Studies* 178).

CHAPTER SIX

1. The mechanisms I describe would manifest in disparate ways in communist dictatorships, but they operate within the parameters I address under corporate capitalism. Corporate ads are forms of propaganda and represent the world's most elaborate and far-reaching system of collective control and disinformation. Ironically,

they often were championed during the Cold War because they stood for a system opposed to communism. Now, as Boštjan Videmšek proposes, China has become "the Party—The [Mother of All] Corporation[s]" (43).

2. Transcendentalism, modernism, and postmodernism of course represent disparate eras and belief systems. When I invoke these concepts in this project, I'm not focused on historicizing them or contextualizing their permutations. I'm instead trying to provide a genealogy for salient concepts of impersonality, and their influence and general development, as they relate to corporate personhood and as they mutated across discourses.

3. Arvidson also indicates that Lewis treats personality and impersonality as a false opposition:

> Whereas "personality" is a front for the impersonality of conformist, unconsciously iterated habit, "impersonality" disguises personally vested motivation. As Lewis argues, "this delusion of impersonality could be best defined as that mistake by virtue of which persons are enabled to masquerade as *things*"; in like fashion, the delusion of personality might be extrapolated as that mistake that allows things to masquerade as persons. These inversions of word and concept confuse human with mechanism and obfuscate the large-scale dynamics of exploitation in which Lewis's democratic masses heedlessly participate. (801–2, emphasis in original)

4. Regarding Gertrude Stein's modernist use of impersonation in her "autobiography" of Alice B. Toklas, see my "The Franklin-Stein Monster."

CHAPTER SEVEN

1. An example of how corporate America co-opts these precepts is evident in remarks of President George H. W. Bush: "The ethic of Native Americans like Chief Seattle must be reborn on this continent. His was a religious understanding that the whole Earth has a soul" (Bush, 1229).

2. The notion of a corporate Frankenstein's Monster often was connected to the legal definition of artificial corporate persons, as well as to the idea of piercing the corporate veil. Siraganian recounts that Maurice Wormser's *Frankenstein, Incorporated* (1931) suggests

> that the corporate form itself tolerates, and maybe even promotes, nefarious results. "Men united" might "do things corporately and collectively which individually they would not think of doing" (100). Yet he interprets this problem as a version of crowd madness, not as the scientific sadism of economic power. For un-fathomable reasons, good individuals "often will stop at nothing when incorporated into a collective unit. Corporations, unlike individuals, unfortunately tend to have no moral standards" (100–101).The consequences are dire: "the artificially created [corporate] monster threatens to injure, if not destroy, much of what Frankenstein holds most dear" (101). ("Dreiser's" 260)

CHAPTER EIGHT

1. See my "Consciousness without Borders" (98).

CHAPTER NINE

1. However, as Chief Justice Roberts writes in his concurrence to *Citizens United*, one must consider media corporations separately in these contexts (558 U.S. at 371, 382–83). Their speech would be different categorically because their business, at least theoretically, is speech.

CHAPTER TWELVE

1. I don't dwell on corporate social responsibility because it's usually a distraction and an even more specious form of advertising. Even when corporations aren't invoking the language of CSR merely to promote themselves, and its underlying premise isn't fraudulent—as it is with BP's cleanups and many corporate educational programs—CSR doesn't alter the nature of corporate personhood.

CHAPTER THIRTEEN

1. Though it doesn't address the trope, Wu's *Master Switch* frequently refers to such octopi, for example Paul Latzke's 1901 novel *A Fight with an Octopus* (50); Carl Laemmle's denunciation of the corporate "film octopus" of Hollywood (66); a theater operator's complaint regarding the way Paramount Pictures tried "to gain a hold for each tentacle of their octopus by threats" (94); the fact that the once centralized entertainment field gave "way to a gang of octopuses" that own diversified properties (235), and so on.

CHAPTER FOURTEEN

1. In consonant terms, Lyons suggests that when "ruinously exposed as a corporate individual, the corporation sought to *disaggregate* its own corporate personhood in order to find a scapegoat that it could sacrifice without bleeding the larger entity dry" (99). What Bose calls the "corporeal identification" of founders or spokespersons with corporations must, however, eventually give way to the aggregation of a fictional corporate body whose mass displaces individual citizens and voters, and in practice is too large to identify, let alone regulate or hold liable (218).

CHAPTER FIFTEEN

1. As Mark Feeney comments, "That last sentence has an ironic cast. DeLillo himself is very much unincorporated. He doesn't teach, he doesn't tour" (491). In "The Power of History," sounding a bit like Acker, DeLillo contends that in *Underworld* he wanted to use language to "unincorporate these [trademarked or too familiar] words, subvert their official status" (63). For a discussion of how DeLillo's characters yearn for a pure speech uninfected by consumer culture, see Paul Maltby.

CHAPTER SIXTEEN

1. My thanks to Jim McClellan for this comment.

2. See also Stuart Sherman's review of *Americans* (*Phoenix*, 318). The passage Lawrence is probably referring to—"If I treat all men as gods, how to me can there be any such thing as a slave?"—is part of one of Emerson's indirect but distinct renunciations of slavery, which Lawrence takes out of context (*Works*, "Lecture on the Times" I, 280).

CHAPTER EIGHTEEN

1. Morawetz, *A Treatise on Private Corporations*, 2nd ed., sec. 1.

2. As one of Wallace's characters in *The Pale King* worries, sounding much like Powers's narrator, corporations "allow for individual reward without individual obligation. . . . We as individual citizens have adopted a corporate attitude" (136–37).

3. Though the issue is outside this book's scope, corporations foster the erosion of privacy in contemporary culture; and the hyper-voyeurism of reality TV and some corporate journalism downplays facts in often consonant ways, and promotes forms of exposure or competition predicated on making the private public.

CHAPTER NINETEEN

1. This evolving racialized trope was contested from the time Thomas Jefferson evoked an immovable black veil that covered the emotions of African Americans. In her introduction to Harriet Jacobs's *Incidents in the Life of a Slave Girl*, Lydia Maria Child associated the veil with slavery, contending that "this peculiar phase of Slavery [the abuse of women] has generally been kept veiled; but the public ought to be made acquainted with its monstrous features, and I willingly take the responsibility of presenting them with the veil withdrawn" (xii). We need to consider the historical as well as legal contexts that are inextricable from granting personhood to an inanimate thing; for centuries, this country considered African Americans things of property

and fractions of persons. It now grants hyper-personhood—since, as the dissent in *Citizens United* emphasizes, few individuals could ever marshal the financial and political resources and power of corporations, 558 U.S. at 469–71—to inanimate things of property. Using the same legal precedent, corporations usurped the principle of personhood that had been restored to former slaves. Personhood always has been a malleable and artificial concept in the United States, which means that one's status as human is alienable.

2. As Ishmael Reed writes in his 1976 novel *Flight to Canada*, paraphrasing Frederick Douglass, "Isn't it strange? Whitman desires to fuse with nature, and here I am, involuntarily, the comrade of the inanimate, but not by choice. . . . I am property. I am a thing" (75). Reed also notes that Stowe's novel *Uncle Tom's Cabin* was originally subtitled "The Man Who Was a Thing" (93). Again, we can glimpse the process in which the properties of nature and corporations are conflated; instead of "fusing" with or transcending the self in nature, one can "transcend" individuality by becoming a corporate person. Pivoting around the Fourteenth Amendment, the law treated slaves as degraded imitations of life, but now treats corporations, which are things, as enhanced imitations of life.

3. Responding to legal challenges to the Civil Rights Act in 1964, the Court stated that "Section 201 (a) of Title II commands that all persons shall be entitled to the full and equal enjoyment of the goods and services of any place of public accommodation without discrimination or segregation on the ground of race, color, religion, or national origin; and § 201 (b) defines establishments as places of public accommodation if their operations affect commerce." *Katzenbach. v. McClung*, 379 U.S. 294, 298 (1964). In effect, the Court had to address the district court's assertion that it had to find a "demonstrable connection between food purchased in interstate commerce and sold in a restaurant and the conclusion of Congress that discrimination in the restaurant would affect that commerce" (at 297). Because of precedent, the Court decided that it could uphold the civil rights law on the grounds that discrimination cumulatively affected interstate commerce. For example, addressing a nineteenth-century civil rights law, the Court had once pronounced that the first two sections of the "'Act to protect all citizens in their civil and legal rights,' are unconstitutional and void" (*United States v. Stanley, et al.*, 109 U.S. 3, 26 [1882]). According to the Court, "The essence of the law is, not to declare broadly that all persons shall be entitled to the full and equal enjoyment of the accommodations, advantages, facilities, and privileges of inns, public conveyances, and theatres; but that such enjoyment shall not be subject to any conditions applicable only to citizens of a particular race or color, or who had been in a previous condition of servitude" (9–10). In other words, congress didn't have the right to legislate equality under the law per se, especially proactively and with regard to race:

> It is absurd to affirm that, because the rights of life, liberty and property (which include all civil rights that men have), are by the amendment sought to be protected against invasion on the part of the State without due process of law, Congress may therefore provide due process of law for their vindication in every case; and that, because the denial by a State to any persons, of the equal protection of the laws, is prohibited by the amendment, therefore Congress may establish laws for their equal protection. In fine, the legislation

which Congress is authorized to adopt in this behalf is not general legislation upon the [civil] rights of the citizen, but corrective legislation. (13)

Even in the 1960s, the Court had to defer to a perceived lack of congressional authority to legislate civil rights as rights of personhood rather than commerce.

CHAPTER TWENTY

1. Throughout this book, I invoke cases whose logic is emblematic—that is, I don't necessarily address holdings for their precedential value, but the way they illuminate the premises that facilitate corporate personhood.

2. As Jake Bernstein notes, a 2011 World Bank survey found that 85 percent of more than 150 cases of grand corruption involved anonymous US corporations (24). To attribute anonymity to corporations is slightly misleading, however, in that doing so implies primarily that particular identities are being shielded, when what's being shielded is the structure of incentives and protections that allow corporations to function without individual liability in perpetuity.

3. In a slightly different context, Franklin suggests that the use of personal language has become vexed in certain academic and other self-narratives: "In the contemporary academy, language that is impersonal, even legalistic, can paradoxically have the most impact personally, and in a way that can be transformative politically" (25). For Franklin, such seemingly impersonal language "can hit hardest on a personal as well as political level, in part because it refuses those in institutionally privileged positions the right to feelings of being marginalized, and instead highlights the often uncomfortable responsibilities of institutional location" (34).

4. In parts of the United States, corporations have become effective monopolies with regard to certain kinds of goods; the corporate product is the only available option, and one can even obtain many government services, from food stamps to Medicare appeals, only through outsourced corporate mediators. As Ghachem observes in other contexts, the charters of the East India Companies created effective monopolies. Modified by economies of scale, our economy has come full circle, with corporations becoming monopolistic in form and practice; especially when three or four dominate national and world markets, giant corporations operate more like the political sectors of Orwell's *1984.*

5. See William Simon ("Rights 1498).

CHAPTER TWENTY-ONE

1. Burkhard Schnepel notes that for the anthropologist Sir Henry Maine, the primary attribute of corporations

is their perpetuity, assured by laws of intestate succession. Maine's maxim that "corporations never die" puts the emphasis on the preservation and devolution of the collectively held universitas juris, the bundle of rights and duties. . . . [Meyer] Fortes writes . . . "It is not their co-existence as 'a plurality of persons collected in one body' that makes a group corporate, but their 'plurality in succession,' their perpetuity in time." Summing up these ideas [in *The King's Two Bodies*, Ernst] Kantorowicz says that "the most significant feature of the personified collectivities and corporate bodies was that they projected into past and future, that they preserved their identity despite changes, and that therefore they were legally immortal." (6)

As such, corporations can displace the cultural centrality of familial succession. Though his work is dated, and according to James Dow conflates the precepts of Maine and Max Weber and generated the "muddled concept of corporation in Anthropology," Fortes focuses on the critically overlooked ontological features of the corporation (905).

2. See also my "World Trade Centers" for a discussion of the false millenarian promise of technology. In exploring the numinous possibilities of the internet, in which one could upload virtual identities, DeLillo narrativized Klein's premise that corporations try to "free [themselves] from the corporeal world of commodities" (22).

CHAPTER TWENTY-TWO

1. According to Žižek, "this 'objective interpellation' actually affects my subjectivity only by means of the fact that I myself am well aware of how, outside the grasp of my knowledge, databases circulate which determine my symbolic identity in the eyes of the social 'big Other.'" (*Ticklish* 260).

2. Numerous critics, including Henry Giroux (*Stealing*; *Zombies*), more generally address the cultural function of zombies under contemporary capitalism.

CHAPTER TWENTY-THREE

1. Quoted in Harvey, *Neoliberalism* 23.

2. Such passages iterate Melville's own sentiments, here voiced in a letter to Hawthorne, regarding whether one can lose oneself in the collective of nature:

You must often have felt it, lying on the grass on a warm summer's day. Your legs seem to send out shoots into the earth. Your hair feels like leaves upon your head. This is the all feeling. (*Correspondence* 193–94)

3. Notably, Melville reverses the usual order of the phrase *hospital corporation*. The friendless man in *The Confidence-Man* states that the New York Corporation Hospital was where he "got worse—pretty much as you see me now" (96). As Foucault notes, the first British workhouses, allied with madhouses and hospitals, also were administered by corporations (*Madness* 44).

4. See https://www.snopes.com/paul-ryan-said-free-lunches-give-children-empty-souls/.

5. One of Wu's limitations is that he sometime acts as an apologist who imagines a priori that many corporate ads endorse appealing products, and therefore can be exculpated on pragmatic grounds. In the generally illuminating *The Attention Merchants*, for example, Wu frequently makes the following kind of qualifications: "He was after all promoting what were, in the 1920s, among the best cars on earth" (59); what brand advertising "offered to adherents is not merely a good product (though often it is)" (79); "when done well and on behalf of a good product, advertising can, in this way, advance human freedom by showing that choices exist and making them seem real" (119). While Wu periodically admits that such choices are largely illusory and meaningless, and that advertisers sell fantasies, not products, he makes some unfounded claims that advertising promotes the dissemination of useful information.

6. Wallace experienced some of his own feelings of inadequacy in terms similar to those he used to evoke the degradations of corporate culture: he described himself as feeling as if he were a fake person who suffered from "imposter syndrome" (Max 8).

CHAPTER TWENTY-FIVE

1. Vernon Shetley suggested in conversation that the episode also references a scene in *Point Blank* in which the gangster Lee Marvin confronts Carroll O'Connor for his payout, only to be told the Organization (a proto-corporation) is in effect virtual and doesn't deal in real currency.

2. Regarding the ways corporations developed management techniques derived from the operations of slave plantations, see Rosenthal, who argues that "the power of masters over their slaves gave them power as managers. Plantations became laboratories for agricultural experimentation, and planters and overseers measured and monitored human capital with great precision. Through accounting, human figures became figures on paper, appearing as interchangeable inputs of production" (735).

3. Evidencing the way advertising precepts can infect every aspect of communication—from tone to morality to aesthetics to basic reasoning—as well as how advertising language often conveys the opposite of what it seems to claim, Frank Viviano, in a piece about branding impresario David Aaker written for the UC Berkeley alumni magazine, asserts, apparently without irony, that at the branding company Prophet "the emphasis is unmistakably on egalitarian democracy. . . . The comparisons to Plato and Newton are not facetious" (24–25).

4. While their tone differs, Melville and Pynchon depict the corporation in terms of similar kinds of reflexive cannibalism. Though he values labor, Ishmael describes whaling as a cannibalistic corporate enterprise: he asks, for example, "Your knife-handle, my civilized and enlightened gourmand dining off that roast beef, what is the handle made of?—what but the bones of the brother of the very ox you are eating?" (300). Emblematically, Ishmael uses whale skin as a transparent bookmark for his "whale books"; this "infinitely thin substance, which . . . invests the entire body of the whale," and is depicted as being akin to a child's skin, is used for every aspect of Ishmael's text, including its parchment and binding, and even the magnifier that sees itself. As Ishmael sardonically concludes, "It is pleasant to read about whales

through their own spectacles" (306). Ishmael also cannot justify "that a man should eat a newly murdered thing of the sea, and eat it too by its own light" (299). Whaling appropriates bodies not only as raw materials, but to commandeer more bodies: it represents an economy of serial killing.

In *Gravity's Rainbow*, we learn that the Slothrops once "were not yet so much involved with paper, and the wholesale slaughtering of trees. They were still for the living green, against the dead white" (268). Recalling Ishmael's sardonic observations that we eat creatures using their own bones as implements, Pynchon's narrator tells us that "Slothrop's intensely alert to trees finally. When he comes in among trees, he will spend time touching them . . . understanding that each tree is . . . aware of what's happening to it, not just some hunk of wood to be cut down. Slothrop's family actually made its money killing trees, amputating them from their roots, chopping them up, grinding them to pulp, bleaching that to paper and getting paid for this with more paper. 'That's really insane'" (552–53).

5. In protest, Acker titles various novels after the works of dead white men, in a sense appropriating their copyrights on language.

CHAPTER TWENTY-SEVEN

1. My thanks to Bill Asquith at Bloomsbury for suggesting that novelty, however, might not be incommensurate with improvement.

2. Outside capitalist societies, people often used surplus production to exchange gifts (or munus) to strengthened community ties. See Hardack, "Bad" 563–65.

3. Critics have addressed how advertisers effectively weaponize language in detail. In *All Marketers Are Liars*, Seth Godin, for example, documents how ads make us feel, an area I reinterpret. For example, advertising isn't just concerned with generating consistent messages and peer admiration, as Godin claims, but a more profound and comprehensive set of beliefs. Godin focuses on ads that tell compelling stories in largely neutral contexts; I examine the price we pay in being exposed to such stories and what our investment in this form of persuasion tells us about faith and logic in US culture.

CHAPTER THIRTY

1. Elizabeth White Nelson traces this phrase, "universal Yankee nation," to the Philadelphia editor Robert Walsh, who used it to rally Western voters to support a Northern candidate (14). It became a term that invoked the idea that the South was sectional, while the North could represent the entire country. Ironically, sectional antipathy, along with anti-corporate activism, now represents one of the few forms of resistance to corporate universality.

2. For a discussion of how transcendental precepts of nature's universality establish some cultural coordinates for corporate universality, see my "The Pan-American Zone."

CHAPTER THIRTY-ONE

1. See, e.g., Bersani 153, and Porter 514.

2. Corporations also play out the tension between our culture's veneration of false novelty and a conservative insistence that the Constitution is an immutable, sacred text whose meaning was handed down and rests only with a conservative rendition of the founders' intentions.

CHAPTER THIRTY-TWO

1. Public broadcasting entities, like cities, have distinct fundraising challenges, but most corporate sponsorships manipulate content, and represent another of the myriad attempts to raise revenue that betray the public trust. In a remarkably unctuous, canned "interview" conducted on September 7, 2014, a brander/marketer for NPR described a new app broadcasters could use to capitalize on undervalued audience share and provide targeted local ads for brands listeners care about. Tellingly, the interviewer remarked that some listeners would worry that NPR would lose its very soul. Advertising is a battle for souls; even if the idea of a soul is another fiction, it carries as much significance as the fiction of corporate personhood.

CHAPTER THIRTY-THREE

1. Žižek observes that streets are no longer public, but private spaces, in which people treat each other civilly primarily when on camera (*Event* 156–57). People are absorbed in their own electronic devices, and the genuinely public forum is disappearing. Few noncommercial spaces are left in which we can interact or communicate information.

CHAPTER THIRTY-FOUR

1. The speciousness of music marketing can be encapsulated in the practice of reissuing albums, particularly as greatest hits packages. Designations such as "greatest hits" reflect the willfully arbitrary nature of advertising language—you can't prescribe what such a package should include. Despite the room for necessary leeway, it would be clear to most listeners that a reissue of his early, uncommercial pastiche of an album *TB Sheets* isn't Van Morrison's greatest hits, but it's repeatedly repackaged

that way. It's just a matter of time before someone calls their first recordings their greatest hits.

CHAPTER THIRTY-SEVEN

1. Some critics might assert that advertising never has been anything but a form of virtually unregulated manipulation and has never pretended to represent anything else. Ads simply distill the viewpoint of sellers in an amoral fashion. Such critics might also contend that fictional corporate spokespersons elide morality because they have no connection with it: they're merely messengers, precisely like lawyers or agents representing other entities. But as I suggest, that structural disconnection also is the basis of the corporate form, which separates owners from actors/managers, and allows for private shareholders to profit at the public's expense, with the public taking on and subsidizing their risk.

2. Advertisers can be held liable for making false claims, but they rarely make the kinds of assertions courts will evaluate, and even more rarely are held accountable. In an exception, in 1992 Wilkinson had to pay $953,000 in damages for violating the Lanham Act, 15 U.S.C.S. § 1125(a), for knowingly misrepresenting in advertisements that its razor was superior to Gillette's, when it could be shown objectively it wasn't. The judge also stipulated that Wilkinson's ad agency share liability because it shaped the "personality" that made the claim. See *Gillette Co. v. Wilkinson Sword, Inc.*, 795 F. Supp. 662 (S.D.N.Y. 1992). Thanks to Jim McClellan for this reference.

CHAPTER THIRTY-EIGHT

1. The original series *Star Trek* episode "The Return of the Archons" dramatizes this Hobbesian premise in depicting inhabitants of a world, run by a personified computer program, who must be "of the body."

2. Meyer and Jepperson propose that in earlier

religious polities, and in the secularized formations that eventually built upon them, spiritual charisma could be distributed across three main locations: (a) in a central institutional complex (a monarchy, a high Church, a state); (b) in the community as an organic body (that is, in a sacralized matrix of relations [e.g., a system of corporate orders]); or (c) in spiritualized subunits (namely, individuals empowered as souls carrying responsibility for responsible action, whether individually or associationally). (109)

But in contemporary contexts, we need to invoke the corporate idiom more literally: in the United States., the role of "organic" community and the public sphere is considerably displaced or supplanted by the artificial corporation. Yet the corporation remains closer to what nature once represented than to the modern state, as it exists beyond conventional social and human ontological limitations, and even individual oversight or management.

3. It's useful to connect Hobbes's evocation of the representative actor to Emerson's conception of the representative man, because both types belong to the lineage of impersonal corporate personhood. Emerson's apparent idealization of American individualism through nature turns out to be a representative proselytization for corporate identity. As noted, Emerson was interested in the self only in so far as it transcends what would commonly be understood as individuality. Nature collects what Emerson refers to as "distributed" individuals into the collective, which uses them to represent it. A version of Tocqueville's immense divine being, the corporation then displaces the function of nature; it bears the collective identity that speaks through us.

Emerson's notions of self-reliance were misappropriated not via social Darwninism, as Howard Horwitz suggests, but by misinterpretations that rely on generic and inapposite definitions of the self. For Emerson, self-reliance entails the evacuation of the self into an archetypal All, a representative or typological entity that eradicates false particularity. The corporate structure of agency Horwitz invokes is Emersonian, but not because Emerson extolled individualism as it's commonly understood, but because his transcendental individual is wholly representative and stripped of individuality (97). The transcendentalist transcends the self by merging into the divine aggregate, whether Nature or the corporation. Emerson is then corporate in ways that are disparate from those that Newfield identifies in other contexts (e.g., *Emerson* 71). Though the unifications of corporate monopolies have some Emersonian overtones, a monopolist such as John D. Rockefeller never could have been an Emersonian representative man, and Emerson's theory of self-reliance would not justify oil trusts.

4. See also my "Bad Faith" for a comparison of how the US government evaluates the worth of individuals and corporations in the context of race, welfare, gifts, and public and private rights.

CHAPTER THIRTY-NINE

1. The anthropologist Richard Price related this narrative to me.

2. For an extended reading of *Avatar* in this context, see my "It's Always Already Too Late for White Men: Personified Nature and Corporate Personhood, from *Moby-Dick* to *Avatar*," forthcoming in *Angelaki* 29.6 (2024).

CHAPTER FORTY

1. In his dissent, Justice Douglas proposes that "Those who have that intimate relation with the inanimate object about to be injured, polluted, or otherwise despoiled are its legitimate spokesmen." *Sierra Club*, 405 U.S. at 745. Justice Douglas's approach, however, relies on a form of commodity fetishism, as he justifies attributing human personality not only to aspects of nature, but things such as ships. See, for example 753, n2. As Justice Douglas argues here, "Permitting a court to appoint a representative of an inanimate object would not be significantly different from customary judi-

cial appointments of guardians *ad litem*, executors, conservators, receivers, or counsel for indigents." Douglas doesn't want to confer the same "highly artificial" status on inanimate objects that corporations achieve, but to allow surrogates to speak for them. Expanding standing rights to the natural world could provide environmental benefits, but not necessarily a basis for remediating the effects of corporate personhood. Indigenous peoples outside the United States have tried to have personhood granted to aspects of the natural world to afford them legal protections, but it's unclear how effective that strategy will prove.

2. The admirably cogent Section 17529, gutted by corporations, stated:

> (e) Like junk faxes, spam imposes a cost on users, using up valuable storage space in e-mail inboxes, as well as costly computer band width . . . and discourages people from using e-mail. (f) Spam filters have not proven effective. (g) Like traditional paper "junk" mail, spam can be annoying and waste time, but it also causes many additional problems because it is easy and inexpensive to create, but difficult and costly to eliminate. . . . (i) Many spammers have become so adept at masking their tracks that they are rarely found. . . . (k) The true beneficiaries of spam are the advertisers who benefit from the marketing derived from the advertisements. . . . (m) [I]t is necessary that spam be prohibited and that commercial advertising e-mails be regulated.

CHAPTER FORTY-ONE

1. See generally, e.g., *Cent. Hudson Gas & Elec. Corp. v. Pub. Serv. Comm'n*, 447 U.S. 557, 558–559 (1980) (holding that regulations of commercial speech that serve substantial government interests, and are not more extensive or burdensome than necessary, are constitutional); *Fla. Bar v. Went For It, Inc.*, 515 U.S. 618, 628 (1995).

2. In fact, the Court didn't validate the concept of corporate personhood in that case; but, forming another perfectly closed loop, it later incrementally adopted and expanded the general principle and legitimized it retrospectively. It took multiple layers of mistakes and miscarriages based on legal solecisms to legitimate corporate personhood. It was appropriately railroads, as Bakan notes, that because they "demanded more capital investment" than partnerships could provide, led middle-class investors to buy corporate shares; it was corporate pressure, and an acknowledgment of commercial reality, that led the Court gradually to grant corporations exceptional rights (11).

3. Some would argue that corporations need to enter the political arena to influence policy or consumers, as Coca-Cola recently did in objecting to Georgia's restrictive voter law. Even if we cannot attribute them to persons and they reflect calculated self-interest, such interventions are laudable. However, they're distractions from the company's business practices. (Paul Hawkens notes [among thousands of examples that would pertain just to this corporation], how absurd it is for Coca-Cola to use Olympic athletes to promote its unhealthy products, to sell Fruitopia, a drink that contains more sugar than even Coke, and to claim on its Indian website that "sugar does not cause heart disease, cancer, diabetes, or obesity," in much the way fossil

fuels don't cause climate change, or Fruitopia/Caltopia doesn't cause brain damage [161]). Such behavior makes sense under our current system, but we should ask why we allow these inhuman commercial entities to speak so loudly in the political as well as most other realms.

CHAPTER FORTY-TWO

1. Many corporate legal assertions also involve forms of commercial speech (but are not advertisements per se). These statements still raise the question of "who" the corporation is; lawyers represent corporations, but one couldn't specify the intent or agency of those corporations beyond, for example, their position in lawsuits. This consideration raises the legal (and perhaps ontological) question of whether corporations can sue or be sued in noneconomic contexts; even recent lawsuits that push the envelope, claiming corporations have religious rights to withhold contraception, must first raise the issue in economic contexts (e.g., whether corporations can be compelled to spend money, provide worker benefits, etc.). Corporations as yet have no free-standing rights that are not tethered to their spending and marketing.

2. As Justice Stevens concurred in part and dissented in part,

> The legal structure of corporations allows them to amass and deploy financial resources on a scale few natural persons can match. The structure of a business corporation, further-more, draws a line between the corporation's economic interests and the political preferences of the individuals associated with the corporation; the corporation must engage the electoral process with the aim "to enhance the profitability of the company, no matter how persuasive the arguments for a broader or conflicting set of priorities."130 S. Ct. at 974.

But even in that limited context, the corporation's speech would be commercial.

CHAPTER FORTY-THREE

1. As Edward St. Aubyn declaims in *Lost for Words*, sounding as if he'd just read Žižek, he was living "in a late capitalist utopia of obligatory permissiveness, with its injunction to gratify ever more perverse desires" (29). Ironically, this text about the ways literary publishing has succumbed to the cult of celebrity features effective endorsements by "pop-culture icons such as Anthony Bourdain and January Jones," appropriately, a mad woman.

CHAPTER FORTY-FOUR

1. Josh Tillman (who records as/with Father John Misty and Fleet Foxes) also used this conceit in noting how Neil Young is among the few who have refused to commodify their music:

Advertising is so enmeshed in our thought life we've developed Stockholm Syndrome. People buy the idea of the '60s and '70s like a product, like it's something you can own by buying things, or conversely, by becoming a product fashioned in the style of the '70s. . . . It's sad how commodified music has become, how people do it to *be* it, instead of doing it because they *are* it. (Crazy Horse, 23)

Stockholm Syndrome remains an appropriate metaphor for consumers, because we pay to be abused and identify with our abusers, those who have captured our culture and hold it hostage.

2. As a representative example, Rod Stewart's corporatized "Live the Life" tour was named using a gibberish slogan, almost a random series of words meant to evoke a positive feeling but meaning nothing. Most music tours are now branded with arbitrary catchphrases to differentiate them—and are attended by advertising slogans such as "Your life your way" that are equally meaningless and transferable. The entire process, from staging to music production, is undertaken with the logic as well as sponsorship of corporate advertising.

CHAPTER FORTY-SEVEN

1. See "Ukrainian Man Renames Himself iPhone 7 to Win the Phone," *Washington Post*, https://www.washingtonpost.com/world/europe/ukrainian-man -renames-himself-iphone-7-to-win-the-phone/2016/10/28/ce2e2584-9d38-11e6-b552 -b1f85e484086_story.html.

CHAPTER FIFTY

1. See https://www.wsj.com/articles/tech-giants-google-facebook-and-amazon -intensify-antitrust-debate-11559966461.

CHAPTER FIFTY-TWO

1. The privatization of education is a corporate directive that manipulates class and racial resentments. The idea of requiring an equal distribution of public education funding can make people become apoplectically self-entitled. John Irving, author of *The World According to Garp*, wrote that

what I have called Marxist about Act 60 [Vermont's law apportioning funds for public schools] is that, in the name of equalizing educational opportunities, the state has declared the achievement of a level playing field simply by penalizing the topmost public schools in the state. But Act 60 isn't chiefly about education—it is chiefly about the redistribution of wealth. (http://www.freerepublic.com/focus/f-news/1032399/posts)

The delusion is that you can make access to education equal without making access to funding equal. Under a corporatist federalist ideology of local control, Irving founded and funded a private school and yanked his child out of the public education system (see http://www.edweek.org/ew/articles/1998/10/28/09vt.h18.html). Of course it's not considered "class warfare" for wealthy towns to spend their property taxes exclusively on their own schools, even when the point of taxation is to pay for the overarching common good. Imagine how absurd it would be if towns paid taxes for only their own stretch of highway, food inspection, courts, and so on. Their citizens wouldn't be paying for civic infrastructure, but pay-to-play services.

CHAPTER FIFTY-THREE

1. See http://www.samefacts.com/2014/10/drug-policy/annals-of-commerce-beerkeley/; http://newsroom.ucla.edu/releases/we-dare-new-ucla-brand-campaign-celebrates-optimists-everywhere.

Acknowledgments

This book is dedicated to the memory of Joanne Hutchinson, Ursula Le Guin, Geoff Nunberg, and my father, Alvin Hardack, all of whose generosity lives on.

My thanks to Kim Benston, for his always insightful comments and encouragement; Marilyn Gewirtz, whose breadth of knowledge is surpassed only by her warmth and kindness; James Martin, for steadfast commiseration and friendship; Deborah Luepnitz, for decades of engaging conversation and camaraderie, her exemplary suggestions, and her belief in this project; Anna Hellen, for being Anna Hellen; Simon Stern, for his generous and astute reading of sections of my manuscript; Sabina Knight, for her empathy and geniality; Sam Weinstein and Jim McClellan, for their helpful recommendations and references; Leila May, Don Palmer, and Toni Wein, no better companions to travel the world with; Peter Briggs, for long-standing support and assistance; Ioram Melcer and Nourit Melcer-Padon, for their interest in this project; Sharif Youssef and Jody Greene; Anne Richardson-Oakes; and Purnima Bose, Laura E. Lyons, Cindy Franklin, Craig Howes, and the participants in the *Biography* seminar, for their hospitality and feedback.

Thanks to Les and Harrod Blank for permission to cite from the film *Burden of Dreams* (1982), directed by Les Blank, with Maureen Gosling, https://lesblank.com/films/burden-of-dreams-1982-2/. Thanks to Seth Kittay for permission to cite from the film *Putney Swope* (1969), directed by Robert Downey. Quotations from *Infinite Jest* by David Foster Wallace, copyright © 1996, are reprinted by permission of Little, Brown and Company, an imprint of Hachette Book Group, Inc.

Sections of this book were published in different form in "New *and* Improved: The Zero-Sum Game of Corporate Personhood"; "Exceptionally Gifted: Corporate Exceptionalism and the Expropriation of Human Rights"; and "Bad Company: The Corporate Acquisition of Nature, Divinity, and Personhood in U.S. Culture."

Bibliography

Abbarno, G. J. M. "Huckstering in the Classroom: Limits to Corporate Social Responsibility." *Journal of Business Ethics* 32.2 (2001): 179–89.

Acker, Kathy. *Don Quixote*. New York: Grove Press, 1986.

———. *Literal Madness: Three Novels*. New York: Grove P: 1988.

Adams, Sean Patrick. "Soulless Monsters and Iron Horses: The Civil War, Institutional Change, and American Capitalism." In *Capitalism Takes Command: The Social Transformation of Nineteenth-Century America*. Ed. Gary Kornblith and Michael Zakim, 119–44. Chicago: University of Chicago Press, 2012.

Allen, David. *Democracy, Inc.: The Press and Law in the Corporate Rationalization of the Public Sphere*. Champaign-Urbana: University of Illinois Press, 2005.

Allman, Matthew. "Swift Boat Captains of Industry for Truth: *Citizens United* and the Illogic of the Natural Person Theory of Corporate Personhood." *Florida State University Law Review* 38.2 (2011): 387–410.

Anderson, Misty G. "Zombie Sovereignty." *Restoration: Studies in English Literary Culture, 1660–1700*, 40.2 (2016): 105–15.

Anonymous. "Carlyle's Works." *The London Quarterly Review* 130 (September 1840): 233–262.

Anonymous. "Spirit and Tendencies of the New School of Philosophy." *The United States Democratic Review* 15 (1844): 23–32.

Aronczyk, Melissa. *Branding the Nation: The Global Business of National Identity*. New York: Oxford University Press, 2013.

Arvidson, Heather. "Personality, Impersonality, and the Personified Detachment of Wyndham Lewis." *Modernism/Modernity* 25.4 (2018): 791–814.

Auleta, Ken. "The Search Party." *The New Yorker*, January 14, 2008: 30–37.

Bakan, Joel. *The Corporation: The Pathological Pursuit of Profit and Power*. New York: Simon & Schuster, 2005.

Banet-Weiser, Sarah. *Authentic™: The Politics of Ambivalence in a Brand Culture*. New York: New York University Press, 2012.

Barnet, Richard. *Roots of War*. New York: Penguin, 1972.

Bartholomew, Mark. *Adcreep: The Case against Modern Marketing*. Stanford, CA: Stanford University Press, 2017.

Bartol, Cyrus. "Transcendentalism." In *Radical Problems*. Boston: Roberts Brothers, 1872. 61–97. Reprinted in *Critical Essays on American Transcendentalism*. Ed. Philip Gura and Joel Myerson. Boston: G. K. Hall, 1982. 108–27.

Baudrillard, Jean. *Selected Writings*. Ed. Mark Poster, trans. Jacques Mourrain. Stanford, CA: Stanford University Press 1988.

Beauman, Ned. *Glow*. New York: Knopf, 2015.

Bellah, Robert, et al. *Habits of the Heart: Individualism and Commitment in American Life*. New York: Harper & Row, 1985.

Bennett, Andrea. "Disaster Advertising." *Adbusters* 20.5 (2012): 7.

Bennett, Jane. *Vibrant Matter: A Political Ecology of Things*. Durham: Duke University Press, 2010.

Berger, John. *Ways of Seeing*. London: BBC/Penguin, 1972.

Bergson, Henri. *Laughter: An Essay on the Meaning of the Comic*. Trans. Cloudesley Brereton and Fred Rothwell. New York: Cosimo, 2005.

Bernstein, Jake. "Loopholes for Kleptocrats." *New York Review of Books*, December 21, 2021: 23–25.

Bersani, Leo. *The Culture of Redemption*. Cambridge, MA: Harvard University Press, 1990.

Bobbio, Norberto. *Thomas Hobbes and the Natural Law Tradition*. Chicago: University of Chicago Press, 1993.

Bose, Purnima. "General Electric, Corporate Personhood, and the Emergence of the Professional Manager." In *Cultural Critique and the Global Corporation*. Ed. Purnima Bose and Laura E. Lyons, 28–63. Bloomington: Indiana University Press, 2010..

Bose, Purnima, and Laura E. Lyons. "Introduction: Toward a Critical Corporate Studies." In *Cultural Critique and the Global Corporation*. Ed. Bose and Lyons, 1–27. Bloomington: Indiana University Press, 2010.

Breeze, Ruth. *Corporate Discourse*. London: Bloomsbury, 2013.

Brito, Tonya. "From Madonna to Proletariat: Constructing a New Ideology of Motherhood in Welfare Discourse." *Villanova Law Review* 44 (1999): 415–44.

Bromley, Patricia, and John W. Meyer. *Hyper-Organization: Global Organizational Expansion*. Oxford: Oxford University Press, 2015.

Bromwich, David. "How Publicity Makes People Real." *Social Research* 68.1 (2001): 145–71.

Brunner, John. *The Shockwave Rider*. New York: Ballantine, 1975.

Buchanan, James. *Modern Atheism: Under Its Forms of Pantheism, Materialism, Secularism, Development, and Natural Laws*. Boston: Gould and Lincoln, 1857.

Bush, George. "Remarks at the Washington Centennial Celebration in Spokane, September 19, 1989." *Public Papers of the Presidents of the United States: George Bush, 1989. Book 2*. Washington, D.C.: United States Government Printing Office, 1989. 1227-29.

Cameron, Sharon. *Impersonality: Seven Essays*. Chicago: University of Chicago Press, 2007.

Canetti, Elias. *Crowds and Power*. Trans. Carol Stewart. New York; Farrar Straus Giroux, 1973.

Carrére, Immanuel. *I Am Alive and You Are Dead: A Journey into the Mind of Philip K. Dick*. New York: Metropolitan Books, (1993) 2004.

Catenaccio, Paola, and Chiara Degano. "Corporate Social Responsibility as a Key to the Representation of Corporate Identity: The Case of Novartis." In *Discourse and Identity in the Professions: Legal, Corporate and Institutional Citizenship*. Ed. Vijay Bhatia and Paola Evangelisti Allori, 79–102. Bern: Peter Lang, 2011..

Cayton, Mary. *Emerson's Emergence: Self and Society in the Transformation of New England*. Chapel Hill: University of North Carolina Press, 1989.

Chai, Leon. *The Romantic Foundations of the American Renaissance*. Ithaca, NY: Cornell University Press, 1987.

Christensen, Lars Thøger, and George Cheney. "Self-Absorption and Self-Seduction in the Corporate Identity Game." In *The Expressive Organization: Linking Identity, Reputation and the Corporate Brand*. Ed. Majken Schultz et al., 246–70. Oxford: Oxford University Press, 2000.

Clare, Ralph. *Fictions Inc.: The Corporation in Postmodern Fiction, Film, and Popular Culture*. New Brunswick, NJ: Rutgers University Press, 2014.

Coburn, Tyler. "Charter Citizen," *e-flux journal* 52 (February 2014). http://www.tylercoburn.com/works.html.

Cooper, James Fenimore. *The Bravo: A Tale*. Venice, Italy: W. A. Townsend, 1859.

Crazy Horse, Kandia. "Out of the Blue, and Into the Black-Renaissance Via Neil Young's *Archives*." *San Francisco Bay Guardian*, July 8–14, 2009, 20–22, 23.

Danesi, Marcel. *Brands*. New York: Routledge, 2006.

Davis, James. *Commerce in Color: Race, Consumer Culture, and American Literature, 1893–1933*. Ann Arbor: University of Michigan Press, 2007.

Davis, Mike. *City of Quartz: Excavating the Future in Los Angeles*. London: Verso, 1990.

Davis-Floyd, Robbie. "Storying Corporate Futures: The Shell Scenarios." In *Corporate Futures: The Diffusion of the Culturally Sensitive Corporate Form*. Ed. George Marcus, 141–76. Chicago: University of Chicago Press, 1998.

Davies, William "Short Cuts." *London Review of Books*, 5 April 2018: 20–21.

DeLillo, Don. *Great Jones Street*. New York: Vintage, 1973.

———. *Mao II*. New York: Viking, 1991.

———. "The Power of History." *New York Times Magazine* 7 Sept. 1997: 60–63.

———. *Ratner's Star*. New York: Vintage, 1989.

———. *Underworld*. New York: Scribner, 1997.

———. *White Noise*. New York: Penguin, 1986.

———. *Zero K*. New York: Scribner, 2016.

Dewey, John. "The Historic Background of Corporate Legal Personality." *Yale Law Journal* 35.6 (1926): 655–73.

Dewey, Joseph. *Understanding Richard Powers*. Columbia: University of South Carolina Press, 2002.

Dewey, Rev. Orville. "Blanco-White—Rationalism." *The Christian Examiner* 39 (July 1845): 195–219.

Dibadj, Reza. "(Mis)Conceptions of the Corporation." *Georgia State University Law Review* 29.3 (2013): 731–82.

Dick, Philip K. *The Divine Invasion*. New York: Simon & Schuster, 1981.

———. *Ubik*. London: Granada, 1978.

Dienst, Richard. *Still Life in Real Time: Theory after Television*. Durham, NC: Duke University Press, 1995.

Dillard, Annie. *Teaching a Stone to Talk: Expeditions and Encounters*. New York: Harper and Row, 1982.

Dix, Reverend Morgan. *Lectures on the Pantheistic Idea of an Impersonal Deity*. New York: Hurd and Houghton, 1864.

Donoghue, Frank. *The Last Professors: The Corporate University and the Fate of the Humanities*. New York: Fordham University Press, 2008.

Dow, James. "On the Muddled Concept of Corporation in Anthropology." *American Anthropologist* 75.3 (1973): 904–8.

Drori, Gili S., John W. Meyer, and Hokyu Hwang. *Globalization and Organization: World Society and Organizational Change*. New York: Oxford University Press 2007.

Du Bois, W. E. B. *The Souls of Black Folks*. New York: Signet, 1969.

Dunbar-Ortiz, Roxanne. *An Indigenous People's History of the United States*. Boston: Beacon Press, 2014.

Eagleton, Terry. "The Slow Death of the University." *The Chronicle Review*, April 10, 2015: B6–B9.

Eliot, T. S. "Tradition and the Individual Talent." In *The Sacred Wood: Essays on Poetry and Criticism*, 47–59. London: Methuen, 1920.

Emerson, Ralph Waldo. *The Complete Sermons of Ralph Waldo Emerson* 1–4. Ed. Albert von Frank et al. Columbia: University of Missouri Press, 1990.

———. *The Complete Works of Ralph Waldo Emerson* 1–12. Boston: Houghton Mifflin, 1904.

———. *The Early Lectures of Ralph Waldo Emerson* 1–3. Ed. Robert Spiller and Wallace Williams. Cambridge, MA: Harvard University Press, 1959, 1964, 1972.

———. *The Journals and Miscellaneous Notebooks of Ralph Waldo Emerson* 1–16. Ed. William Gilman, et al. Cambridge, MA: Harvard University Press, 1960–82.

———. *Uncollected Lectures by Ralph Waldo Emerson*. Ed. Clarence Gohdes. New York: William Rudge, 1932.

Enoch, Simon John. "The Potemkin Corporation: Corporate Social Responsibility, Public Relations and Crises of Democracy and Ecology." PhD diss. Ryerson University and York University (Canada), 2009. http://berkeley.worldcat.org/title /potemkin-corporation-corporate-social-responsibility-public-relations-and-crises -of-democracy-and-ecology/oclc/718168763&.

d'Errico, Peter. "Corporate Personality and Human Commodification." *Rethinking Marxism* 9.2 (1996): 99–113.

Esposito, Roberto. *Bíos: Biopolitics and Philosophy*. Trans. Timothy Campbell. Minneapolis. University of Minnesota Press, 2008.

Feidelson Jr., Charles. *Symbolism and American Literature*. Chicago: University of Chicago Press, 1953.

Fichtelberg, Joseph. *The Complex Image: Faith and Method in American Autobiography*. Philadelphia: University of Pennsylvania Press, 1989.

Fisher, Mark. *Capitalist Realism: Is There No Alternative?* Winchester, UK: Zero Books, 2009.

———. *The Weird and the Eerie*. London: Repeater, 2016.

Fisher, Phillip. "Democratic Social Space: Whitman, Melville, and the Promise of American Transparency." *Representations* 24 (Fall 1988): 60–101.

Foster, Robert. "Corporate Oxymorons and the Anthropology of Corporations." *Dialectical Anthropology* 34.1 (2010): 95–102.

Foucault, Michel. "Technologies of Self." *Technologies of the Self: A Seminar with Michel Foucault*. Ed. Luther Martin et al., 16–149. Amherst: University of Massachusetts Press, 1988.

———. *Madness & Civilization: A History of Insanity in the Age of Reason*. Trans. Richard Howard. New York: Vintage: 1973.

Fox, Stephen. *The Mirror Makers: A History of American Advertising and Its Creators*. New York: William Morrow, 1984.

Frank, Thomas. "Free Markets Killed Capitalism: Ayn Rand, Ronald Reagan, Wal-Mart, Amazon and the 1 Percent's Sick Triumph Over Us All." Salon. http://www.salon.com/2014/06/29/free_markets_killed_capitalism_ayn_rand_ronald_reagan_wal_mart_amazon_and_the_1_percents_sick_triumph_over_us_all/.

———. *One Market under God: Extreme Capitalism, Market Populism, and the End of Economic Democracy*. New York: Doubleday, 2000.

Franklin, Cynthia. *Academic Lives: Memoir, Cultural Theory, and the University Today*. Athens: University of Georgia Press, 2009.

French, Peter. "The Corporation as a Moral Person." *American Philosophical Quarterly* 16.3 (1979): 207–15.

Gaakeer, Jeanne. "*Sua Cuique Persona*? Some Reflections of the Fiction of Legal Personhood." Address to the Legal Bodies Conference, Leiden University Centre for Arts in Society, May 2014.

Garnett, Richard. *Life of Ralph Waldo Emerson*. London: Walter Scott, 1888.

Garrett, Jan Edward. "Persons, Kinds, and Corporations: An Aristotelian View." *Philosophy and Phenomenological Research* 49.2 (1988): 261–81.

Ghachem, Malick. "The Forever Company: How to Narrate the Story of an Eighteenth-Century Legal Person (The Case of the *Campaignie des Indes*)." Keynote address at The Legal Bodies Conference: Corpus, Persona, Communitas" symposium, Leiden University (Leiden, the Netherlands), May 17, 2014.

Giles, Paul. *The Global Remapping of American Literature*. Princeton, NJ: Princeton University Press, 2011.

Girard, René. *Deceit, Desire and the Novel*. Trans. Yvonne Freccero. Baltimore: Johns Hopkins University Press, 1965.

Giroux, Henry. *Stealing Innocence: Corporate Culture's War on Children*. New York: Palgrave Macmillan: 2001.

———. *Zombie Politics and Culture in the Age of Casino Capitalism*. New York: Peter Lang, 2011.

Godin. Seth. *All Marketers Are Liars*. New York: Penguin, 2005.

Görlach, Manfred. "A Linguistic History of Advertising, 1700–1890." In *Sounds, Words, Texts and Change*. Ed. Teresa Fanego et al., 83–104. Amsterdam: Benjamins, 2002.

Graeber, David. *The Democracy Project: A History, a Crisis, a Movement*. New York: Penguin, 2013.

Grear, Anna. *Redirecting Human Rights: Facing the Challenge of Corporate Legal Humanity*. New York: Palgrave Macmillan, 2010.

Haineault, Doris-Louise, and Jean-Yves Roy. *Unconscious for Sale: Advertising, Psychoanalysis, and the Public*. Trans. Kimball Lockhart and Barbara Kerslake. Minnesota: University of Minnesota Press, 1993.

Hakim, Danny. "Google Is Target of European Backlash on U.S. Tech Dominance." *The New York Times*, September 9, 2014, A1, B2.

Hardack, Richard. "Bad Faith: Race, Religion, and the Reformation of Welfare Law." *Cardozo Public Law, Policy and Ethics Journal* 4.3 (2006). 539–649.

_____. "Consciousness without Borders: Narratology in *Against the Day* and the Works of Thomas Pynchon." *Criticism* 52.1 (2010). 91–128.

———. "Exceptionally Gifted: Corporate Exceptionalism and the Expropriation of Human Rights." In *Human Rights after Corporate Personhood: An Uneasy Merger*. Ed. Jody Greene and Sharif Youssef (Toronto: University of Toronto Press, 2020). 141–74.

———. "Fictitious Lives: the Fantastic Nature of Corporations," version of talk delivered to the Utopia & Dystopia Conference on the Fantastic in Media Entertainment," the University of Southern Denmark, Odense, Denmark, May 2020, available at https://www.imaginingtheimpossible.com/post/fictitious-lives-the-fantastic-nature-of-corporations.

———. "The Franklin-Stein Monster: Ventriloquism and Missing Persons in American Autobiography." In *Writing Lives: American Biography and Autobiography*. Ed. Hans Bak and Hans Krabbendam, 16–28. Amsterdam: VU University Press, 1998.

———. "New *and* Improved: The Zero-Sum Game of Corporate Personhood." Special Issue on Life-Writing and Corporate Personhood. *Biography: An Interdisciplinary Quarterly* 37.1 (2014): 36–68.

———. *"Not Altogether Human": Pantheism and the Dark Nature of the American Renaissance*. Amherst: University of Massachusetts Press, 2012.

———. "The Pan-American Zone: Emerson, Melville and the Transcendental Colonization of the Pacific." *Passages: Journal of Transnational and Transcultural Studies* 1.1 (1999). 53–83.

———. "Pure Formalities: Living with the Nescient Dead, or the Dead Who Don't Know They Are Dead." *Contemporary Literature* 59.2 (2018). 161–203.

———. "What They Don't Want You to Hear: Beltone, Ticketmaster, and the Failure of Antitrust Policy." *Boston U Journal of Science & Technology Law* 284 (2003): 284–325.

———. "World Trade Centers and Word-Wide Webs: From Over-Soul to *Underworld* in Don DeLillo." *Arizona Quarterly* 69.1 (2013). 151–83.

Harris, David Evan. "São Paulo: A City without Ads." *Adbusters*, August 3, 2007. https://www.adbusters.org/magazine/73/Sao_Paulo_A_City_Without_Ads.html

Hartmann, Thom. *Unequal Protection: the Rise of Corporate Dominance and the Theft of Human Rights*. San Francisco: Berrett Kohler, 2002.

Harvey, David. *A Brief History of Neoliberlism*. Oxford: Oxford University Press, 2011.

———. *The Condition of Postmodernity*. Oxford: Basil Blackwell, 1990.

———. *The Enigma of Capital and the Crises of Capitalism*. Oxford: Oxford University Press, 2010.

Hawken, Paul. *Blessed Unrest: How the Largest Movement in the World Came into Being and Why No One Saw It Coming*. New York: Viking, 2007.

Hawthorne, Nathaniel. *The House of the Seven Gables. The Centenary Edition of the Works of Nathaniel Hawthorne*, vol. 2. Ed. William Charvat, et al. Columbus: Ohio State University Press, 1965.

———. *The Marble Faun: or the Romance of Monte Beni. The Centenary Edition*, vol. 4. Ed. William Charvat, et al. Columbus: Ohio State University Press, 1968.

Hine, Thomas. *The Total Package: The Secret History and Hidden Meanings of Boxes, Bottles, Cans, and Other Persuasive Containers*. Boston: Back Bay Books, 1997.

Hitchcock, Ethan Allen. *Fifty Years in Camp and Field: Diary of Major General Ethan Allen Hitchcock*. Ed. W. Croffut. New York: Knickerbocker Press, 1909.

Hobbes, Thomas. *Leviathan; or, The Matter, Forme & Power of a Commonwealth, Ecclesiasticall and Civil*. Ed. A. R. Waller. Cambridge, Cambridge University Press, 1904.

Holmes, Edmond. *All Is One: A Plea for the Higher Pantheism*. London: R. Corbden-Sanderson, 1921.

Hood, Edwin. *Swedenborg: a Biography and an Exposition*. London: Arthur Hall, 1864.

Horwitz, Howard. "The Standard Oil Trust as Emersonian Hero." *Raritan* 6.4 (1987): 97–119.

Hovenkamp, Herbert. "The Classical Corporation in American Legal Thought." 76 *Georgetown Law Journal* 76 (1988): 1593–689.

Howe, Craig. Comments delivered to the seminar to workshop the special issue of *Biography* on "Life-Writing and Corporate Personhood," the Center for Biographical Research at the University of Hawai'i at Manoa, August 2013.

Hunt, John. *Pantheism and Christianity*. 1884. Port Washington, New York: Kennikat Press, 1970.

Huxley, Aldous. *Brave New World*. New York; Bantam, 1958.

Ignatieff, Michael. *Fire and Ashes*. Cambridge, MA: Harvard University Press, 2013.

Irwin, John. *American Hieroglyphics: The Symbol of the Hieroglyphics in the American Renaissance*. New Haven, CT: Yale University Press, 1980.

Iscoe, Adam. "Man's Best Friend: The Smell Test." *The New Yorker*, March 1, 2021, 16–17.

Jacobs, Harriet (Linda Brent). *Incidents in the life of a Slave Girl*. Ed. Lydia Maria Child. Introd. Lydia Maria Child; introd. Walter Teller. New York: Harcourt Brace, 1973.

Jameson, Frederic. *Postmodernism; or, the Cultural Logic of Late Capitalism*. Durham, NC: Duke University Press, 1991.

Jhally, Sut. *The Codes of Advertising: Fetishism and the Political Economy of Meaning in the Consumer Society*. New York: Routledge, 1987.

Johnson, Charles. *Oxherding Tale*. New York: Grove Press, 1982.

———. *Middle Passage*. New York: Plume, 1990.

Orczak, Jennifer. "'Not Like You and Me': Hobby Lobby, the Fourteenth Amendment, and What the Further Expansion of Corporate Personhood Means For Individual Rights." *Brooklyn Law Review* 80.1 (2014): 285.

Kallayli, Gopi. *The Internet to the Innernet*. Carlsbad, CA: Hay House: 2015.

Katchadourian, Raffi. "The Doomsday Invention: Will Artificial Intelligence Bring Us Utopia or Destruction?" *The New Yorker*, November 23, 2015: 64–79.

Kennedy, Michael D. "Rewriting the Death and Afterlife of a Corporation: Bethlehem Steel." *Biography* 37.1 (2014): 246–78.

Klein, Naomi. *No Logo*. New York: Picador, 2000.

Lawrence, D. H. "Pan in America." In *Phoenix*. Ed. Edward McDonald, 22–31. New York: Viking, 1936.

———. *Phoenix*. Ed. Edward McDonald. New York: Viking, 1936.

———. *Studies in Classic American Literature*. New York: Penguin Books, 1964.

Lears, Jackson. *Fables of Abundance: A Cultural History of Advertising*. New York: Basic Books, 1995.

LeClair, Tom. *In the Loop: Don DeLillo and the Systems Novel*. Urbana: University of Illinois Press, 1987.

Levine, Lawrence. *The Unpredictable Past: Explorations in American Cultural History*. New York: Oxford University Press, 1993.

Lewis, Wyndham. *Wyndham Lewis: An Anthology of His Prose*. London: Methuen, 1969.

Ligotti, Thomas. *My Work Is Not Yet Done: Three Tales of Corporate Horror*. New York: Ebury, 2011.

Liss, David. *The Devil's Company: a Novel*. New York: Random House, 2009.

List, Christian, and Philip Pettit. *Group Agency: The Possibility, Design, and Status of Corporate Agents*. Oxford: Oxford University Press, 2011.

Locke, John. *Second Treatise on Civil Government*. Ed. Thomas Reardon. Indianapolis, IN: Bobbs Merrill, 1952 (1690).

Lynn, Barry. *Cornered: The New Monopoly Capitalism and the Economics of Destruction*. Hoboken, NJ: John Wiley & Sons, 2009.

Lyons, Laura E. "'I'd Like My Life Back": Corporate Personhood and the BP Oil Disaster." *Biography* 34.1 (2011): 96–107.

Madsen, Deborah. "The Business of Living: *Gravity's Rainbow*, Evolution, and the Advancement of Capitalism." *Pynchon Notes* 40–41 (1997): 144–58.

Maliszewski, Paul. "The Business of *Gain*." In *Intersections: Essays on Richard Powers*. Ed. Stephen Burn and Peter Dempsey, 162–86. Champaign, IL: Dalkey Archive, 2008.

Maltby, Paul. "The Romantic Metaphysics of Don DeLillo." *Contemporary Literature* 37.2 (1996): 258–77.

Manning, Rev. Jacob M. *Half Truths and the Truth*. Boston: Lee and Shepard, 1871.

Manring, M. M. *Slave in a Box: the Strange Career, of Aunt Jemima*. Charlottesville: University Press Virginia, 1998.

Marchand, Roland. *Creating the Corporate Soul: The Rise of Public Relations and Corporate Imagery in American Big Business*. Berkeley: University of California Press, 1998.

Marcuse, Herbert. *One-Dimensional Man: Studies in the Ideology of Advanced Industrial Society*. Boston: Beacon Press, 1964.

Mark, Gregory. "The Personification of the Business Corporation in American Law." *University of Chicago Law Review* 54.9 (1987): 1444–74.

Marx, Karl. *The Economic and Philosophical Manuscripts: Early Writings*. Trans. Rodney Livingstone and Gregor Benton. Harmondsworth, UK: Penguin Books, 1975.

Marx, Leo. *The Machine in the Garden: Technology and the Pastoral Idea in America*. London: Oxford University Press, 1964.

Max, D. T. *Every Love Story Is a Ghost Story: A Life of David Foster Wallace*. New York: Viking, 2012.

Mayhew, Henry. *The London Street-Folk*. Mineola, NY: Dover, 1968.

McCarthy, Tom. *Satin Island*. New York: Knopf, 2015.

Meier, Harry. "Companies Turn Tables on Human Rights Lawyers." *The New York Times* March 6, 2015, B1–B2.

Melville, Herman. *The Confidence-Man*. Ed. Harrison Hayford et al. Evanston, IL: Northwestern University Press, 1984.

———. *Correspondence*. Ed. Lynn Horth. Evanston, Il: Northwestern University Press, 1993.

———. *Mardi*. Ed. Hayford et al. Evanston, Il: Northwestern University Press, 1970.

———. *Moby-Dick*. Ed. Hayford et al. Evanston, Il: Northwestern University Press, 1988.

———. *Pierre*. Ed. Hayford et al. Evanston, IL: Northwestern University Press, 1968.

———. *Redburn*. Ed. Hayford et al. Evanston, IL: Northwestern University Press, 1969.

———. *White Jacket*. Ed. Hayford et al. Evanston, IL: Northwestern University Press, 1970.

Menand, Louis. "Change Your Life: The Lessons of the New Left." *The New Yorker*, March 22, 2021, 46–53.

———. *American Studies*. New York: Farrar Straus and Giroux, 2002.

Meyer, John W., and Patricia Bromley. "The Worldwide Expansion of 'Organization.'" *Sociological Theory* 31.4 (2013): 366–89.

Meyer, John W., and Ronald Jepperson. "The "Actors" of Modern Society: The Cultural Construction of Social Agency." *Sociological Theory* 18 (2000): 100–120.

Meyers, Virginia. "University Inc. The Pernicious Effects of Corporate Influence." *AFT On Campus* (Summer 2015). https://www.aft.org/periodical/aft-campus/summer-2015/university-inc.

Michaels, Walter Benn. *The Gold Standard and the Logic of Naturalism*. Berkeley: University of California Press, 1987.

Mitchell, David. *Black Swan Green*. New York: Random House, 2006.

———. *Ghostwritten*. New York: Vintage, 1999.

———. *Utopia Avenue*. New York, Random House, 2020.

Moore, Anne Elizabeth. *Unmarketable: Brandalism, Copyfighting, Mocketing, and the Erosion of Integrity*. New York: New Press, 2007.

Nelson, Elizabeth White. "The Land of Pumpkin Pies": Humor and the Crafting of Sectional Identity in the North, 1790–1870." On file with the author, University of Nevada, Las Vegas.

Newfield, Christopher. "Corporate Culture Wars." In *Corporate Futures*. Ed. George Marcus, 23–62. Chicago: University of Chicago Press.

———. *The Emerson Effect: Individualism and Submission in America*. Chicago: University of Chicago Press, 1996.

Norton, Andrews. *A Discourse on the Latest Form of Infidelity*. 1839. Port Washington, NY: Kennikat Press, 1971.

O'Brien, John. *Literature Incorporated: The Cultural Unconscious of the Business Corporation, 1650–1850*. Chicago: University of Chicago Press, 2016.

Osmos, Evan. "Cleveland Postcard." *The New Yorker*, August 1, 2016, 16–17.

Packard, Vance. *The Hidden Persuaders*. New York: Penguin (1957) 1981.

Pask, Gordon, and Susan Curran. *Micro Man: Computers and the Evolution of Consciousness*. New York: Macmillan, 1982.

Piety, Tamara. "Advertising as Experimentation on Human Subjects." *Advertising & Society Quarterly* 19.2 (2018). Project MUSE, doi:10.1353/asr.2018.0015.

Pocock, J. G. A. *The Machiavellian Moment: Florentine Political Thought and the Atlantic Republican Tradition*. Princeton, NJ: Princeton University Press, 1975.

Porter, Carolyn. "What We Know That We Don't Know." *American Literary History* 6 (Fall 1994): 467–526.

Powers, Richard. *Gain*. New York: Farrar, Straus and Giroux, 1998.

———. *The Gold Bug Variations*. New York: William and Morrow, 1991.

———. "Making the Rounds." In *Intersections*. Ed. Burn and Dempsey, 305–10.

———. *The Overstory*. New York: Norton, 2018.

Putney Swope. Dir. Robert Downey. Cinema V, 1969. Film.

Pynchon, Thomas. *Against the Day*. New York: Penguin, 2006.

———. *Bleeding Edge*. New York: Penguin, 2013.

———. *Gravity's Rainbow*. New York: Penguin, 1995 (1973).

———. *Mason & Dixon*. New York: Harry Holt, 1997.

Rand, Ayn. *Night of January 16*. In *Three Plays*. New York: Signet, 1968.

Reed, Ishmael. *Flight to Canada*. New York: Avon, 1976.

Ries, Al and Jack Trout. *Bottom-Up Marketing*. New York: Penguin, 1990.

Ritzenberg, Aaron. "The Corporation and the Transformation of American Culture." In *The Routledge Research Companion to Law and Humanities in Nineteenth-Century America*. Ed. Nan Goodman and Simon Stern, 35–55. New York: Routledge, 2017.

———. *The Sentimental Touch: The Language of Feeling in the Age of Managerialism*. New York: Fordham University Press, 2012.

Rives, Rochelle. *Modernist Impersonalities: Affect, Authority, and the Subject*. New York: Palgrave Macmillan, 2012.

Rosenthal, Caitlin. "From Memory to Mastery: Accounting for Control in America, 1750–1880." *Enterprise & Society* 14.4 (2013): 732–48.

Runciman, David. "Diary." *London Review of Books*, January 25, 2018, 38–39.

Rushkoff, Douglas. *Life Inc: How Corporatism Conquered the World and How We Can Take It Back*. New York: Random House, 2001.

Safina, Carl. "Occupy Corporations." *Adbusters* 20.2 (2012): 41–45, 47.

———. *Present Shock: When Everything Happens Now*. New York, Penguin, 2013.

Said, Edward. *Beginnings: Intention and Method*. New York, Columbia University Press, 1985.

Saisset, Emile Edmond. *Modern Pantheism: An Essay on Religious Philosophy* 1–2. Trans. anonymous. Edinburgh: T. and T. Clark, 1863.

Sands, Robert. *The Writings of Robert C. Sands*. Vol. 2. New York: Harper & Brothers, 1834.

Santos, Boaventura de Sousa. "The Americas: Social Movements and Resistance against U.S. Imperialism." Talk delivered to the 5th Conference of the International Association of Inter-American Studies, Reinventing the Social: Movements and Narratives of Resistance, Dissension and Reconciliation in the Americas, The University of Coimbra, Portugal, March 24, 2018.

Scanlan, Margaret. "Writers among Terrorists: Don DeLillo's *Mao II* and the Rushdie Affair." *Modern Fiction Studies* 40.2 (1994): 229–52.

Schnepel, Burkhard. "Corporations, Personhood, and Ritual in Tribal Society: Three Interconnected Topics in the Anthropology of Meyer Fortes." *Journal of the Anthropological Society of Oxford* 21.1 (1990): 1–31.

Schudson, Michael. *Advertising, the Uneasy Persuasion: Its Dubious Impact on American Society*. New York: Basic Books, 1984.

Schwartz, Nelson. "Recovery in U.S. Is Lifting Profits, but Not Adding Jobs." *The New York Times*, March 4, 2013: A1, 3.

Sealts, Jr., Merton. *Emerson on the Scholar*. Columbia: University of Missouri Press, 1992.

Sepinwall, Amy. "*Citizens United* and the Ineluctable of Question Corporate Citizenship." *Connecticut Law Review* 44.3 (2012): 575–615.

Simon, William. "Rights and Redistribution in the Welfare System," *Stanford Law Review* 38.6

Siraganian, Lisa. "Dreiser's Anti-Corporate Tools: Veil-Piercing and the Novel of Corporate Agency." *American Literary History* 30.2 (2018): 249–77.

———. *Modernism and the Meaning of Corporate Persons*. Oxford: Oxford University Press, 2020.

————. "Theorizing Corporate Intentionality in Contemporary American Fiction." *Law & Literature* 27.1 (2015): 99–123.

Sivulka, Juliann. *Soap, Sex and Cigarettes: A Cultural History of American Advertising.* Belmont, CA: Wadsworth, 1998.

Skinner, Quentin. "Hobbes and the Purely Artificial Person of the State." *The Journal of Political Philosophy* 7.1 (1999): 1–29.

Slotkin, Richard. *Regeneration through Violence.* Middletown, CT: Wesleyan University Press, 1973.

Sovacool, Benjamin. "Broken by Design: The Corporation as a Failed Technology." *Science, Technology & Society* 15:1 (2010): 1–25.

Sprague, Robert, and Mary Ellen Wells. "The Supreme Court as Prometheus: Breathing Life into the Corporate Supercitizen." *American Business Law Journal* 49.3 (2012): 507–56.

St. Aubyn, Edward. *Lost for Words.* New York: Farrar, Straus and Giroux, 2014.

Steiner, George. *Errata: an Examined Life.* New Haven: Yale University Press, 1997.

————. *Language and Silence: Essays on Language. Literature and the Inhuman.* New York: Athenaeum, 1986.

Stoller, Matt. *Goliath.* New York: Simon & Schuster, 2019.

Stone, Christopher. *Should Trees Have Standing? Toward Legal Rights for Natural Objects.* Berkeley: University of California Press, 1974.

Stowe, Harriet Beecher. *Uncle Tom's Cabin.* New York: Dodd, Mead & Co., 1952 (1852).

Surowiecki, James. "Twilight of the Brands." *The New Yorker*, February 17 & 24, 2014, 40.

Taub, Jennifer. "Is Hobby Lobby a Tool for Limiting Corporate Constitutional Rights?" *Constutional Commentary* 30 (2015): 403.

Thomas, Brook. "*The House of the Seven Gables*: Hawthorne's Legal Story." *The University of Mississippi Studies in English* 5 (1987): 249–71.

Thoreau, Henry David. *Journals* 1–4. Ed., John Broderick et al. Princeton, NJ: Princeton University Press, 1992.

Titolo, Matthew, "The Corporation's Neoliberal Soul?" In *Human Rights after Corporate Personhood.* Ed. Jody Greene and Sharif Youssef, 27–51. Toronto: University of Toronto Press.

Tocqueville, Alexis De. *Democracy in America* 1–2. The Henry Reeve Text, Rev. Francis Bowen, Ed. Phillips Bradley. New York: Knopf, 1953.

Todorov, Tzvetan. *The Fantastic: A Structural Approach to a Literary Genre.* Trans. Richard Howard. Ithaca, NY: Cornell University Press, 1970.

Trachtenberg, Alan. *The Incorporation of America: Culture and Society in the Gilded Age.* New York: Hill and Wang, 1982.

Tracy, Marc. "Nike Got Ducks, Under Armour Gets Terrapins." *The New York Times*, August 26, 2015, A1, B11.

Tucker, Anne. "Flawed Assumptions: A Corporate Law Analysis of Free Speech and Corporate Personhood in *Citizens United.*" *Case Western Reserve Law Review* 61.2 (2010): 496–548.

Turnbull, Andy. *The Synthetic Beast: When Corporations Come to Life*. Toronto: Red Ear Publishing 2002.

Videmšek, Boštjan. "China Inc. The Mother of All Corporations." *Adbusters* 24.23 (2013): 40–43.

Viviano, Frank. "The Plato and Newton of Branding." *California* 125.1 (2014): 22–27.

Wallace, David Foster. "Discussion: Rick Moody and David Foster Wallace." Commonwealth Club, Herbst Theater, San Francisco, November 28, 2005.

———. *Infinite Jest*. Boston: Little Brown, 1996.

———. *The Pale King*. New York: Little, Brown, 2011.

———. *A Supposedly Fun Thing I'll Never Do Again*. Boston: Little, Brown, 1997.

Waugh, Charles. "We Are Not a Nation, So Much as a World": Melville's Global Consciousness." *Studies in American Fiction* 33.2 (2005): 203–28.

Weiner, Tim. *Legacy of Ashes: A History of the CIA*. New York: Random House, 2007.

"What We Talk about When We Talk about Persons: The Language of a Legal Fiction." *Harvard Law Review* 114, no. 6 (2001): 1745–68. https://doi.org/10.2307/1342652.

Whitehead, Colson. *Apex Hides the Hurt*. New York: Doubleday, 2006.

Whitman, Walt. *Complete Poetry and Selected Prose*. Ed. James Miller, Jr. Boston: Houghton Mifflin, 1959.

Wicke, Jennifer. *Advertising Fictions: Literature, Advertisement and Social Reading*. New York: Columbia University Press, 1988.

Wieseltier, Leon. "Among the Disrupted." *The New York Times Book Review*, January 18, 2015: 1, 14–15.

Wu, Tim. *The Attention Merchants: The Epic Scramble to Get Inside Our Heads*. New York: Vintage, 2017.

———. *The Master Switch: The Rise and Fall of Information Empires*. New York: Knopf, 2010.

Zheutlin, Peter. "Product Placement." *The New Yorker*, January 18, 2010: 5.

Žižek, Slavoj. *Absolute Recoil: Towards a New Foundation of Dialectical Materialism*. New York: Verso, 2014.

———. *Enjoy Your Symptom! Jacques Lacan in Hollywood and Out*. New York: Routledge.

———. *Event: A Philosophical Journey through a Concept*. Brooklyn: Melville House, 2014.

———. *The Fragile Absolute*. London: Verso, 2001.

———. *How to Read Lacan*. New York: Norton, 2007.

———. *In Defense of Lost Causes*. London: Verso, 2009.

———. *The Indivisible Remainder: on Schelling and Related Matters*. London: Verso, 2007.

———. *Interrogating the Real*. Ed. Rex Butler and Scott Stephens. New York: Continuum, 2006.

———. "Introduction." *Mapping Ideology*. Ed. Žižek. London: Verso, 1995. 1–33.

———. *Less Than Nothing: Hegel and the Shadow of Dialectical Materialism*. London, Verso, 2012.

————. *Living in the End Times*. New York: Verso, 2010.

————. *The Parallax View*. Cambridge, MA: MIT Press, 2006.

————. *The Ticklish Subject: The Absent Centre of Political Ontology*. London: Verso, 2000.

————. *The Universal Exception*. Ed. Butler and Stephens. New York: Continuum, 2006.

Zuboff, Shoshana. *The Age of Surveillance Capitalism: The Fight for a Human Future at the New Frontier of Power*. New York: Hachette, 2019.

Zwicker, Heather. "To Build a Better World: Bechtel, a Family Company." In *Cultural Critique*. Ed. Purnima Bose and Laura E. Lyons, 102–27. Bloomington: Indiana University Press, 2010.

Index

Abbarno, G. J. M., 312

Acker, Kathy, 198, 334n5; *Don Quixote*, 179, 181–82, 215; *Literal Madness: Three Novels*, 50

Adams, Sean Patrick, 166

advertising, 1–6, 9–15, 16–23, 25–27, 30–31, 36, 42, 56, 63 65, 69, 72–73, 76, 88, 91, 95–96, 100–106, 111, 113–29, 138–40, 144, 155–59, 166–67, 170–71, 177, 179, 182–83, 185–89, 191–92, 195–97, 199–209, 211–13, 215–30, 234, 240, 247, 252, 255, 257–59, 265–87, 289–305, 307, 311–14, 319–24, 325n2, 328n1, 333n5,n3, 334n3, 335n1,n1, 336n1, 338n2, 339–40n1,n2, *passim*

Agency, 5–6, 11–14, 16–17, 31, 33–35, 47, 55, 61–62, 64, 66, 73, 75, 83–86, 91, 126, 130, 143–44, 164, 166, 168–69, 172, 179, 206, 234–40, 243–45, 249, 297–98, 326n1

Aliens, 7, 17, 54, 123, 130, 176, 242, 245, 247–49. *See also* vampires, zombies

Alien films, 103, 248–51

AI, *see* artificial intelligence

Allen, David, 171

Anderson, Benedict, imagined communities, 205

Anderson, Misty G., 97

animism, and animation (attributing life or spirit to the world, commodities, and inanimate things), 59, 62–64, 91–92, 241, 251, 337n1. *See also* pantheism, soul

Anonymous, "Carlyle's Works," 326n1

Anonymous, "Spirit and Tendencies of the New School of Philosophy," 46

Aronczyk, Melissa, 204, 239, 301

The Arrangement, 186

artificial intelligence, and artificiality, 3, 14, 36, 64–66, 71–72, 75, 87, 96, 128–29, 156, 158–59, 162–63, 166, 170, 186, 206, 226, 236, 238, 244, 249, 258, 272, 275–76, 286. *See also* bodies, virtuality

Avatar (and Pandora) 61, 248–51. *See also* animism, pantheism

Arvidson, Heather, 56, 327n3

Auleta, Ken, 275

Bakan, Joel, 14, 51, 99, 135, 168, 171, 211, 311, 338n2

Banet-Weiser, Sarah, 204

Barnet, Richard, 199, 202, 230

Bartholomew, Mark, 275

Bartol, Cyrus, 43

Baudrillard, Jean, 299–300

About the Author

Richard Hardack was a Javits fellow at UC Berkeley, at which he received his doctorate in English and JD. He has taught at UC Berkeley and Bryn Mawr and Haverford Colleges; published more than fifty articles in American Studies and law; and presented more than one hundred conference papers in twenty countries. His first book, *"Not Altogether Human": Pantheism and the Dark Nature of the American Renaissance*, which focused on Melville and Emerson, was published by the University of Massachusetts Press. He is also project editor for the history of NASA's Juno Mission to Jupiter.